Outside the Pale

Reading
WOMEN
Writing

a series edited by
Shari Benstock and Celeste Schenck

Reading Women Writing is dedicated to furthering international feminist debate. The series publishes books on all aspects of feminist theory and textual practice. *Reading Women Writing* especially welcomes books that address cultures, histories, and experience beyond first-world academic boundaries. A complete list of titles in the series appears at the end of the book.

Outside the Pale

CULTURAL EXCLUSION,
GENDER DIFFERENCE, *and the*
VICTORIAN WOMAN WRITER

Elsie B. Michie

Cornell University Press

ITHACA AND LONDON

First published 1993 by Cornell University Press.

Library of Congress Cataloging-in-Publication Data

Michie, Elsie B. (Elsie Browning), 1948-
   Outside the pale : cultural exclusion, gender difference, and the Victorian woman writer / Elsie B. Michie.
      p.   cm.—(Reading women writing)
   Includes bibliographical references and index.
   ISBN 0-8014-2831-9 (cloth).—ISBN 0-8014-8085-X (pbk.)
   1. Women authors, English—19th century—Social conditions. 2. English literature—Women authors—History and criticism. 3. Women and literature—Great Britain—History—19th century. 4. English literature—19th century—History and criticism. 5. Authorship—Sex differences.   I. Title.   II. Series.
PR115.M46   1993
820.9′9287′09034—dc20   93-2458

Printed in the United States of America

⊗ The paper in this book meets the minimum requirements of the American National Standard for Information Sciences— Permanence of Paper for Printed Library Materials, ANSI Z39.48–1984.

Contents

Acknowledgments

I am grateful for a Louisiana State University Research Fellowship which helped me to complete the book manuscript. I also acknowledge the encouragement I received from a number of colleagues at different stages of the project: Deirdre David, Charlotte Feierman, Margaret Homans, Rosan Jordan, Elizabeth Kirk, Michelle Massé, Beth Newman, and Lisa Walker. I thank Bernhard Kendler of Cornell University Press for his unfailing courtesy during the editorial process and Mary Poovey and Rosemarie Bodenheimer for their careful reading of my manuscript. Finally, I want to express the warmest gratitude to Laurie Langbauer and Robin Roberts for their support as I completed the project.

Short sections of Chapter 1 appeared as "Production Replaces Creation: Market Forces in *Frankenstein*," in *Nineteenth-Century Contexts* 12 (Spring 1989): 27–33, and as "*Frankenstein* and Marx's Theories of Alienated Labor," in *Approaches to Teaching Shelley's "Frankenstein,"* ed. Stephen C. Behrendt, 93–98 (New York: MLA, 1990). A version of Chapter 2 appeared as "From Simianized Irish to Oriental Despots: Heathcliff, Rochester, the Brontës, and Race," in *NOVEL: A Forum in Fiction* 25 (Winter 1992): 125–40. Copyright NOVEL Corp. © 1992.

E. B. M.

Outside the Pale

Introduction: "Excluded from Discourse and Imprisoned within It": The Position of the Nineteenth-Century Woman Writer

> Class and race ideologies are . . . steeped in and spoken through the language of sexual differentiation. Class and race meanings are not metaphors for the sexual, or vice versa. It is better, though not exact, to see them as reciprocally constituting each other through a kind of narrative invocation, a set of associative terms in a chain of meaning. To understand how gender and class—to take two categories only—are articulated together transforms our analysis of each of them.
>
> —Cora Kaplan, *Sea Changes*

Feminist theorists from Simone de Beauvoir onward have taught us to see femininity as a quality of the second sex. From this point of view, the feminine is that which is repressed, denied, or excluded by the dominant culture, which appears to be universal but in fact implicitly defines itself as masculine. The difficulty with such a position is that the feminine territory that is excluded by the dominant culture can come to seem monolithic and unchanging, the space of the "other." To counter this difficulty, the cultural exclusion of femininity has come increasingly to be read in terms of history. That is: at any point in time the dominant culture defines itself by excluding or denying some of its elements, but the excluded elements vary as the culture changes shape under the pressure of economic, political, and social developments. As a result, while femininity continues to be positioned as the "other" of masculinity, the way femininity is constructed at different points in history varies because what is repressed or denied as the dominant culture changes. In this book, I read the works of five nineteenth-century authors—Mary Shelley, Charlotte and Emily Brontë, Elizabeth Gaskell, and George Eliot—in light of the differing definitions of femininity which were foregrounded during the time that each woman was writing. In each case the particular model of gender difference that positioned the woman writer was shaped by the social concerns that were dominant at the moment she was writing, concerns about modes of production, class difference, property owning, colonial relations, and access to education. Each chapter focuses on the interconnections between a specific model of sexual difference and other discursive structures that have, apparently, nothing to do with gender.

The cultural exclusion of femininity was dramatized with particular clarity in the case of these five authors because of the contradiction inherent in their position as women writers; in the nineteenth century to become a professional writer was to enter a territory implicitly defined as masculine. What this contradiction meant for Shelley, the Brontës, Gaskell, and Eliot was that the figures who surrounded and influenced them as they wrote, the individuals who functioned as mentors, literary role models, and gatekeepers to the world of publishing, tended to be men, either family members or literary professionals, often both at once. The figure who most dominated the scene when Mary Shelley began her literary career by writing *Frankenstein* was Percy Shelley, who helped prepare the lists of the texts she read in the months when she was working on the novel and who read and revised the manuscript when it was finished. Emily and Charlotte Brontë also wrote in the presence of a male family member who was a literary figure, their father, the Reverend Patrick Brontë, who had achieved his own social status by learning and teaching literature and who wrote and published sermons, stories, and poems. Patrick Brontë shaped his daughters' taste by determining what volumes were available in their library and by encouraging them to read authors, such as Milton, who had been important to him in his personal advancement. Elizabeth Gaskell too began her writing career by working with a male family member, her husband. However, the figure under whose aegis she began an extensive career of publishing, first with *Household Words* and later with *All the Year Round*, was Charles Dickens, who edited much of what she wrote between 1850 and 1863 and helped to define her position as a professional writer. In her career as a journalist, translator, and novelist, George Eliot worked with several male literary colleagues, the most significant of whom was George Henry Lewes, who was also both a family member, her "husband" as she chose to call him, and a professional critic. Lewes's numerous published articles in the *Westminster Review* and elsewhere meant that Eliot was extremely familiar with his opinions about the novel in general and about women's writing in particular before she began her own career as a novelist. In their private life together, Lewes pursued a course of reading with Eliot and both advised her about her writing and publishing and consulted her about his own.

Although all these male mentors were supportive, encouraging the women artists they lived with or whose work they published to write, each man also stood in and, in some sense, stood *for* a literary realm that excluded the nineteenth-century woman writer because of her gender. Percy Shelley, for example, identified himself as a member of a major literary movement of his time, as a Romantic poet, and, as a result, could position himself as an inheritor of the Wordsworthian and Coleridgian belief in the power of the poetic imagination. As a number of critics have pointed out, however, in analyzing the work not just of Mary Shelley but also of Dorothy Wordsworth and Emily Brontë, Romantic ideology was constructed in such a way that a woman writer found it difficult to define herself as possessing the imaginative power that made it possible to be a Romantic poet.[1] In the case of the Brontës, the Reverend Patrick Brontë was able, in educating himself, to move from being an illiterate Irish weaver to becoming an English clergyman with a university degree. In doing so, he enacted a mid-century fantasy of upward mobility, the fantasy of the "self-made man," a fantasy whose popular title identifies those it excludes. As women, Charlotte and Emily Brontë were unable to do what their father did; they could not use their education—their knowledge of literature—to achieve professional status in Victorian society. In the case of Elizabeth Gaskell, her editor Charles Dickens and some male writers who worked for him, including Wilkie Collins and Edward Bulwer-Lytton, received enormous public rec-

1. For a very interesting reading of the problems raised for Dorothy Wordsworth and Emily Brontë by Romantic models of poetic inspiration, see Margaret Homans, *Women Writers and Poetic Identity: Dorothy Wordsworth, Emily Brontë, and Emily Dickinson* (1980). For a discussion of Mary Shelley's troubled relationship to Romanticism, see Mary Poovey, *The Proper Lady and the Woman Writer: Ideology as Style in the Works of Mary Wollstonecraft, Mary Shelley, and Jane Austen* (1974).

ognition for their work, in part because they were able to control its reception through advertising and the way in which it was published in such periodicals as *Household Words*. As a mid-Victorian woman, Elizabeth Gaskell found that she was excluded from active participation in the literary marketplace; she could publish her writing but had no means of controlling its appearance and reception. In the case of George Eliot, liberal intellectual writers of her time, such as George Henry Lewes and Matthew Arnold, were active advocates of an ideal of "high culture" that was to became available to all through the new systems of higher education then being developed. Eliot found, however, that as a woman she was excluded from full participation in those educational systems and, by extension, in the concomitant intellectual celebration of "culture."

Each of these nineteenth-century women writers found herself, in the words of Teresa de Lauretis, "at once excluded from discourse and imprisoned within it."[2] Each was prevented from taking a discursive position, from speaking or writing as a Romantic poet or a self-made man or a professional editor or a disciple of "culture," because she was also imprisoned within discourse. She was excluded from a realm implicitly defined as masculine because she was imprisoned within a limiting definition of femininity. Mary Shelley, for example, describes herself and other women as having a "material mechanism"[3] as contrasted to her husband who is, an "ethereal Being who did not belong to the gross & palpable world."[4] Shelley is unable to exercise the abstract powers of the imagination as a Romantic poet should because, as a woman, she is associated with the palpable, material world. The Brontës confronted a conception of femininity which defined women as excluded from the realm of the marketplace, the realm one critic of their novels describes as "the political, colonial and mercantile activities of the English people."[5] That critic goes on to explain that while the spirit of enterprise makes it possible for men to redress

2. Teresa de Lauretis, *Alice Doesn't: Feminism, Semiotics, Cinema* (1984), 7.

3. "To Maria Gisborne, 11 June 1835," in *The Letters of Mary Wollstonecraft Shelley,* 3 vols., ed. Betty T. Bennett (1983), 2:246.

4. Cited in *The Journals of Mary Shelley*, 2 vols., ed. Paula R. Feldman and Diana Scott-Kilvert (1987), 2:437n.

5. Eugène Forçade, "Review," from *Revue des deux mondes*, in *The Brontës: The Critical Heritage*, ed. Miriam Allott (1974), 102.

the inequities of their position, "it is different for women."[6] Elizabeth Gaskell confronted a definition of femininity as split between a proper, private realm, the home, and an improperly public one, the "streets." As Luce Irigaray puts it, "As soon as a woman leaves the house, someone starts to wonder, someone asks her: how can you be a woman and be out here at the same time?"[7] Gaskell was unable to participate fully in professional literary life because her activities as a professional author might make her seem an "improper" woman in the eyes of the Victorian public. George Eliot confronted a definition of femininity as fragmented, as opposed to masculinity, which was defined as whole. That model of gender difference was invoked repeatedly in late-nineteenth century arguments about whether women had the ability to take part in higher education. Eliot found herself excluded from the Arnoldian concept of culture because, as a woman, she was defined as having a "broken" biological nature that made it impossible for her to comprehend higher intellectual subjects.

All the models of gender difference discussed in the previous paragraph are, of course, extremely familiar. Feminist theorists, perhaps most prominently Luce Irigaray, have discussed at length how the cultural construction of woman has repeatedly been associated with the material as opposed to the spiritual, the home sphere as opposed to the marketplace, the private as opposed to the public, and the fragmentary as opposed to the comprehensive. When one reads Irigaray's powerfully persuasive descriptions of this excluded feminine territory, one is tempted to view these definitions of woman as "other" as if they are universal, monolithic, and unchanging. Such a temptation is what the recent feminist emphasis on history is designed to counter. As Joan Scott explains, "the point of new historical investigation is to disrupt the notion of fixity, to discover the nature of the debate or repression that leads to the appearance of timeless permanence in binary gender representation. This kind of analysis must include a notion of politics and reference to social institutions and organizations."[8] In the cases of Shelley, the Brontës, Gaskell, and Eliot, as one moves from

6. Ibid.

7. Luce Irigaray, *This Sex Which Is Not One*, trans. Catherine Porter with Carolyn Burke (1985), 144–45.

8. Joan Scott, "Gender: A Useful Category of Historical Analysis," in *Coming to Terms: Feminism, Theory, Politics*, ed. Elizabeth Weed (1989), 94.

1818 to 1870, one can see that different aspects of the traditional definition of femininity become foregrounded at different moments in time. In each case, the shift in what was emphasized in the models of gender difference these writers confronted was, as Scott explains, linked to political, social, and economic issues, both those that were being debated and those that were being repressed at this particular historical moment.

In the chapters that follow, I analyze the particular definition of femininity which positioned each of these five women writers and read it against the backdrop of the specific economic, political, and social debates which helped determine the shape of that model of gender difference. In Chapter 1, I read the opposition between masculine spirituality and feminine materiality which appears over and over again in Shelley's letters as linked to early nineteenth-century debates about society's dependence on production and its increasing materialism. The model of gender difference, which opposed masculine spirituality to feminine materiality, provided a means for early capitalist society to repress or deny the materialism that made it so uncomfortable. In Chapter 2, I read the exclusively masculine narrative of self-making, which the Reverend Patrick Brontë enacted and which the Brontë sisters encoded in the stories of Heathcliff and Rochester, as connected to midcentury colonial thinking. By looking at caricatures of the Irish and fantasies about "oriental despots" in both the Brontë novels and other texts of the time, one can examine the imperialist subtext that grounded Victorian fantasies of upward mobility. In Chapters 3 and 4, I read the split between the private and public woman, which troubled Elizabeth Gaskell as a professional woman writer, within the context of mid-nineteenth-century debates about controlling prostitution and the spread of venereal disease that led eventually to the passage of the Contagious Diseases Acts. Such legislative measures functioned to police the boundary between the home and the streets by locking up or confining what was defined as a dangerously "public" woman. In Chapter 5, I read the definition of femininity as fragmentary, which George Eliot confronted in her professional career, against the backdrop of late nineteenth-century debates about education and "culture." Although the Arnoldian ideal of "culture" was supposedly open to everyone, in fact liberal intellectuals also mapped out a territory in which some were defined as naturally incapable of higher education. While such a territory was overtly associated with women, who were defined by anthropologists, doctors, and others as physically unfit for strenuous intellectual work, it was covertly associated with the working classes who could then simultaneously be offered culture and defined as naturally excluded from it.

The intent behind *Outside the Pale* is not simply to identify the historical concerns that motivated a particular definition of femininity, but to analyze *how* discourses having to do with gender work together with discourses having to do with politics, economics, colonial thinking, or class relations. As Gilles Deleuze and Félix Guattari note, "The unconscious poses no problems of meaning, solely problems of use. The question posed by desire is not 'What does it mean?' but rather '*How does it work?*' "[9] The critical methodologies most useful in analyzing how a symbolic economy works are those developed by poststructural theory. My own approach may seem at odds with the premises of poststructuralism since, rather than allowing for the full play of différance, I have identified the authors I analyze as women writers—though the gendered identity of each of these writers is somewhat problematized when she is read as confronting and resisting particular definitions of femininity. The purpose of *Outside the Pale* is, however, less to explore the theoretical questions raised by the tension between poststructuralism and historical specificity than to develop critical readings of literary texts which would take into account *both* the specificity of gender roles as they were articulated at a particular historical moment *and* the play of differences which allows a symbolic system to function.[10] My analyses of Shelley, the Brontës,

9. Gilles Deleuze and Félix Guattari, *Anti-Oedipus: Capitalism and Schizophrenia* (1986), 109.

10. Debates about the tension between the indeterminacy of poststructuralist theory and the political need to identify a historically specific subject abound not just in the recent writings of feminist critics but also in the writings of postcolonial critics. For a feminist debate about the tension between poststructuralist approaches and the need to specify the gender of the subject, see Peggy Kamuf, "Replacing Feminist Criticism," Nancy K. Miller, "The Text's Heroine: A Feminist Critic and Her Fictions," and Peggy Kamuf and Nancy K. Miller, "Parisian Letters: Between Feminism and Deconstruction," in *Conflicts in Feminism*, ed. Marianne Hirsch and Evelyn Fox Keller (1990), 105–33. For a feminist critic who is working toward finding a middle ground between these two positions, see Linda Alcoff, "Cultural Feminism versus Post-Structuralism: The Identity Crisis in Feminist Theory," *Signs* 13.3 (1988):

Gaskell, and Eliot are intended, as R. Radhakrishnan put it, to "historicize and situate the radical politics of 'indeterminacy.' "[11] Those analyses are positioned in what I see as a blind spot in the work of such deconstructive critics in Neil Hertz, D. A. Miller, and Gayatri Spivak, whose analyses of *Middlemarch, Bleak House,* and *Jane Eyre* have been crucial to the development of my own critical readings of these texts.

All these critics reach a point where the poststructuralist insistence on indeterminacy keeps them from making local, circumstantial, and historical identifications[12] not only of the models of gender difference but also of the political, economic, and social debates that underlie the texts they analyze. In "Recognizing Casaubon," for example, Neil Hertz brilliantly analyzes the section of *Middlemarch* where Dorothea Brooke confronts the "stupendous fragmentariness" of Rome in terms of classic nineteenth-century accounts of the sublime. He compares the scene from *Middlemarch* to a series of analogues from Kant to Locke, all of which involve a spectator's sense of being overwhelmed by a sensory experience that cannot immediately be comprehended. Hertz's poststructuralism leads him, however, to blur questions of gender difference in analyzing Eliot's novel; all the spectators he cites as analogues for Dorothea Brooke are male. It is here that we might choose *not* to remain in the realm of indeterminacy but to situate or historicize the Rome scenes from *Middlemarch* by taking into account not only the general question of gender, which would involve asking what difference it makes to have a female spectator of the sublime, but also the question of what historically specific definition of femininity underlies Eliot's depiction of Dorothea's inability to comprehend Rome. At the time when Eliot was writing *Middlemarch,* debates about access to higher education led to a proliferation of

405–36. For a similar debate in cultural criticism, see the critique of Homi Bhabha's poststructuralism in Abdul JanMohamed, "The Economy of Manichean Allegory: The Function of Racial Difference in Colonialist Literature," *Critical Inquiry* 12.1 (1985): 59–87. For someone attempting to chart a middle ground in cultural studies, see R. Radhakrishnan, "Ethnic Identity and Post-Structuralist Differance," *Cultural Critique* 6 (1987): 199–220. For an attempt to collapse the two poles of this debate in a number of different arenas including feminism and cultural criticism, see Diana Fuss, *Essentially Speaking: Feminism, Nature, and Difference* (1989).

    11. Radhakrishnan, "Ethic Identity," 199.
    12. Here I echo the words of Radhakrishnan, "Ethnic Identity," 213.

arguments which asserted that women were biologically broken and therefore, as Mr. Brooke puts it early in Eliot's novel, "deep studies, classics, mathematics, that kind of thing, are too taxing for a woman."[13] The scene in which Dorothea is depicted as unable to comprehend the fragmentation of Rome both resembles and differs from Kant's description of his first overwhelming vision of St. Peter's. Eliot's Victorian readers would have interpreted Dorothea's response to Rome in the context not just of classic descriptions of the sublime but also of contemporary definitions of the limitation of the female mind. By taking this historically specific model of gender difference into account, we can begin to understand the symbolic gestures Eliot makes in representing her heroine in Rome, gestures that evoke traditional accounts of the sublime but also resist the late nineteenth-century emphasis on femininity as fragmented.

In his brilliant analysis of the disciplinary structures in *Bleak House*, D. A. Miller also emphasizes indeterminacy by asserting, in characteristically deconstructive fashion, that in Dickens's novel surveillance is not fixed or located but all-pervasive. What we have learned, however, particularly from critics writing about the treatment of homosexuality in the nineteenth century, is that while policing may be everywhere, it makes a good deal of difference what population is defined as the object of disciplinary actions. We can historicize questions of gender and policing in *Bleak House* by reading that novel in light of a form of midcentury surveillance that was directed at women as a group through the policing and imprisonment of prostitutes in order to control the spread of venereal disease. In *Bleak House*, when the all-pervasive systems of surveillance, the law, and the police, focus on and pursue a single figure who effectively stands as a scapegoat for the rest of society, that figure is a woman, Lady Dedlock, whose sexual transgression and ability to elude the police by walking the streets in disguise link her to the figure of the Victorian prostitute, particularly in a novel so obsessed with the spread of a disease that threatens to mark the face even of an "innocent" woman. By reading *Bleak House*

---

13. George Eliot, *Middlemarch*, ed. Gordon S. Haight (1956), vol. 1, chap. 7., p. 48. All further references to this book (hereafter abbreviated *MM*) appear in the text.

in light of the historically specific model of gender difference associated with the treatment of prostitutes, one can begin to understand the function of such figures as Lady Dedlock and Esther Summerson. One can also read even so apparently benign a figure as the rescue worker Alan Woodcourt as the appropriate agent to accompany Inspector Bucket in the final pursuit of the errant Lady Dedlock, the medical man working together with the police. For my purposes, such a historically specific reading of *Bleak House* also allows one to compare it with Gaskell's *Ruth*, which is similarly concerned with a "fallen" woman whose sexuality is figuratively linked to the spread of disease. Gaskell's novel, however, represents the policing of female sexuality quite differently from Dickens's, because Gaskell's relation to the model of gender difference implied by the midcentury treatment of prostitutes differs from Dickens's in light of her gender.

Miller's analysis of *Bleak House*, furthermore, shows how a critical reading that insists on indeterminacy can unwittingly replicate the arguments of the historically specific issues it overlooks. In describing *Bleak House*, Miller tends to invoke exactly the kind of logic that was characteristic of mid-nineteenth century social texts on prostitution. For example, when he argues that the detective story in Dickens's novel "sanctions the deviate erotic desire that inspires it and that it releases into action" and further, that "the unsavory sexual secrets that ultimately gratify this desire are themselves subversive of socially given arrangements,"[14] he shows how Dickens's novel resembles the writings of William Acton and William R. Greg. Although these authors were fascinated by the sanctioned social deviance of prostitution, they also argued that, as an unsavory sexual practice, it threatened, through the spread of venereal disease, to disrupt given social structures. Miller goes on to explain that in *Bleak House* "what keeps the production of this desire [for the detective story] from being dangerously excessive—what in fact turns the dangerous excess back into profit—is that the detective story . . . produces among *its* effects the desire for its own . . . regulatory agency."[15] Here Miller's language echoes precisely the logic of those who argued that prostitution was a locus where

14. David A. Miller, *The Novel and the Police* (1988), 72.
15. Ibid., 73.

illicit sexuality could and should be made profitable, but who also asserted that if that sexuality was not to become dangerously excessive, it required medical and police supervision. Miller's descriptions of *Bleak House* accurately reflect the way Dickens's novel itself presents contemporaneous discussions about the treatment of prostitutes. But because, in his analysis of *Bleak House*, Miller overlooks that historically specific instance of policing, he replicates the ideological patterns of Dickens's novel without gaining critical distance from them.

Of the three deconstructive critics discussed here, Spivak, in "Three Women's Texts and a Critique of Imperialism," is the most interested in a specific historical issue, the way that what she calls the axiomatics of midcentury imperialism occlude the third world woman.[16] In the midst of a brilliant critique of feminist analyses of *Jane Eyre*, Spivak, however, like Hertz and Miller, has at least one moment when she insists on emphasizing indeterminacy. At the point where she addresses the question of the author, Spivak explains that she will deal only with the novel and not with Brontë's biography because "to touch Brontë's 'life' in such a way . . . would be too risky here."[17] Presumably the risk is of labeling Brontë imperialist or racist, as Spivak explains toward the end of her argument when she asserts that "readings such as this one do not necessarily accuse Charlotte Brontë the named individual of harboring imperialist sentiments."[18] When she broaches the subject of Brontë's life initially, Spivak states that she does not want to "undermine the excellence of the individual artist" but instead to "incite a degree of rage against the imperialist narrativization of history, that it should produce so abject a script for [Brontë]."[19] We can situate *Jane Eyre* and analyze the particularity of the imperialist scripts which were produced for Brontë precisely by addressing the historical specificity of Brontë's background. By raising the question of the Reverend Patrick Brontë's Irish past and mid-

16. For an interesting critical reading of "Three Women's Texts and a Critique of Imperialism," which is quite different from mine but which I also find persuasive, see Benita Parry, "Problems in Current Theories of Colonial Discourse," *Oxford Literary Review* 9 (1987): 27–58.

17. Gayatri Spivak, "Three Women's Texts and a Critique of Imperialism," in *"Race," Writing, and Difference*, ed. Henry Louis Gates, Jr. (1986), 263.

18. Ibid., 276.

19. Ibid., 263.

century Victorian characterizations of the Irish, one can begin to analyze how those representations of local colonialism are connected, in Charlotte's and also Emily's novels, to the more exotic representations of India and the West Indies that Spivak discusses in her essay.

Spivak's analysis of *Jane Eyre* also exemplifies the critical difficulties that arise not from a deconstructive emphasis on indeterminacy but from the opposite impulse, the impulse to name and bring to the foreground a pattern in the text which has hitherto remained invisible. Spivak begins her article by criticizing apparently "radical" feminist readings of *Jane Eyre* for their complicity in rendering the racial otherness of the third world woman, Bertha Mason, invisible. In her reading of Brontë's novel, Spivak effectively turns the tables on those earlier feminist readers by bringing the occluded questions of race and imperialism to center stage. The difficulty with such a critical gesture is, however, that when you foreground one set of images, others tend to move into the background and become invisible. As with optical illusions which cause you to see either a vase or two people kissing but not both at the same time, it is hard to look simultaneously at the patterns that structure racial differences and those that structure gender differences.[20] In emphasizing questions of race, Spivak's analysis of *Jane Eyre* tends to overlook questions of gender difference. By identifying the points in *Jane Eyre* where the "unquestioned ideology of imperialist axiomatics"[21] is most clearly displayed, Spivak analyzes first Rochester's description of his dealings with Bertha Mason and later the description of St. John Rivers pursuing his mission in India. At this point Spivak does not ask, as I think she might, whether there is a difference between these explicitly masculine articulations of imperialism and the position of the feminine in the novel—a difference that, though it does not free the female characters or Brontë herself from the burden of imperialism, makes them differently complicit because their relation to the power struc-

20. As Jane Gaines notes in describing Barry Gordy's film *Mahogany*, "racial conflict surfaces or recedes . . . rather like the perceptual trick in which, depending on the angle of view, one swirling pattern or the other pops out at the viewer" (Jane Gaines, "White Privilege and Looking Relations: Race and Gender in Feminist Film Theory," in *Issues in Feminist Film Criticism*, ed. Patricia Ehrens [1990], 207).
21. Spivak, "Three Women's Texts," 267.

ture of British society is different from that of figures like Rochester and St. John.

In order to avoid the problem with foregrounding that occurs in Spivak's essay, I have attempted in my analyses always to keep two structuring forces in view: both the particular definition of femininity which positioned each of the women writers discussed, and another discourse, political, economic, or colonial, which was interconnected with that model of gender difference. This double focus may unsettle the reader since, like the viewer of the optical illusion, we are more comfortable when we see either one clear image or the other and the overall picture makes sense. Spivak's article suggests, however, that if we do not pay attention to more than one discourse at the same time, we risk not simply occluding the discourse we ignore but also oversimplifying our analysis of the discourse we address. If we choose to look at the discourse of imperialism and to allow the discourse of gender difference to fall into the background, the discourse of imperialism may appear to function in a more homogeneous, more monolithic fashion than it actually does in the text we are analyzing. In the case of *Jane Eyre* and *Wuthering Heights*, for example, it is by analyzing the way that gender difference cuts across and intersects with Victorian definitions of racial difference that we can begin to understand better how both discourses worked at midcentury.

In order for each chapter in *Outside the Pale* to focus on the intersection of two different discourses, each must draw from a field of diverse sources to set up its argument. Despite their intertexual complexity, all the chapters have a similar structure. Each begins by identifying the historical moment in which the writer worked and the political, social, racial, or economic debates that were central at that moment. Each chapter also opens with an outline of the particular model of gender difference which positioned the woman writer. Documents including journals, letters, diaries, and contemporaneous reviews of her own and other women's novels allow us to see how the author in question responded to and internalized the definitions of femininity and masculinity which she confronted as a woman and a writer. Each chapter also draws on extraliterary texts: the writings of Marx on alienated labor, of Greg and Acton on prostitution, of ethnographers like James Beddoe on the racial constitution of the Irish, and of anthropologists on the effects of menstruation on women's mental abilities. Analyzing the rhetoric and imagery of these texts shows the particular model of gender difference the woman writer confronted appearing in and structuring forms of social discourse other than her novels. (The writings of Marx reappear in Chapters 1, 2, and 4 not only because he is an extremely accurate analyst of nineteenth-century economic and social issues but also because the figurative language that appears in his analyses provides vivid examples of the way the Victorian political unconscious used images of race and gender difference.) Once this network of discourses has been mapped out, each chapter proceeds to analyze the way the interconnection between gender and social, political, or economic issues works in the novels of the woman writer in question.

The book essentially moves through three time periods: the early nineteenth century when Mary Shelley wrote *Frankenstein*, the late 1840s and early 1850s when the Brontës wrote *Wuthering Heights* and *Jane Eyre* and Gaskell and Dickens had their editorial dealings, and the 1870s when George Eliot wrote Book Two of *Middlemarch*. As one moves from decade to decade, one can see that economic and social debates change their emphasis from production in the early 1800s, to class difference and property owning at midcentury, to difference in access to culture and education in the latter half of the century. Nonetheless, the Brontës and Gaskell, who were writing at almost the same time (*Jane Eyre* and *Wuthering Heights* appeared in the same year as *Mary Barton*) and therefore responding to a definition of femininity shaped by similar economic pressures, experience that definition differently because of their own personal histories. The Brontës feel frustration because the split between the marketplace and the domestic realm means that women are unable to enact the narrative of the self-made man; Gaskell feels anxiety because the split between public and private women threatens to make her activities as a professional woman writer improper.

Moreover, in responding to the models of gender difference which constrain them, these women authors use differing strategies of resistance. In *Frankenstein*, *Jane Eyre*, and *Wuthering Heights*, Shelley and the Brontës respond to the constraint of their own position by providing critical representations of the definition of masculinity which excludes them. These representations expose exactly what that dominant position ordinarily represses or denies, and what it hides. In *Frankenstein*, Shelley exposes the materiality denied by the definition of masculinity as abstract. In *Wuthering Heights* and *Jane Eyre*, Emily and Charlotte Brontë expose the colonial subtext that is repressed in masculine fantasies of upward mobility. Because Chapters 1 and 2 are primarily concerned with the construction of masculinity, they contain relatively little discussion of the position of women in the novels under consideration. Chapters 3 and 4 show Elizabeth Gaskell responding to the model of gender difference which constrains her by seeking not to criticize the masculine position that excludes her but to redefine or resist the definition of femininity that imprisons her. Because Gaskell's gestures of resistance are difficult to see without a contrast, I have, in Chapters 3 and 4, borrowed the strategy used by Shelley and the Brontës and introduced the masculine position that is the correlative of Gaskell's feminine one, by analysing both Dickens's editorial dealings with Gaskell and the novels of his which parallel hers. Finally, in the Rome scenes of *Middlemarch*, we have, in a relatively small textual space, Eliot's meticulous attempts both to criticize a masculine position, as represented by Casaubon and Rome, and to redefine its feminine correlative, as represented by Dorothea's response to Casaubon and Rome.

In Chapter 1, I argue that in *Frankenstein* Mary Shelley resists the theories of abstract creativity espoused by Percy Shelly, Coleridge and the other Romantic poets, because those theories implicitly define creativity as masculine. Shelley's own narrative, in the "Author's Introduction" to the 1831 version of *Frankenstein*, of how she differed from those male writers in not being immediately "inspired" to write a ghost story marks her sense that as a woman she was excluded from such theories of poetic inspiration. In her novel, she describes Victor's making of the monster in a way that rewrites abstract creation as material production. In doing so, Shelley tells the story of a maker becoming alienated from what he makes, a depiction that resembles Marx's later descriptions of the alienated worker confronting his product "as an alien being, as a power independent of the producer."[22] Shelley's novel exposes the anxieties about production which were repressed by the Romantic

22. Karl Marx, "Alienated Labour," from *Economic and Philosophical Manuscripts*, in *Selected Writings*, ed. David McLellan (1977), 78.

theories of creativity and allows us to read those theories as associated with the moment when, as Marx argues, the alienation of labor begins—the moment in which products or commodities, like the monster, were becoming increasingly fetishized.

In Chapter 2, I argue that in *Jane Eyre* and *Wuthering Heights*, Charlotte and Emily Brontë represent the classic Victorian fantasy of the self-made man in the figures of Heathcliff and Rochester, both of whom leave home at an early age in order to return enriched and empowered. Both novels expose the unspoken imperialist fantasies that underlie such masculine narratives of class advancement. In *Jane Eyre*, as Gayatri Spivak has pointed out, the imperialist underpinnings of Rochester's advancement are clearly represented through his involvement with Bertha Mason. But Rochester and Heathcliff are themselves represented through classic Victorian images of racial difference. When they are characterized as oppressed, outcast, or "other," both are associated with mid-nineteenth century stereotypes of the simianized Irish. When they are in a position of dominance, they are characterized as "oriental despots." The Brontë novels thus show the implicitly masculine narrative of upward mobility realized by Heathcliff and Rochester to be an enactment of the desire to dominate, a desire which is troubling when its effects can be seen in locations close to home such as Ireland, but which can be projected as fantasy onto more distant and racially differentiated oriental scenarios.

In Chapters 3 and 4, I read Gaskell's and Dickens's literary interactions in the context of mid-nineteenth-century discussions of prostitution. Because that model of gender difference was articulated in light of discussions that led to the passage of the Contagious Diseases Acts and therefore was itself inherently politicized, I have broken my analysis of Dickens and Gaskell into two chapters. The first deals solely with the model of gender difference implicit in midcentury discussions of prostitution. It shows how, because both Dickens and Gaskell viewed Gaskell's professional writing as threatening to make her an improperly public woman, their editorial dealings were structured by the model of gender difference implicit in discussions of prostitution. This chapter further analyzes the way in which Gaskell's and Dickens's differing positions on the treatment of prostitutes, that emerged in their discussions of Victorian rescue work and structured their editorial dealings, were also articulated in *Bleak House* and *Ruth*, two novels which, with their concerns about disease and illicit female sexuality, reflect the differing positions being taken in the years prior to the Contagious Diseases Acts. In Chapter 4, the second of the two chapters on Gaskell and Dickens, I consider how the discourse of gender difference, so prominent in discussions of prostitution, was also linked to the discourse of economics, specifically of property owning. I discuss the way in which the interconnection between the erotic and the economic in the figure of the prostitute provided a double means to defuse midcentury, middle-class anxieties about class conflict. On the one hand, the economic discourse which surrounded the prostitute and defined her as property made it possible to conceive of the working classes as ineligible to become property owners. On the other hand, the erotic discourse which surrounded the prostitute deflected the Victorian audience's attention away from what it sensed was basically an unresolvable economic conflict. In Chapter 4, I analyze *Ruth*, *Hard Times*, and *North and South* as a series of texts in which increasing concerns about manufacturing and the relations between masters and workers continue to be associated with the story or image of the "fallen" woman.

In Chapter 5, I argue that in the Rome scenes in Chapter 20 of *Middlemarch*, George Eliot resists the traditional Victorian opposition between masculine wholeness and feminine fragmentation (the opposition Freud was to encode in his theories of castration anxiety). That model of gender difference raised particular difficulties for George Eliot because it was intertwined with the opposition between culture and anarchy which was so important to liberal intellectuals of the 1860s and 70s, such as Matthew Arnold and George Henry Lewes. The interconnection between those two models of difference meant that if Eliot endorsed the Arnoldian ideal of cultural wholeness, she was effectively supporting a sphere of knowledge which was implicitly defined as masculine and from which women were excluded because of their gender. (In the late nineteenth century, women were literally excluded from this ideal of "culture" on the basis of their bodies. They were defined as incapable of the higher education that would grant them access to "culture" because their biology, particularly the fact that they menstruated, rendered them too "broken" to comprehend deep subjects.) If, on the other hand, Eliot chose to resist the idea of masculine wholeness, she was implicitly placing herself on the side opposed to culture, the position of anarchy or rebellion. In the Rome scenes in *Middlemarch*, Eliot evokes the various political positions which could be articulated through the opposition between masculine wholeness and feminine fragmentation and, at the same time, refuses to reify that opposition. In making such a gesture of resistance, she exposes that apparently essentialist or biological model of gender difference as a discursive structure, which was particularly useful to such liberal critics as George Henry Lewes. The Rome scenes from *Middlemarch* make it possible to see that, in his posthumous review of Dickens (published at the same time as Book II of *Middlemarch*), Lewes uses the opposition between masculine wholeness and feminine fragmentation to define Dickens, as a popular artist, as feminine and therefore excluded from the wholeness of "high" culture in much the same way that Dorothea finds herself excluded from Rome.

In the readings performed in each of these chapters, I seek both to map out a particular corner of the nineteenth-century symbolic economy and to show how a knowledge of the way discourses intersect within that small segment of the symbolic economy changes our readings of even extremely familiar texts. Understanding the political and the sexual or gendered unconscious that structures these texts seems particularly important because without such an understanding our criticism will replicate the ideological structures these women writers struggle to resist. The problem, as Teresa de Lauretis has argued, is that "male narratives of gender... bound by the heterosexual contract... persistently tend to reproduce themselves in feminist theories. They *tend to*, and will do so unless one constantly resists, suspicious of their drift."[23] I have already indicated, in the case of D. A. Miller, how a brilliant analysis of *Bleak House* can also reiterate the logic of those arguing in favor of the Contagious Diseases Acts, a position that not only justified the imprisonment of prostitutes but also confined women who attempted to enter what the Victorians defined as an "improperly" public sphere. Each of the chapters which follows ends with a

---

23. Teresa de Lauretis, *Technologies of Gender: Essays on Theory, Film, and Fiction* (1987), 25.

similar analysis of the way that modern criticism of these authors has become caught up in replicating rather than analyzing the ideological patterns which structure their works. Such a gesture may appear to dehistoricize the models of gender difference I am analyzing. My point throughout the book is, however, that these definitions of femininity persist over time, but take different forms at different moments in history. It is by analyzing the way a model of gender difference permeates a diverse field of rhetoric at a specific moment in time that we can come to understand how it works. Only then can we begin to resist the replication of these models of gender difference in our own work.

"Matters That Appertain to the Imagination": Accounting for Production in *Frankenstein*

You will understand why, in this book, the word 'creation' is suppressed and systematically replaced by 'production.'
—Pierre Macherey, *A Theory of Literary Production*

In this chapter, *Frankenstein* is read as having been produced at a stage early in the economic development of the nineteenth century when, as Marx puts it, commodities were beginning to be fetishized.[1] During the period when Shelley and the Romantic poets were writing, the English economy was becoming increasingly dependent on the production of commodities. Marx explains that, at that economic juncture, commodities came to be perceived as extremely powerful and desirable objects. However, in order for society to establish and maintain its investments in the commodity as a fetish, the commodity's material, manufactured, or produced nature had to be ignored or denied. Written in the same time period as E. T. A. Hoffmann's "The Sandman," Shelley's novel shares with that story what Chris Baldick describes as "a series of Frankensteinian problems, most obviously a complex involving the fusion of productive labour and sexual obsession."[2] Like Marx, both

---

1. While *Frankenstein* was traditionally read, as Robert Kiely and Masao Miyoshi read it, as a Romantic novel, recent criticism, especially George Levine's *The Realistic Imagination*, has tended to see it as a precursor to the Victorian novel. I place Shelley's novel in a nineteenth-century tradition but also mark it as coming out of the same historical moment as Romanticism. See Robert Kiely, *The Romantic Novel in England* (1972), Masao Miyoshi, *The Divided Self: A Perspective on Literature of the Victorians* (1969), and George Levine, *The Realistic Imagination: English Fiction from Frankenstein to Lady Chatterly* (1981).
2. Chris Baldick, *In Frankenstein's Shadow* (1987), 67. Baldick provides a fascinating analysis not just of "The Sandman" but also of "The Mines of Falun," a Hoffmann story in which the hero Elis becomes fascinated with mining. "Like other tales of Hoffmann," Baldick writes, "it pursues the conflict between normal bonds of af-

Hoffmann and Shelley are fascinated by the process of production. In their fiction they represent the manufactured object as initially attractive beyond its market value but also as subsequently repulsive. In *Frankenstein* in particular, Shelley explores at length what Marx describes as the natural consequence of the fetishization of commodities, the alienation of labor. In her descriptions of Victor's relation to the thing he has made, Shelly provides what is virtually a narrative representation of the theoretical assertion Marx makes in *Economic and Philosophical Manuscripts of 1844*, that "the object that labour produces, its product, confronts it as an alien being, as a power independent of the producer."[3]

The Romantic poets were aware of and troubled by what they saw as the increasing materialism of their time. As Coleridge remarks in a lay sermon written in 1817, the year that Shelley was finishing the first version of *Frankenstein*: "We are . . . a busy, enterprising, and commercial nation. The habits attached to this character must, if there exist no adequate counterpoise, inevitably lead us, under the specious names of utility, practical knowledge, and so forth, to look at all things thro' the medium of the market, and to estimate the Worth of all pursuits and attainments by their marketable value."[4]

The counterpoise Coleridge proposes to his nation's growing dependence on commodities was, as Catherine Gallagher has noted, "establishing the existence of a separate realm of spiritual values."[5] The Romantic poets thus privileged the spiritual, ideal,

---

fection and a professional 'mystery' which exacts a single-minded devotion from its followers. It gives us not just a Freudian nuptial trauma but an image of the world of work as a rival to the sexual claims of the fiancée. Only when Elis hears that there is more to mining than the mundane value of 'vile profit' does he become embroiled in its fantasized appeal" (ibid.).

3. Karl Marx, "Alienated Labour," from *Economic and Philosophical Manuscripts*, in *Selected Writings*, ed. David McLellan (1977), 78. All references to this book (hereafter abbreviated *SW*) appear in the text.

4. "A Lay Sermon," in *Lay Sermons*, ed. R. J. White, *The Collected Works of Samuel Taylor Coleridge* (1972), 189. Catherine Gallagher cites this passage in the course of discussing Coleridge's political opposition to Bentham and goes on to explain that "in the second decade of the century, when Coleridge adopted his idea of the state from the German Idealists, he explicitly contrasted it to the marketplace" (Gallagher, *The Industrial Reformation of English Fiction: Social Discourse and Narrative Form, 1832–1867* [1988], 190).

5. Gallagher, *Industrial Reformation of English Fiction*, 190.

or abstract over the material, an emphasis Mary Shelley was careful to maintain in describing her husband and his poetry. In the notes and prefaces to the annotated edition of Percy Shelley's *Poetical Works*, which Mary Shelley published while preparing the revised edition of *Frankenstein*, she characterizes her husband as having, "an abstract and etherealized inspiration" and as "taking more delight in the abstract and the ideal than in the special and tangible."[6] In her journal of 1822, he is invoked as "a spirit caged, an elemental being enshrined in a frail image," and in Harriet de Boinville's letter to Mary Shelley, he is described as "an ethereal Being who did not belong to the gross & palpable world."[7]

For Mary Shelley, the difficulty raised by the Romantic opposition of the spiritual to the material was that it implicitly articulated a model of gender difference; it opposed masculine spirituality or abstraction to feminine materiality. This model leads Shelley, almost invariably, to characterize herself and her own work in terms diametrically opposed to those she uses to discuss the male Romantic poets. In the Author's Introduction to the 1831 edition of *Frankenstein*, for example, she represents herself as writing from within but also as positioned outside the circles of Romanticism; she depicts herself as a silent listener when Byron and Shelley talk about galvanism, and also as the one who fails to think of story when two Romantic poets are immediately inspired to write. She characterizes Byron's *Childe Harold* as "clothed in all the light and harmony of poetry, [which] seemed to stamp as divine the glories of heaven and earth" and Percy Shelley himself as "apt to embody ideas and sentiments in the radiance of brilliant imagery and in the music of the most melodious verse that adorns our language," but associates her own writing with the "common-place" and the "machinery of a story."[8] Describing of the contrast between herself and her husband in her letters, she writes, "I was never the Eve of any Paradise, but a human creature blessed by an elemental spirit's company & love—an angel who imprisoned in flesh could

---

6. Percy Shelley, The *Poetical Works*, ed. Edward Dowden, 2 vols. (1893), 1:224, 20.

7. *The Journals of Mary Shelley*, ed. Paula R. Feldman and Diana Scott-Kilvert, 2 vols. (1987), 2:437. For the citation of Harriet de Boinville's letter, see *Journals*, 2:437n.

8. Mary Shelley, *Frankenstein* (1965), viii, ix. All further references to this book (hereafter abbreviated *F*) appear in the text.

not adapt himself to his clay shrine."[9] The contrast between Percy's ethereal nature and Mary Shelley's earthly or material one recurs throughout the journals and letters, revealed for example, in her anxiety about the worldliness Percy's friends accuse her of after his death. It is inscribed as a difference not just between her fiction and Romantic poetry or between Mary and Percy Shelley but as the difference between genders. As she puts it when asked about women's intellect, "the sex of our material mechanism makes us quite different creatures [from men]—better though weaker."[10]

Shelley's gender thus means that she is inherently associated with the materiality that Romantic writers such as Coleridge hoped to counter with their ideal of spirituality. It is, however, precisely because she writes from the position of the material—of that which is repressed not only by the Romantic poets but also in early nineteenth-century society in general—that Shelley ultimately tells a story which anticipates Marx's theory of alienated labor with uncanny accuracy. Marx developed that theory out of his opposition to the German Romantics, including Hegel, who insisted on privileging the spiritual over the material. Hegel argues that because alienation takes place only at an abstract level, the mind can, in a dialectical process, reappropriate the alienated object as it moves towards absolute self-knowledge. In Marx's words, Hegel asserts:

9. "To Jane Williams, 18 September, 1822," in *The Letters of Mary Wollstonecraft Shelley*, ed. Betty T. Bennett, 3 vols. (1980–88), 1:264. That Percy Shelley, as the male half of the couple, was unaware of the gender difference that Mary, as the female half, experienced so intensely is suggested by his comment to Jefferson Hogg in 1814: "I do not think that there is an excellence at which human nature can arrive, that she does not indisputably possess, or of which her character does not afford manifest intimations. I speak thus of Mary now—& so intimately are our natures now united, that I feel whilst I describe her excellencies as if I were an egoist expatiating upon his own perfections" (*Letters of Percy Bysshe Shelley*, 1:402). Mary Poovey cites this passage as an example of how Percy Shelley's egotism was initially beneficial to Mary, leading him to promote her interests (Poovey, *The Proper Lady and the Woman Writer: Ideology as Style in the Works of Mary Wollstonecraft, Mary Shelley, and Jane Austen* [1984], 120). It also seems clear that the stance Percy Shelley takes here is the one that allows him to write the preface of the 1818 edition of *Frankenstein* as if he were speaking in Mary Shelley's voice. From his position as the male Romantic poet, her gender difference does not make a difference. From hers, it is crucial.

10. "To Maria Gisborne, 11 June [1835]," in *Letters*, 2:246. For a reading of the opposition I am describing here in terms of androgyny, see William Veeder, *Mary Shelley and Frankenstein: The Fate of Androgyny* (1986).

the subject knowing itself as absolute self-consciousness, is therefore God, absolute spirit, the idea that knows and manifests itself. Real man and real nature become mere predicates or symbols of this hidden, unreal man and unreal nature. The relationship of subject and predicate to each other is thus completely inverted: a mystical subject-object or subjectivity reaching beyond the object, absolute subject as process (it externalizes itself, returns to itself from its externalization and at the same time re-absorbs its externalization); a pure and unceasing circular movement within itself. (SW 109)

The power that Hegel asserts the subject has in relation to the world outside itself resembles the power the Romantic poets abrogated to the imaginative self. For example, when Coleridge, whom Baldick describes as "the British avatar of German Idealism,"[11] characterizes his poetic activity as "the eternal act of creation in the infinite I AM," he is, in effect, articulating his version of the absolute subject as God, knowing and manifesting itself. Similarly, when Wordsworth says, "I was often unable to think of external things as having external existence, and I communed with all that I saw as something not apart from, but inherent in, my own immaterial nature," he is talking about a relation in which, to use Hegelian terms, he reaches beyond the objective world and becomes absolute subject in the process.[12]

The Romantic poets' belief in the power of abstract creativity, which both Coleridge and Wordsworth celebrate, is precisely the imaginative power Mary Shelley cannot appropriate for herself because of her self-acknowledged woman's material mechanism. However, just as Marx counters Hegel's abstract idealism by insisting that the alienated object has an external or material existence and therefore cannot be reappropriated simply by a gesture of the mind, Shelley counters the Romantic belief in abstract creativity by telling the story of a creator, Victor Frankenstein, whose imagination produces a figure neither idealized nor etherealized but

11. Baldick, In Frankenstein's Shadow, 34.
12. The passage from Wordsworth is cited in de Man, "The Rhetoric of Temporality," in Interpretation: Theory and Practice, ed. Charles S. Singleton (1969), 180. De Man's essay provides a salutary corrective to my tendency to totalize Romantic theories of creativity by placing them all under the rubric of abstraction. De Man explores the variety of positions the Romantic poets and critical readers of their poetry take on the relation of the self to the world outside it.

emphatically material. In the words of Robert Kiely: "In making that monster a poor grotesque patchwork, a physical mess of seams and wrinkles, she introduces a consideration of the material universe which challenges and undermines the purity of idealism. In short, the sheer concreteness of the ugly thing which Frankenstein has created often makes his ambitions and his character—however sympathetically described—seem ridiculous and even insane."[13] Using the terms of Marx's analysis of Hegel to characterize *Frankenstein*, one might say that, in telling the story of Victor and the monster, Shelley depicts a subject who externalizes himself thinking he will become a god but discovers instead that he can neither return to himself from that externalization nor reabsorb it.[14]

In rendering the material product of invention visible in the form of the monster, Shelley's novel almost inevitably engages the same kind of issues of alienation and labor which Marx deals with in his early critical responses to Hegel. Passages such as the following, from Marx's *Economic and Philosophical Manuscripts of 1844* sound like virtual descriptions of Victor's relation to the thing he makes:

> The more the worker externalizes himself in his work, the more powerful becomes the alien, objective world that he creates opposite himself. . . . The worker puts his life into the object and this means that it no longer belongs to him but to the object. . . . So the greater this product the less he is himself. The externalization of the worker in

13. Kiely, *Romantic Novel in England*, 161. After this brilliant description of the materiality of the monster, Kiely goes on to reinscribe, without criticism, the model of gender difference which opposes masculine spirituality to feminine materiality. He notes that in *Frankenstein* "the arguments on behalf of idealism and unworldly genius are seriously presented, but the controlling perspective is that of an earthbound woman" (161).

14. Miyoshi argues that Percy Shelley had already begun to separate himself from early Romantics, including Coleridge and Wordsworth. According to Miyoshi, in *Alastor*—the poem critics such as Margaret Homans have read as lying behind *Frankenstein*—Shelley depicts "the ultimate failure of the Romantic shapership" (Miyoshi, *Divided Self*, 71). Miyoshi then reads Mary Shelley's novel as an extension of Percy Shelley's critique, asserting that "in this tale, as in the Shelley poem, there is a projection or reproduction of the self; nor is a reunion of the two ultimately possible, for the pursuit ends only with the death of the pursuer. For this reason primarily, the story is a commentary on Romantic alienation, although, like her husband, Mary Shelley is finally quite ambivalent toward the Romantic quest" (ibid., 85). By reading *Frankenstein* in terms of Romantic alienation, Miyoshi ignores, I think, the crucial change that results from Mary Shelley's insistence, like Marx's, that the alienated object has a material being.

his product implies not only that his labour becomes an object, an exterior existence but also that it exists outside him, independent and alien, and becomes a self-sufficient power opposite him, that the life he has lent to the object affronts him, hostile and alien. (78–9)

To read Marx's early writings alongside *Frankenstein* is to see that Shelley carefully chronicles the experience of the making of the monster not as an act of creation but as a process of production during which the producer inevitably becomes alienated from what he has made.[15]

In telling her story, Shelley is relatively uninterested in the moment when the monster is given life. Instead, she focuses the reader's attention on the process leading up to that moment, the separation that follows it, and the way in which both lead to Victor's alienation. Victor thus tells us, "I revolved in my mind . . . the whole train of my progress towards the creation, the appearance of the work of my own hands alive at my bedside, its departure" (*F* 7.74). Because Shelley's novel shows production as a process, it vividly conveys what Marx describes as the "alienation [which] shows itself not only in the result, but also in the act of production, inside productive activity itself" (*SW* 80). As Marx explains, in-

---

15. Several critics have suggested that a Marxist reading of *Frankenstein* would involve reading the monster as an emblem of the alienated laborer. Spivak points out, for example, that "other 'political' readings—for instance, that the monster is the nascent working class—can also be advanced" ("Three Women's Texts and a Critique of Imperialism," in *"Race," Writing and Difference*, ed. Henry Louis Gates, Jr. [1986], 276). Franco Moretti performs precisely such a reading of *Frankenstein* ("Dialectic of Fear," in *Signs Taken for Wonders: Essays in the Sociology of Literary Forms* [1983], 83–90). I would agree that the monster can be read as an emblem of the working classes, but I think *Frankenstein* was written at a point in the nineteenth century when economic anxieties and fantasies were focused more on the arena of production than on that of class difference. The parallels Lee Sterrenburg has so brilliantly noted between the monster and the French Revolution and Paul O'Flinn's reminders that, during the years Shelley was writing *Frankenstein*, she, Percy Shelley, and Byron were involved in responses to the Peterloo Massacre suggest that a general sense of class uprising underlies *Frankenstein* (see Lee Sterrenburg, "Mary Shelley's Monster: Politics and Psyche in *Frankenstein*," in *The Endurance of Frankenstein: Essays on Mary Shelley's Novel*, ed. George Levine and U. C. Knoepflmacher [1979], 143–71, and Paul O'Flinn, "Production and Reproduction: The case of *Frankenstein*," in *Popular Fictions: Essays in Literature and History*, ed. Peter Humm et al. [1986], 196–221). But it is really not until midcentury that the monster begins to be used as an explicit figure for the working classes, as, for example, in Gaskell's 1848 novel *Mary Barton*.

volvement in the process of manufacture alienates the worker not only from the object produced but also from nature and from any connection with fellow beings. All these symptoms of alienation are represented in *Frankenstein*, which shows Victor, as he works on the monster, as isolating himself from the human community by shutting himself up "in a solitary chamber, or rather cell, at the top of the house, and separated from all the other apartments" (4.53). Eventually Victor ceases even to notice the external world; he declares, "It was a most beautiful season; never did the fields bestow a more plentiful harvest or the vines yield a more luxuriant vintage, but my eyes were insensible to the charms of nature" (4.53). Once produced, the monster functions as an active principle of alienation, literally cutting Victor off from family and friends, severing any connection he might have to what Marx describes as the worker's "species-being." In the end, Victor himself perfectly articulates his own alienated condition when he exclaims, "I abhorred the face of man. Oh, not abhorred! They were my breth-ren, my fellow beings, and I felt attracted even to the most repulsive among them, as to creatures of an angelic and celestial mechanism. But I felt that I had no right to share their intercourse" (22.176).[16]

In Shelley's novel, as in Marx's writings, the worker's alienation from the external world and from the object produced leads inev-itably to self-alienation. *Frankenstein* shows the process of produc-tion dividing Victor from himself. On the one hand, he experiences the act of making as so attractive that, despite all that subsequently happens to him, Victor still says to Walton on the last pages of the novel, "even now I cannot recollect without passion my reveries while the work was incomplete. I trod heaven in my thoughts, now exulting in my powers, now burning with the idea of their effects" (24.201). At the same time, despite this almost obsessive enthusiasm, he describes himself as experiencing the "horrors" of "toil" in a "workshop of filthy creation" (4.53) during the process of making the creature. Echoing Marx's worker whom productive

16. Shelley added this passage to the 1831 version of *Frankenstein*, where she seems to have heightened Victor's awareness of his alienation. She also added the following passage in which Victor laments his isolation from his family: "I felt as if I were placed under a ban—as if I had no right to claim their sympathies—as if never more might I enjoy companionship with them" (17.142).

labor alienates "from his own body, nature exterior to him, and his intellectual being, his human essence" (83), Victor finds that, "often did my human nature turn with loathing from my occupation, whilst, still urged on by an eagerness which perpetually increased, I brought my work near to a conclusion" (4.53). In the novel, he describes his experience of making the monster by saying, "I appeared rather like one doomed by slavery to toil in the mines, or any other unwholesome trade than an artist occupied by his favorite employment" (4.54–55). In Marx's terms, as a worker, Victor "does not confirm himself in his work, he denies himself, feels miserable instead of happy, deploys no free physical and intellectual energy, but mortifies his body and ruins his mind" (80).

The suggestion of mortification or "deadness" that infuses Marx's descriptions of the worker's experience of production is literally represented in *Frankenstein* through the materials Victor has to work with—the parts of dismembered corpses.[17] That it is not simply dead matter but the parts of bodies that Victor uses provides an apt image of production. As Elaine Scarry and others have noted, Marx repeatedly characterizes the worker, as "working" over his (or her) own body and also the figurative "body" of the physical world.[18] In *Frankenstein*, Victor's revulsion toward the materials he has to work with becomes particularly clear when he describes making the second monster. Here his thinking reflects the gendered opposition Shelley articulates in her diaries between masculine spirituality and feminine materiality. In making the first *male* monster, Victor imagines himself to have trod heaven in his thoughts; in making the second *female* monster, he finds himself

17. As Elaine Scarry has noted, in Marx, the worker is generally represented as a reanimator of dead matter revealed, for example, in his assertion that "yarn with which we neither weave nor spin is cotton wasted. Living labour must seize on these things, awaken them from the dead" (quoted in Scarry, *The Body in Pain: The Making and Unmaking of the World* [1986], 247). While in Marx's writings this gesture of awakening has a utopian potential for the worker, Shelley focuses primarily on the producer's sense of being involved with dead matter.

18. Several recent critics have noted the importance of the image of the human body in Marx's writings. Scarry notes that Marx "throughout his writings assumes that the made world is the human being's body" (ibid., 244). Similarly, John McMurtry argues that "private-property appropriation of [the] means of production is for [Marx] . . . the dismemberment of those whose 'external organs' are cut off by such exclusive appropriation" (McMurtry, *The Structure of Marx's World View* [1978], 64).

completely earthbound. The second monster evokes no dreams of greatness; she stands as an emblem of nothing except the materiality inherent in the process of production. In Victor's words, "it was, indeed, a filthy process in which I was engaged. During my first experiment, a kind of enthusiastic frenzy had blinded me to the horror of my employment; my mind was intently fixed on the consummation of my labour, and my eyes were shut to the horror of my proceedings. But now I went to it in cold blood, and my heart often sickened at the work of my hands" (19.156–57).

Victor's description of making both monsters suggests that such acts of production raise questions about visibility and about what is actually seen. To understand the relationship between vision and production, it may help, to turn to Marx's comments on the fetishism of commodities in *Capital*. To explain how "the products of labour become commodities, social things whose qualities are at the same time perceptible and imperceptible by the senses" (*SW* 436), Marx uses the following analogy:

> In the same way the light from an object is perceived by us not as the subjective excitation of our optic nerve, but as the objective form of something outside the eye itself. But, in the act of seeing, there is at all events, an actual passage of light from one thing to another, from the external object to the eye. There is a physical relation between physical things. But it is different with commodities. There, the existence of things *qua* commodities, and the value relation between the products of labour which stamps them as commodities, have absolutely no connection with their physical properties and with the material relations arising therefrom. There it is a definite social relation between men, that assumes, in their eyes, the fantastic form of a relation between things.[19]

In this passage, by way of a curious twist, Marx moves toward his final assertion that the commodity's value is in its social or fantastic form. He first asserts the sensuousness of the commodity, then links that material presence to the process of sight, then denies that the physical relation so carefully invoked through the analogy with vi-

19. My attention was called to this passage from *Capital* by Ann Cvetkovich's use of it in her article "Ghostlier Determinations: The Economy of Sensation and *The Woman in White*," *Novel* (Fall 1989): 40.

sion has anything to do with the commodity's value. Marx's passage not only asserts but also illustrates that in order for the product of labor to have value as a commodity, its visible, material, or produced nature needs to be repressed or denied, to remain unseen.

In *Frankenstein*, the monster is monstrous because its manufactured, material nature is relentlessly visible.[20] Here we might remember the etymology of the word *monster*, which originally meant something displayed, as opposed to something repulsive or horrifying. Baldick notes that "As Michel Foucault reminded us in his discussion of the public performances put on by the inmates of lunatic asylums until the early nineteenth century, a 'monster' is something or someone to be *shown*. (Cf. Latin, *monstrare*; French, *montrer*; English, demonstrate.)"[21] From the beginning the monster is repulsive because the things that make it work are overtly displayed rather than covered or hidden. In Victor's words, its "yellow skin scarcely covered the work of muscles and arteries beneath" (5.56). As critics such as Barbara Johnson have noted, the creature is also horrifying because it is visibly a collection of parts. It has been described as an aggregate, an assemblage, a fabrication, "the meticulous gathering of heterogeneous ready-made materials."[22] The fact that the creature's monstrosity inheres in its manufactured nature is protrayed in the various cinematic images of it which almost invariably represent the monster as terrifying because of its enormous size, the seams on its face, and the bolts in its head. These signature traits emphasize the monster's massiveness, its sheer material presence, and its constructed nature, the fact that it is sutured or bolted together, and made up of component parts.

In *Frankenstein*, the monster functions as what Marx calls a social hieroglyph; it shows or makes visible what early nineteenth-century society wished to deny, the materiality inherent in the act of production. Shelley demonstrates in her novel that such a denial involved refusing to see and to recognize both the manufactured nature of the product and the material presence of the worker. In the scenes at the De Laceys' and in later scenes when Victor is

20. Anne Mellor devotes an entire chapter to the various references to sight in *Frankenstein* and also "reads" the monster's visibility semiotically ("Problems of Perception," in *Mary Shelley: Her Life, Her Fiction, Her Monsters* [1988], 127–40).

21. Baldick, *In Frankenstein's Shadow*, 10.

22. Barbara Johnson, "My Monster/My Self," in *A World of Difference* (1987), 151.

pursuing the monster across the wastes of Russia, individuals are shown as willing to accept the fruits of the labors of others so long as the laborer remains invisible. The De Laceys find firewood at their door and wish to believe that they are being helped by "an invisible hand" or a " 'good spirit' " (12.109).[23] During his pursuit of the monster, Victor finds food ready for him, a happening that he explains by saying, "Sometimes, when nature, overcome by hunger, sank under the exhaustion, a repast was prepared for me in the desert that restored and inspired me. The fare was, indeed, coarse, such as the peasants of the country ate, but I will not doubt that it was set there by the spirits that I had invoked to aid me" (24.194).[24] Victor's language in this passage evokes both the Bible and Romantic poetry. His allusion, however, to texts that are associated with spirituality and creation is undercut by the fact that it is the monster who actually maintains him. In terms of the opposition with which this chapter begins, both the De Laceys and Victor wish to believe that the being who provides them with necessities is abstract or immaterial, an etherealized spirit. As soon as the physical presence of the being who works for them becomes visible, the De Laceys cast it out completely.

In *Frankenstein*, the materiality inherent in production is embodied not soley in the figure of the monster but also in a written text, the laboratory notebooks Victor keeps during the making of the monster. His notebooks function as a vehicle both for the repression of the material and for its inevitable return. While Victor asserts

23. The scenes set at the De Laceys' raise the issue of work in a way that the rest of the novel does not, because the loss of their fortune forces the De Laceys to work. In these scenes, as the monster becomes educated and begins to see itself for the first time as society would see it, it comes to understand its position as similar to that of the worker. Franco Moretti notes Marx's description of the worker in *Economic and Philosophical Manuscripts of 1844*: "the more his product is shaped, the more misshapen the worker; the more civilized his object, the more powerless the worker; the more intelligent the work, the duller the worker and the more he becomes a slave of nature. . . . It is true that labour produces . . . palaces, but hovels for the worker. . . . It produces intelligence, but it produces idiocy and cretinism for the worker" (Moretti, "Dialectic of Fear," 87).

24. Margaret Homans cites this passage from *Frankenstein* and notes that while Victor wants to assert that he is being helped by spirits, he acknowledges a few pages later that he knows the monster aids him. As she points out, "Frankenstein, it would seem, deliberately misinterprets the demon's guidance and provisions for him as belonging instead to a spirit of good" (Homans, *Bearing the Word: Language and Female Experience in Nineteenth-Century Women's Writing* [1986], 110).

that throughout the process of working on the monster he had always intended to create ideal beauty and expresses horror when he beholds the final result of his labors, his notebooks tell a different story. They reveal that he was always aware of the material nature of the thing he made and that he recorded that awareness in writing. The notebooks contain all that Victor repressed or denied about the process of manufacture.[25] In the words of the monster: "Everything is related in them which bears reference to my accursed origin; the whole detail of that series of disgusting circumstances which produced it is set in view; the minutest description of my odious and loathsome person is given, in language which painted your own horrors and rendered mine indelible" (15.124). Reading the laboratory notebooks forces the monster to face its own materiality, a materiality that it, too, would like to deny. In showing the monster turning from *Paradise Lost*, a fiction it takes for true history, to the laboratory notebooks, Shelley once again reveals the desire to believe in spiritual creation disrupted by visible evidence of material production. Peter Brooks comments that this shift in reading "substitutes for myths of creation a literal account of the Monster's manufacture."[26]

The gesture the monster makes as it turns from *Paradise Lost* to the laboratory notebooks is paradigmatic of the gesture readers are repeatedly asked to make in *Frankenstein*. In approaching Shelley's narrative, we resemble Victor when he climbs the Alps, calling on the "wandering spirits" of nature for solace, and what responds is not the experience of the sublime that one might expect from such a paradigmatic Romantic scenario but the monster itself, whose massive physical presence makes it the antithesis of "the aerial creations of the poets" (2.36).[27] Similarly, as readers of *Frankenstein*, we continue to have our expectations upended as the story unfolds. Shelley's novel so frequently refers to the Romantic poets,

25. Margaret Homans notes the discrepancy between Victor's journal entry and his self-conscious account of the production of the monster (ibid., 108).

26. Peter Brooks, " 'Godlike Science/Unhallowed Arts': Language, Nature, and Monstrosity," in *Endurance of Frankenstein*, 210.

27. The phrase "aerial creations of the poets" (2.36), which appears in the section describing Elizabeth Lavenza's taste, was originally written by Percy Shelley and can presumably be taken as his definition of his own works. It is, of course, a definition that tallies with the way Mary Shelley describes both him and his poetry especially after his death.

biblical images, and narratives such as *Paradise Lost* that the reader repeatedly anticipates a creation story. What we read instead is something rather more akin to Victor's laboratory notebooks: the account of production and alienation I have been tracing in *Frankenstein*. But Shelley's novel never gives us an account of pure production; we never actually read Victor's laboratory notebooks. Unlike Pierre Macherey's *A Theory of Literary Production*, where "the word 'creation' is suppressed, and systematically replaced by 'production,' "[28] Shelley's novel focuses on the moment of slippage when creation is being replaced by production, a moment when characters and readers experience a sense of vertigo because the creative stories they expected are suddenly disrupted by the visible presence of materiality. In Shelley's novel it is as if material production is always present but invariably repressed or denied; it is always coming to the surface but never quite able to be directly represented or acknowledged.

It is in the Author's Introduction, appended to the 1831 edition of her novel, that Shelley most systematically replaces the Romantic belief in abstract creativity with her own theory of literary production. The overall strategy she uses in that new introduction is to narrate the series of events which led to the writing of *Frankenstein*, a gesture which makes that prologue a document analogous to Victor's laboratory notebooks; both provide accounts of "that series of disgusting circumstances which produced" an "accursed origin" (15.124). In her introduction, Shelley stresses prehistory by telling us what led to the writing of the novel, and further, by noting that she originally began the story at the moment the creature awakens, a comment which informs her readers that when she expanded *Frankenstein* what she added was an account of the prehistory of Victor's making of the monster.[29] By using the introduction to make visible what Pierre Macherey describes as the

28. Pierre Macherey, *A Theory of Literary Production* (1978), 68. All further references to this book (hereafter abbreviated *TLP*) appear in the text.

29. In the 1831 edition, Shelley's revisions of the early parts of Victor's story also make the prehistory of the making of the monster parallel the prehistory of the making of the novel. For example, she modifies the scene in which the oak tree is destroyed by lightning by adding to it an anonymous scholar who discourses on electricity and galvanism while Victor listens. That scene then parallels the scene in the introduction where she describes herself listening to Percy Shelley and Byron discourse on galvanism.

"determinate conditions" (68) under which the novel came into being, Shelley positions her own work of art not as an "etherealized" creation emerging out of nothing but as the end product of a series of specific events. Like the monster, her novel is constructed out of prior materials. Though her new introduction is apparently just an autobiographical anecdote, it, in fact, functions in much the same way that classic Romantic introductions such as Wordsworth's and Coleridge's preface to *The Lyrical Ballads* do. It is implicitly an artistic manifesto, a manifesto that, in the case of *Frankenstein*, represents the work of literature as produced rather than created.

Throughout the introduction, Shelley carefully selects the terms she uses to refer to her own novel. She never talks about her creativity, calls herself a creator, or refers to *Frankenstein* as a creation. Instead, from the very beginning, when discussing the publishers' request that she write the introduction, she calls her novel "a former production" (vii). Later she discusses whether she could "produce anything worthy of notice" (viii) and describes fiction, in contrast to poetry, as involving the need to "invent the machinery of a story" (ix). Language that links the work of literature with production also appears in another addition Shelley made to the 1831 edition of *Frankenstein*, the long passage added to one of Walton's letters where he discusses being influenced by the "Ancient Mariner." Within a very short space in that passage, Walton highlights words and phrases such as "work," "practically industrious," "workman," and "labour," (21) and refers to Coleridge's poem as "that production of the most imaginative of modern poets" (21). He also credits "The Rhyme of the Ancient Mariner" with sparking his enthusiasm for his arctic exploration; that is, with inspiring in him an ambitious drive that the novel will show is parallel to Victor Frankenstein's.[30] By adding Walton's discussion of Coleridge to the 1831 version of her novel, Shelley suggests that the points she makes in her introduction are applicable not just to

30. In showing Coleridge's poem inspiring Walton to move away from rather than toward his bonds with the rest of his species, Mary Shelley is directly countering Percy Shelley's argument in the "Defence of Poetry" that, as Mary Poovey explains, "true poetry . . . strengthens the individual's moral sense because it exercises and enlarges the capacity for sympathetic identification, that is for establishing relationships" (*Proper Lady*, 130).

Frankenstein but to other works of the imagination as well, including the writings of the Romantic poets. All these "imaginative creations" are material products whose effects are neither necessarily moral nor capable of being controlled by the intentions of those who produce them.

Once the introduction is read as working to replace the idea of creation with that of production, Shelley's anecdote about her initial "failure" to think of a ghost story, when the male writers Percy Shelley, Byron, and even Polidori were immediately inspired, then takes on a new significance. It conveys not so much Shelley's inability to be inspired as it does her position outside the system of inspiration the Romantic poets espoused. As Macherey notes: "the way in which the conditions of its possibility *precede* the work (a fact which is so obvious but which centuries of criticism have ignored) systematically censures in advance any psychology of inspiration, even if this psychology is expressed in a theory of an intellectual will, to produce novel beauty" (*TLP* 197). Shelley describes her "lack" of inspiration by saying that she "felt that blank incapability of invention which is the greatest misery of authorship, when dull Nothing replies to our anxious invocations" (x). The terms of this phrase are picked up in the following paragraph where Shelley, in discussing cosmogony, asserts that: "invention, it must be humbly admitted, does not consist in creating out of void, but out of chaos; the materials must, in the first place, be afforded: it can give form to dark, shapeless substances but cannot bring into being the substance itself" (x). In "humbly" insisting that creation does not come out of nothing, Shelley here suggests that her earlier assertion that "nothing" responded to her invocation marks the fact that her novel was not *created* out of nothing but *produced* out of something.

The discussion of cosmogony is the turning point in Shelley's introduction. It is the only paragraph in which she does not relay autobiographical anecdotes, appearing between her early characterizations of herself as a not yet successful creator (she has not lived up to her parents' fame, did not produce imaginary works as a child, is not inspired as the Romantic poets are) and her later account of the series of events which led to the production of *Frankenstein*. To understand why Shelley debunks the biblical concept of creation *ex nihilo* in moving from creativity to productivity, it may help to look again at *Economic and Philosophical Manuscripts of 1844*. There Marx's critique of the biblical concept of creation functions as a bridge between his discussion of the alienation involved in production and his critique of Hegel's overemphasis of the spiritual. Marx opens his discussion of creation by stating that "the idea of the creation of the world received a severe blow from the science of geogeny, the science which describes the formation and coming into being of the earth as a process of self-generation" (*SW* 94–95). Having made this point, Marx is impelled, nevertheless, to address imaginary readers who seek to know about their origins:

> Now it is easy to say to the single individual what Aristotle already said: you are engendered by your father and your mother and so in your case it is the mating of two human beings, a human species-act, that has produced the human being. You see, too, that physically also man owes his existence to man. So you must not only bear in mind the aspect of the infinite regression and ask further: who engendered my father and his grandfather, etc. . . . But you will answer: . . . the progression . . . pushes me ever further backwards until I ask, who created the first man and the world as a whole? I can only answer you: your question itself is a product of abstraction. . . . When you inquire about the creation of the world and man, then you abstract from man and the world. You suppose them non-existent and yet require me to prove to you that they exist. I say to you: give up your abstraction and you will give up your question. (95)

In her introduction, Shelley too refuses to define creation as a moment in which something comes out of nothing. Instead she uses Eastern cosmogony to illustrate a regressive movement back to a time before the moment of origin, similar to what Marx describes; she reminds us that "the Hindus give the world an elephant to support it, but they make the elephant stand upon a tortoise" (x).[31] In wording which emphasizes the materiality of the most

31. Marta Weigle has pointed to the general tendency of European culture to privilege the idea of creation out of nothing over other versions of the creation myth, which it attributes to non-Western cultures. As an example of this privileging, she quotes from Franz Boas's description of American Indian cosmogony, which he reads as more materialist and hence less abstract than the creation myths that

abstract of mental activities, she concludes by insisting that even in *"matters . . . that* appertain to the imagination" (x, emphasis added), invention consists of being able to seize on the possibilities inherent in the materials available.

The final figure Shelley uses to represent the imagination going to work on prior substances involves a glancing allusion to Columbus showing Queen Isabella an egg in order to persuade her of the earth's being round. In this anecdote the egg stands, as the material does generally in the novel, as a grounding that the male imagination seizes upon. The image of an egg, however, also suggests a feminocentric account of creation out of substance as a replacement for male-centered myths of creation out of nothing.[32] Appearing at the very end of Shelley's discussion of cosmogony, the egg is the first in a series of terms that begin to emerge at this point in the introduction, terms linked to reproduction, which will be combined with terms associated with industry and production. In the paragraph immediately following her discussion of cosmogony, in which Shelley represents male figures conversing about scientific reanimation (Percy Shelley and Byron discuss Darwin and vermicelli), she uses terms such as "galvanism," "component parts," and "manufactured" (x). In the following paragraph, where she describes her own dream of how such a reanimation might occur, she refers to an "engine" powering the creature's awakening as well as to "the cradle of life" (xi). In discussing her own work, Shelley uses an amalgam of terms; words such as "workshop," "component part," and "manufacture" are juxtaposed with words like "offspring," "progeny," and "abortion." The language of the

---

came out of Western civilization: "The idea of creation, in the sense of a projection into objective existence of a world that pre-existed in the mind of a creator, is also almost entirely foreign to the American race. The thought that our world had a previous existence only as an idea in the mind of a superior being, and became objective reality by a will, is not the form in which the Indian conceives his mythology. There was no unorganized chaos preceding the origin of the world. Everything has always been in existence in some objective form somewhere" (Boas, *Race, Language and Culture* [1940], 468.).

32. Weigle points out that creation *ex nihilo* is androcentric as well as ethnocentric because it is implicitly defined as masculine and privileged over other more material creation myths, i.e., those in which the universe emerges from prior materials like an egg. Her book goes on to explore various feminocentric myths of creation.

introduction invites the reader not to separate production and re-production but to consider them together, linking both, I would argue, to materiality and alienation.[33]

Ellen Moers's reading of *Frankenstein* in terms of childbirth dove-tails beautifully with a reading of the novel in terms of alienation and production. As Moers points out in her chapter "Female Gothic," the descriptions of the monster's grotesque physical ap-pearance and Victor's initial "revulsion against [the] newborn life" he has brought into being encode a common reaction of women to the first sight of their babies.[34] In an anti-repressive gesture that mimics the ones Shelley makes in her novel, Moers quotes Dr. Spock's description of the physical appearance of a newborn baby, making visible to her readers what they may not normally see.[35] Moers asserts that childbirth, like the manufacture of commodities, is an arena where society denies or represses the material aspects of a process of production by insisting that the child is always beautiful and that there could not possibly be a moment of maternal alienation. In fact, the alienation inherent in childbearing can be extended from the mother's immediate response to the physical appearance of the child to her later relation to that child. Similar to the worker facing the alien power of the object he or she has made, the mother recognizes, as Helene Deutsch explains in *The*

33. For an extensive theoretical discussion of the unacknowledged ways in which production and reproduction are linked, see Mary O'Brien, "Production and Re-production," in *The Politics of Reproduction* (1981), 140–84.

34. Ellen Moers, *Literary Women: The Great Writers* (1976), 93.

35. The full quotation from Dr. Spock's *Baby and Child Care* has a very prominent position in Moers's chapter "Female Gothic." It stands as the epigraph and reads: "A baby at birth is usually disappointing-looking to a parent who hasn't seen one before. His skin is coated with wax, which, if left on, will be absorbed slowly and will lessen the chance of rashes. His skin underneath is apt to be very red. His face tends to be puffy and lumpy, and there may be black-and-blue marks. . . . The head is misshapen . . . low in the forehead, elongated at the back, and quite lopsided. Occasionally there may be, in addition, a hematoma, a localized hemorrhage under the scalp that sticks out as a distinct bump and takes weeks to go away. A couple of days after birth there may be a touch of jaundice, which is visible for about a week. . . . The baby's body is covered all over with fuzzy hair. . . . For a couple of weeks afterward there is apt to be a dry scaling of the skin, which is also shed. Some babies have black hair on the scalp at first, which may come far down on the forehead" (cited in Moers, *Literary Women*, 90).

Psychology of Women, "she who has created this new life must obey its power; its rule is expected, yet invisible, implacable."[36]

For the woman writer, childbirth may be a particularly interesting locus in which to examine production because, as Barbara Johnson points out in her analysis of *Frankenstein,* in the mother-child bond, alienation runs in both directions. The mother may not only be horrified by or alienated from the child, the child may also be alienated from the mother. In a reading which resembles Moers's in linking Shelley's life to her novel, Johnson reminds us that Mary Shelley's own mother, Mary Wollstonecraft, died shortly after, and as a result of, giving birth to her daughter. Noting this, Johnson indicates how repeatedly *Frankenstein* invokes the elimination of the mother. The novel thereby depicts both the mother's repulsion at the child and the child's fear of, but also perhaps need or desire for, "somehow effecting the death of [its] own parents."[37] Shelley's sense of the double movement of alienation inherent in reproduction may explain the difference between her narrative of production and that of Hoffmann, a male writer, who, while he depicts his hero's fascination with the automaton, does not tell the story from the automaton's point of view. Shelley, in contrast, in depicting the alienation inherent in production, narrates the tale from the position of the producer and of the commodity, as well as from the point of view both of the repressor and of that which is repressed and denied.[38]

Moers's reading of *Frankenstein* implies that we should view the

36. Helene Deutsch, *Motherhood,* vol. 2 of *The Psychology of Women: A Psychoanalytic Interpretation* (1943), 215.

37. Johnson, "My Monster/My Self," 152.

38. Margaret Homans notes a different kind of feminine experience of alienation which might also apply here. She argues that Shelley's novel represents women's feelings of alienation at having to occupy the position of man's object of desire. Reading *Frankenstein* as a response to Percy Shelley's *Alastor,* she sees Mary Shelley as literalizing her husband's description of the pursuit of a beautiful but unrealizable feminine ideal in Victor's creation of the monster as his object of desire. According to Homans, Shelley's novel in effect asks the question "What if the hero of *Alastor* actually got what he thinks he wants? What if desire were embodied, contrary to the poet's deepest wishes?" (Homans, *Bearing the Word,* 107–8). With its presentation of part of the narrative from the monster's point of view, "*Frankenstein* is the story of what it feels like to be the undesired embodiment of romantic imaginative desire" (ibid., 108).

making of the monster not as an isolated, aberrant, or transgressive event but rather, like birth, as something common, aspects of which seem monstrous because we repress or deny them. Such a reading is borne out in Shelley's novel where the act of making something or bringing it into being effectively takes place three times: the making of the monster, Walton's recording of Victor's story, and Shelley's writing of the novel. All three events are characterized in similar terms. In describing the transcription of the manuscript, Walton and Victor use language that echoes the earlier description of the making of the monster. In Walton's words: "Frankenstein discovered that I made notes concerning his history; he asked to see them and then himself corrected and augmented them in many places, but principally in giving the life and spirit to the conversation he held with his enemy. 'Since you have preserved my narration,' said he, 'I would not that a mutilated one should go down to posterity' " (24.199). This passage also echoes the descriptions Mary Shelley provides of her experience of writing the novel. In the introduction, Shelley characterizes herself as writing down her dream in much the same way that Walton transcribes Victor's story. And, as Victor edits Walton's text, so Percy Shelley edited and corrected Mary Shelley's manuscript. Shelley, of course, parallels the writing of her own novel to the making of the monster in the famous envoi of the introduction where she exclaims, "I bid my hideous progeny go forth and prosper" (xii).

That envoi marks the distance Shelley has come over the course of her introduction in moving from an opening paragraph where she refers to *Frankenstein* as a "hideous idea" (vii) to a penultimate paragraph where she refers to it as a "hideous progeny" (xii). Shelley's move, from referring to the novel as an idea to referring to it as a progeny, by way of a narrative of the concrete events that led to its being produced, emphasizes that in the course of her introduction, she is repositioning *Frankenstein*, defining it not as an abstraction but as a material object. As a material object, it is also something from which Shelley must inevitably be alienated, as she acknowledges in the envoi both by calling it hideous and by wanting it to go forth and prosper. If we take seriously the implications of Shelley's apparently contradictory closing admonition to her novel, we should read the making of the monster not only as a nontransgressive act but as an act exemplary of the making of the work of art. If we make that gesture, then much of what is apparently monstrous about the being Victor makes can be read as characteristic of the work of art when viewed as production rather than creation.

The monster represents the very qualities that Pierre Macherey argues theories of creativity seek to deny or repress about the work of art. As he puts it:

> The writer, as the producer of a text, does not manufacture the materials with which he works. Neither does he stumble across them as spontaneously available wandering fragments, useful in the building of any sort of edifice; they are not neutral transparent components which have the grace to vanish, to disappear into the totality they contribute to, giving it substance and adopting its forms. . . . even when they are used and blended into a totality they retain a certain autonomy; and may, in some cases, resume their particular life. (TLP 41–42)

The monster, too, as we have seen, is made of parts that fail to cohere because they are visible as the separate materials out of which it is created. Once the work of art is defined as a product rather than a creation, and the materials of which it is made are examined rather than repressed, then it no longer conforms to our assumptions about what "art" should be: "Some of these assumptions have already been pointed out: the postulate of beauty (the work conforms to a model), the postulate of innocence (the work is self-sufficient, its discourse abolishes even the memory of that which it is not), the postulate of harmony or totality (the work is perfect, completed, it constitutes a finished entity)" (TLP 80). As Shelley's novel makes clear, Victor fails in his attempt to assert his "individual will to produce novel beauty" (TLP 197). The monster is neither beautiful nor harmonious nor innocent. Nor does Shelley's novel seem to conform to these artistic ideals, which may explain why one contemporary critic angrily wrote, "it inculcates no lesson of conduct, manners, or morality. . . . it gratuitously harasses the heart, and only adds to the store, already too great, of painful sensations."[39] But perhaps this is what the novel demonstrates, that the work of art is not necessarily moral, beautiful, and

---

39. *Quarterly Review*, January 1818, cited in Poovey, *Proper Lady*, 122.

harmonious; rather, it is a product whose material nature cannot be covered over or repressed but must be monstrously displayed.

The problem for modern critics of the novel is that in the commodity culture in which we live creativity continues to be privileged over productivity.[40] As a result, it is difficult to read *Frankenstein* and avoid replicating the gesture the novel so insistently criticizes, the gesture of repressing the materiality inherent in the process of production. Ironically, even avowedly materialist critics such as Chris Baldick, Paul O'Flinn, and Mary Poovey become inadvertently caught up in making such a gesture of denial. All three critics use similar logic to define Victor's making of the monster as a deviant or transgressive act and, in doing so, verge over into a surprisingly moralistic tone. For Baldick and O'Flinn, the making of the monster is an instance of "bad" capitalist production because it takes place in private. As O'Flinn explains, "scientific advance pursued for private motives and with no reining and directing social control or sense of social responsibility leads directly to catastrophe."[41] In a similar vein, Mary Poovey reads Victor's act as an instance of "monstrous self-assertion," an egotistical gesture which threatens to break the bonds of domestic harmony.[42] In her words, the introduction to the 1831 version of the novel defines the creator of the monster as "transgress[ing] the bounds of propriety through his art."[43]

Both O'Flinn and Poovey view Robert Walton as the figure who represents the corrective to Victor's negative assertion of individual

40. The very difficulty that readers and critics experience in referring to the being made by Victor suggests the contradictions inherent in social attitudes toward production. While Shelley calls it by a number of names (a phantasm, a demon, a thing, a being, a man, a creature, a monster, a demoniacal corpse, a mummy, a wretch, a figure, an object), critics tend to reduce this plurality to a choice between referring to it as a creature or a monster. The contributors to a recent anthology on *Frankenstein* were all asked to refer to the thing Victor makes as "the creature" rather than "the monster." Such a word choice demonstrates the limits of our language; if one does not imply that the being was created by calling it a creature, one must call it a monster. To imply that it is manufactured or produced automatically makes it monstrous. The reduction of names to the dichotomy between creature and monster and the privileging of creature over monster replicates exactly the ideology Shelley attempts to criticize in her novel.

41. O'Flinn, "Production and Reproduction," 202.

42. Poovey, *Proper Lady*, 122.

43. Ibid., 138.

desire. For them, as for other critics, Walton functions as what Fredric Jameson calls a "horizon figure";[44] he stands on the edge or limit of *Frankenstein*, never fully realized, but representing a fantastic resolution to the contradictions that the narrative has elsewhere been unable to resolve. For the Marxist critic, Walton's being forced to acknowledge the demands of his crew and turn back represents Shelley's acknowledgment that labor is social and takes place within a group. (O'Flinn argues that Shelley actually describes a strike on the part of the crew.) The feminist critic interprets Walton's listening to his crew and also his return to his sister as Shelley's recognition that transgressive individual desires can and must be contained or controlled within the domestic circle. While I grant the accuracy of these observations, it seems important to point out that Walton is able to make what critics read as the key gesture of turning back because his enterprise differs crucially from Victor's; he is an explorer, *not* a producer. Walton can function as a "horizon figure" in *Frankenstein* only in an ironic sense; he stands as the apparent solution to the problem Victor represents precisely because his ambition has not made him productive.

The fact that so many critics read Walton as a corrective to Victor Frankenstein suggests, as I think is true, that the novel does not criticize Walton's actions in the same way that it criticizes Victor's. I would read Walton's exoneration as an indication not that the novel has found a way to overcome the alienation inherent in production but that Shelley herself has become absorbed in denying the materiality of a different kind of alienation. In Shelley's novel Walton is associated with imperialist rather than industrial or productive drives. Prior to the opening of the narrative, he is characterized as having abandoned his desire to be a poet, a desire which, if it had been effective, would have allowed him to live in "a paradise of [his] own *creation*" (letter 1.16, emphasis added). Walton seeks to *find* rather than *make* a paradise. In her author's introduction, Shelley refers to two distinct imaginative activities, "discovery and invention" (x). Walton is involved in discovery and therefore needs to be linked with the character Clerval who wishes to learn foreign languages in order to travel to India. Walton's

44. For Jameson's discussions of horizon figures, see *The Political Unconscious: Narrative as a Socially Symbolic Act* (1981), 168–69, 181–84.

implicitly imperialist thinking is articulated perhaps most clearly in the scene where he encounters first the monster and then Victor in the arctic. Walton distinguishes between the two by saying that Victor "was not, as the other traveller seemed to be, a savage inhabitant of some undiscovered island, but a European" (letter 4.23).[45] Here again, the monster embodies material alienation, in this case the alienation of those who are colonized. But, in her depiction of Walton, Shelley does not criticize his imperialist or colonial ambitions in the same way that she criticizes Victor's productive ones. It is the absence of this critical perspective on Walton that allows him to appear to represent a solution to the problems presented in Victor's story. By insistently dramatizing gestures that repress or deny materiality, *Frankenstein* provides the tools which allow the critic to identify the novel's own contradictions.

The chapters that follow will explore the issues which remain peripheral in *Frankenstein*, questions of class difference and colonial relations, which become both more crucial and more problematic for women writing later in the nineteenth century. Because Shelley is writing at a point early in the economic development of her century, she addresses the question of cultural exclusion at the level not of identifiable social groups but of ideological gestures; she shows the way the materiality of production is repressed or denied when creativity is privileged. By midcentury, Elizabeth Gaskell will use the image of Frankenstein's monster to represent a conflict of class interests rather than ideas. Speaking as the voice of the middle class, the narrator of *Mary Barton* asserts that "the actions of the uneducated seem to me typified in those of Frankenstein, that monster of many human qualities. . . . Why have we made them what they are; a powerful monster, yet without the

45. Walton's descriptions of his first encounters with Victor and the monster in the Arctic are apparently an instance of what Spivak describes as "incidental imperialist sentiment in *Frankenstein*" (Spivak, "Three Women's Texts," 273). Despite Spivak's insistence that Shelley's novel "does not deploy the axiomatics of imperialism" (ibid.), it seems clear that Shelley has much less anxiety about imperialist or exploratorial ambitions than she does about entrepreneurial or productive ones. Not only does she allow Walton to return unscathed from his enterprise, she also characterizes Clerval as an innocent victim of the monster, at the same time adding to the 1831 edition of the novel the two passages in which she discusses the fact that he is studying languages to prepare for going out to India (see *Frankenstein: The 1818 Text*, ed. James Reiger [1974], 243, 254). Thus in her revisions she makes the novel's imperialist strain much more explicit without anywhere criticizing it.

inner means for peace and happiness?"[46] Chapters 3 and 4 analyze how the definitions of femininity that Elizabeth Gaskell confronted as a professional woman writer working for Dickens were implicated in midcentury efforts to exclude the working classes from full access to their economic rights. But, before we address the question of class conflict as it is represented in Dickens's and Gaskell's novels of the 1850s, we will look first at Emily Brontë's *Wuthering Heights* and Charlotte Brontë's *Jane Eyre*, where questions of class difference are inscribed as fantasies of upward mobility but where those fantasies are also represented as implicated in midcentury colonial thinking. The imperialist subplot that Shelley seems to feel comfortable representing as relatively innocent in *Frankenstein* takes on more sinister overtones in the two Brontë novels, where it is shown to depend on cultural exclusions founded on emerging conceptions of racial difference.

46. Elizabeth Gaskell, *Mary Barton: A Tale of Manchester Life* (1970), 15.219–20.

2

"The Yahoo, Not the Demon":
Heathcliff, Rochester, and
the Simianization of the Irish

> By acceding to the wildest fantasies (in the popular
> sense) of the colonizer, the stereotyped other reveals
> something of the fantasy (as desire, defence) of that po-
> sition of mastery.
> —Homi Bhabha, "The Other Question"

As one moves from the early 1800s, the era of *Frankenstein*, to
the late 1840s, the era of *Wuthering Heights* and *Jane Eyre*, the implicit
economic focus of the novel shifts from the arena of production to
that of class relations. At the time Emily and Charlotte Brontë were
writing, Victorian audiences were fascinated by stories of individuals who were able to change their class status, stories such as the
one lived by the Reverend Patrick Brontë when he transformed
himself from an illiterate Irish weaver into a university-educated
English clergyman, and those depicted in *Wuthering Heights* and
Jane Eyre, when Heathcliff and Rochester respectively leave home
without money only to return having acquired wealth, family position, and, in Heathcliff's case, education and gentility. Stories
like these appealed to midcentury audiences because they suggested that everyone could overcome the limitations of their social
situation, but such stories tended to be articulated in a colonial
context. While the Victorian audience recognized that it was extremely difficult to redress social inequities at home, they could
fantasize that the unlimited expansion of the empire made it easy
to do so abroad. The colonial grounding of fantasies of upward
mobility, however, also made visible what mid-Victorian audiences
wished to deny: that the desire to elevate oneself in class implicitly
involved a desire to dominate others. Heathcliff's and Rochester's
stories show how, at midcentury, the desires for domination, which
were part and parcel of fantasies of class elevation, could not be
acknowledged when they were seen at work in places close to

home such as Ireland, but could be allowed free rein when they were projected onto more exotic locales—when they were, as Perry Anderson aptly puts it, "extroject[ed] onto the 'Orient.' "[1]

The mid-Victorian fantasy of upward mobility that linked questions of class difference to questions of colonial dominance was also explicitly gendered; it was a version of what we have come to call the story of the self-made *man*. That avenue of advancement was therefore never open to Victorian women, as Eugène Forçade articulates in his 1848 review of *Jane Eyre*:

> The political, colonial and mercantile activities of the English people, that spirit of enterprise that takes Anglo-Saxons to every corner of the world, do it is true redress, for men, the effects of the law of primogeniture. It is not quite the same for women; they have not the same means of winning a place in the sun. Among the middle classes especially, how many girls belonging to the junior branch of the family, must decline through poverty to dependence and destitution! How often must one find, especially among these Englishwomen, that inner conflict, that fatality arising from their situation, so cruelly felt by our needy middle classes, and which grows out of a disharmony between birth, education and fortune. It is in this class that our author has chosen the heroine of her novel.[2]

The Brontë sisters' gender thus implied that they were defined as excluded from enacting narratives of upward mobility. Writing from their position as outsiders, Emily and Charlotte Brontë depict male figures following a trajectory of advancement in *Wuthering Heights* and *Jane Eyre*, but do so in a manner that allows readers to see the repressed colonial subtext that undercuts the mid-Victorian fantasy that the idea of the self-made man will redress social inequities.

To map out the patterns of Victorian colonial thinking that underlie *Jane Eyre* and *Wuthering Heights*, we need first to consider Anglo-Irish relations at the time the two novels were written. In England, the immediate effect of the cataclysmic 1840s Irish potato famine was a sudden influx of Irish immigrants that exacerbated

1. Perry Anderson, *Lineages of the Absolutist State* (1979), 463.
2. Eugène Forçade, Review of *Jane Eyre*, from *Revue des deux mondes*, in *The Brontës: The Critical Heritage*, ed. Miriam Allott (1974), 102.

the already longstanding English xenophobia about the Irish.[3] As L. Perry Curtis has demonstrated, the English tendency to caricature the Irish and represent them as an alien people, which persisted from the Renaissance onward, was intensified in the mid-nineteenth century in a process Curtis describes as the simianization of the Irish.[4] By the 1860s, that process, which was in its early stages in the 1840s, had crystallized, and the English public had become familiar, in both cartoons and political commentary, with characterizations such as the following, sketched by an unknown satiric writer in *Punch* in 1862: "A creature manifestly between the Gorilla and the Negro is to be met with in some of the lowest districts of London and Liverpool by adventurous explorers. It comes from Ireland, whence it has contrived to migrate; it belongs in fact to a tribe of Irish savages: the lowest species of the Irish Yahoo. When conversing with its kind it talks a sort of gibberish."[5] As this passage suggests, to associate the Irish with simians was, for the Victorians, to link them to the same kind of stereotypes that were being used to describe blacks. Such a linkage was supported by mid-nineteenth-century ethnographic thinking, exemplified in the writings of John Beddoe, a founding member of the Ethnological Society and later president of the Anthropological Institute from 1889 to 1891. Beddoe became famous for establishing what he called the "Index of Nigresence," a pseudoscientific formula that allowed him to determine the relative amount of melanin

3. In interviewing Raymond Williams the editors of the *New Left Review* argue that in the 1840s, "there occurred a cataclysmic event, far more dramatic than anything that happened in England, a very short geographical distance away, whose consequences were directly governed by the established order of the English state. That was, of course, the famine in Ireland—a disaster without comparison in Europe. Yet if we consult the two maps of either the official ideology of the period or the recorded subjective experience of its novels, neither of them extended to include this catastrophe right on their doorstep, causally connected to socio-political processes in England" (Raymond Williams, "The Long Revolution," in *Politics and Letters: Interviews with New Left Review* [1979], 170). I am suggesting that the Irish cataclysm is not so much absent from the Brontës' novels as it is present but virtually invisible. This chapter attempts to map out the various structures of feeling that occlude the traces of Irishness in these texts.

4. L. Perry Curtis's *Anglo-Saxons and Celts: A Study of Anti-Irish Prejudice in Victorian England* (1968) and his *Apes and Angels: The Irishman in Victorian Caricature* (1971) provide a wealth of information about English attitudes toward the Irish in the mid-Victorian period.

5. Quoted in Curtis, *Apes and Angels*, 100.

in the hair, skin, and iris of the eyes, and the relative proportion of "dark" persons to light in any population. He used that index to confirm that a much greater percentage of what he described as "Africanoid celts" were to be found in Wales and Ireland than in central England.[6]

This kind of thinking was so pervasive at midcentury that it is replicated even in the writings of those attempting to pay close attention to the complexities of Anglo-Irish relations. A revealing passage from Charles Kingsley's letters to his wife in which he describes his travels in Ireland allows us to see how a Victorian writer who was aware of the problematic English treatment of the Irish still could not avoid becoming imbricated in Victorian racist and imperialist logic. Kingsley writes:

> I am haunted by the human chimpanzees I saw along that hundred miles of horrible country. I don't believe they are our fault. I believe there are not only many more of them than of old, but that they are happier, better, more comfortably fed and lodged under our rule than they ever were. But to see white chimpanzees is dreadful; if they were black, one would not feel it so much, but their skins, except where tanned by exposure, are as white as ours.[7]

In this passage, the Irish occupy the position aptly described by Homi Bhabha as "not quite/not white,"[8] a state of racial indeterminacy that Kingsley finds peculiarly unsettling and resists by introducing what Bhabha would call an "epidermal schema."[9] As

6. John Beddoe, *The Races of Britain* (London, 1885), 5. Beddoe is cited and discussed in Curtis, *Apes and Angels* (19–20) and *Anglo-Saxons and Celts* (71–72). Beddoe's ethnographic studies demonstrate that at midcentury the concept of racial difference or "race" was not fixed but was in the process of being defined as a term.

7. *Charles Kingsley: His Letters and Memories of His Life*, ed. by Frances Kingsley (1877), 2:107, cited in Curtis, *Anglo-Saxons and Celts*, 84.

8. Homi Bhabha, "Of Mimicry and Man: The Ambivalence of Colonial Discourse," *October* 28 (Spring 1984): 132.

9. Homi Bhabha, "The Other Question: Difference, Discrimination and The Discourse of Colonialism," in *Literature, Politics and Theory: Papers from the Essex Conference 1976–84*, ed. Francis Barker et al. (1986), 165. While Bhabha uses terms such as "epidermal schema," which he adopts from the writings of Franz Fanon, and "not quite/not white" to describe the way it feels to be in the position of the stereotyped other, his terms can also be used, as I do here, to analyze the psychic mechanisms of those who are doing the stereotyping.

Kingsley turns from looking at the Irish to thinking about "blacks," difference in skin color makes "racial" difference seem more absolute and therefore less troubling. Kingsley's passage is paradigmatic of the way Victorian colonial thinking generally worked; it shifted attention away from the oppressions of local colonialism, which were uncomfortably close to home, and focused instead on oppressions that seemed more acceptable because they involved peoples conceived as more distant, more exotic, and more easily defined in terms of stereotypes of "racial" difference. [10]

The kind of shift that occurs at the end of Kingsley's meditation repeats itself over and over again in the rhetoric of those writing about the British empire, typified by the description of the Chinese as the "Irish of the orient," as well as by Marx's comment in the opening of his 1852 article on British rule in India that "Hindustan is not the Italy, but the Ireland of the East. . . . a world of voluptuousness and a world of woes." [11] Marx provides a particularly interesting instance of colonial thinking since, unlike a number of Victorian writers, he did not turn a blind eye to the English treatment of the Irish but condemned it, asserting that "England never has and never can—so long as the present relations last—rule Ireland otherwise than by the most abominable reign of terror and the most reprehensible corruption." [12] Such assertions lead one to expect Marx to be similarly critical of English domination in India. In places, he is critical, as in the conclusion of his article "The Future Results of British Rule in India," where he asserts that in India "the profound hypocrisy and inherent barbarism of bourgeois civilization lies unveiled before our eyes, turning from its home, where it assumes respectable forms, to the colonies, where it goes naked." [13] When Marx condemns the British for their naked barbarity, an attribute usually associated not with the colonizers but

10. For an extended discussion of the idea of local or "internal colonialism" with reference specifically to the Irish, see Michael Hechter, *Internal Colonialism: The Celtic Fringe in British National Development, 1536–1966* (1976).

11. Karl Marx, "The British Rule in India," in *The Portable Karl Marx*, ed. Eugene Kamenka (1984), 329.

12. "To Kugelmann, 29 November 1869," in *Selected Writings*, ed. David McLellan (1977), 591.

13. Karl Marx, "The Future Results of British Rule in India," in *Selected Writings*, 335.

with the colonized, his imagery prefigures the subsequent change in the direction of his argument. As Marx turns his attention from England to the colonies, his logic shifts in much the same way that Kingsley's does as he turns from white to black chimpanzees; the oppression that makes Marx uncomfortable at home turns out to be necessary, even beneficial, when it is practiced in India.

Although Marx begins his 1853 article "The British Rule in India" by criticizing the British destruction of the Indian village system, his argument changes at midpoint, and he proceeds instead to criticize native rule for its "aimless, unbounded forces of destruction," its slavery, its degradation, and "brutalizing worship of nature."[14] Once he has defined Indian government as regressive, Marx is able, at least fleetingly, to characterize British actions in India as progressive. He concludes by arguing that, despite its brutality, the British destruction of the Indian economy and village system moved India out of the stagnation of the past and into a modern, industrial future. As he describes it:

> England, it is true, in causing a social revolution in Hindustan was actuated only by the vilest interests, and was stupid in her manner of enforcing them. But . . . can mankind fulfil its destiny without a fundamental revolution in the social state of Asia? If not, whatever may have been the crimes of England she was the unconscious tool of history in bringing about that revolution.[15]

As Marx moves from the local colonization of the Irish to the more distant colonization of the Indians, he conceptualizes the act of domination, which seems wholly oppressive at home, as having two forms, one of which (the Indian) is defined as reactionary, the

14. Marx, "The British Rule in India," in *Portable*, 335–36.
15. Ibid., 336. The particular image Marx has of India, as a place of stagnation and oppression that needs, in effect, to be "raped" by the British in order to be moved into modern history, seems to be characteristic of the kind of fantasies which can be engaged about a culture that is racially different or even one that involves racial difference. Cora Kaplan describes the function of the pre–Civil War South in *Gone with the Wind* with a logic that replicates Marx's; "that imaginary historical landscape was both Edenic and poisoned—by slavery, by illusion—and its violent disruption necessary so that the South could enter modern industrial capitalist society. Sherman's rape of Georgia, Rhett's violent seduction of Scarlett, are analogous events in the text, progressive events if you like, which take place in a world tinged with unbearable emotional nostalgia" (Cora Kaplan, *Sea Changes: Essays on Culture and Feminism* [1986], 119).

other (the British) as potentially revolutionary. This split in Marx's thinking is characteristic of the way the colonized become a locus where the colonizers can articulate both what they fear and what they desire. As Bhabha explains, in colonial discourse the stereotyped other functions as both phobia and fetish.[16] The stereotype that allows Marx to articulate both his fears and desires about domination is the figure of the "oriental despot."[17]

Echoing the passages from Kingsley and Marx, in the Brontë novels, a shift in Victorian thinking from the racial indeterminacy of the Irish to images of racial difference that seem more absolute leads to the emergence of such stereotypes as the oriental despot. The Brontës would have been particularly aware of the issues surrounding the Irish at midcentury since their father, the Reverend Patrick Brontë, had been born in Ireland to an uneducated working-class family but had become a university-educated clergyman living comfortably in England. Their novels, however, contain few explicit references to Ireland, and those references tend to be occluded by allusions to peoples thought of as more exotic and more clearly racially differentiated than the Irish. In *Shirley*, for example, when Charlotte Brontë introduces Malone, one of the few identifiably Irish characters to appear in her novels, she sketches him as

> a tall, strongly-built personage, with real Irish legs and arms, and a face as genuinely national: not the Milesian face—not Daniel O'Connell's style, but the high-featured, North-American-Indian sort of visage, which belongs to a certain class of the Irish gentry, and has a petrified and proud look, better suited to the owner of an estate of slaves, than to the landlord of a free peasantry.[18]

As soon as the narrator attempts to pin down what makes Malone Irish, the passage shifts to associating him with explicitly colonized figures, the American Indians, and to describing him, as Marx does

16. Bhabha, "Other Question," 159.

17. Considering Marx's writings on India along with other Victorian writings such as ethnographies of the Irish, Kingsley's letter, and the Brontë novels may help us to understand, as Said puts it, "how Marx's moral equation of Asiatic loss with the British colonial rule he condemned gets skewed back towards the old inequality between East and West" (Edward Said, *Orientalism* [1979], 154). Said discusses Marx's views on India in *Orientalism*, 153–57.

18. Charlotte Brontë, *Shirley*, ed. Andrew and Judith Hook (1974), 1.42.

in criticizing Indian government, not as oppressed but as an oppressor of others, a slaveholder, thus a kind of despot.

Similarly, in *Wuthering Heights* and *Jane Eyre*, allusions to the Irish are masked by references to more exotic manifestations of racial difference. Indeed, for most London readers, the representations of "savagery" in the Brontë novels were triply distanced, first by their location in Yorkshire, then by covert references to the Irish, and finally, by more explicit references to the orient and the West Indies. Nevertheless, for some readers the violence depicted in those novels felt disturbingly close to home. As one reviewer remarks, "It is with difficulty that we can prevail upon ourselves to believe in the appearance of such a phenomenon, so near our own dwellings as the summit of a Lancashire or Yorkshire moor."[19] The reviewer here refers to Heathcliff, a figure whose "difference" Victorian critics deplored in terms reminiscent of midcentury caricatures of the Irish. Another critic says of Heathcliff, expanding the reference to include the Brontë novels in general, "It is the yahoo, not the demon, that they select for representation."[20] There are unidentified traces of Irishness in the descriptions of both Heathcliff and Rochester. But, like the Kingsley passage, where the indeterminate racial difference of the Irish is unsettling, or the critical response, where the idea of Heathcliff in Yorkshire seems too close, references to the local colonization of the Irish in *Wuthering Heights* and *Jane Eyre* are covered over by images that suggest both more explicit "racial" difference and more distant colonies.

19. "Unsigned review of *Wuthering Heights*," from the *Examiner*, in Allott, *The Brontës: The Critical Heritage*, 221.

20. E. P. Whipple, "Novels of the Season," in *North American Review*, from Allott, *The Brontës: The Critical Heritage*, 247. This kind of comment, which associates both the Brontës and the characters in their novels with images of racial and cultural difference, appears throughout the early reviews of both *Wuthering Heights* and *Jane Eyre*. Elizabeth Rigby describes Jane as having "the strength of a mere heathen mind which is a law unto itself," and Catherine and Heathcliff as "too odiously and abominably pagan to be palatable even to the most vitiated class of English readers" ("Unsigned review," from *Quarterly Review*, in Allott, *The Brontës: The Critical Heritage*, 109, 111). Heathcliff is described as "the black gipsy-cub [who] might possibly have been raised into a human being," as having "no Christian virtue implanted in his heathenish soul, no English grace softening his obdurate visage," and, as "the untrained doomed child of some half-savage sailor's holiday" (Charlotte Brontë, "To W. S. Williams, 14 August 1848"; John Skelton, "Unsigned review," from *Fraser's Magazine*; A. Mary F. Robinson, "The Origin of *Wuthering Heights*"; all cited in Allott, *The Brontës: The Critical Heritage*, 246, 337, 435).

Heathcliff is described as a heathen, a lascar, a gypsy, and an Indian or Chinese prince. Rochester is called a Paynim, an emir, a sultan, a bashaw, and the Grand Turk. (Even his horse Mesrour is named after the executioner at the court of Harun al-Raschid from the *Arabian Nights*.) In both novels, however, behind these overt references to orientalism lie details which link Heathcliff and Rochester to contemporary stereotypes of the Irish.

As Winifred Gérin has pointed out, the depiction of Heathcliff, particularly when he first appears at the Heights, may have had its origin in the Victorian representations of the Irish children who were pouring into England in the late 1840s as a result of the potato famine. When Nelly characterizes Heathcliff as "a dirty, ragged, black-haired child; big enough both to walk and talk . . . yet, when it was set on its feet, it only stared round, and repeated over and over again some gibberish that nobody could understand,"[21] her language is strikingly similar to that used in the satiric sketch cited earlier from the 1862 *Punch*. Gérin explains the events that may have led Brontë to include such a characterization in her novel:

> In August 1845 Branwell was sent to Liverpool. . . . It was the time when the first shiploads of Irish immigrants were landing at Liverpool and dying in the cellars of the warehouses on the quays. Their images, and especially those of the children, were unforgettably depicted in the *Illustrated London News*—starving scarecrows with a few rags on them and an animal growth of black hair almost obscuring their features. The relevance of such happenings within a day's journey from Haworth (collections were made in Haworth Church for the victims of the Irish Famine) cannot be overlooked in explaining Emily's choice of Liverpool for the scene of Mr. Earnshaw's encounter with "the gipsy brat" Heathcliff. . . . Branwell's visit to Liverpool was in August 1845; the writing of *Wuthering Heights* belongs to the autumn and winter of that year.[22]

When Heathcliff is later described as having hair as long as "a colt's mane" (7.45), a "slouching gait, and ignoble look" (8.53) by which

---

21. Emily Brontë, *Wuthering Heights* (1990), chap. 4, p. 29. All further references to this book (hereafter abbreviated *WH*) appear in the text.

22. Winifred Gérin, *Emily Brontë: A Biography* (1971), 225–26. This passage was first called to my attention by James H. Kavanaugh, who cites it in the introduction to *Emily Brontë* (1985), 11–12.

he "contrived to convey an impression of inward and outward repulsiveness" (8.52), these details all reinforce his resemblance to mid-nineteenth-century stereotypes of the Irish. Brontë's depiction of Heathcliff's childhood treatment also resonates with the kind of uneasiness one senses in Kingsley's description of the Irish people he saw along the road during his travels. Does Heathcliff become brutish because of Hindley's neglect, as the Irish may have been made chimpanzees by the English treatment of them? Or is Heathcliff inherently savage, as racist caricatures imply the Irish are? Like the passage from Kingsley, *Wuthering Heights* leaves its Victorian readers with no clear or comforting answer to such troubling questions.

Although Rochester does not share Heathcliff's mysterious origins or his oppressed childhood, he, like Heathcliff, is marked out from other characters in the novel by his differing physical makeup. From the moment of his first appearance, Rochester is characterized, recurrently, almost obsessively as having a "dark face,"[23] "heavy brow" (12.145), "broad and jetty eyebrows" (13.151), "deep eyes" (17.204), "full nostrils" (13.151), and a body with "unusual breadth of chest, disproportionate almost to his length of limb"(14.163–64), all of which leads Jane to assert that "I am sure most people would have thought him an ugly man" (14.164). These details of Rochester's appearance, which he calls "personal defects" and Céline Varens "deformities" (15.175), conform to the simianized images of the Irish that were beginning to proliferate at the time *Jane Eyre* was written.[24] Later in the novel, Rochester's dark, gnomelike physiognomy is contrasted to the true "English" type, St. John Rivers, whom Jane describes as

> tall, slender; his face riveted the eye; it was like a Greek face, very pure in outline: quite a straight, classic nose; quite an Athenian mouth and chin. . . . He might well be a little shocked at the irregularity of my lineaments, his own being so harmonious. His eyes were large

23. Charlotte Brontë, *Jane Eyre* (1965), chap. 12, p. 145. All further references to this book (hereafter abbreviated *JE*) appear in the text.

24. As Curtis notes, "The process of simianizing Paddy's features took place roughly between 1840 and 1890 with the 1860s serving as a pivotal point in this alteration of the stereotype" (Curtis, *Apes and Angels*, 29).

and blue, with brown lashes; his high forehead, colourless as ivory, was partially streaked over by careless locks of fair hair. (29.371)

Such comparisons were a staple in Victorian ethnographic writing, as in "The Comparative Anthropology of England and Wales," where Daniel MacKintosh delineates the Celtic type by comparing it to the "pure" Saxon who is distinguished by

> features excessively regular: face round, broad, and shortish, mouth well formed, and neither raised nor sunk. Chin neither prominent nor receding. Nose straight and neither long nor short. Underpart of face a short ellipse. Low cheek bones. Eyes rather prominent, blue or bluish grey and very well defined. Eyebrows semicircular, horizontally placed. Forehead semicircular.... Hair light brown. Chest and shoulders of moderate breadth.... Total absence of all angles and sudden projections or depressions. [25]

Victorian ethnologists studying the racial characteristics of the Celts and the Irish emphasized differences not just of appearance but also of personality. For them, "the interdependence of pigment, complexion and facial features on the one hand and national and racial character on the other was regarded as axiomatic." [26] The violent intensity of Heathcliff's and Rochester's personal attachments and the emotional volatility both men exhibit are characteristic of Victorian stereotypes of Irish national or racial behavior. When Heathcliff, for example, expresses his desire to "have the privilege of flinging Joseph off the highest gable, and painting the house-front with Hindley's blood!" (6.38), he exemplifies what the 1834 *Edinburgh Review* described as typically Irish personality traits: a "desperate recklessness of the consequences of actions" and "a spirit of revenge, not to be satiated except by blood." [27] With his extreme, almost feminine sensitivity, morbidity, and mood swings, Rochester also conforms to contemporary descriptions of the Irish as "quick in perception, but deficient in depth of reasoning power; headstrong and excitable; tendency to oppose; strong in

25. Daniel Mackintosh, "The Comparative Anthropology of England and Wales," *Anthropological Review and Journal*, vol. 4:17, cited in Curtis, *Apes and Angels*, 18.

26. Curtis, *Apes and Angels*, 10–11.

27. *Edinburgh Review* 59 (April 1834), 119, 235, cited in Curtis, *Anglo-Saxons and Celts*, 54.

love and hate; at one time lively, soon after sad, vivid in imagination."[28]

Given the Reverend Patrick Brontë's origins, it is not surprising
that he was also characterized, both in the family mythology and
in biographers' anecdotes, as engaging in the kind of volatile, emotional behavior the Victorians considered typically Irish. The stories
about him going into his wife's closet and cutting her silk dresses
to ribbons or shooting off his shotgun in the house, which we now
take to be apocryphal, are all characteristic of mid-nineteenth-
century stereotypes of Irish behavior. As Elizabeth Gaskell says in
her biography of Charlotte Brontë: "His strong, passionate, Irish
nature was, in general, compressed down with resolute stoicism;
but it was there notwithstanding all his philosophic calm and dignity of demeanor."[29] This passage, in which Gaskell both denies
and affirms Brontë's Irish nature, is characteristic of the way she
generally deals with the potentially unsettling question of his racial
difference from the English. When describing his physical appearance, for example, she both notes that he is Irish and, at the
same time, describes him in terms that make him sound like Charlotte's characterization of St. John Rivers as the true English type:
"Mr Brontë has now no trace of his Irish origin remaining in his
speech; he never could have shown his Celtic descent in the straight
Greek lines and long oval of his face."[30] Here, too, Gaskell asserts
racial difference at the very moment she attempts to deny it. In
the process of characterizing Brontë as "purely" English, she uses
the word "trace," suggesting that, for her, as well as for her Victorian readers, Brontë would have been indelibly "marked" by his
Irish origins.

28. Mackintosh, "Comparative Anthropology," 1–15, 16, cited in Curtis, *Anglo-Saxons and Celts*, 71.

29. Elizabeth Gaskell, *The Life of Charlotte Brontë*, ed. Winifred Gérin (1971), 75.

30. Ibid., 64. For Gaskell and other critics writing at midcentury, the Brontës'
Irish ancestry and the traces of Irishness in their novels needed to be suppressed
and denied. By the end of the century, the attitude toward the Irish was very
different. In 1899–1900, a reviewer such as Mrs. Humphry Ward could ask: "In the
first place, has it ever been sufficiently recognized that Charlotte Brontë is first and
foremost *an Irishwoman*, that her genius is at bottom a Celtic genius? The main
characteristics indeed of the Celt are all hers—disinterestedness, melancholy, wild-
ness, a wayward force and passion, for ever wooed by sounds and sights to which
other natures are insensible" (Mary Ward, from the "Preface to the Haworth edition
of the Brontës's work," in Allott, *The Brontës: The Critical Heritage*, 449).

Questions of race remain, however, denied or repressed in writings about Patrick Brontë and in his own stories about his life which emphasize instead the way he overcame class difference. According to his biographers and critics, the Reverend Patrick Brontë realized a Victorian fantasy of upward mobility by leaving his Irish working-class background behind and transforming himself into a university-educated clergyman, thus becoming an established member of the English professional classes. This transformation appears to have been completed when he was at Cambridge and changed his name from Prunty to Brontë, thereby taking, in place of an identifiable Irish name, a surname associated with both Lord Nelson and the aristocracy. In his later retellings of his life, however, Brontë located its turning point somewhat earlier, at the moment when he, still a poor, self-educated Irish weaver, was standing in the midst of a field declaiming *Paradise Lost*, a text he had memorized because it moved him so powerfully. At that moment, the Reverend Andrew Harshaw rode by, saw him, and exclaimed, "You are a natural gentleman."[31] In practical terms, Harshaw made Brontë's social advancement possible, initially by offering him a teaching job and eventually by helping him to go to Cambridge, thus enabling him to leave behind his working-class, Irish origins. This description of encountering Harshaw conveys, however, less the practical realities of class advancement than an image, as Tom Winnifrith puts it, in his 1988 biography of Charlotte Brontë, of Patrick Brontë heroically "leaping at one bound a great class barrier."[32] The Miltonic tone of Winnifrith's comment echoes Brontë's own emphasis on *Paradise Lost* and suggests accurately, as Charlotte and Emily's novels bear out, that the unspoken literary analogue for Patrick Brontë's leap upward in class is Satan's flight from Pandemonium to Eden.

In Brontë's telling of his own life and in *Wuthering Heights* and *Jane Eyre*, the references to *Paradise Lost* help us to uncover the colonial subtext of narratives which are apparently about class elevation. Both Heathcliff and Rochester enact, in differing ways, a trajectory of upward mobility that resembles Patrick Brontë's, and,

31. The story of Patrick Brontë, *Paradise Lost*, and Reverend Harshaw is told in a number of places. See John Cannon, *The Road to Haworth: The Story of the Brontës' Irish Ancestry* (1980), 77–80.
32. Tom Winnifrith, *A New Life of Charlotte Brontë* (1988), 8.

in both cases, the literary figure associated with their self-advancement is Milton's Satan. When Heathcliff transforms himself from a semiliterate member of the serving classes to a "gentleman," perhaps, as Lockwood speculates, by getting "a sizer's place at college" (10.70), the pattern of his life seems particularly close to Patrick Brontë's. After he returns to the Heights educated and wealthy, Heathcliff is also repeatedly compared to Satan; he has become, in Charlotte Brontë's apt image, "a magnate of the infernal world."[33] Because, for Rochester, the trajectory of upward mobility involves not overcoming class difference but acquiring money, his story reveals itself more overtly than Heathcliff's to be imperialistic. The literary model he uses to structure the story of his return from the colonies is, as Gayatri Spivak has noted, Satan's flight from hell to earth. In telling Jane about his relation to Bertha Mason, Rochester says:

"One night I had been awakened by her yells . . . it was a fiery West Indian night . . . The air was like sulphur-streams—I could find no refreshment anywhere. . . .

'This life,' said I at last, 'is hell: this is the air—those are the sounds of the bottomless pit! I have a right to deliver myself from it if I can. . . . let me break away, and go home to God!'. . . .

A wind fresh from Europe blew over the ocean and rushed through the open casement. . . .

'Go,' said Hope, 'and live again in Europe' " (27.335–36)[34]

Rochester's representation of Jamaica as Pandemonium and England as Eden is typical of the way *Paradise Lost* was used in colonial rhetoric of the time period. In discussing the Irish question, for example, the noted historian W. E. H. Lecky uses a similar set of images from Milton's poem to assert that Ireland needs firm English

33. Charlotte Brontë, from "Biographical Notice" to the second edition of *Wuthering Heights* and *Agnes Grey*, in Allott, *The Brontës: The Critical Heritage*, 287.

34. While Gayatri Spivak cites these passages as an instance of the "unquestioned ideology of imperialist axiomatics" of *Jane Eyre* (Spivak, "Three Women's Texts," 267), I would argue that the imperialist discourse here is both curiously foregrounded, because of Rochester's anomalous status in the novel, and also undercut, because it is put in the mouth of a male speaker. See my comments in the introduction on the limits of Spivak's approach.

rule "on the Indian model" because Home Rule would lead to "the most perfect of all earthly realisations of Pandemonium."[35]

Rochester's use of *Paradise Lost* in his colonial narrative suggests what Patrick Brontë's story of his own life occludes: that the image of one's heroic ability to overcome class or economic differences covers over the problem that to leave Ireland behind is not to leave one's Irishness behind. If, as Gayatri Spivak remarks, Rochester uses his Miltonic narrative to "inscribe the field of imperial conquest . . . as Hell,"[36] he also, like Satan, brings what he defines as "hell" back with him by returning to England with Bertha Mason, a sign of his continued connection to the colonized. Though both Heathcliff and Rochester move from a position of oppression to one of dominance, neither escapes being characterized in terms that associate him with Victorian stereotypes of racial difference. When oppressed, both are linked to the images of the simianized Irish. When dominant, both are described as Chinese princes or sultans, thus as "oriental despots." Emily and Charlotte Brontë's characterizations of Heathcliff and Rochester allow us to map out the colonial thinking that made idealized mid-Victorian narratives of upward mobility possible. While *Jane Eyre* focuses almost exclusively on Rochester after he has achieved a position of dominance, *Wuthering Heights* shows both stages but concentrates on Heathcliff's childhood oppression which is linked to images of racial difference.

Consciousness of class difference enters *Wuthering Heights*, as Terry Eagleton has pointed out, when Cathy and Heathcliff escape from Wuthering Heights and have their first vision of Thrushcross Grange.[37] In that scene, the difference between classes is, however,

---

35. Elisabeth Lecky, *A Memoir of the Rt. Hon. William E. H. Lecky* (New York, 1910), 158, cited in Curtis, *Anglo-Saxons and Celts*, 87–88.

36. Spivak, "Three Women's Texts," 266.

37. Terry Eagleton describes the economic and social differences between the Grange and the Heights in the following manner: "The delicate spiritless Lintons in their crimson-carpeted drawing-room are radically severed from the labour which sustains them; gentility grows from the production of others, detaches itself from that work (as the Grange is separate from the Heights), and then comes to dominate the labour on which it is parasitic. In doing so, it becomes a form of self-bondage; if work is servitude, so in a subtler sense is civilisation. To some extent, these polarities are held together in the yeoman-farming structure of the Heights. Here labour and culture, freedom and necessity, Nature and society are roughly complementary. The Earnshaws are gentlemen yet they work the land; they enjoy the

immediately underwritten by assertions of racial difference. As soon as the two interlopers are caught, Mr. Linton takes one look at Heathcliff, calls him a Lascar and a heathen, and defines him as a criminal solely on the basis of his appearance, exclaiming that " 'the villain scowls so plainly in his face, would it not be a kindness to the country to hang him at once, before he shows his nature in acts, as well as features?' " (6.39). When Cathy returns to the Heights after her five-week stay at the Grange, she is differentiated from Heathcliff on the basis of her hands, which have been "whitened" by the Lintons' pampering, while Heathcliff, as Cathy herself now notices, has "dusky fingers" that might dirty her dress. The differing appearance of their hands raises issues of who works and who does not, who is dirty and who is not, but illustrates those differences, potentially of both class and gender, by emphasizing a difference in skin color. [38] The novel here establishes the kind of

freedom of being their own masters, but that freedom moves within the rough discipline of labour; and because the social unit of the Heights—the family—is both 'natural' (biological) and an economic system, it acts to some degree as a mediation between Nature and artifice, naturalising property relations and socialising blood-ties. Relationships in this isolated world are turbulently face-to-face, but they are impersonally mediated through a working relation with Nature" (Eagleton, *Myths of Power: A Marxist Study of the Brontës* [1975], 105). For a discussion of the effect of the Grange on Cathy and Heathcliff, see pp. 106–9.

38. Catherine and Heathcliff's first encounter with the world of the Grange teaches them not only class but also gender difference. Sandra Gilbert and Susan Gubar describe the effect the Grange has on Cathy in the following manner: "Barefoot, as if to emphasize her 'wild child' innocence, Catherine is exceptionally vulnerable, as a wild child must inevitably be, and when the dog is 'throttled off, his huge, purple tongue hanging half a foot out of his mouth . . . his pendant lips [are] streaming with bloody slaver.' 'Look . . . how her foot bleeds,' Edgar Linton exclaims, and 'She may be lamed for life,' his mother anxiously notes (chap. 6.). Obviously such bleeding has sexual connotations, especially when it occurs in a pubescent girl. Crippling injuries to the feet are equally resonant, moreover, almost always signifying symbolic castration, as in the stories of Oedipus, Achilles and the Fisher King. Additionally, it hardly needs to be noted that Skulker's equipment for aggression—his huge purple tongue and pendant lips, for instance—sounds extraordinarily phallic. In a Freudian sense, then, the imagery of the brief but violent episode hints that Catherine has been simultaneously catapulted into adult female sexuality *and* castrated. . . . the hypothesis that Catherine Earnshaw has become in some sense a 'social castrate,' that she has been 'lamed for life,' is borne out by her treatment at Thrushcross Grange . . . For assuming that she is a 'young lady,' the entire Linton household cossets the wounded (but still healthy) girl as if she were truly an invalid. Indeed, feeding her their alien rich food—negus and cakes from their own table—washing her feet, combing her hair, dressing her in 'enormous slippers,' and wheeling her about like a doll, they seem to be enacting some sinister

"epidermal schema" Kingsley uses in responding to the Irish. Images of differences in skin, hair, and eye color—what Dorothy Van Ghent describes as "notions of somatic change"—pervade this section of the novel.[39] For example, Cathy, on her return from the Grange, exclaims at her first sight of Heathcliff, " 'Why, how very black and cross you look! and how—how funny and grim! But that's because I'm used to Edgar and Isabella Linton' "(7.41). Such responses teach Heathcliff not only to see himself as visibly different from the upper-class Lintons but also to be dissatisfied with that difference. Following their contact with the Grange, Heathcliff comes, like Pecola Breedlove in Toni Morrison's *The Bluest Eye*, to wish that instead of his own dark appearance he had "light hair and a fair skin" and "Edgar Linton's great blue eyes and even forehead" (7.44).

At this juncture in *Wuthering Heights*, Heathcliff is repositioned; to use Kingsley's images, he is no longer seen as a "white" but as a "black chimpanzee." And, as soon as his indeterminate racial status becomes fixed as "other," Heathcliff begins to function, as Bhabha argues stereotypes of racial difference generally do, as both "phobia and fetish," thereby "open[ing] the royal road to colonial fantasy."[40] In Brontë's novel, class difference determines whether Heathcliff becomes a locus of fear or of desire. From the point of view of a member of the gentry, Mr. Linton, Heathcliff's blackness makes him a potential thief come to rob the landlord on rent-day. From the point of view of a servant, Nelly, it makes him a potential prince. Nelly articulates her fantasies about Heathcliff in response to his expressed longing to have the same fair appearance as the Lintons. To console and motivate him, she offers him the kind of advice the British classically offered the peoples they colonized. She tells him that washing and a change in attitude will make him the equal of the civilized, white Lintons. As she puts it:

> A good heart will help you to a bonny face, my lad . . . *if you were a regular black*. . . . You're fit for a prince in disguise. Who knows but

---

ritual of initiation. . . . For five weeks now, she will be at the mercy of the Grange's heavenly gentility" (Gilbert and Gubar, *The Madwoman in the Attic: The Woman Writer and the Nineteenth-Century Literary Imagination* [1979], 272–73).

39. Dorothy Van Ghent, *The English Novel: Form and Function* (1953), 205.

40. Bhabha, "Other Question," 159.

your father was Emperor of China, and your mother an Indian queen, each of them able to buy up, with one week's income, Wuthering Heights and Thrushcross Grange together? And you were kidnapped by wicked sailors, and brought to England. Were I in your place, I would frame high notions of my birth. (7.44–5, emphasis added)

Nelly's speech functions as a microcosm of the paradigmatic shift we saw in Kingsley and Marx and also provides a key to the subsequent movement of *Wuthering Heights*. It shows the moment when redefining Heathcliff as racially different—as a "regular black"— makes it possible to have a fantasy about him which is both "royal" and "colonial," a fantasy that can only be articulated in oriental imagery. In terms of the overall movement of the novel, Cathy's and Heathcliff's first encounter with the Lintons opens up the possibility of upward mobility—for her, through marriage to Edgar, for him, through leaving and "making his fortune." And, when he eventually returns to the world of the Heights and the Grange, having fulfilled this classic Victorian fantasy of self-making by acquiring both money and an education, Heathcliff enacts both the fears and desires that were articulated about him as a figure of racial difference. The novel is purposefully vague about how much money Heathcliff actually accumulates during his mysterious absence. As a result, his actions subsequent to his return can be read either, in old Mr. Linton's terms, as a process of stealing, first from the Heights and later, more extensively, from the Grange, or, in Nelly's terms, as his having enough money to buy the Heights and the Grange together. Whether Heathcliff is viewed as someone who appropriates a fortune or as someone who has already amassed it, when he returns home and takes up a "position of mastery," he is characterized in terms which conform to the contemporary stereotype of the "oriental despot."

The oriental despot became a staple in western political thinking from the enlightenment onward, particularly during the colonial period. According to Montesquieu, Hegel, and others, such despotism arose because "Asiatic States lacked stable private property or a hereditary nobility, and were therefore arbitrary and tyrannical in character."[41] In a passage that Marx later cited and approved,

41. Anderson, *Lineages*, 464. Anderson provides an extensive discussion of the

Bernier defined the oriental despot as "actuated by a blind passion, ambitious to be more absolute than is warranted by the laws of God and of nature, the Kings of Asia grasp at everything, until at length they lose everything; coveting too many riches, they find themselves without wealth, or far less than the goals of their cupidity."[42] It is this image of despotism that Marx invokes in 1853 to condemn native Indian governments as reactionary and to praise British intervention.[43] This is also the stereotype of racial difference which, in *Wuthering Heights* and *Jane Eyre*, lies behind the depictions of Heathcliff and Rochester when they are in positions of dominance. Both are linked to the oriental despot not only because they are described as sultans and Chinese princes, but also because the details of their anomalous positions in their respective stories fit Bernier's definition of what constitutes an oriental despot.

Both Heathcliff and Rochester are positioned at the start of their careers as excluded from the realm of private property and inheritance either because of having an extrafamilial origin or because of their rank as second son. As a result, they, like the oriental despot, must acquire power and wealth through conquest or appropriation. Both are characterized as having a powerful desire for accumulation, described in the novels as cupidity or avarice. And, having amassed their wealth, both return home to act the part of the tyrant, assuming a semi-godlike status, taking the law into their own hands, and delighting in mastery almost to the point of torture. As Heathcliff says to Cathy: "The tyrant grinds down his slaves and they don't turn against him, they crush those beneath them. You are welcome to torture me to death for your amusement, only allow me to amuse myself a little in the same style" (11.87). For both, the wealth they have accumulated is bound to their own physical persons. In *Wuthering Heights*, Heathcliff wishes that at

---

history of the concept of oriental despotism from Aristotle up to Marx in *Lineages*, 462–72.

42. Bernier, *Travels in the Mogul Empire*, 232–33, cited in Anderson, *Lineages*, 473n.

43. For discussions of Marx's use of the idea of oriental despotism or the asiatic mode of production, see Perry Anderson, *Lineages*, pp. 473–95; and Barry Hindess and Paul Hirst, *Pre-capitalist Modes of Production* (1975), chap. 4. For an attempt to apply Marx's theories of oriental despotism, see Karl Wittfogel, *Oriental Despotism* (1957), a book soundly criticized by Perry Anderson. Here I am considering not the vexed question of the historical validity or applicability of Marx's category of the oriental despot but solely the function of that figure in Victorian colonial fantasies.

his death he could " 'annihilate [his property] from the face of the earth' " (34.252). Similarly, in *Jane Eyre*, when Rochester's body is mutilated during the burning of Thornfield, his property appears to diminish simultaneously almost as if by sympathetic magic. Though Heathcliff dies and Rochester survives, both end as Bernier describes the oriental despot ending—deprived of the power and wealth they sought to amass.

Of the two novels, *Jane Eyre* more extensively explores Victorian fantasies about the oriental despot, in part because it depicts that figure from the perspective of a woman who is herself excluded from direct participation in the trajectory of upward mobility that Heathcliff and Rochester enact. *Wuthering Heights* suggests that there are three positions women can take relative to the narrative of the self-made man. They can be like Catherine Earnshaw and advance themselves through marriage—the position Jane initially appears to occupy in relation to Rochester. Or, they can be like Isabella Linton and function as conduits through whom money and property pass to the men who are moving upward—the position Bertha Mason occupies in *Jane Eyre*. Or, they can be like Nelly Dean, positioned outside male narratives of self-advancement yet taking vicarious pleasure in them—the position, I would argue, Jane occupies in telling her story and that of Rochester. *Jane Eyre* essentially enacts the moment in *Wuthering Heights* when Nelly fantasizes about Heathcliff as a Chinese or Indian prince by expanding it into a whole story. It is as if Nelly were telling the story of Heathcliff not by suppressing her feelings, as she does in *Wuthering Heights*, but by articulating the frustrations that arise from her position as a woman and a servant and the desires for advancement that she can only project onto male figures who are apparently free to overcome the limitations of their situations.

When *Jane Eyre* opens, Jane is in the position of the outsider or the "other" in the Reed family, a position from which, if she were a man she could potentially enact the kind of narrative of upward mobility that Heathcliff and Rochester accomplish. From the beginning, she is also characterized in terms that associate her with racial difference. On the first page of the novel, for example, when Jane describes herself appropriating the Reeds' book and going behind the curtain to read it, she says that she sat "cross-legged, like a Turk" (1.39). Later, when Brocklehurst condemns Jane's ungrateful conduct in front of the whole school at Lowood, he describes her as "worse than many a little heathen who says its prayers to Brahma and kneels before Juggernaut" (7.98). This assessment is reiterated in the critical response to the novel in the *Church of England Quarterly Review* which warned that for any real sign of Christianity discernable in Jane Eyre she "might have been a Mohammedan or a Hindoo."[44] Like Heathcliff and Rochester, Jane stands initially in the position of the oppressed or the colonized but also seeks herself to be dominant. Her early desire to escape into such books as *The Arabian Nights* and *Gulliver's Travels* and her fantasies about the "savage" countries of Lilliput and Brobdingnag, which she takes to be real places, are part and parcel of the kind of colonial thinking that later allows Rochester to condemn Bertha for her "pigmy intellect" and "giant propensities" (27.334).

Charlotte Brontë's novel suggests that while women may be shut out from the narratives of upward mobility, exemplified by Heathcliff and Rochester, the desire to dominate, associated with the figure of the oriental despot, is not limited to men but is felt by women as well. In *Jane Eyre*, what Barthes would call the "semes" of the oriental despot are attached not only to Rochester but also to female figures such as Mrs. Reed, who is described as having an "imperious, despotic eyebrow" (21.259), and Blanche Ingram's mother, who wears "a shawl turban of some gold-wrought Indian fabric, [which] invested her (I suppose she thought) with a truly imperial dignity" (17.201). Blanche herself is noted for her imperiousness. (Blanche's physical similarity to Bertha and her name, which conveys the idea of "blanching" or "whitening," suggest that the semes of racial difference, like those of despotism, are not fixed to one character but can always float from one to another.) But *Jane Eyre*'s relentlessly negative characterizations of domineering female figures like Mrs. Reed and the Ingrams—both mother and daughter—imply that it is wrong for women to desire direct access to the power encoded through the figure of the oriental despot. The narrative of Jane's childhood therefore shows her being educated out of a desire to dominate, a desire which Helen Burns describes as a doctrine similar to the ones that "heathens and savage tribes hold" (6.90). Lowood performs a kind of missionary

44. *Church of England Quarterly Review*, April 1848, 491–92.

function for Jane by teaching her to "civilize" her "savage" emotions. (The school is linked indirectly both to the oppression of the Irish—the girls' burnt porridge is compared to rotten potatoes and they are described as experiencing a famine—and to the perilous effects of missionary work in the Americas and elsewhere. In essence, Lowood brings disease and death to those it seeks to civilize.)

Once Jane has been taught to control what are later described as "passions [which] may rage furiously, like true heathens, as they are" (19.230), she can then participate in the scenario of oriental despotism only vicariously through her relationship to Rochester. The first time Jane and Rochester meet, the novel emphasizes the power differential between them, a difference represented initially in terms of size and gender, later of class and wealth, through oriental imagery. In that first meeting Rochester is thrown from his horse, an incident which Gilbert and Gubar argue allows for a reversal of gender difference with Jane helping Rochester.[45] But the scene also emphasizes that, even while injured and needing help, Rochester is able to "master" a horse Jane cannot control. Rochester characterizes his own power in godlike, oriental terms, saying, "I see . . . the mountain will never be brought to Mahomet, so all you can do is to aid Mahomet to go to the mountain" (12.146). That Rochester's "orientalism" attracts Jane is suggested a little later in the novel when she tries to paint a portrait of the kind of woman who would appeal to Rochester and fantasizes that Blanche Ingram has "raven ringlets, the oriental eye." At the moment of articulating the word oriental, Jane breaks off, acknowledging that she has "revert[ed] to Mr. Rochester as a model!" (16.191).

For Jane to participate in the scenario of the oriental despot from the position of being a woman is, in essence, to fantasize not about dominating but about being dominated.[46] Shortly after the scene

45. As Gilbert and Gubar put it: "What are we to think of the fact that the prince's first action is to fall on the ice, together with his horse, and exclaim prosaically 'What the deuce is to do now?' Clearly the master's mastery is not universal. Jane offers help, and Rochester, leaning on her shoulder, admits that 'necessity compels me to make you useful' " (Gilbert and Gubar, Madwoman, 351–52).

46. See the opening section of Cora Kaplan's "The Thorn Birds: Fiction, Fantasy, Femininity" for an interesting discussion of her own and other women readers' fantasies of being dominated. She describes herself as "held . . . captive" by such narratives as Jane Eyre and Gone with the Wind, and later asserts that in contrast to

in which she attempts to paint Blanche's portrait, Jane describes herself as virtually enslaved by precisely those traits of Rochester's which make him seem most racially different: "My master's colourless, olive face, square, massive brow, broad and jetty eyebrows, deep eyes, strong features, firm, grim mouth—all energy, decision, will—were not beautiful, according to rule; but they were more than beautiful to me: they were full of an interest, an influence that quite mastered me—that took my feelings from my own power and fettered them in his" (17.203–4). As the courtship progresses, Jane describes Rochester with increasing frequency and explicitness in terms characteristic of the mid-nineteenth-century conception of the oriental despot. At the charades, for example, when Rochester is dressed as Eliezer, it is a kind of apotheosis for Jane who recognizes that "his dark eyes and swarthy skin and Paynim features suited the costume exactly: he looked the very model of an Eastern Emir, an agent or a victim of the bowstring" (18.212). The charades are played immediately after Rochester brings Blanche Ingram back to Thornfield, an action which makes Jane extremely conscious of the class difference that separates her from her more powerful "master." Appropriately, in terms of the relative positioning of Ireland and the "Orient" in Victorian colonial rhetoric, when Rochester pretends he is about to marry Blanche, a woman of his own class, he threatens to exile Jane, a penniless woman of a lower class, to Mrs. Dionysus O'Gall of Bitternutt Lodge, Connaught (23.279).

It is during the period of the engagement, after Jane is formally tied to Rochester, that she begins to conceive of their relationship in terms not just of his role as oriental despot but also of her matching role as harem inmate. The image of the harem began to appear in French literature with more frequency at about the same time and in many of the same texts that contained discussions of oriental despotism such as the writings of Montesquieu.[47] It was

women, the working classes, and colonial peoples, middle-class men in the late eighteenth century, when the novel was beginning to develop, "were felt to have a fixed positionality; radical discourses presented them as the origin of their own identities, as developing independent subjects, the makers and controllers of narrative, rather than its *enthralled* and *captive* audience" (Kaplan, *Sea Changes*, 117, 124, emphasis added).

47. For a discussion of Montesquieu and other eighteenth-century French de-

an image that also appeared in eighteenth-century English literature notably, among other texts, in Johnson's *Rasselas*, the novel
Helen Burns is reading when Jane first meets her, and in Mary
Wollstonecraft's *Vindications of the Rights of Women*.[48] It was to continue to appear in the British novel as late as George Meredith's
Diana of the Crossways where the despotic hero Dacier is described
in terms strikingly reminiscent of, though somewhat more sinister
than, Brontë's description of Rochester. He is "in the dominion of
Love a sultan of the bow-string and chopper period, sovereignly
endowed to stretch a finger for the scimitared Mesrour to make
the erring woman head and trunk with one blow."[49] Like oriental
despotism, which Marx argues is a state existing between early
communal societies and the foundation of capitalism,[50] for the Victorians, the harem and the whole attendant concept of the buying
and selling of wives was defined as a state which came before
modern civilized marriage. For example, in the series of charades
that Rochester and his guests perform in *Jane Eyre*, the representation of Eliezer buying Rebecca as a wife for Isaac—a pointedly
oriental transaction—is positioned between the dramatic representation of a proper Victorian wedding and that of Rochester re-
gressed to a state of savagery.

Similar to the image of the oriental despot, through which it was
possible to articulate both a fascination with and a fear of the desire
to dominate, the correlative image of the harem was, from its early
uses in the eighteenth century onward, double-edged. It conveyed
both submission and resistance to dominance. In Montesquieu's
Lettres persanes, for example, "a rebellious dying harem-inmate declares to her master: 'I may have lived in servitude, but I have

---

pictions of the harem, see Pauline Kra, "The Role of the Harem in Imitations of
Montesquieu's *Lettres persanes*," *Studies in Voltaire and the Eighteenth Century* 182
(1979): 272–83.

48. For an interesting discussion of the image of the harem in Wollstonecraft's
writings and its relevance to the oriental figure of Safie in *Frankenstein*, see Joyce
Zonana, " 'They Will Prove the Truth of My Tale': Safie's Letters as the Feminist
Core of Mary Shelley's *Frankenstein*," *Journal of Narrative Technique* 21 (Spring 1991):
170–84.

49. George Meredith, *Diana of the Crossways*, ed. Arthur Symons (n.d.), chap.
34, p. 289.

50. This positioning of oriental despotism as coming immediately before capitalism would fit with Fredric Jameson's characterization of Heathcliff as a "proto-
capitalist" figure (Jameson, *Political Unconscious*, 128).

always been free. I have amended your laws according to the laws of nature, and my mind has always remained independent.' "[51] Similarly in *Rasselas*, the reader is told that a woman "with a mind accustomed to stronger operations" would be bored by the "childish play" of the harem.[52] In *Vindications of the Rights of Women*, the repeated image of the harem becomes a means for Wollstonecraft both to describe women's oppression and to assert the need for resistance to that oppression:

> In a seraglio, I grant, that all these arts are necessary: the epicure must have his palate tickled, or he will sink into apathy; but have women so little ambition as to be satisfied with such a condition? Can they supinely dream life away in the lap of pleasure, or the languour of weariness, rather than assert their claim to pursue reasonable pleasures and render themselves conspicuous by practising the virtues which dignify mankind?[53]

This double-edged image of the harem is invoked in *Jane Eyre* to convey both the fantasies and frustrations of women caught in a society where they are excluded from the paths of advancement open to men.

In *Jane Eyre*, as Jane approaches the moment of her marriage to Rochester, the harem becomes an image through which she is able to articulate fantasies not just of submission but also of rebellion. When he seeks to shower Jane with gifts, a gesture which emphasizes the money he has and she lacks, she describes him as bestowing on her a smile "such as a sultan might, in a blissful and fond moment, bestow on a slave his gold and gems had enriched" (24.297). Playing along with Jane's fantasy, Rochester asks her what she will do when he becomes a sultan with a seraglio, and she replies:

> "I'll be preparing myself to go out as a missionary to preach liberty to them that are enslaved—your harem inmates amongst the rest. I'll

51. Montesquieu, *Persian Letters* (1973), 280, cited in Zonana, "They Will Prove," 183, n.16.

52. Samuel Johnson, *Rasselas*, in *Selected Poetry and Prose*, ed. Frank Brady and W. K. Wimsatt (1977), cited in Zonana, "They Will Prove," 184, n.16.

53. Mary Wollstonecraft, *A Vindication of the Rights of Women*, ed. Charles W. Hagelman, Jr. (1967), 62–63.

get admitted there, and I'll stir up mutiny; and you, three-tailed
bashaw as you are, sir, shall in a trice find yourself fettered amongst
our hands: nor will I, for one, consent to cut your bonds till you have
signed a charter, the most liberal that despot ever yet conferred."
(24.297–98)

Here Jane uses the image of the seraglio to reverse her earlier sense
of being fettered to Rochester and to voice the possibility of her
fettering him and, furthermore, of her rousing a group of women
to rebel against a man who owns and oppresses them.[54] In this
instance, women's resistance to male domination is thus linked
rhetorically to resistance as it was acted out by the working classes.
Jane's use of the words "mutiny" and "charter" is the closest Brontë
comes, in this novel written during a time of intense political unrest, to referring directly to Chartism.[55]

It is tempting, therefore, particularly for the feminist critic, to
read Jane's speech as a moment of radical resistance to oppression.
We need, however, to remember that Jane is depicted not as re-
belling against Rochester but as imagining a gesture of rebellion
within the context of ongoing fantasies about oriental despotism.[56]

---

54. At least one contemporary critic read Charlotte Brontë's strategies as an
author in terms which make them resemble the resistant gesture Jane makes when
she fantasizes that she would refuse to accept her subordinate status as a member
of the seraglio. Eneas Sweetland Dallas argues that Charlotte Brontë chooses what
Gilbert and Gubar will later call "plain Janes" to be her heroines because she
"deem[s] the lovely *houris* of fiction to be a mistake" ("Unsigned review," from
Blackwood's Magazine, in Allott, *The Brontës: The Critical Heritage*, 362, emphasis
added).

55. The other moment in *Jane Eyre* when Jane's and women's rebellions are linked
to class rebellion is the long internal monologue at the beginning of Chapter 12
where Jane asserts that "nobody knows how many rebellions besides political rebellions ferment in the masses of life which people earth" (12.141). This passage
has, of course, been made famous by Virginia Woolf's analysis of it in *A Room of
One's Own* (1929), 71–72.

56. The scenario depicted fantastically in *Jane Eyre*, of someone preaching wom-
en's rights in an oriental setting, was actually a common colonial scenario. Improving the status of women was often used as a justification for disrupting local
government in India. Contemporary Indian feminists have become increasingly
suspicious of the colonial logic behind these apparently feminist arguments. As
Lata Mani puts it, "We have accepted for too long and at face value, the view that
colonization brings with it a more positive reappraisal of the rights of women. It is
of course true that women become critical matter for public discourse in the nineteenth century. But does this signify concern for women, or do women become the
currency, so to speak, in a complex set of exchanges in which several competing

Jane's imaginary portrait of herself stirring up revolution among the harem inmates is, I would argue, analogous to the imaginary portrait Nelly paints of Heathcliff as the son of an Indian queen and the emperor of China. Both Nelly and Jane are aware that their gender prevents them from taking direct action that would allow them to "leap at one bound a great class barrier." Instead both these female figures of uncertain class position—one a housekeeper, the other a governess—use oriental imagery to construct a fantastic scenario in which an individual overcomes social inequities. In envisioning Heathcliff as a prince or a king, Nelly articulates an implicitly conservative, almost royalist fantasy; she maintains the social hierarchy but imagines someone of servant status being able to attain extreme class elevation. In contrast, in representing a group of female slaves overturning a male tyrant, Jane articulates a potentially radical fantasy. But both women are able to fantasize about overcoming the differences of class and gender that oppress them only by grounding their fantasies in a scenario based on the assumption of racial or cultural difference— the scenario of the oriental despot. Neither Nelly's nor Jane's speeches can then be read as radically disruptive because in both, as Bhabha states in a slightly different context, "cultural otherness functions as the moment of *presence* in a theory of *différance*."[57]

The Brontë novels eventually deal with the troubling and fascinating presence of racial difference by exorcising it. By the end of *Wuthering Heights* and *Jane Eyre*, the figures who stand most explicitly on the borderline of the non-white, Heathcliff and Bertha Mason, are dead. At the same time, both novels conclude by representing the rude or savage other being "civilized" (*WH* 32.239), a process which, as *Wuthering Heights* makes clear, involves being made white. The last chapters of *Jane Eyre* show Jane "rehumaniz[ing]" (37.461) Rochester, who is depicted, in a series of images reminiscent of earlier descriptions of Bertha Mason, as "savage" and "wild" as if he were some "wronged and fettered wild beast" (36.452, 37.456). The last chapters of *Wuthering Heights* show the second Cathy educating Hareton, thereby "enlightening the

projects intersect?" (Lata Mani, "Contentious Traditions: The Debate on *Sati* in Colonial India," in *Recasting Women: Essays in Indian Colonial History*, ed. Kumkum Sangari and Sudesh Vaid [1989], 119).

57. Bhabha, "Other Question," 151.

darkness in which he had been reared" (31.228) and teaching him
to shake off "clouds of ignorance and degradation" (33.244). Nelly
again voices the implicit epidermal schema and the aristocratic
fantasies here when she describes how Hareton's "brightening
mind brightened his features, and added spirit and nobility to their
aspect" (33.244). The dynamics of both scenes emphasize lack of
dominance; women educate men and those formerly separated by
class difference—Jane and Rochester, Cathy and Hareton (a racially
acceptable stand-in for Heathcliff)—learn to perceive one another
as equals. If, as Bhabha asserts, imperialism is "at once a civilizing
mission and a violent subjugating force,"[58] then the final scenes
of *Jane Eyre* and *Wuthering Heights* represent the fantasy that it
would be possible to split those two impulses, depicting as they
do interactions which civilize without subjugating.

Of the two, the conclusion of *Jane Eyre* depicts more explicitly
the desire to subjugate being exorcised, along with images of racial
difference, in its final evocation of St. John Rivers in India. In terms
of Jane's story, Rivers illustrates how the desire to dominate, which
appeals when it is projected onto an orientalized figure like Rochester, repels when it takes an explicitly English form like Rivers's.
When Jane has to deal with Rivers at home, she characterizes him
as the epitome of "hardness and despotism" (34.432). Yet, as Spivak has pointed out, once Rivers is "extrojected" to India, his
dominance can be rewritten as progressive. In the final paragraphs
of the novel, Jane describes how "firm, faithful, and devoted, full
of energy and zeal, and truth, he labours for his race; he clears
their painful way to improvement" (38.477). The shift in Brontë's
tone as she moves from describing Rivers in England to describing
him in India is analogous to the evident shift in Marx's writings
when he moves from criticizing English despotism at home to
praising how in India, "European despotism planted upon Asiatic
despotism" can clear a painful way for improvement.[59] As the
figure who appears in the last lines of *Jane Eyre*, St. John Rivers in
India perfectly embodies what I have been arguing in this chapter;
in essence, that for the Victorians, forms of despotism or domination that are experienced as negative at home can be rewritten

58. Ibid., 148.
59. Marx, "The British Rule in India," in *Portable*, 330.

as desirable when they are projected onto scenarios conceived in terms of racial difference.

Those images of racial difference that, within the Brontë novels, are shown to elicit "the wildest fantasies of the colonizer"[60] elicit similar fantasies in critics of those novels. Spivak has already noted how "radical" feminist readings of *Jane Eyre* are implicated in the imperialist thinking that exorcises Bertha Mason by making her invisible.[61] Similarly, in the criticism of *Wuthering Heights*, particularly in discussions of Heathcliff, writers who make radical assertions about class and gender often find themselves enmeshed in replicating the racist or imperialist stereotypes that the novel itself critiques. In Terry Eagleton's analysis of *Wuthering Heights*, for example, he asserts that Heathcliff occupies a position outside the constraints of class. As Eagleton points out, "The obscurity of his origins . . . frees him of any exact social role; as Nelly Dean muses later, he might equally be a prince."[62] This comment appears in the context of Eagleton's argument that Heathcliff initially represents a pre- or extrasocial figure, a position strikingly similar to the one taken by Gilbert and Gubar in *The Madwoman in the Attic*. In their discussion of *Wuthering Heights*, they assert that Heathcliff is outside gender relations; he is both masculine and feminine, an alter ego, who gives Catherine extraordinary "fullness of being."[63] For both Marxist and feminist critics, Heathcliff functions, as Bhabha suggests the colonized do in general, as a fetish, something that allows the disavowal of difference[64]—for Eagleton, the disavowal of class difference, and for Gilbert and Gubar, the disavowal of gender difference.[65] But, for all these critics, the disavowal of

60. Bhabha, "Other Question," 170.

61. The reading I have just done of *Jane Eyre* could, of course, be criticized in precisely these terms. Though I have alluded to Bertha as a parallel for Jane, in the course of examining the way the fantasies of the colonizers work in the Brontës' novels, I have replicated those fantasies to the extent of rendering the third world woman invisible.

62. Eagleton, *Myths of Power*, 102.

63. Gilbert and Gubar, *Madwoman*, 265.

64. For a discussion of the stereotyped other as fetish, see Bhabha, "Other Question," 161–72.

65. Gilbert and Gubar describe Heathcliff's function for Catherine in terms that are quite startlingly fetishistic. They depict his as "a complementary addition to her being who fleshes out all her lacks the way a bandage might staunch a wound" (Gilbert and Gubar, *Madwoman*, 265).

gender or class difference is based on an assumption of race difference, in the same way that Nelly's initial fantasy of Heathcliff as a prince is made possible by her having defined him previously as "a regular black" or that Jane's fantasy of resisting Rochester is made possible only after their relationship has been represented in terms of a sultan and his harem. It is not surprising then that, in the midst of praising Heathcliff, critics of *Wuthering Heights* fall back on stereotypical images of racial difference, with Eagleton associating Heathcliff with "a darkness . . . [which] is at once fearful and fertilizing,"[66] and Gilbert and Gubar characterizing him as embodying "dark energies [which] seem . . . limitless."[67]

Such powerful and fantasizing responses to Heathcliff appear elsewhere than in the writings of contemporary critics concerned with issues of class and gender. From very early on, critical readers of *Wuthering Heights* found, as George Henry Lewes put it in 1850, that "Heathcliff, devil though he be, is drawn with a sort of dusky splendour which fascinates."[68] One can recognize that fascination not only in the writings of Eagleton and Gilbert and Gubar but also, for example, in Dorothy Van Ghent's "On *Wuthering Heights*" in *The English Novel: Form and Function*. From the beginning, the images Van Ghent uses to convey the novel's strangeness, which she associates with Heathcliff, suggest racial difference without explicitly naming it. She compares Brontë's novel to Chinese paintings and to Conrad's *Heart of Darkness*, and throughout the essay, uses a series of terms to talk about Heathcliff which are usually associated with the study of other cultures: he shows "cannibal unregeneracy," his relation to Cathy is "taboo," he is "anthropologically rudimentary."[69] In the essay's final paragraph, where Heathcliff is invoked as the "dark child," he becomes the locus of a fantasy of completion similar to the ones implicit in the fetishistic imagery used by Gilbert and Gubar and Eagleton.

To reach her conclusion, Van Ghent traces a pattern of bright and dark children in Emily Brontë's poetry and *Wuthering Heights*, a pattern into which, as she acknowledges, the texts often do not

66. Eagleton, *Myths of Power*, 102.
67. Gilbert and Gubar, *Madwoman*, 298.
68. G. H. Lewes, "Unsigned review," from the *Leader*, in Allott, *The Brontës: The Critical Heritage*, 292.
69. Van Ghent, *English Novel*, 190, 194.

fit.[70] Though she does not mention it, her characterization of the first Catherine as a "golden" child with whom Heathcliff, the "dark" child, must be united, is itself problematic given that Catherine Earnshaw has neither the blond hair nor the fair skin of her daughter. (The novel makes it clear that those "light" attributes come from the Lintons. "Golden" is therefore an appropriate term for them given the novel's interest in differences of class and wealth.) In effect, Van Ghent has to enforce what is implicitly a racial or epidermal opposition (one defined solely in terms of coloring and appearance) before she can then fantasize a final idyllic moment in which the two might have come together had the novel ended differently:

> Perhaps, had the ideal and impossible eventuality taken place, had the "inside" and the "outside," the bright child and the dark one, become identified in such a way that they could freely assume each other's modes, then perhaps the world of the animals and the elements—the world of wild moor and barren rock, of fierce wind and attacking beast, that is the strongest palpability in *Wuthering Heights*— would have offered itself completely to human understanding and creative intercourse.[71]

The utopian tone of this passage reflects the period in which the essay was written—the years immediately following the second world war when the modern civil rights movement had its beginnings. But, like Eagleton's and Gilbert and Gubar's descriptions of Heathcliff, this is also a fantasy in which the "dark other" functions as the fetish that when joined to its "golden" half brings about completeness.

The Brontë novels themselves may help us recognize the moments when we as critics are likely to become caught up in stereotypical thinking about racial difference. *Jane Eyre* and *Wuthering*

70. Van Ghent finds herself having to bend her examples to fit the pattern of blond and dark she has established. For example, when she analyzes a poem from the Gondal cycle, she has to explain "the fact that, in the poem, both the infant and the spectral lover have golden hair seem[ing], in this elusive fantasy, to be a mark of perversion of the metamorphic sequence, at least of its having gone awry (as in the case, too, of young Cathy and Linton, who is not dark but fair)" (ibid., 205).

71. Ibid., 207.

Heights demonstrate how an uneasiness about indeterminate racial difference—a difference which is itself never explicitly named—gets covered over by more explicit and exotic stereotypes of otherness that quickly, in Bhabha's terms, become the vehicle for the "wildest fantasies . . . of the colonizer."[72] Indeed, the Brontë novels dramatize the incredible adaptability of these racial stereotypes, the way in which they can accommodate fantasies about both dominance and submission, about both class advancement and rebellion. Precisely because these stereotypes of otherness are so flexible it is difficult to avoid replicating them in our critical readings. Analysis of the Brontë novels suggests that in order to become aware of this tendency toward replication, we need first to identify the moment at which issues of racial difference enter the argument—in the case of the Brontës, to identify the concern with the Irish which remains unspoken in their texts. But, it is not enough simply to locate the historically specific context that triggers a particular strain of racist or imperialist thinking. We need also to analyze the way in which that strain of imperialist thinking works, as here we have explored various ramifications of the Victorian fascination with oriental despotism. This will allow us to understand how and why particular stereotypes of racial difference function so effectively as screens onto which we can project our own varied fantasies as colonizers.

In Chapter 2, in the process of bringing to the foreground the colonial and racial subtexts implicit in narratives of upward mobility that are defined as open only to men, I have moved questions about the position of women into the background. In the following two chapters, I examine what has been overlooked here. In Chapter 3, I consider the model of femininity implicit in the Brontës' sense that they were excluded from the story of the self-made man, the model which defines women as excluded from the realm of the marketplace because their only appropriate place is in the home. In Chapter 4, the definition of femininity that splits the private woman from the inappropriately public one is read in the context of anxieties about class conflict which were intensifying throughout the 1850s. If the Brontë novels encode one response to changing social structures at midcentury—the fantasy that it might be pos-

72. Bhabha, "Other Question," 170.

sible for anyone to overcome the limitations of class difference—
Gaskell's and Dickens's novels of the 1850s encode another—the
middle-class fear that those below will attempt to leap out of their
class position. While Chapter 4 foregrounds questions of class and
economic difference, we will see, running through the background
of Gaskell's and Dickens's novels, images of racial difference that
are part of the pattern of colonial thinking so clearly laid out in the
Brontë novels.

3

"My Story as My Own Property": Gaskell, Dickens, and the Rhetoric of Prostitution

> How can a woman writer be a proper lady? The cultural
> construction of woman seems to foreclose any alternative
> to the one in which experience equals ruin.
> —Laurie Langbauer, *Women and Romance*

This chapter examines the model of femininity implicit in the Brontës' experience of being unable to participate in the story of the self-made man, the model which defines it as appropriate for women to be in the home and inappropriate for them to be out in the public realm of the marketplace. It does so by reading Elizabeth Gaskell's literary interactions with Charles Dickens against the backdrop of a contemporary social discourse that highlighted the figure of the inappropriately public woman, the discourse surrounding the treatment of prostitutes. Debates about prostitution flourished during the period of Dickens's and Gaskell's editorial dealings which began in 1850 and ended in 1863. Concern about prostitution was heightened at midcentury with the publication of Mayhew's articles on prostitutes in the *Morning Chronicle* in 1849 and 1850, W. R. Greg's "Prostitution" in the *Westminster Review* in 1850, and Acton's early reviews and treatises in 1848 and 1851.[1] In

---

1. As Mary Poovey explains, "Prostitution initially attracted widespread attention in Britain in the 1840s. . . . The first British analysts of prostitution were either doctors or laymen influenced by Evangelicism or journalists interested in mapping the previously undifferentiated mass of the laboring and indigent poor. Some of the most influential Evangelical contributions to the literature were Dr. Michael Ryan's *Prostitution in London* (1839), Ralph Wardlaw's *Lecture on Female Prostitution* (1842), and James Beard Talbot's *The Miseries of Prostitution* (1844). The most important 'sociological' study of prostitutes was that section of Henry Mayhew's *Morning Chronicle* series entitled 'The Metropolitan Poor.' Mayhew's reports were originally published between October 19, 1849, and December 12, 1850" ("Speaking of the Body: Mid-Victorian Constructions of Female Desire," in *Body/Politics: Women*

the years following, agitation about the problem of prostitution increased in intensity, leading to the passage of the first of the Contagious Diseases Acts in 1864, a bill which made it legal to detain prostitutes and force them to undergo medical examination. Both Gaskell and Dickens were actively involved in mid-Victorian efforts to "rescue" prostitutes, she through her work with refuges for "fallen" women in Manchester, and he through his work with Urania Cottage, the "Home for Homeless Women" he founded with Angela Burdett Coutts. But Gaskell and Dickens took differing positions on how prostitutes could be saved, a difference of opinion which is reflected in their representations of "fallen" women in *Bleak House* and *Ruth*, and which also colored the way in which they dealt with Gaskell's "public" position as a professional woman writer in their editorial dealings.

As Judith Walkowitz explains, there was a double impulse at the heart of midcentury work with prostitutes and discussions of prostitution; in the 1850s, "hand in hand with the tremendous expansion of evangelical rescue homes in the metropolis came police crackdowns on the night haunts of prostitutes and their open solicitation in the West End."[2] Together these two impulses literally enforced the split between the public and the private woman; through them, the prostitute was defined as either criminally out in the streets or safely locked up in rescue homes. As the phrase "locked up" suggests, rescue homes were not separate from but part of mid-Victorian efforts at policing. While refuges like Urania Cottage were characterized as "homes," they also functioned to imprison the women who were taken into them. Dickens himself makes clear that the women who became inmates in the "home" he founded with Coutts were kept under rigorous surveillance. They were "constantly employed, and always overlooked,"[3] confined and continuously tested in order to bring out the "good,

---

and the Discourses of Science, ed. Mary Jacobus, Evelyn Fox Keller, and Sally Shuttleworth [1990], 30–31).

2. Judith Walkowitz, *Prostitution and Victorian Society: Women, Class, and the State* (1980), 42. Walkowitz's book offers a comprehensive discussion of the various movements associated with the passage and repeal of the Contagious Diseases Acts.

3. Charles Dickens, "A Home for Homeless Women," *Household Words* 7 (23 April 1853): 170.

excellent, steady characters [they had] when under restraint."[4] Dickens thought of Urania Cottage not as a prison but as a place of "penitential discipline" where "fallen" women prepared themselves for a new life abroad. But he himself noted that the prostitutes he talked to about his "Home for Homeless Women" often had difficulty distinguishing his attempts to "rescue" them from society's attempts to punish them. As he puts it, "In the course of my nightly wanderings into strange places, I have spoken to several women and girls, who are very thankful, but make a fatal and decisive confusion between emigration and transportation."[5]

In contrast to Dickens, Gaskell did not view emigration as a solution to the problem of prostitution, instead insisting that "fallen" women could be redeemed by being taken into the domestic sphere. In taking this position, Gaskell anticipated and also helped to inspire a belief in what Josephine Butler, the founder of the Ladies National Association, was later to call the "home influence."[6] Yet while Gaskell believed in the power of the home sphere as a solution to the problem of prostitution, Victorian society's insistence that the public and private woman be kept separate made it extremely difficult for her to put that belief into practice. As a result, we find her writing to Dickens in 1850 requesting his help to find a way for Pasley, a young needlewoman who had been seduced into prostitution, to emigrate. Although Gaskell turns to Dickens, the tone of her request conveys her frustration at having to resort to a solution she does not herself advocate. She writes:

Some years since I asked Mr Burnett to apply to you for a prospectus of Miss Coutts's refuge for Female prisoners, and the answer I re-

4. "To Miss Burdett Coutts, 26 May 1846," in *The Letters of Charles Dickens*, ed. Madeline House, Graham Storey, and Kathleen Tillotson, 6 vols. (1965-), 4:554–55.

5. "To Miss Burdett Coutts, 12 April 1850," in *Letters*, 6:83.

6. As Judith Walkowitz notes about Butler, "In 1869 she edited a collection of essays, entitled *Women's Work and Women's Culture*. In her introduction, she acknowledged that women's sphere was the home, but called for the diffusion of the 'home influence' in the general society. She celebrated the feminine form of philanthropy, 'the independent, individual ministering, the home influence' against the masculine form, 'the large comprehensive measure, the organization, the system planned by men and sanctioned by Parliament'" (Josephine Butler, *An Autobiographical Memoir* [1928], 81–83, cited in Walkowitz, *Prostitution and Victorian Society*, 117).

ceived was something to the effect that you did not think such an establishment could be carried out successfully anywhere, *unless connected with a scheme of emigration, as Miss Coutts was.* (as I have written it it seems like a cross question & crooked answer, but I believe Mr Burnett told you the report was required by people desirous of establishing a similar refuge in Manchester.)[7]

In *Ruth*, Gaskell was to return to the problem presented by Pasley and to write a novel depicting a "fallen" woman who is not forced to emigrate but rather, taken into a home and enabled to become part of "normal" Victorian society. In her own professional life, however, Gaskell experienced a sense of frustration similar to what she felt at being incapable of helping Pasley, a "public" woman, enter the domestic sphere. As a domestic woman who became a professional writer, Gaskell, too, crossed the boundary between private and public, but found, as she did so, that it was impossible for her to be out in public and not have her behavior characterized in terms of deviance, waywardness, or impropriety.

Gaskell articulated her sense that being a professional writer made her a scandalously "public" woman most explicitly after the publication of *Ruth*. Describing herself, after the controversial reception of her novel, as ill of " 'Ruth' fever,"[8] Gaskell conflates her position as author with that of the "fallen" heroine of her novel, who dies of a fever contracted from her erstwhile seducer. The public response to *Ruth* makes Gaskell feel the contradictions of being a woman out in public. As Luce Irigaray puts it:

> How can one be a "woman" and be "in the street"? That is, be out in public, be public—and still more tellingly, do so in the mode of speech. We come back to the question of the family: why isn't the woman, who belongs to the private sphere, always locked up in the

7. "To Charles Dickens, 8 January [1850]," letter 61 in *The Letters of Mrs. Gaskell,* ed. J. A. V. Chapple and Arthur Pollard (1967), 98. Dickens's initial response to Gaskell's request was, "I am very much afraid I cannot help you. . . . unless she first came into the Home, and enabled us to form a personal knowledge of her from our own observation. And I doubt Miss Coutts's inclination to admit her, as she is not altogether a helpless outcast" ("To Mrs. Gaskell, 9 January 1850," in *Letters*, 6:6–7). While Angela Burdett Coutts did not take Pasley into Urania Cottage, she did help Gaskell find a couple who would allow Pasley to accompany them when they emigrated.

8. "To Eliza Fox, [?Early February] 1853," letter 150, in *Letters*, 222.

house? As soon as a woman leaves the house, someone starts to wonder, someone asks her; how can you be a woman and be out here at the same time?[9]

Like the Irigarayan woman out in the streets in the mode of speech, Gaskell publishes her novel and is then troubled by the way others perceive and address her. As she says, "I hate publishing because of the talk people make, which I always feel as a great impertinence, *if they address their remarks to me* in any way."[10] Shortly after the first public responses to *Ruth*, Gaskell writes to ask her friend Eliza Fox: "Now *should* you have burnt the 1st vol. of Ruth as so *very* bad? even if you had been a very anxious father of a family? Yet *two* men have; and a third has forbidden his wife to read it; they sit next to us in Chapel and you can't think how 'improper' I feel under their eyes."[11] While Gaskell sounds here as if it is others who see her as improper, she states earlier in her letter that she must *be* an "improper" woman because she "so manage[s] to shock people."[12] The tone of uneasiness that pervades these letters about *Ruth* comes, I would argue, from Gaskell's sense that as a professional woman writer she risks internalizing the public perception of her as improper.

If Gaskell, with the publication of *Ruth*, expressed anxieties about being out in the public sphere, when she was on the brink of beginning her professional career with Dickens, she expressed anxieties about leaving the safety of the home sphere. As she writes to Eliza Fox less than a month after Dickens first asked her to contribute to *Household Words*:

9. Luce Irigaray, *This Sex Which Is Not One*, trans. Catherine Porter and Carolyn Burke (1985), 144–45.

10. "To Marianne Gaskell, [15 November 1852]," letter 140, in *Letters*, 209.

11. "To Eliza Fox, [?Early February 1853]," letter 150, in *Letters*, 223. What is particularly interesting about these comments is that Gaskell herself exaggerated the negative responses to her novel. As the authors of *The Woman Question* point out: "Responses to *Ruth* are less simple-minded than Gaskell suggests. Private and public praise is generous, and adverse comments are often astute" (*The Woman Question: Society and Literature in Britain and America 1837–1883*, ed. Elizabeth Helsinger, Robin Lauterbach Sheets, and William Veeder, 3 vols. [1983], 3.114). Such an exaggeration on Gaskell's part suggests that she was particularly sensitive to critical descriptions of the novel which made her look and feel like a scandalous public woman.

12. "To Eliza Fox, [?Early February 1853]," letter 150, in *Letters*, 223.

One thing is pretty clear, *Women*, must give up living an artist's life,
if home duties are to be paramount. It is different with men, whose
home duties are so small a part of their life. However we are talking
of women. I am sure it is healthy for them to have the refuge of the
hidden world of Art to shelter themselves in when too much pressed
upon by daily small Lilliputian arrows of peddling cares.[13]

Here Gaskell appears to endorse the definition of femininity that
would prevent her from being an artist but at the same time attempts to negotiate a space where it would be possible for her to
practice her art. Gaskell's use of the term "refuge"[14] at the turning
point of her argument suggests that thinking about being a professional artist or writer makes her feel as if she comes dangerously
close to being a "fallen" woman, as if she needs a place of refuge
where she can practice her art without betraying the home sphere.[15]
For Gaskell, *Household Words*, a periodical dedicated to domestic

13. "To Eliza Fox, [c. February 1850]," letter 68, in *Letters*, 106. The image Gaskell
uses in this passage of being pressed upon by Lilliputian arrows recurs in slightly
different form in her later description of how she felt after the publication of *Ruth*:
"The only comparison I can find for myself is to St. Sebastian tied to a tree to be
shot at with arrows" ("To Anne Robson, [Before 27 January 1853]," letter 148, in
Letters, 220–21).

14. This letter was written when Gaskell was intensely involved in working with
"fallen" women in refuges in Manchester. Gaskell wrote to Dickens about Pasley
in January of 1850. He wrote asking her to contribute to *Household Words* later that
month. She wrote the letter to Eliza Fox about women, art, and household duties
in February of 1850, at the time when she was beginning to work on her first story
for *Household Words*, "Lizzie Leigh," the tale of a working woman's fall into prostitution.

15. As Catherine Gallagher puts it in discussing George Eliot and professional
writing, "Art and prostitution are *alternatives* in women's lives, but alternatives with
such similar structures that their very alternativeness calls attention to their
interchangeability" (Gallagher, "George Eliot and *Daniel Deronda*: The Prostitute
and the Jewish Question," in *Sex, Politics, and Science in the Nineteenth-Century Novel*,
ed. Ruth Bernard Yeazell [1986], 54). Gallagher is less interested in connecting her
analysis of George Eliot to nineteenth-century discussions of prostitution than in
tracing the association of writing with prostitution back to the classical period. She
notes, however, that this longstanding association raised particular problems for
the nineteenth-century woman writer: "When women entered the career of authorship, they did not enter an inappropriately male territory, but a degradingly
female one. They did not need to find a female metaphor for authorship; they
needed to avoid or transform the one that was already there. The historical association—disabling, empowering and central to nineteenth-century consciousness—
that I would like to discuss is not the metaphor of the writer as father, but the
metaphor of the author as whore" (ibid., 40).

virtues, must have appeared to be just such a refuge. Over the course of her editorial dealings with Dickens, however, Gaskell was to find that his periodical was less a safe haven that allowed her, as a private woman, to enter the public sphere than a place where the Victorian separation between the public and private woman was enforced.

Dickens's first letters to Gaskell reveal him as caught up in a discursive system that inevitably divides femininity between a proper domestic sphere and an improperly public one. In asking Gaskell, the wife of a minister, to contribute to his periodical, Dickens is obviously extremely anxious about questions of propriety. As a result, when he addresses her, he is careful to emphasize religious or domestic virtues, but he uses terms which are so strong they almost invariably suggest their opposite. So, for example, in the opening sentence of his first letter to Gaskell, in which he asks her to contribute to *Household Words*, Dickens asserts, somewhat playfully, that he does not know what her "literary vows of temperance or abstinence may be."[16] Such a comment links Gaskell to the Christian virtues of temperance and abstinence but at the same time cannot help but imply that writing for him would involve breaking those vows.[17] Later in the same letter, he refers to the payment Gaskell will receive for her work, by remarking, "I should set a value on your help, which your modesty can hardly imagine."[18] Like his opening assertion, this statement describes Gaskell flatteringly, in domestic terms, as a woman who is modest (particularly about her abilities as a writer); at the same time, however, it equates her being well paid for her writing with immodesty or impropriety.

In a follow-up letter in which he continues to encourage Gaskell

16. "To Mrs Gaskell, 31 January 1850," in *Letters*, 6:22.

17. Dickens's reference to temperance in writing to Gaskell is particularly telling since "temperance" was one of the domestic virtues he thought should be taught to prostitutes in refuges. As he explains, in describing the elaborate system which allowed prostitutes to earn good and bad marks in Urania Cottage: "The mark table is divided into the nine following heads. Truthfulness, Industry, Temper, Propriety of Conduct and Conversation, Temperance, Order, Punctuality, Economy, Cleanliness. The word Temperance is not used in the modern slang acceptation, but in its enlarged meaning as defined by Johnson, from the English of Spenser: 'Moderation, patience, calmness, sedateness, moderation of passion' " (Dickens, "A Home for Homeless Women," 171).

18. "To Mrs. Gaskell, 31 January 1850," in *Letters*, 6:22.

to overcome any insecurities or doubts she may have about her work, he assures her, "I am morally certain that nothing so true and earnest as your writing, *can* go wrong under your guidance."[19] Once again, in emphasizing the morality of Gaskell's writing—its truth and earnestness—Dickens uses phrasing which evokes, in the act of denying it, the possibility that her writing could, like a "fallen" woman, "go wrong." The double-edged quality implicit in Dickens's early comments to Gaskell becomes more explicit in their later editorial dealings. While Dickens continues to praise Gaskell to her face, behind her back he begins to articulate the obverse or critical side which remains unspoken in his initial compliments. For example, in the first of a pair of comments in which Dickens positions himself as if his editorial relation to Gaskell almost literally necessitates him standing in the place of her husband, he tells Gaskell, "I receive you, ever, (if Mr Gaskell will allow me to say so) with open arms."[20] But to W. H. Wills, his editorial assistant on *Household Words*, he comments, "If I were Mr. G. Oh Heaven how I would beat her!"[21] These two comments not only reify the split between the "good wife" and the "wayward" or deviant woman, they also define Dickens's position relative to that divided femininity. His function as editor is to be a disciplinarian;

19. "To Mrs. Gaskell, 5 February 1850," in *Letters*, 6:29.

20. "To Elizabeth Gaskell, 13 April 1853," cited in Winifred Gérin, *Elizabeth Gaskell: A Biography*, 142.

21. Quoted in Annette B. Hopkins, *Elizabeth Gaskell: Her Life and Works* (1952), 152. Gaskell was not the only woman Dickens invited to contribute to his newly founded periodical and subsequently criticized. He was eventually to describe Harriet Martineau, for example, in a comment to W. H. Wills, by saying, "I do not suppose that there never was such a wrong-headed woman born—such a vain one—or such a Humbug" ("To W. H. Wills, 6 January 1856," cited in *Charles Dickens as Editor*, ed. Rudolph C. Lehmann [1912], 200). As Ellen Moers points out, Dickens, "as editor of *Household Words* . . . had practical reason to think about (as we know he did) the talent of a number of rising women writers, starting with Mrs. Gaskell" (Moers, "*Bleak House*: The Agitating Women," *The Dickensian* 69 [January 1973]: 24). Moers makes this observation in the context of analyzing how Dickens contains or controls agitating women through his negative portrayals of them in *Bleak House*. I argue that we see a similar containment of women in his editorial dealings with Gaskell. The adjective "agitating" is particularly apt for the women Dickens sought as contributors to his magazine. Almost all of them were writing on a variety of social issues and could thus be viewed as "improperly" public figures. But, by publishing their writing in a magazine dedicated to household duties, Dickens effectively returned these potentially "wayward" women to what the Victorians would have defined as their proper sphere.

he must keep Gaskell's professional behavior within the limits of what is proper and thus prevent her and her writing from "going wrong."[22]

Initially, Gaskell was happy to publish anonymously with Dickens because she believed that that position would give her "free swing."[23] In fact, however, from the very beginning, *Household Words* was less a place of freedom for Gaskell than one where she lost control of her writing. The publication history of "Lizzie Leigh," the first Gaskell story to appear in *Household Words*, provides a perfect example of the way a writer's work could be controlled when it was appearing in a Dickensian periodical. "Lizzie Leigh" was one of a series of early stories Gaskell contributed to *Household Words*, all of which were centered on figurative or literal "falls." Dickens became so annoyed with this recurrent pattern that he commented to Wills that he "wish[ed] to Heaven, [Gaskell's] people would keep a little firmer on their legs!"[24] Dickens's anger may have arisen because, in these stories, Gaskell was moving toward the position she was eventually to articulate in *Ruth*, that "fallen" women could be redeemed and returned to "normal" Victorian society. The case of "Lizzie Leigh," however, shows how Dickens's position as editor made it possible for him to influence even a story's implications. Because "Lizzie Leigh," the story of working woman's "fall" into prostitution, was positioned as the first article in a volume of *Household Words* that ended with a series of letters praising the benefits of emigration, the whole issue ap-

22. I am suggesting that for women writers, *Household Words* could function in much the same way that Urania Cottage functioned for "fallen" women. When Dickens founded *Household Words*, he described its goals as "the raising up of those that are down" and, as its name implies, the propagation of "all home affections and associations" ("To Mrs Gaskell, 31 January 1850," "To Mrs Howitt, 22 February 1850," in *Letters*, 6:22, 6:41). When founding Urania Cottage three years earlier, he had explained to Angela Burdett Coutts that his intent was to "raise up" the women who entered the refuge and to teach them "the whole routine of household duties" ("Home for Homeless Women," 169–70). Dickens repeatedly linked *Household Words* to Urania Cottage, describing himself, for example, while working on *Bleak House* and *A Child's History of England*, as overwhelmed because of his simultaneous involvement with "Household Words . . . and Miss Coutts' home" (quoted in Edgar Johnson, *Charles Dickens: His Tragedy and Triumph* [1952], 2:757). He eventually recommended that W. H. Wills, his editorial assistant on *Household Words*, also function as Angela Burdett Coutts's secretary.

23. "To George Smith, [?1 October 1859]," letter 442, in *Letters*, 577.

24. "To W. H. Wills, 12 December 1850," in *Letters*, 6:231.

peared to argue in favor of Dickens's position that emigration was the solution to the problem of prostitution. Even the prestigious position of the story—as the lead article in the opening issue of a new periodical—led not to Gaskell's aggrandizement but to Dickens's. Though the story was anonymously published, like all contributions to *Household Words*, its placement led readers to assume that it had been written by Dickens. In America, it was subsequently reprinted under his name.[25]

Gaskell was not the only writer to experience the format of Dickensian periodicals as giving her little or no credit for her work. When Dickens asked Douglas Jerrold to write for *Household Words*, asserting, as he had to Gaskell, that the periodical was anonymous throughout, Jerrold pointed to the phrase, "Conducted by Charles Dickens," which appeared on the top of every page and described it instead as "*mon*onymous throughout."[26] After Wilkie Collins replaced Gaskell as the major contributor to Dickensian periodicals from 1853 onward, he also complained about not receiving enough recognition for his work. Both these male authors, however, managed to gain some measure of control over their literary productions. Jerrold refused to publish with Dickens, choosing instead to run his own periodicals, working first as a founding editor of *The Shilling Magazine* and *Punch in London* and later as an associate editor of *Punch*. Collins negotiated with Dickens who offered him a position on the staff of *Household Words* as, in Dickens's own words, compensation "for not getting his name before the public."[27] Before Collins accepted this editorial position, he also persuaded Dickens to change the advertising policy of his periodical so that, while Collins's novels continued to appear anonymously, they were advertised in *Household Words* before their publication under the author's own name.[28]

25. For a discussion of the publication history of "Lizzie Leigh," see Margaret Homans, *Bearing the Word: Language and Female Experience in Nineteenth-Century Women's Writing* (1986), 229.

26. Quoted in Johnson, *Charles Dickens: His Tragedy and Triumph*, 2:704.

27. Quoted in Gerald Grubb, "Dickens's Editorial Methods," *Studies in Philology* 40 (1945): 90.

28. For an extensive discussion of Dickens's dealings with his authors, specifically with Wilkie Collins, Charles Lever, and Bulwer-Lytton, see J. A. Sutherland, "Dickens as Publisher," in *Victorian Novelists and Publishers* (1976), 166–87. For discussions of Dickens's editorial relations in general and also his specific dealings

Gaskell's gender, however, meant that while she had the same experience of having her work appropriated that Jerrold and Collins had, she did not have recourse to the same means of countering that appropriation. The options of running her own periodical or seeking greater publicity for her name were not open to her; such gestures would have simply reinforced what already made her uneasy about her professional activities, her status as a "public" woman. Her correspondence with Dickens also suggests that he would have responded differently to attempts on her part to claim credit for her own writing than he did to such attempts on the part of his male contributors. On the one occasion when Gaskell did accuse Dickens of stealing her work (she asserted that he had taken a ghost story she told at parties and made it the basis of one of his published tales),[29] he simply refused to take her accusation seriously.[30] He responded to Gaskell's charge of appropriation by playfully addressing her as his "Dear Scheherazade," exaggerating his own wealth in fantastic terms reminiscent of *The Arabian Nights*, and, in jest, offering her a princely remuneration for a story he simultaneously argues he never stole.[31] Dickens's choice to address Gaskell as Scheherazade has the peculiar double-edged quality of his early comments to her. On the one hand, given his own fascination with *The Arabian Nights*, it was clearly a way of complimenting Gaskell by characterizing her as an all-engrossing storyteller. On the other, it also reminded Gaskell of her position in their editorial dealings by associating her with the figure of a

---

with Gaskell, see Gerald Grubb, "Dickens's Influence as an Editor," *Studies in Philology* 42 (1945): 611–23; Gerald Grubb, "Dickens's Pattern of Weekly Serialization," *ELH* 9 (June 1942), 141–56; Gerald Grubb, "The Editorial Policies of Charles Dickens," *PMLA* 58 (December 1943): 1110–24. For an essay that addresses only Dickens's dealings with Gaskell, see Annette B. Hopkins, "Dickens and Mrs. Gaskell," *Huntington Library Quarterly* 9 (August 1946): 357–85.

29. As Gaskell said to a friend, "Wretch that he is to go and write MY story of the lady haunted by the face; I shall have nothing to talk about now at dull parties" ("To ?Eliza Fox, [?17 November 1851]," letter 108a, in *Letters*, 172).

30. This response contrasts markedly with the anger Dickens usually expressed when he thought contributors to *Household Words* had appropriated materials from others or had had their own materials appropriated by others. Significantly, in light of the publishing history of "Lizzie Leigh," he was particularly enraged at the pirating of his own works in America. For a discussion of Dickens's position on plagiarism, see Grubb, "The Editorial Policies of Charles Dickens": 1113–14.

31. "To Mrs. Gaskell, 25 November 1851," in *Letters*, 6:545.

woman who is compelled to continue to produce stories for a figure of masculine authority.[32]

The playful comments Dickens makes about his wealth in this letter also reflect the general tenor of his economic dealings with Gaskell. He consistently paid her rather well for her work, another gesture that could easily be read as a sign of his support and generosity.[33] And, as Gaskell was initially happy to have her work published anonymously, she was also happy because, as she says "I never fixed any price on what I did then, nor do I know at what rate he pays me."[34] Like her anonymity, the indefiniteness of her financial dealings with Dickens may have assuaged Gaskell's anxieties about being a professional writer, in this case, anxieties about the taint of commercialism. As time went on, however, Gaskell became increasingly aware that the gestures that protected her status as a "proper" lady also constrained her. Dickens's indeterminate munificence, for example, placed her in a position of constant indebtedness to the magazine. The implicit economics of Gaskell's position are spelled out by Charlotte Brontë when she describes Gaskell's dealings with Dickens over the publication of *North and South* in terms of usury, stating that "Mr. Dickens may, I think, have been somewhat too exacting, but if she found or thought her honour pledged, she does well to redeem it to the best of her ability."[35] Eventually, several years after the publication of *North and South*, Gaskell sought to translate her literary debt back into a financial one by writing "directly to Mr. Wills, to ask again

32. When Dickens calls Gaskell "Scheherazade," he emphasizes that his relation to her is not, in the words Eliza Lynn Linton used to describe Dickens's relation to Wilkie Collins, that of "a literary Mentor to a young Telemachus" (quoted in Grubb, "Dickens's Editorial Methods," 92).

33. Biographers of Dickens have traditionally characterized him as financially supportive of writers such as Gaskell, and her own comments appear to convey a sense of delight at how much she was paid. Nevertheless, Sutherland notes that Dickens paid Gaskell 400 pounds and Bulwer-Lytton 1500 pounds for comparable pieces of work. Annette Hopkins also notes that, as Gaskell became increasingly frustrated with Dickens as an editor, she began shifting her patronage to *The Cornhill Magazine* where she was paid substantially more than she had received from *Household Words* (Hopkins, "Dickens and Mrs. Gaskell," 382).

34. "To Unknown, 7 February [1863]," letter 520, in *Letters*, 699.

35. "To Caroline Winkworth, July 27, 1854." Quoted in Dorothy W. Collin, "The Composition of Mrs. Gaskell's *North and South*," *Bulletin of the John Rylands Library* 54 (August 1971): 74. Brontë's language presumably reflects the way Gaskell talked about her dealings with Dickens over *North and South*.

how much I was indebted to Household Words, & who was the real personal creditor to whom I owed the money, which I shd be very glad to repay with interest &c."[36] During the bulk of the time she was writing for *Household Words*, however, Gaskell found herself in the Scheherazadian position of being always compelled to tell more stories in order to "pay off" her "debt" to the magazine. In the years between 1850 and 1863, she produced fourteen pieces of short fiction, *Cranford*, and *North and South* for anonymous publication in Dickensian periodicals. (If one includes verses, essays, and reviews, as Annette Hopkins does, the tally comes to more than thirty titles.[37])

Even when Gaskell sought to sever her connection with Dickensian periodicals and to publish elsewhere, she still experienced herself as having almost no control over her work.[38] She made reference to writing to Wills regarding her financial obligation to *Household Words* in a letter to Charles Eliot Norton where she goes on to ask, "If I try to keep my story as my own property for a month longer, will you send me word what any body will give for it in America, & how it may best be kept *out of England*."[39] Ironically, the gesture Gaskell makes here as a final effort in regard to her own writing mimics what happened when she originally appealed to Dickens on behalf of the fallen needlewoman, Pasley. Although Gaskell ended up asking him to help Pasley emigrate, she made the request with very negative feelings, writing: "Pray don't say you can't help me for I don't know any one else to ask, and you see the message you sent about emigration some years ago has been the mother of all this mischief."[40] When she wrote this, Gaskell was caught in a system in which she disagreed with Dickens's belief that emigration would solve the problem of prostitution, yet, at the same time, emigration turned out to be the only relief she

36. "To Charles Eliot Norton, 9 March [1859]," letter 418, in *Letters*, 535.
37. Hopkins, "Dickens and Mrs. Gaskell," 357.
38. Gaskell sought to break from Dickens after he had published a justification of his marital difficulties in *Household Words*. As she explained to Charles Eliot Norton in the same letter in which she asked him to find a home for her writing in America, she shared with the general public a "well-grounded feeling of dislike to the publicity he has given to his domestic affairs" ("To Charles Eliot Norton, 9 March [1859]," letter 418, in *Letters*, 535).
39. "To Charles Eliot Norton, 9 March [1859]," letter 418, in *Letters*, 536.
40. "To Charles Dickens, 8 January [1850]," letter 61, in *Letters*, 99.

could seek for her protegée. So, too, in the arena of professional writing, by getting her stories out of England and sending them to America, she is, in effect, choosing "emigration" for her writing. But the only place she can imagine sending her work is also the place where, as we saw with the publication of "Lizzie Leigh," it was originally most fully coopted. As a professional woman writer, Gaskell finally finds little or no way for her stories to remain her own property.

Gaskell's sense that her stories were not her own can usefully be read in light not just of Dickens's editorial dealings with her but also of his dealings with "fallen" women in Urania Cottage. There, too, he emphasized the importance of women having to tell stories, in this case, the stories of their own lives. As he explains in "A Home for Homeless Women": "The history of every inmate, taken down from her own mouth—usually after she has been some little time in the Home—is preserved in a book. She is shown that what she relates of herself she relates in confidence, and does not even communicate to the Superintendents. She is particularly admonished by no means to communicate her history to any of the other inmates."[41] As this passage suggests, the prostitute was discouraged, virtually prohibited, from telling her story either to the other inmates or to the matrons of the house—that is to other women—but was compelled to tell it to the cottage's directors, all male, with Dickens present but often listening in while remaining hidden. This kind of invisible masculine surveillance of female sexuality was characteristic of the way Victorian social authority dealt generally with prostitution, though it tended more frequently to be discussed in terms of overseeing than of overhearing. Thus, for example, later in the century, Josephine Butler and the Ladies National Association would describe the all-male commission that investigated the Contagious Diseases Acts as involved in voyeurism, asserting that "the Royal Commission gives a number of gentlemen the opportunity of being acquainted in the indecent details of an odious system."[42] The accusation of voyeurism could have been addressed not just to the commission dealing with pros-

41. Dickens, "Home for Homeless Women," 170.
42. "Second Annual Report of the Ladies National Association for the Repeal of the Contagious Diseases Acts," *LNA Annual Reports, 1870–1886,* Butler Collection, Fawcett Library, London, cited in Walkowitz, *Prostitution in Victorian Society,* 138.

titution but to a number of Victorian institutions and individuals involved in the study or scrutiny of outcast groups, a scrutiny that necessitated both watching people's behavior and listening to their tales of themselves. As Leonore Davidoff points out:

> The passion for collecting information on and statistics about the working class, particularly working-class women, has a streak of voyeurism which can be sensed behind the work of a journalist such as Mayhew, as well as in the detailed accounting of moral depravity in the pages of staid publications such as the *Journal of the Royal Statistical Society*. This voyeurism also appears in both the lives and writings of men like George Gissing and Somerset Maugham. "Rescue" work among fallen women or simply the compulsion to nocturnal wanderings in search of conversation with "women of the streets," which figure in the lives of men like Gladstone, have some close affinity to the sexual scoring and collecting described at length in the notorious diary *My Secret Life*.[43]

It is in *David Copperfield*, a novel written during the early years of Urania Cottage, that Dickens connects the masculine oversight of female sexuality with professional writing. In that novel, Dickens dramatizes, at least twice, the moment when a male listener overhears and, in the process, appropriates the story a "fallen" woman tells of her own life. The first such appropriation occurs in the scene where Emily is brought back from the streets and from the brink of prostitution to find herself in Martha's room confronted by Rosa Dartle. This scene corresponds to the moment of the prostitute's entry into Urania Cottage; in it, the truth of Emily's repentance is tested, as prostitutes were tested when they entered the refuge, with David listening unseen and unseeing, as Dickens himself listened to the prostitutes' tales. In Dickens's novel, the transference which results from such a scene of eavesdropping becomes explicit when David listens to Rosa's cruel diatribe and exclaims, "How long could *I* bear it?"[44] The ordeal is no longer

43. Leonore Davidoff, "Class and Gender in Victorian England: The Diaries of Arthur J. Munby and Hannah Cullwick," *Feminist Studies* 5 (Spring 1979): 101. We might here recall Dickens describing his "nightly wanderings into strange places" and his conversations with prostitutes about Urania Cottage ("To Miss Burdett Coutts, 12 April 1850," in *Letters*, 6:83).

44. Charles Dickens, *David Copperfield*, ed. Trevor Blount (1956), chap. 50, p. 790, emphasis added.

Emily's; it has become his. A similar appropriation occurs later in the novel when the story of Emily's awakening as a "fallen" woman is finally told. Instead of Emily herself telling what happened to her after she left Steerforth's protection, Mr. Pegotty relays her tale with such "fidelity"—a term that suggests both sexual and narrative constancy—that it becomes the experience of the male listener. As David says, emphasizing his own position as an author, "I can hardly believe, writing now long afterwards, but that I was actually present in these scenes."[45]

It is through the image of Scheherazade that *David Copperfield* links fallen women and their stories to the storytelling involved in professional writing. Early in the novel, when David first becomes a storyteller he is characterized as playing Scheherazade to Steerforth. But, after he introduces Steerforth to Emily, she takes David's place as the nighttime entertainer of his aristocratic friend. In the process she becomes a kind of voiceless Scheherazade, living a tale that, as we have seen, does not remain hers but becomes the property of the male listener or storyteller in much the same way that her body and sexuality become the property of her seducer.[46] Such a symbolic exchange allows David to assuage any anxieties he might have had about the "feminization" of his early position as a storyteller and move on as an adult to become a professional writer. As both Catherine Gallagher and Mary Poovey have argued, in the nineteenth century, the terrain of professional writing may have been seen as generally feminized. Gallagher asserts that the model of professional writing as prostitution was applicable not just to women writers but to everyone who entered the field of commercial writing. In a slightly different vein, Poovey argues that, at midcentury, the commercialization of literary work led to a desire to characterize that work as non-alienated, a desire which meant that writing was associated with the domestic sphere, the one arena

45. Ibid., 51.793.
46. As Laurie Langbauer points out, "In Dickens's most self-revelatory novel, *David Copperfield*, which chronicles his growth as a writer, young David's entry into storytelling involves putting himself in a *woman's* place—David's love for Steerforth prompts him to become his Scheherazade (and his telling Steerforth nightly tales stands in for and also forestalls a different kind of nightly activity that could grow out of their desire)" (Laurie Langbauer, "Dickens's Streetwalkers: Women and the Form of Romance," *ELH* 53 [1986]: 428).

that was defined as safe from the ravages of the marketplace.[47] *David Copperfield* shows how easily, for the male writer, any anxieties arising out of this sense of the feminization or prostitution of professional writing might be managed by projecting them onto and literalizing them through a female figure.

While, at a practical level, Gaskell's gender kept her from countering Dickens's control of her writing in *Household Words*, at a symbolic level, her femininity kept her from projecting anxieties about her writing onto the figure of a woman. As a woman writer, Gaskell herself was in the position not of appropriating someone else's story but of having her own stories appropriated. The history of her editorial dealings with Dickens suggests that the only way she could respond to her situation was to seek to resist masculine appropriation of her work. From almost the very beginning of her literary interactions with Dickens, Gaskell made private gestures of rebellion, for example, by donating some of the money from "Lizzie Leigh" towards the very refuges Dickens disapproved of for prostitutes. She also countered Dickens's attempts to stand in as her "husband" by allowing her husband to "stand in" as her editor. Such a gesture allowed her to tell Dickens that he did not need to edit her work since, "Mr Gaskell has looked this piece well over, so I don't think there will be any carelessnesses left in it."[48] This strategy, of choosing to deal with a different, though domestically appropriate, masculine authority, gave Gaskell only partial control over her own work, as is evident when she describes her experience of being paid for "Lizzie Leigh" in her letter to Eliza Fox: "Do you know they sent me 20 £ for Lizzie Leigh? I stared,

47. See Catherine Gallagher, "George Eliot and *Daniel Deronda*: The Prostitute and the Jewish Question," and Mary Poovey "The Man-of-Letters Hero: *David Copperfield* and the Professional Writer," in *Uneven Developments: The Ideological Work of Gender in Mid-Victorian England* (1988), 89–125. Although Poovey discusses primarily the feminization of male writers, specifically Dickens, she does touch on the question of what happened when a Victorian woman entered the generally feminized sphere of professional writing: "If the feminization of authorship derived its authority from an idealized representation of woman and the domestic sphere, then for a woman to depart from that idealization by engaging in the commercial business of writing was to collapse the boundary between the spheres of alienated and nonalienated labor. A woman who wrote for publication threatened to collapse the ideal from which her authority was derived and to which her fidelity was necessary for so many other social institutions to work" (Poovey, *Uneven Developments*, 125).

48. "To Charles Dickens, [?17 December 1854]," letter 220, in *Letters*, 323.

and wondered if I was swindling them but I suppose I am not; and Wm has composedly buttoned it up in his pocket. He has promised I may have some for the Refuge."[49] Positioned between her editor and her husband, Gaskell is only briefly in possession of the money she earned for her story.

Gaskell also tried to resist Dickens more directly, for example, by depicting a character in *Cranford* being run over by a train while reading *The Pickwick Papers*. That detail has the peculiar double-edged quality characteristic of so many of Dickens's comments to Gaskell. As an image, it compliments Dickens by suggesting that he is an all-engrossing storyteller; but, at the same time, it conveys a covert sense of aggression against him. Such a detail might have allowed alert readers to identify the story as not being written by him. But Dickens used his editorial prerogative to remove the reference to him, explaining to Gaskell that "with my name on every page of Household Words there would be—or at least I should feel—an impropriety in so mentioning myself."[50] Gaskell also resisted Dickens's editorial oversight by repeatedly refusing to meet his deadlines or to conform to the limits set to her as to the number of pages per issue. The problem with such gestures of resistance, however, was that they could easily be read as signs not of Gaskell's independence but of her "waywardness." In her editorial dealings with Dickens, the difficulty for Gaskell was that no matter what gesture she made she could not escape the configuration that defined her as the deviant one and him as the patient one who must control or restrain her deviance. This nineteenth-century model of gender difference is so persistent that modern critics continue to replicate its terms with startling clarity, as in one recent biography of Gaskell, where Dickens's editorial policy is described as "humor[ing]" Gaskell by not drawing the "leading-strings too tight."[51]

49. "To Eliza Fox, 26 April 1850," letter 70, in *Letters*, 113.

50. "To Mrs Gaskell, [4] December 1851," in *Letters*, 6:549.

51. Winifred Gérin, *Elizabeth Gaskell: A Biography*, 126. Gérin is not alone in describing Dickens's editorial dealings with Gaskell in this manner. Kathleen Tillotson, for example, asserts that "Dickens was severe with contributors, and had particular difficulty with Mrs. Gaskell over *North and South*." She cites the passage where Dickens exclaims that he wants to beat Gaskell, and concludes that "Dickens's insistence that each weekly installment should end at an arresting point, [was] a tough order especially for so leisurely an author" (Tillotson, *Novels of the Eighteen-*

Gaskell, however, increasingly came to experience Dickens's "humor" and "patient discipline" as constraints. Her resistance to Dickens intensified over the course of their editorial dealings and reached its peak, as Annette Hopkins has noted, during the serial publication of *North and South* in *Household Words* in 1854–55. At that time, Gaskell most consistently refused to meet deadlines or conform to page limits and also began not just to "act out" her frustrations with Dickens and *Household Words* but also to put them into words. In her letters, she describes her experience of producing *North and South* as one of having her work "crammed & stuffed" into individual numbers of the periodical, and herself as having "infringe[d] all the bounds & limits they set me as to quantity" and yet, at the same time, as being "compelled to desperate compression."[52] Gaskell's sense that *North and South* was being confined in *Household Words* is confirmed by Dickens's private comment to Wills that her novel needed to be "kept down" because otherwise it might "ruin" his periodical.[53] (*North and South* was the only full novel Gaskell published with Dickens. His early description of her as being able to guide her "short fiction" suggests that perhaps he was already anticipating that she would "go wrong" on a novel or longer fiction.) By this point, late in

Forties [1954], 32). This passage implicitly defines Dickens as a severe or tough disciplinarian and Gaskell as a leisurely or errant woman.

52. "To ?Charles Dickens, [?17 December 1854]," letter 220, in *Letters*, 323; "To Anna Jameson, Sunday Evening [January 1855]," letter 225, in *Letters*, 328–29.

53. "To W. H. Wills, 20 August 1854," quoted by Lehmann in *Charles Dickens as Editor*, 143. Catherine Gallagher argues that Dickens became angry with Gaskell during the publication of *North and South* because the novel revealed their ideological differences. She sees Gaskell as asserting the importance of "domestic ideology" in *North and South*, a philosophy that contrasted directly with the "social paternalism" Dickens had advocated in *Hard Times*, the novel which immediately preceded *North and South* in *Household Words*. As Gallagher puts it, Dickens was angered by the argument implicit in *North and South* that "the moral influence women indirectly exert on men is said to be the force connecting public and private life" (Gallagher, *The Industrial Reformation of English Fiction: Social Discourse and Narrative Form 1832–1867* [1985], 168). Dickens may also have been angry with *North and South* because in that novel Gaskell anticipated the position Josephine Butler and the Ladies National Association later used to justify their public protests against the Contagious Diseases Acts. In *North and South*, instead of simply showing a "fallen" woman redeemed within the domestic sphere, as she had in *Ruth*, Gaskell revealed domestic ideals, as embodied in the figure of Margaret Hale, emerging from that private sphere to become active in the public realm by reforming the actions of Captains of Industry such as John Thornton.

their editorial dealings, Dickens defines Gaskell as potentially ruinous and needing to be constrained, and Gaskell experiences that constraint as inescapable no matter how hard she tries to resist or exceed the limits set to her. Both articulate the subtext which, I would argue, runs beneath their editorial dealings from the very beginning: that *Household Words* is less a refuge for Gaskell's writing than its prison.

If Gaskell, as a private woman in the public sphere of professional writing, found no way to avoid being defined as deviant or wayward and thus no way to avoid losing control of her writing, in her fictional characterization of a "fallen" woman in *Ruth*, she could at least imagine a breakdown of the barrier which separated the public and the private spheres. By depicting an impure or sexual woman taken into the home, Gaskell refused the logic implicit in the arguments in favor of the policing of prostitutes, arguments that led to the passage of the Contagious Diseases Acts. That logic associated the deviant or wayward woman with disease and therefore defined her as needing to be kept absolutely separate from the rest of Victorian society. A place such as Urania Cottage effectively kept the domestic sphere, defined as both home and nation, free from contamination by quarantining "fallen" women until they could be sent abroad. Dickens's *Bleak House* provides the clearest symbolic equivalent both of the strategy behind Urania Cottage and of the arguments that were to be made in favor of the Contagious Diseases Acts. In that novel, illicit female sexuality is associated with two figures, one of whom, Esther Summerson, is defined as pure and confined to the home, while the other, Lady Dedlock, is defined as contaminated and exorcised from the novel. This is the symbolic strategy that Gaskell resists in *Ruth*, a novel which, like its immediate Dickensian precursor, *Bleak House*, associates women's extramarital sexuality with images of dirt, contagion, and disease that must be controlled by the presence of a medical authority.[54]

54. In defining prostitution or illicit female sexuality as a disease that needs to be controlled by the medical profession, both *Ruth* and *Bleak House* imply that this makes medicine in some sense the bastard child of prostitution. Both novels associate medical authorities with illegitimacy. In *Ruth*, Mr. Davis, the doctor, turns out to have helped Ruth because he himself is the illegitimate son of a "fallen" woman, and, in the end, he adopts Ruth's illegitimate son to train him as a doctor.

Of the two novels, *Bleak House* shows most clearly how the logic of the arguments about prostitution, which led to the passage of the Contagious Diseases Acts, was a perfect instance of what Foucault calls "bio-politics." As Deleuze explains:

When the diagram of power abandons the model of sovereignty in favour of a disciplinary model, when it becomes the 'bio-power' or 'bio-politics' of populations, controlling and administering life, it is indeed life that emerges as the new object of power. At that point law...allows itself to produce all the more...genocides...in the name of race, precious space, conditions of life and the survival of a population that believes itself to be better than its enemy, which it now treats not as the juridical enemy of the old sovereign but as a toxic or infectious agent, a sort of "biological danger."[55]

In *Bleak House*, Lady Dedlock represents that which cannot be contained by juridical power but must instead be tracked down by the less visible and more pervasive control of the police.[56] In Dickens's novel, she is characterized by her errancy, her ability not only to move from one class to another but also to disguise herself and

---

In *Bleak House*, Mrs. Woodcourt is obsessed with her doctor son's lineage and legitimacy. But, despite her concern, he ends up marrying Esther, the illegitimate daughter of another "fallen" woman.

55. Gilles Deleuze, *Foucault* (1988), 92. As Judith Walkowitz has remarked, in describing England in the 1850s, "For mid-Victorians, prostitution constituted a distressing street disorder that threatened to infect 'healthy' neighborhoods, but it no longer represented a social inequity that could spark a revolution" (Walkowitz, *Prostitution and Victorian Society*, 41). While Dickens's and Gaskell's novels of the 1850s tended to associate the sexuality of the "fallen" woman with images of disease, their earliest novels, *Oliver Twist* and *Mary Barton*, represented the prostitute more as, to use Foucault's term, a juridical enemy; she is linked to other criminals and therefore easily identified and confined by the police.

56. For a brilliant analysis of the general collapse of juridical systems in *Bleak House* and their replacement by a different system of power, see David A. Miller, "Discipline in Different Voices: Bureaucracy, Police, Family, and *Bleak House*," in *The Novel and the Police* (1988), 58–106. While Miller argues, accurately I think, that this new form of policing is all-pervasive, in so doing, he ignores the moment when Lady Dedlock becomes an emblem of or scapegoat for those who are controlled by this power. See my comments in the introduction on what I see as a blind spot in Miller's approach.

move from the home to the streets and back again.[57] As a figure who slips unnoticeably from one place to another and proves threateningly difficult to control, she becomes the object of the novel's final pursuit, the figure who must be exorcised before the home and society as a whole can be declared free from contamination.

The law's inability to locate and contain Lady Dedlock's wandering sexuality is dramatized most explicitly in the scene where Tulkinghorn, as a representative of the court, does not follow the pointing finger of the figure painted on his ceiling to look out the window and see the woman passing by. As the narrator explains: "Why should Mr Tulkinghorn, for such no-reason, look out of window? Is the hand not always pointing there? So he does not look out of window. . . . And if he did, what would it be to see a woman going by? . . . What would it be to see a woman going by, even though she were going secretly?"[58] Tulkinghorn's general failure to uncover Lady Dedlock's secrets will lead him, as agent of the law, to call in the new and more pervasive force of the police, in the figure of Inspector Bucket.[59] But the moment when Tulkinghorn fails to look out the window can insightfully be read in light of the "Appeal to Fallen Women," where Dickens characterizes Angela Burdett Coutts, the philanthropist who helped him found Urania Cottage, in similar terms as "a lady in this town, who, from the windows of her house, has seen such as you going past at night, and has felt her heart bleed at the sight. She is what is called a great lady; but she has looked after you with compassion,

57. The initial characterization of Lady Dedlock as both restless and in a freezing mood would link her to contemporaneous stereotypes of prostitutes. As Walkowitz notes, "According to rescue workers and others, . . . a restlessness, and a desire for independence frequently characterized the young women who moved into prostitution" (Walkowitz, *Prostitution and Victorian Society*, 20). "Writers . . . emphasized the prostitute's sterility, frigidity" (ibid., 37).

58. Charles Dickens, *Bleak House*, ed. Norman Page (1971), chap. 16, p. 276. All further references to this book (hereafter abbreviated *BH*) appear in the text.

59. The descriptions of Bucket's ability to penetrate so effectively into the houses of his suspects echo contemporary descriptions of the police actions it was thought would help control prostitution. W. R. Greg writes "that the police [detectives] should have authority, *suo periculo*, and under due restrictions, to enter, without notice, any houses which they *know* to be used for improper purposes" (Greg, "Prostitution," *Westminster Review* 53 [1850]: 487).

as being of her own sex and nature."[60] The difference between these two figures, both safely ensconced in their middle or upper-class houses, is that while Tulkinghorn cannot or will not "see" Lady Dedlock as she walks the streets, Angela Burdett Coutts "looks after" the streetwalkers she hopes to rescue. The figure of Coutts thus suggests that dangerously errant female sexuality should be controlled or contained not through juridical means but through what Victorian society considered "rescue" work.

The final pursuit of Lady Dedlock shows Victorian "rescue" work as inextricably linked with gestures of policing. While Inspector Bucket fails in what he characterizes as his attempt to "save" or "rescue" Lady Dedlock, he succeeds in driving her out of the Dedlock mansion—that is out of the private, upper-class family in which she has hidden—onto the streets, and into the clothes of a working-class woman. By forcing Lady Dedlock to acknowledge her status as a public woman, Bucket effects precisely what the policing of the period was designed to do to prostitutes. As Acton asserts in praising Parent-Duchâtelet's work, "The great object of the system adopted in France is to repress private or secret, and to encourage public or avowed prostitution."[61] And, when Alan Woodcourt joins Bucket in the final discovery of Lady Dedlock's body, we see Dickens anticipating exactly the logic of those who were to argue in favor of the passage of the Contagious Diseases Acts. Of all the characters in *Bleak House*, Alan Woodcourt most fully exemplifies the ideal Victorian "rescue" worker. With his commitment to sacrifice his own advancement for the sake of the urban poor and his literal rescue of those who are shipwrecked, he is a hero whose altruism appears to make him virtually flawless. Indeed, Woodcourt's benevolence is so great that it is difficult to think of him or, by extension, the medical profession he represents, as disciplinary in any sense. Yet, when the pursuit of Lady Dedlock comes to its close and the novel moves, in its last chapters, to show

60. "[An Appeal to Fallen Women]," appendix D, in *Letters*, 5:698.
61. William Acton, *Prostitution*, ed. Peter Fryer (1969), 97. As Walkowitz explains, "This medical and police supervision in turn created an outcast class of 'sexually deviant' females, forcing prostitutes to acknowledge their status as 'public' women and destroying their private association with the general community of the laboring poor" (Walkowitz, *Prostitution in Victorian Society*, 5).

Alan Woodcourt helping Bucket examine and identify her body, that scene represents precisely the strategy that writers such as Greg and Acton argued the English should adopt from the French system of regulation: In it, the "girls . . . are subject to the constant surveillance of authorized inspectors and medical men."[62]

The disease that marks Esther's face and forces her to go veiled for much of the latter half of the novel suggests that she as well as Lady Dedlock should be linked to midcentury discussions of prostitution. Writers such as Greg and Acton almost invariably represent their approach to the subject of prostitution as similar to lifting the veil from the face of a woman who has been scarred by a disfiguring disease. In his 1850 article "Prostitution," for example, Greg tells his audience that the circumstances of prostitution have been "star[ing]" Victorian England "in the face," but the subject has not been discussed because society has been willing to say "to the unfortunate prostitutes and their frequenters—'As long as you . . . but throw a decent veil over your proceedings, we shall not interfere with you, but shall regard you as an inevitable evil.' "[63] In his 1851 book on generative diseases, William Acton develops the same imagery at greater length, asserting that

> it is time to burst through the veil of that artificial bashfulness which has injured the growth, while it has affected the features of genuine purity. Society has suffered from that spurious modesty which lets fearful forms of vice swell to rank luxuriousness, rather than point at their existence—which coyly turns its head away from the "wounds and putrefying sores" that are eating into our system, because it would have to blush at the exposure.[64]

If Lady Dedlock, in *Bleak House*, is associated with a dangerously transgressive female sexuality that must, because of its contaminating effects, be exorcised from the novel, Esther Summerson displays the abjection and humility which, for reformers such as

62. Greg, "Prostitution," 483.

63. Ibid., 493.

64. William Acton, *A Practical Treatise on Diseases of the Urinary and Generative Organs*, 2d ed. (1851), 2, cited in Jacqueline Rose, "George Eliot and the Spectacle of Woman," in *Sexuality in the Field of Vision* (1986), 112. For a fuller discussion of Rose's argument about how Victorian discussions of prostitution scrutinized the woman's body, see my discussion of Gaskell and Dickens in Chapter 4.

Greg, Acton, and Dickens, made it possible to define the prostitute as capable of redemption. From her childhood onward, Esther is associated with sexual transgression because of her illegitimacy and the way Miss Barbary brings her up. She is placed in a position, like that of the "fallen" women who were taken into rescue homes, of having to prove that she does not carry a sexual taint if she wants to lead a "normal" life. As Dickens says, addressing the women who might want to enter Urania Cottage, you should do so "if you have ever wished . . . for a chance of rising out of your sad life, and having friends, a quiet home, means of being useful to yourself and others, peace of mind, self-respect."[65] In an earlier letter to Angela Burdett Coutts, he insists that the women who enter the home be told that theirs has to be a "*useful* repentance" and that they must be "steady and firm, . . . cheerful and hopeful."[66] The formulations Dickens uses to discuss his repentant inmates are echoed almost precisely in the descriptions of Esther's behavior in *Bleak House*. To counter the potential contamination of her mother's actions, Esther resolves to "strive . . . to be industrious, contented, and kind-hearted, and to do some good to some one, and win some love to myself" (*BH* 3.65). This resolution leads to the notoriously excessive humility that has troubled critics about Esther, behavior which, I would argue, conforms to what was expected of women who were taken into homes like Urania Cottage and had to prove the sincerity of their repentance.

Esther also exhibits the kind of self-restraint that Dickens argued was necessary for the women who came into Urania Cottage if they were to achieve the positive goals he had set out for them. As he says, "You must resolve to set a watch upon yourself, and to be firm in your control over yourself, and to restrain yourself; to be patient, gentle, persevering, and good-tempered."[67] The self-surveillance Dickens describes here is part of the general sense in which Urania Cottage is a home that is also a prison. As he puts it: "Keys are never left about. The garden gate is always kept locked. . . . Any inmate missing from her usual place for ten minutes would be looked after. . . . A girl declaring that she wishes to

65. "[An Appeal to Fallen Women]," appendix D, in *Letters*, 5:698.
66. "To Miss Burdett Coutts, 16 May 1846," in *Letters*, 4:553, 554.
67. "[An Appeal to Fallen Women]," appendix D, in *Letters*, 5:699.

leave, is not allowed to do so hastily, but is locked in a chamber by herself."[68] In *Bleak House*, Esther shows herself to be invariably "patient, gentle, persevering and good-tempered." Like the women in Urania Cottage, she exercises self-restraint by practicing the whole routine of household duties at Bleak House. The housekeeping keys that she carries and constantly jingles suggest that she is, in effect, her own jailer, keeping her emotions in check and herself confined to the domestic realm. She acts out her impulse toward self-imprisonment most explicitly when she catches the mysterious fever that subsequently marks her face and locks herself in her room to avoid contaminating others. With this gesture, Esther replicates, on a personal level, the strategies that were being advocated at an institutional level by those in favor of the Contagious Diseases Acts.[69]

The split in *Bleak House* between Lady Dedlock and Esther is a version of the split between the public and the private woman discussed earlier in the chapter, but here, the presence of Alan Woodcourt also marks it as a split between the toxic and the healthy, or, in simpler terms, between the dirty and the clean. This split is represented perhaps most clearly in the final image of the first prostitute Dickens depicted, the image of Nancy in her death scene in *Oliver Twist*. In that scene, as the prostitute is beaten to death, she is described as so battered and bloody that she cannot see and her face cannot be seen. At the same time, however, she holds up to Heaven the spotlessly clean white napkin given to her by the "pure" woman, Rose Maylie.[70] The imagery of dirt and cleanliness evoked in Dickens's final image of Nancy appears throughout the rhetoric of contemporary social texts on prostitu-

68. Dickens, "Home for Homeless Women," 172–73.

69. That the domestic self-restraint which Esther embodies and which Dickens advocated for the inmates of Urania Cottage is intended to control women's deviant sexuality, not only on an individual but also on a social level, is suggested by the fact that Esther joins with Bucket and eventually Woodcourt in the final pursuit of Lady Dedlock. In *Bleak House* the domestic realm is shown acting in concert with the police and medical authorities.

70. With this image, Nancy is represented as literally "upholding" an emblem of the virtue of the middle-class woman, a strategy which, Mary Poovey has argued, was characteristic of mid-Victorian social texts on prostitution. As she explains, Greg, in his 1850 article "Prostitution," represents "the prostitute as innately moral," thereby aligning her "with—rather than in opposition to—the virtuous middle-class woman" (Poovey, "Speaking of the Body," 33).

tion. Acton, for example, describes involvement with prostitutes as being like touching "moral pitch,"[71] a figurative description that becomes literal toward the end of his book *Prostitution*, when he insists that the best work redeemed prostitutes could be trained for would be doing laundry. Dickens's earliest iconographic representation of Nancy makes it clear, however, that the purity offered to the prostitute is never really her own but rather, a fetish, a part which can be separated off from the rest of her and valued while she is sacrificed. In terms of the logic of the control of disease, the dirty or contaminated half must be exorcised before the half that remains can be fully purified, as, in *Bleak House*, Lady Dedlock must die before Esther Summerson can be certified as healthy in the realm of her own home. And it is the medical authority, Woodcourt, who, in testifying on the last page of the novel that Esther's face is no longer marked by disease, testifies to the health of the pure woman confined to the home as surely as he testified to the death of the impure woman shut out in the streets.[72]

In *Ruth*, Gaskell refuses to separate femininity into pure and impure halves. She portrays a "fallen" woman taken into the sanctity of the domestic sphere, thereby representing in her novel the practical solution that was not available to her when she was actually dealing with the problem of the "fallen" needlewoman, Pasley. By depicting Ruth becoming a member of the family circle of a dissenting minister as well as a wealthy manufacturer, Gaskell transgressed the boundary that writers such as Dickens, Acton, and Greg worked to maintain. The idea of the prostitute crossing over the threshold of the home was abhorrent to these writers, as is dramatized in Acton's 1848 *Quarterly Review* article on prostitution in which he speaks in the voice of the reformed prostitute in order to have her say, "Take me anywhere but home first; let me not pass at once from the fume of my guilty life into that pure circle."[73] By showing Ruth passing directly into the home, Gaskell's

71. Acton, *Prostitution*, 59.
72. As Foucault notes, in the Victorian era, "Sexuality was carefully confined; it moved into the home" (*The History of Sexuality*: vol. I. *An Introduction*, trans. Robert Hurley [1980], 3).
73. William Acton, "Review of *A Short Account of the London Magdalene Hospital* and *De la prostitution dans la Ville de Paris* par A. J. B. Parent-Duchâtelet," *Quarterly Review* 83 (September 1848): 366.

novel allows, to adapt a phrase from Greg's 1850 article "Prostitution," "the introduction of filth into the pure sanctuary of the affections."[74] Gaskell's novel was so disturbing to Victorian readers because it represented the transgression of a boundary that seemed as if it should be absolute. As Kristeva notes: "it is thus not lack of cleanliness or health that causes abjection but what disturbs identity, system, order. What does not respect borders, positions, rules. The in-between, the ambiguous, the composite."[75]

In *Ruth*, Gaskell refuses the split between purity and impurity not simply at the level of action, by showing what happens to Ruth, but also at the level of figuration, in the imagery she associates with her. In depicting her heroine, Gaskell refuses the cultural construction of femininity that separates "whores" from "madonnas." Ruth's early work as a needlewoman, her seduction by a "gentleman," and her subsequent "fall" are all details that associate her with stereotypical Victorian accounts of how women became prostitutes. Gaskell's readers would have assumed that a story which had such a beginning could have only one end. As Ruth's seducer Bellingham says, "There was but one thing that could have happened."[76] Or as Jemima's dressmaker remarks, "One knows they can but go from bad to worse, poor creatures!" (25.321). However, as Hilary Schor has commented, *Ruth* tells the familiar story of a "fallen" woman by using religious motifs; "Gaskell is playing off readers' expectations about fallen women to create her own female passion play, one worked out in more specifically Christological terms than have been noted."[77] In Gaskell's descriptions, Ruth is associated with saintliness, purity, suffering, and maternal love. She is thereby characterized as a madonna, a parallel Gaskell makes explicit when she quotes from Milton's "On the Morning of Christ's Nativity" to describe the morning on which Ruth's illegitimate son is born.

The gesture Gaskell makes in representing Ruth as simulta-

74. Greg, "Prostitution," 450.

75. Julia Kristeva, *Powers of Horror: An Essay in Abjection*, trans. Leon S. Roudiez (1982), 4.

76. Elizabeth Gaskell, *Ruth*, ed. Alan Shelston (1976), chap. 23, p. 278. All further references to this book (hereafter abbreviated *R*) appear in the text.

77. Hilary Schor, "The Plot of the Beautiful Ignoramus: *Ruth* and the Tradition of the Fallen Woman," in *Sex and Death in Victorian Literature*, ed. Regina Barreca (1990), 158–59.

neously pure and impure potentially allows Victorian women to recognize the split inherent in contemporaneous definitions of femininity. *Ruth* dramatizes this kind of recognition in the scene where Jemima, who has previously admired Ruth's virtuous conduct, suddenly learns of her friend's having been seduced and abandoned. In describing the effect this new knowledge has on Jemima, Gaskell emphasizes the tremendous boundary a proper domestic woman has to cross simply to know about sexual experiences like Ruth's. She uses the following analogy: "The diver, leaving the green sward, smooth and known, where his friends stand with their familiar smiling faces, admiring his glad bravery—the diver, down in an instant in the horrid depths of the sea, close to some strange, ghastly, lidless-eyed monster, can hardly more feel his blood curdle at the near terror than did Jemima now" (25.323). Jemima finds the knowledge she has gained about Ruth so terrifying that her immediate impulse is to separate the realm of the sexual from that of the pure. She thinks about the Ruth she has known in her home and the Ruth with the scandalous past, and hopes, for a moment, that there are two different women named Ruth Hilton. But, in Gaskell's novel, the same woman incorporates both these apparently contradictory experiences, a fact that Jemima finally acknowledges by describing Ruth as if she had two antithetical characters. On the one hand, Ruth continues to seem the same pure figure who has, throughout the novel, been associated with the whiteness of snow and marble. On the other, because of her sexual "fall," she now seems, "stained," as if she has "a memory blackened by sin," and had been "darkened ... into a treacherous hypocrite, with a black secret shut up in her soul" (25.324–25). In contemplating Ruth, Jemima sees the contradiction inherent in the Victorian cultural construction of femininity. As Leonore Davidoff puts it: "In viewing Victorian women it is as if we are looking at a picture through a double exposure. Indeed, the dual vision of women, as woman and lady, becomes mixed with other polarities such as those between white and black."[78] Though in the end of her novel, Gaskell cannot escape the Victo-

78. Davidoff, "Class and Gender in Victorian England," 91. For the way in which this discourse of black and white is linked to images of racial difference, see my discussion of Greg, Gaskell, and Dickens in Chapter 4.

rian logic which demands that the sexually experienced woman be sacrificed or exorcised, she can, in the middle of her story, represent one woman recognizing the way in which that logic divides women from themselves and from each other, as she does in depicting Jemima's suddenly changed perception of Ruth.

Gaskell's transgression of the boundary that kept the "pure" separate from the "contaminated" was, I would argue, what made her novel have such a galvanizing effect on its Victorian readership. While some, as we saw earlier in the chapter, were shocked by *Ruth*, others viewed the symbolic gesture Gaskell made as liberating. Elizabeth Barrett Browning noted that Gaskell's novel "contains truths purifying and purely put, yet treats of a subject scarcely ever boldly treated of except when taken up by unclean hands."[79] For Josephine Butler, the gesture Gaskell made in *Ruth*, and the Victorian audience's subsequent refusal to accept that gesture, helped make visible what needed to be changed in her society. As Butler explains in her autobiographical memoir, the reception of Gaskell's novel was one of the events that led her eventually to work with the Ladies National Association in opposition to the Contagious Diseases Acts:

> A book was published at that time by Mrs. Gaskell, and was much discussed. This led to expressions of judgement which seemed to me false—fatally false. . . . A pure woman, it was reiterated, should be absolutely ignorant of a certain class of evils in the world, albeit those evils bore with murderous cruelty on other women. One young man seriously declared that he would not allow his own mother to read such a book as that under discussion—a book which seemed to me to have a very wholesome tendency, though dealing with a painful subject. Silence was thought to be the great duty of all on such subjects.[80]

If readers such as Elizabeth Barrett Browning and Josephine Butler approved of Gaskell's transgression of the boundary that sep-

79. R. D. Waller, *Letters Addressed to Mrs. Gaskell by Celebrated Contemporaries* (1935), 42, cited in Gérin, *Elizabeth Gaskell: A Biography*, 140.

80. Josephine Butler, *An Autobiographical Memoir*, ed. George W. and Lucy A. Johnson (1915), 31. Butler was also frustrated because, in the responses to Gaskell's *Ruth*, "a moral lapse in a woman was spoken of as an immensely worse thing than in a man; there was no comparison to be formed between them" (ibid., 31).

arated the pure from the impure, a reader like W. R. Greg responded to *Ruth* by working to separate the categories that Gaskell so carefully joins in her novel. In "The False Morality of Lady Novelists," Greg praises the novel but concludes by criticizing Gaskell, arguing that "if she designed to awaken the world's compassion for the ordinary class of betrayed and deserted Magdalenes, the circumstances of Ruth's error should not have been made so innocent, nor should Ruth herself have been painted as so perfect. If she intended to describe a saint (as she has done), she should not have held conventional and mysterious language about her as a grievous sinner."[81] Greg introduces his comments about *Ruth* by asserting that, from his point of view, "Mrs Gaskell scarcely seems at one with herself in this matter."[82] In fact, of course, he is troubled because Gaskell incorporated into *one* figure, Ruth, two categories that seem to him as if they should be kept absolutely separate by being divided into two figures, as they are in *Bleak House*. His review thus works to rearticulate the split that he feels Gaskell's novel collapses, both by insisting that it should be present in the novel and that Gaskell herself should not be divided. It was precisely such a unified position that, as we saw from her editorial dealings with Dickens, the mid-Victorian cultural construction of femininity made it impossible for Gaskell to maintain.

The impulse to define Gaskell as a writer who is divided also permeates contemporary critical evaluations of her work. She tends to be described as split between being a writer of domestic fiction in such works as *Cranford* and *Wives and Daughters* and a writer of social fiction in *Mary Barton* or *North and South*. Interestingly, *Ruth*, the novel in which Gaskell systematically attempts to collapse the split between public and private woman, is often simply left off these lists as if it were not worthy of critical consideration. Such assessments of Gaskell replicate the split between the private and the public which already confined her as a mid-nineteenth-century professional woman writer who was also deeply identified with domestic ideology. Indeed when Gaskell is described, as she frequently is, as a talented though "limited" writer, we might note

81. William Rathbone Greg, "The False Morality of Lady Novelists," *National Review* 7 (1869): 167.
82. Ibid., 167.

that such descriptions reiterate her experience of being confined to the domestic realm and of having her novel *North and South* crammed and stuffed into the various issues of *Household Words*. In describing Gaskell's relation to Dickens, modern critics tend to replicate not only the split within Victorian definitions of femininity but also the relative positions of femininity and masculinity.[83] Critics often describe Dickens as if he had "made" Gaskell as a writer, thereby ignoring the fact that she had already published *Mary Barton* and established herself as a valuable "property" before he had ever approached her for his periodical. Characterizations of Dickens's editorial position relative to Gaskell almost invariably reiterate the scenario in which Gaskell is defined as "wayward," difficult, or undisciplined and Dickens as the patient figure who needs to take her in hand. These nineteenth-century categories are so deeply imbued in our thinking that, in the index to a recent biography of Gaskell—a place where one would expect to find the least ideologically fraught or most "factual" topics—one finds instead, under the heading of Charles Dickens, the category "EG's wayward dealings with."[84]

In writing about Gaskell, I have attempted to refuse the traditional split between the public and the private woman and to ask what happens when we read her gestures as signs of resistance rather than waywardness. The difficulty for Gaskell is that, unlike Mary Shelley and the Brontës, she does not use the position of feminine exclusion to criticize the masculine position which excludes her. Instead she attempts to resist and redefine the feminine position assigned to her by her culture. Such resistance is difficult, as we see from her editorial dealings in which she finds almost no way to avoid being defined as a wayward woman and having her writing appropriated. Even in her novel *Ruth*, where, as I have argued, there is a little more room for resistance, Gaskell still ends up sacrificing her "fallen" heroine to contamination in much the

83. Modern critics also tend to echo the curiously sexual tone of Dickens's initial approaches to Gaskell. Ellen Moers characterizes him as "soliciting" Gaskell (Moers, *"Bleak House*: The Agitating Women," 23), Fred Kaplan as "seducing" her (Fred Kaplan, *Dickens: A Biography* [1989], 266), and Annette Hopkins as "attracted" to her writing and therefore "keeping after" her in order to establish an "intercourse" with her (Hopkins, "Dickens and Mrs. Gaskell," 357).

84. Gérin, *Elizabeth Gaskell: A Biography*, 314.

same way that Lady Dedlock is sacrificed at the end of *Bleak House*. Gaskell's gestures of resistance are also difficult to locate because the model of gender difference that associates femininity with deviance, and masculinity with the patience needed to control that deviance, is, as we see from biographies and criticism of Gaskell, so extraordinarily persistent that it appears as "truth" rather than a cultural construct. In order to make Gaskell's gestures visible, I have, as it were, borrowed a page from the novels of Mary Shelley and the Brontës. In this chapter, I have chosen to make the gesture Gaskell never makes, to examine and criticize the masculine position that is correlative to hers. I have performed this critique through Charles Dickens because Gaskell had extensive dealings with him in the realms both of rescuing prostitutes and of literary professionalism. The intent of the chapter is not, however, to criticize Dickens as an individual but to show the position he inevitably comes to occupy given the mid-Victorian constructions of masculinity and femininity, a position similar to that occupied by writers such as Greg and Acton. It is through Dickens's editorial dealings with Gaskell, as well as his depiction of rescue workers in *Bleak House*, that we can begin to see how gestures of apparent benevolence and patience also function as constraints. By reading Gaskell's actions as resisting that control, we can learn to see them not as deviance but as attempts to refuse the split between the "deviant" public woman and the proper private one which felt so confining to Gaskell.

In Chapter 3, unlike Chapters 1 and 2, I have examined a model of gender difference without connecting it to other discursive structures. The difficulty with the model of gender difference that positioned Gaskell is that it was also the one which was being articulated in contemporaneous discussions of prostitution. As a result, the split between the public and the private woman was, as the term "bio-politics" suggests, already politicized at midcentury. Because of this politicization, in this chapter, I have explored at length the complex and varied forms that model of gender difference takes in Gaskell's and Dickens's editorial dealings, their work with prostitutes, and their novels. The model of gender difference, which splits the public from the private woman, was, however, also connected to other discursive structures. Gaskell's assertion that she was unable to keep her stories her own property identifies the subtext that runs through midcentury discussions of prostitution and representations of "fallen" women. It was an economic subtext which dealt with questions of who should own property and who should not. In Chapter 4, I continue to examine Gaskell's and Dickens's novels, particularly those that contain representations of conflicts between masters and workers, in order to explore the connection between the figure of the improperly public woman and middle-class anxieties about property-owning.

4

"Those That Will Not Work": Prostitutes, Property, Gaskell, and Dickens

> The body of the prostitute is clearly the meeting place of Eros and commerce.
> —Peter Brooks, *Reading for Plot*

This chapter continues to focus on Victorian social discourse about prostitution but reads that discourse in light of the mid-1850s economic anxieties about class conflict. If the Brontë novels discussed in Chapter 2 inscribe midcentury fantasies of overcoming class inequities through upward mobility, the novels discussed in this chapter represent the middle-class fear of such desires for advancement on the part of the working classes. In terms of the fiction it addresses, Chapter 4 resumes where Chapter 3 left off by reading *Ruth* and the Dickens and Gaskell novels which followed it, *Hard Times* and *North and South*, as a sequence of interconnected texts, all of which contain depictions of middle-class manufacturing families. This chapter also glances back at Gaskell's *Mary Barton* because, like Dickens's and Gaskell's novels of the mid-1850s, it contains explicit depictions of conflicts between manufacturers and workers.[1] All these novels represent but also work to occlude a

---

1. *Mary Barton* may have influenced Dickens, who read it while working on *David Copperfield*; both novels contain representations of prostitutes. Esther, the prostitute from Gaskell's earliest novel, also seems to haunt *Bleak House*, not only in the name of its heroine but also in the scene in which Lady Dedlock's body is found on the threshold of the paupers' burial ground clad in the clothes of Jenny, the bricklayer's wife. When Esther Summerson exclaims, "It was my mother, cold and dead" (59.869), the scene is reminiscent of the one in Gaskell's novel in which Esther, the prostitute, returns home disguised in the clothes of a respectable working-class woman, and Mary Barton sees in her "a form, so closely resembling her dead mother, that [she] never doubted the identity, but exclaimed . . . 'Oh! mother! mother! You are come at last' " (Elizabeth Gaskell, *Mary Barton: A Tale of Manchester Life*, ed. Stephen Gill [1970], chap. 20, p. 287. All further references to this book [hereafter abbreviated as *MB*] appear in the text).

crucial contradiction in mid-nineteenth-century attitudes toward property-owning. While one of the driving forces behind laissez-faire economics was the belief that everyone should be encouraged to want to own property, the middle classes, in fact, also feared the working-class desire to become property owners. As Margaret Hale says in *North and South*, "the workpeople speak as though it were in the interest of the employers to keep them from acquiring money—that it would make them too independent if they had a sum in the savings' bank."[2] The contradiction implicit in Victorian economics was, as Mary Poovey argues, that "the unregulated market relations celebrated by the middle classes did not actually entail equal access to available resources but institutionalized class exploitation."[3] Mid-nineteenth-century rhetoric about prostitution defused the potential threat of working-class desires to own property both by creating an arena in which it was possible to define individuals as property and by defining some desires to possess property as negative, in essence, as stealing or appropriation.[4]

The definition of femininity being addressed in this chapter is essentially the same as the one discussed in Chapter 3 where women experienced themselves as split between a proper private sphere and an improperly public one. But here, rather than examining women's anxieties about leaving the domestic sphere, I consider the social and economic concerns that motivated the insistent mid-Victorian foregrounding of the image of the improperly public or "fallen" woman. This chapter examines the connection between the economic and the sexual in mid-Victorian discussions of prostitution and in Gaskell's and Dickens's novels of the mid-

---

2. Elizabeth Gaskell, *North and South*, ed. Dorothy Collin (1970), chap. 15, p. 165. All further references to this book (hereafter abbreviated *NS*) appear in the text.

3. Poovey, "Speaking of the Body," 36. Poovey argues that the contradictory representations of women in Greg's 1850 article "Prostitution" "displace and seem to resolve another contradiction—the contradiction inherent in the bourgeois image of laissez-faire social relations" (ibid., 35–36).

4. The questions of whether a worker's labor is his or her property or whether to be a worker means one is defined as property were also critical problems in the world of nineteenth-century publishing. As Mary Poovey states in "The Man-of-Letters Hero: *David Copperfield* and the Professional Writer": "In the first place, because of the peculiarities of literary composition, this activity exposed the arbitrariness of the definition of labor to which wages were affixed. . . . In the second place, the problematic nature of literary property revealed how slippery a concept 'private property' could be" (Poovey, *Uneven Developments*, 105).

1850s. It maps out the ideological space where "the body of the prostitute" becomes "the meeting place of Eros and commerce,"[5] an interconnection that is both more complex and less transparent than the epigraph to this chapter might suggest. The interconnection of the economic and the erotic in the rhetoric of prostitution provides a double means for managing midcentury anxieties about class conflict. On the one hand, as suggested above, the economic discourse which surrounded the figure of the prostitute allowed for the apparent resolution of the contradictions implicit in middle-class attitudes toward the working classes. On the other, the erotic discourse which surrounded the figure of the prostitute and led to the specularization of the body of the "fallen" woman worked to occlude unresolvable economic conflicts by deflecting the Victorian audience's attention away from them.

A brief look at *Mary Barton* will help us to see how the prostitute functions as a middle ground between the erotic and the economic in mid-Victorian thinking. As critics have noted, Gaskell's earliest novel is divided so equally between two stories, one about workers and strikes and one about women and seduction, that it is hard to know whether it should have been called *John Barton*, as Gaskell originally intended, or *Mary Barton*, as the publisher eventually decreed.[6] The figure Gaskell positions between these two stories and links to both is Esther, the sister of Mary Barton's mother, a factory girl, who early in the novel is seduced into prostitution. As a "fallen" woman, Esther is obviously a parallel for Mary Barton; she represents what Mary will become if she succumbs to her upper-class seducer. In *Mary Barton*, the prostitute is also, however, paralleled to the rebellious worker. Esther's and John's life stories follow an almost identical pattern. Both the "fallen" woman and the striking worker begin by wanting something better than their condition as factory workers. They fail in striving for that improved life and instead find themselves barely struggling to survive. Both

---

5. Peter Brooks, *Reading for Plot: Design and Intention in Narrative* (1984), 144.

6. As Raymond Williams notes: "It was originally to be called *John Barton*. . . . The change of emphasis which the book subsequently underwent, and the consequent change of title to *Mary Barton*, seem to have been made at the instance of the publishers, Chapman and Hall. The details of this matter are still obscure, but we must evidently allow something for this external influence on the shape of the novel" (Williams, *Culture and Society: 1780–1950* [1958], 88–89).

lose children because of the poverty of their situation and grieve inconsolably over those unnecessary deaths. Both eventually respond to the unbearable pain of their lives by giving in to the deadening effects of a drug, Esther to alcohol and John Barton to opium. These parallel lives end with John Barton and Esther buried in a single grave

> without name, or initial, or date. Only this verse is inscribed upon the stone which covers the remains of these two wanderers
>   Psalms ciii. v. 9—'For He will not always chide, neither will He keep his anger forever.' (MB 38.465)

Not identified as separate individuals, the striking worker and "fallen" woman are characterized here as children who have strayed but whom their father will forgive, a familial image that is repeated in both *Ruth* and *Hard Times*.

Though Esther has crucial symbolic significance, standing as she does between the stories of John and Mary Barton, she appears only briefly at *Mary Barton*'s beginning and again toward its end. The figure who takes her place between the novel's erotic and economic plots and who is effectively her counterpart is Harry Carson, the mill owner's son. Young Carson links the two halves of the novel because he is both the one who attempts to seduce Mary Barton and the one who takes the most extreme hard line toward the workers, persecuting and ridiculing them so severely that they strike back. The narrator of *Mary Barton* emphasizes that Carson's economic and erotic predations take place simultaneously and seem almost to reinforce one another: "With all his letter-writing, his calling, his being present at the New Bailey, when investigations of any case of violence against knob-sticks was going on, he beset Mary more than ever" (15.224). Carson thinks about seducing Mary by using the same economic logic that he uses to think about getting labor out of his workers; he is determined "that at any price he must have her, only that he would obtain her as cheaply as he could" (11.180). What makes Harry Carson such a negative figure in *Mary Barton* is that he treats both women and workers as if they were property or goods to be bought and sold. Because of his treatment of others, he, as well as Esther, would be associated with the idea of "prostitution" in Victorian thinking. If the "fallen" woman is the one who has been prostituted, then the seducer/mill owner is the one who prostitutes others. As Marx writes in a footnote to the *Economic and Philosophical Manuscripts of 1844*, "Prostitution is only a particular expression of the general prostitution of the worker, and because prostitution is a relationship which includes both the person prostituted and the person prostituting—whose business is even greater—thus the capitalist, too, etc., is included within this category." (*Selected Works*, 90n.)

If Harry Carson's treatment of women and workers in *Mary Barton* is conceived as an act of prostitution, John Barton's stance as a rebellious worker is also associated with prostitution in terms that resemble those Marx uses to discuss workers and property-owning in the *Economic and Philosophical Manuscripts*. In Gaskell's novel, the position that John Barton makes seem most prostituted is articulated when, in arguing with a fellow worker about what differentiates masters from workers, he asserts, " 'You'll say (at least many a one does), they'n getten capital an' we'n getten none. I say, our labour's our capital and we ought to draw interest on that' " (6.104). In the *Economic and Philosophical Manuscripts of 1844*, Marx criticizes early communist impulses such as Barton's. According to Marx, the problem with defining labor as capital and assuming that class inequities could be overcome if everyone were in equal possession of property is that, "the relationship of the community to the world of things remains that of private property" (87). As Marx goes on to argue:

Finally, this process of opposing general private property to private property is expressed in the animal form of opposing to marriage (which is of course a form of exclusive private property) the community of women where the woman becomes the common property of the community. One might say that the idea of the community of women reveals the open secret of this completely crude and unthinking type of communism. Just as women pass from marriage to universal prostitution, so the whole world of wealth, that is the objective essence of man, passes from the relationship of exclusive marriage to the private property owner to the relationship of universal prostitution with the community. (87)

While Gaskell and Marx have diametrically opposed views of workers (she sees an argument such as Barton's as potentially threatening middle-class values; he sees it as imbued with those same values), both conceptualize the linkage between workers and prostitution in strikingly similar terms. Both implicitly define two positions, one feminine, one masculine. The feminine position, which is occupied by the prostitute, involves being defined as, in the words of Laurie Langbauer, "a symbol for property, the thing possessed."[7] The masculine position involves being associated with an indiscriminate desire to own property, a desire both Gaskell and Marx characterize as negative by linking it with prostitution. These two symbolic positions are articulated throughout the rhetoric of midcentury social texts on prostitution and in Gaskell's *Ruth* and Dickens's *Hard Times*.

The writings of those such as Acton and Greg, who address the subject of prostitution, directly spell out the economic argument that necessitates the symbolic equation of the prostitute with property in mid-nineteenth-century rhetoric. Economic images and language appear throughout social texts on prostitution, displayed, for example, by Acton's characterization of prostitution as a "free trade in female honour"[8] or by his description of prostitutes as women of "bankrupt" character who bring "discredit" on their homes.[9] Greg's 1850 *Westminster Review* article "Prostitution" allows us to see the whole of the implicit economic argument that motivates this persistent rhetoric. Greg concludes his article by arguing that the English should deal with prostitution and the spread of venereal disease by adopting a system of medical and police supervision modeled on the French system described by Parent-Duchâtelet. In order to reach this conclusion, however, Greg first makes an economic argument based on defining prostitution as analogous to the slave trade.[10] He introduces the concept

7. Laurie Langbauer, *Women and Romance: The Consolation of Gender in the English Novel* (1990), 115.

8. Acton, *Prostitution*, 211.

9. Acton, "Review of *A Short Account of the London Magdalene Hospital*," 366. W. R. Greg also describes seducers as men who "profit" by "women's hearts" (Greg, "Prostitution," 459). Acton picks up this same economic imagery and applies it not just to prostitution but to his own activity of writing about prostitution, arguing that "it will not be without profit to consider . . . the condition to which these unhappy women are reduced" (Acton, *Prostitution*, 58). Even as a subject of discourse, the prostitute is defined as a source of profit.

10. This analogy between slavery and prostitution was to be virtually institutionalized in the phrase "white slave trade." Acton refers to the prostitute as the

of slavery early in "Prostitution" when he describes prostitutes as "far more out of the pale of humanity than negroes on a slave plantation, or fellahs in a pasha's dungeon."[11] By associating prostitutes with images of those considered absolutely different from himself because of their race, Greg is also able, while eliciting sympathy for prostitutes, to define them as property.[12]

Greg begins his final economic argument by asserting that efforts to abolish the slave trade had proved not only useless but harmful; in his words, "our attempts to repress the slave traffic by an armed force are not only in a great measure answerable for its *increase . . .* but have actually been the *cause* of its having quadrupled in suffering and atrocity."[13] As Greg contends, the problem is one of economics; one cannot "prevent *any* demand from being met by an adequate supply."[14] Following laissez-faire logic, the demand for slaves cannot and should not be limited, and thus the only "humane" choice is to limit or control the supply, or in Greg's words, *"to regulate the number of slaves per tonnage."*[15] With this assertion, Greg turns from slavery to prostitution, arguing by anal-

---

"white slave of her proprietor" (Acton, *Prostitution*, 43). In fact, it was not until later in the century that the discourse of white slavery was fully developed. William Thomas Stead published a series of articles in the *Pall Mall Gazette* in July 1885 entitled "The Maiden Tribute of Modern Babylon" that led to the passage of the Criminal Law Amendment Act, by which the age of consent for girls was raised from thirteen to sixteen. For a discussion of images of women in Stead's essay, see Joseph Kestner, *Mythology and Misogyny: The Social Discourse of Nineteenth-Century British Classical-Subject Painting* (1989), 3–23.

11. Greg, "Prostitution," 450.

12. Here Greg introduces what I have called in Chapter 2, following Homi Bhabha, an "epidermal schema." By associating prostitutes with images of those defined primarily in terms of their difference in skin color, Greg is comfortable defining prostitutes not as full subjects but as objects to be bought and sold. For a discussion of the way in which images of prostitutes were consistently associated with images of racial difference in nineteenth-century rhetoric, see Sander Gilman, "Black Bodies, White Bodies: Toward an Iconography of Female Sexuality in Late Nineteenth-Century Art, Medicine and Literature," in *Difference and Pathology: Stereotypes of Sexuality, Race, and Madness* (1985), 76–108.

13. Greg, "Prostitution," 490.

14. Ibid., 489. Acton begins his argument in favor of the control of prostitution with a similar insistence on laissez-faire economics when he asserts, "Regret it as we may, we cannot but admit that a woman if so disposed may make a profit of her own person and that the state has no right to prevent it" (Acton, *Prostitution*, 26).

15. Greg, "Prostitution," 489.

ogy that, because the demand for prostitutes also cannot and should not be limited, prostitution is a trade that cannot be abolished but must instead be "regulated." While the term regulation, when used in the context of mid-Victorian discussions of prostitution, usually refers to the regulation or control of disease, here it is introduced not in a medical but economic context.[16] Greg uses the analogy between prostitution and slavery to define prostitutes as objects to be bought and sold, a supply of goods that can be controlled to meet market demands. By equating prostitutes with property, he is able to reconcile two apparently contradictory economic positions; he can insist on the importance of unregulated market relations and, at the same time, argue for one arena in which regulation is desirable.

Defining prostitutes as property and arguing implicitly that the desire for property should be unlimited, however, potentially exacerbated middle-class anxiety about working-class desires to own property. In the rhetoric about prostitution, this potentially threatening position is defused by associating prostitutes with a negative desire for property, the desire to acquire money without working for it. In nineteenth-century social texts on prostitution, women's sexual transgressions are frequently associated with crimes such as swindling, forgery, or embezzlement. Acton, for example, in his 1848 review of Parent-Duchâtelet's *De la prostitution*, lists "drunkenness, thefts, forgeries, [and] embezzlements" as linked to and aggravated by prostitution.[17] Similarly, in a series of articles that appeared in the *Morning Chronicle* in 1850, Mayhew groups prostitutes, beggars, thieves, and swindlers together, asserting that "the pickpockets—the beggars—the prostitutes—the street-sellers—the street-performers—the cabmen—the coachmen—the watermen—the sailors and such like" are similar because "these classes . . . partake more or less of the purely vagabond, doing nothing whatsoever for their living, but moving from place to place

16. At the end of his *Quarterly Review* essay on Parent-Duchâtelet's *De la prostitution*, Acton similarly associates a biological argument with an economic one by asserting that one way to ameliorate the problem of prostitution would be for the men who have sinned to give money, "penitential contributions to those asylums which are devoted to the reformation of fallen women" (Acton, "Review of *A Short Account of the London Magdalene Hospital*," 376).

17. Ibid., 368.

preying upon the earnings of the more industrious portions of the community."[18] Mayhew's case studies of the women who became prostitutes almost invariably depict a woman who works with feverish industry at a job that does not pay enough for her to support herself—usually some form of needlework—and is then forced to take to the streets. Such narratives implicitly define prostitution as the opposite of the hard labor the woman previously performed. That definition is borne out by the title of the section of Mayhew's four volume work published in 1861 which dealt with thieves, swindlers, beggars, and prostitutes: "Those That Will Not Work."[19] It is also borne out in the irony with which prostitutes continue to be referred to as "working girls" as if what they do has nothing to do with work. Such rhetoric suggests, as Acton spells out, the assumption that prostitutes are motivated by the desire to "obtain the greatest amount of income procurable with the least amount of exertion."[20]

The logic of articles such as Mayhew's, however, implies less that prostitutes themselves are defined as desiring to obtain money than that the desire to obtain money without work is defined as analogous to prostitution. As Langbauer notes, in Marx's writings, prostitution becomes "*the* symbol of . . . man's reification, his fall

18. Henry Mayhew, *London Labor and the London Poor: A Cyclopedia of the Condition and Earnings of Those That Will Work, Those That Cannot Work, and Those That Will Not Work,* (1861), 1: 2–3, cited in Catherine Gallagher, "The Body versus the Social Body in the Works of Thomas Malthus and Henry Mayhew," *Representations* 14 (Spring 1986): 90. In that article and in "George Eliot and *Daniel Deronda*: The Prostitute and the Jewish Question," Gallagher argues that Victorian thinking was hostile "toward groups that seem to represent a realm of exchange divorced from production" (Gallagher, "George Eliot and *Daniel Deronda*," 43). In discussing *Daniel Deronda,* she notes that prostitution is positioned as analogous to pawnbroking, which she describes as "the unnatural generation of money, which, in usury, proliferates through mere circulation but brings nothing qualitatively new into being" (ibid., 40). Mayhew's description of the classes he discusses as "purely vagabond" might remind us of Gaskell's final characterization of Esther and John Barton as "two wanderers."

19. The linkage between prostitutes and those who will not work continues to be assumed in texts such as the 1990 movie *Pretty Woman,* in which Julia Roberts's prostitution is defined as analogous to Richard Gere's profession of buying up companies, breaking them in pieces, and selling them. The two can be redeemed only when she ceases to practice prostitution and he decides to build ships—in essence, when both apparently choose work and productivity over buying and selling.

20. Acton, *Prostitution,* 60.

into the painful materialism of capitalism."[21] Langbauer uses the word "man" advisedly since in Marx's and also in Greg's and Acton's writings, the position of wanting to own property is implicitly occupied by a man;[22] it is the masculine correlative to the seductions that lead women into prostitution. Dickens makes the parallel between economic and sexual temptation explicit in an early letter to Angela Burdett Coutts on Urania Cottage, the "Home for Homeless Women," which the two were founding together. In that letter, Dickens advocates strict discipline and constant testing for the "fallen" women who were to be taken into the refuge, arguing that they needed to be taught to resist temptation. The analogy he uses to explain his rationale for such a stringent disciplinary system exemplifies the way in which mid-Victorian thinking paralleled female erotic and male economic transgressions. Dickens tell Coutts that in establishing a refuge for "fallen" women she must ask herself

> whether there are not, at the Banking House in the Strand, many young men whose lives are one exposure to, and resistance of, temptation. And whether it is not a Christian act to say to such unfortunate creatures as you purpose, by God's blessing, to reclaim "Test for yourselves the reality of your repentance and your power of resisting temptation, while you are *here*, and before you are in the World outside, to fall before it![23]

In this letter, written in 1846, in which Dickens characterizes young men as exposed to temptation in banking houses, he anticipates his 1854 portrait of Tom Gradgrind in *Hard Times*, a portrait also

21. Langbauer, *Women and Romance*, 116.

22. As Mary Poovey has noted, in Greg's essay, it is *only* men who feel sexual desire (Poovey, "Speaking of the Body," 34). Poovey makes a similar argument about Victorian women being defined as without desire in her discussion of *David Copperfield*, and comments in a note to that essay that "this helps explain both why male desire became the paradigm for Freud's model of 'universal' psychological development and why female desire, that 'dark continent,' was assumed to follow a trajectory different than male desire" (Poovey, *Uneven Developments*, 231n.). Poovey's comment suggests the way in which, in Freud's imagery as well as in Greg's argument about prostitution and slavery, masculine sexual desire is positioned as analogous to the imperialist drive to dominate or possess other races.

23. "To Miss Burdett Coutts, 25 July 1846," in *Letters*, 4:588.

modeled on Gaskell's depiction of Richard Bradshaw in her 1853 novel *Ruth*.[24]

In *Ruth*, Gaskell represents a man's economic crimes as parallel to a woman's sexual transgression. She introduces the story of Richard Bradshaw's forgery and embezzlement late in her novel in order to show the self-righteous Mr. Bradshaw learning to forgive his son and subsequently being able to forgive the unforgivable, a woman's sexual fall. Echoes of *Ruth* in *Hard Times* suggest that Dickens may also have intentionally positioned Tom Gradgrind's economic crime of stealing from Bounderby the banker as parallel to sexual falls like Ruth's.[25] In *Hard Times*, Dickens picks up an image from *Ruth*, the image of the "blackamoor," which in Gaskell's novel is used to denote Ruth's guilt, and uses it to denote Tom's. In *Ruth*, when Mr. Bradshaw finds out about Ruth's past and condemns the Bensons for allowing a "fallen" woman to become a member of a respectable middle-class family, he exclaims, "I know there are plenty of sickly sentimentalists just now who reserve all their interest and regard for criminals—why not pick one of these to help you in your task of washing the blackamoor

24. Critics have often noted that the depiction of the Gradgrind family in Dickens's novel was based on Gaskell's depiction of the Bradshaws in *Ruth*. As Alan Shelston remarks in his introduction to *Ruth*, "In the specific instance of the Bradshaw family—from the overall conception down to the details of the criminality of the son and heir—we have a clear anticipation of the Gradgrinds of Dickens's *Hard Times*. (Dickens, it should be recorded, was much involved with Mrs Gaskell in the early 1850s; he expressed his admiration of *Ruth* when it first appeared in 1853, and began work on *Hard Times* in January 1854)" (xviii).

25. There is no actual "fallen" woman in *Hard Times*, though I will come back to the question of Harthouse's attempted seduction of Louisa. The figure in Dickens's novel who occupies the same structural position as Ruth in Gaskell's novel—the position of being taken into the home of a family associated with manufacturing—is Sissy Jupe. Sissy is also associated with Ruth through the openings of both novels. In the first chapter of *Ruth*, Ruth is characterized as taking pleasure in the painted panels of the old house where she works as a seamstress because on them "were thrown with the careless, triumphant hand of a master—the most lovely wreaths of flowers . . . so real-looking, that you could almost fancy you smelt their fragrance" (1.6). In the second chapter of *Hard Times*, Sissy responds to Gradgrind's question about whether she would carpet a room with representations of flowers by saying, " 'If you please, sir, I am very fond of flowers. . . . They wouldn't crush and wither, if you please sir. They would be pictures of what was very pretty and pleasant, and I would fancy' " (Charles Dickens, *Hard Times* [1964], bk. 1, chap. 2, p. 6. All further references to this book [hereafter abbreviated *HT*] appear in the text).

white?" (27.349). At the end of *Hard Times*, Dickens literalizes Brad-shaw's image by depicting Tom Gradgrind hiding out in Sleary's Circus disguised as a comic blackamoor who will have to be washed clean in beer. (We should note that while Ruth is *defined* as a blackamoor, Tom is only dressed as one and therefore, presumably, can be washed clean of his sins.) Overall, it is Gaskell's portrait of the sanctimonious manufacturer, Mr. Bradshaw, and his oppres-sive dealings with both his son and daughter that Dickens finds most useful in depicting the Gradgrind family in *Hard Times*.[26]

In *Hard Times* and *Ruth*, the two economic positions that I have argued are associated with the discourse of prostitution—being defined as property or wanting to acquire property illicitly—are occupied by the daughters and sons of manufacturers. In both fictional families, the father is a businessman whose harsh behavior alienates his daughter and son. While the sons, Richard Bradshaw and Tom Gradgrind, will not work but instead appropriate money belonging to others through forgery, embezzlement, and theft, the daughters, Jemima Bradshaw and Louisa Gradgrind, find them-selves treated as if they were property to be bartered in business dealings. Early in *Hard Times*, the narrator asks the novel's readers to consider an "analogy between the case of the Coketown pop-ulation and the case of the little Gradgrinds" (1.5.23). Such an analogy should, I think, be extended to the Bradshaws in *Ruth*. It would suggest that, in both novels, we read the father's tyrannical treatment of his children as analogous to the masters' treatment of the workers and, moreover, that the two positions the children occupy—being treated as property or acting as thieves—represent not the workers themselves but two middle-class attitudes toward the working class.[27]

26. Bradshaw seems generally to have struck a strong chord with mid-Victorian readers. While W. R. Greg was, as we have seen in Chapter 3, critical of Gaskell's depiction of Ruth, he loved her depiction of Bradshaw. Greg writes: "Among the members of Mr. Benson's congregation is a wealthy and influential merchant, Mr. Bradshaw,—the very distilled essence of a disagreeable Pharisee; ostentatious, pa-tronizing, self-confident, and self-worshiping; rigidly righteous according to his own notion, but in our eyes a heinous and habitual offender; a harsh and oppressive tyrant in his own family without perceiving it, or rather without admitting that his harshness and oppression is other than a sublime virtue; yet driving by it one child into rebellion and another into hypocrisy and crime . . . " (Greg, "The False Morality of Lady Novelists," 166).

27. Richard and Jemima Bradshaw and Tom and Louisa Gradgrind must, of

In the descriptions of Jemima Bradshaw's courtship in *Ruth* and Louisa Gradgrind's courtship and marriage in *Hard Times*, Gaskell and Dickens both represent marriage in virtually the same terms that Marx uses in his comments on private property. For both manufacturing daughters, marriage involves being treated as property in a way that borders on prostitution. As Greg puts it in "Prostitution," "For one woman who thus, of deliberate choice, sells herself to a lover, ten sell themselves to a husband."[28] Jemima Bradshaw and Louisa Gradgrind do not, however, sell themselves but are sold by businessmen—their fathers and brothers. Both heroines end up married to their fathers' business partners in what verges on being a purely financial transaction. When Mr. Bradshaw contemplates his daughter's potential marriage to Mr. Farquhar, he virtually acknowledges its economic use to him: "The fitness of the thing had long ago struck him; her father's partner—so the fortune he meant to give her might continue in the business; a man of such steadiness of character, and such a capital eye for a desirable speculation as Mr. Farquhar" (20.216). The narrator of *Hard Times* uses similar economic terms to characterize Louisa's marriage to Bounderby: "Love . . . on all occasions during the period of betrothal, took a manufacturing aspect. Dresses were made, jewellery was made, cakes and gloves were made, settlements were made." (I.16.100). Louisa's role in this transaction is spelled out early in the novel when Tom speculates on how he will profit from his sister's marriage to the banker and describes her as a "capital girl" (I.14.89). In both *Ruth* and *Hard Times*, the daughters clearly realize that they are being treated as property. When Jemima first learns that her father has encouraged Mr. Farquhar to court her, "she felt as if she would rather be bought openly, like an Oriental daughter, where no one is degraded in their own eyes by being parties to such a contract"(21.240–41).[29]

---

course, be read as hybrid figures because they are characterized literally as members of middle-class families while, at the same time, they stand in the symbolic position of the working class. When, in *Hard Times*, Tom Gradgrind is shown attempting to palm his stealing off on Stephen Blackpool, it suggests Dickens's awareness that what is at stake in figures such as Tom and Richard Bradshaw is the middle-class desire to project its own anxieties and guilt onto figures of the working classes.

28. Greg, "Prostitution," 458.

29. In this passage from *Ruth*, as in Greg's use of the analogy of slavery in "Prostitution," the definition of women as objects to be bought and sold is artic-

In contrast to the daughters who attempt to obey their father's rules only to find themselves treated as property, the sons, Richard Bradshaw and Tom Gradgrind, covertly rebel. In both novels, the father's hard treatment has evidently made the son what he is. As Mr. Farquhar explains in *Ruth*, Richard has been "cowed by his father into a want of individuality and self-respect" (31.411) and, as a result, has learned to ignore "all ideas not bearing upon his own self-interests" (26.333). Self-interest is, of course, the business principle Mr. Gradgrind teaches must always come first. Their fathers' harsh treatment makes the Bradshaw and Gradgrind sons not industrious but idle in a way that is explicitly associated with the idleness of the workers in *Hard Times*. As Bitzer tells Mrs. Sparsit, Tom "is as improvident as any of the people in this town. And you know what *their* improvidence is" (II.1.110). Bitzer characterizes Tom in exactly the same way that the manufacturers in *Mary Barton* characterize laid-off workers such as John Barton: if those workers were not so improvident they would have saved up enough money to last out factory closings. When workers like Barton seek to claim their labor as their own property by striking or rioting against the knobsticks who are brought in to replace them, they are then seen as thieves. The position of the manufacturer is, as Mrs. Thornton articulates in *North and South*, that workers are striking for " 'the mastership and ownership of other people's property' " (15.162). In *Ruth* and *Hard Times*, this middle-class view of workers is represented through the figures of improvident sons who rebel against their businessman fathers by seizing or appropriating property which is not their own.

Together the daughters and sons of manufacturing fathers represent the contradiction inherent in middle-class attitudes towards the working classes, a contradiction that eventually leads mid-Victorians to turn their attention away from what seems to be an unresolvable economic conflict of interest. The depictions of daughters in both *Ruth* and *Hard Times* clearly point out that it is wrong to treat individuals as if they were property. However, the gesture

---

ulated through images of racial and cultural difference. In her comment, Jemima uses the oriental imagery that in Chapter 2 we saw used in *Jane Eyre*, portrayed, for example, in the scene of the charades at Thornfield, where Eliezer buying Rebecca as a wife for Isaac is represented as the kind of economic exchange that lurks behind the facade of "proper" Victorian marriages.

of sympathy implicit in the descriptions of Jemima Bradshaw and Louisa Gradgrind also elicits middle-class uneasiness. If workers are not seen as objects but as subjects, they must potentially be thought of as property owners. This threatening possibility is defused by the figures of the two brothers through whom the desire to own property can be represented as negative, criminal, and resulting from idleness. *Mary Barton* reaches the same kind of impasse as *Hard Times* when it moves toward its conclusion. Gaskell obviously condemns treating other people as property in her negative characterization of Harry Carson. When, however, the workers rebel against Carson's treatment by killing him, guilt is immediately transferred from the masters to the workers, who are represented as threatening to the middle class. Having reached an impasse in the representation of class conflict, both novels veer away from economic issues to focus on an erotic story—in *Hard Times*, the story of Harthouse's attempted seduction of Louisa, and in *Mary Barton*, the story of Harry Carson's pursuit of Mary which is foregrounded in the trial scene. The shift that takes place at the end of *Hard Times* and *Mary Barton* resembles the shift at the end of Greg's argument in "Prostitution" when he moves from talking about prostitutes as property to be regulated in an economic sense to talking about them as bodies to be regulated in a medical sense. Greg's argument and Dickens's and Gaskell's novels all conclude by allowing the body of the "fallen" or potentially "fallen" woman to become the center of the reader's attention, which is then deflected away from uncomfortably contradictory attitudes toward economic issues raised earlier in the text.[30]

As Jacqueline Rose has pointed out in "George Eliot and the Spectacle of Woman," mid-Victorian discussions of prostitution, with their emphasis on examining the body of the diseased woman, made female sexuality into a spectacle. Citing a passage from Acton's early treatise on generative diseases where he compares his

30. The figure of the "fallen" woman functions doubly to screen economic issues in *Hard Times*. Not only are the implications of Tom Gradgrind's crime hidden by the novel's focus on Harthouse's seduction of Louisa, but also the emblematic worker of the text, Stephen Blackpool, expresses overt concern not about the workplace but about his wife, who sounds suspiciously like a "fallen" woman in the narrator's description of her, "a creature so foul to look at, in her tatters, stains and splashes, but so much fouler than that in her moral infamy, that it was a shameful thing even to see her" (1.10.64).

own work of writing about prostitution to lifting the veil from the face of a woman who has been marked or scarred by disease, Rose argues that in the 1850s[31]

> the prostitute . . . becomes the publicly sanctioned image against which society measures its moral consciousness of self. But if morality is a sexual matter, it is not just because of the reference to the prostitute and the explicit discourse of purity and vice. It is also because of the sexual fantasy, the relentless and punishing scrutiny of the woman, which supports it. In the second half of the nineteenth century, morality makes a spectacle of itself.[32]

As Rose later explains, "the sexual fantasy" which makes the woman "the privileged object of investigation and control" is contaminated "by all the questions about social inequality and misery which this attention directed at the woman serves to displace."[33] *Hard Times* and *Mary Barton* allow us to analyze this gesture of displacement because we can see their plots turning away from unresolvable economic conflicts to focus on the image of the "fallen" woman's body.

In *Hard Times*, as soon as Tom commits his theft and attempts to blame it on Stephen Blackpool, the narrative swerves away from its concentration on masters and workers or fathers and children to focus on James Harthouse's attempted seduction of Louisa Gradgrind.[34] That story represents the only possibility of resolution in the novel; by rejecting Harthouse and returning to her father,

31. For a full citation of the passage from Acton, see my discussion of Esther Summerson's scarred face in *Bleak House* in Chapter 3.

32. Rose, *Sexuality in the Field of Vision*, 112.

33. Ibid., 113.

34. While Tom's stealing occurs in chapter 6 of Book II of *Hard Times*, chapters 7 through 12 describe Harthouse's attempted seduction of Louisa. The novel implicitly parallels Tom's economic crime with Harthouse's sexual one; both seek to break into something that has been locked up, a bank vault, Louisa's repressed feelings. But the representations of seductions in *Hard Times* and also in *Ruth* are kept fairly separate from the economic realm because, unlike the seducer in *Mary Barton*, the seducers in Gaskell's and Dickens's later novels are clearly defined as *not* directly part of the world of manufacturing. Dickens appears to have modeled Harthouse on Bellingham, the man responsible for Ruth's fall in Gaskell's novel; both are idle, upper-class rakes, who eventually become political candidates. These later novels keep the economic and erotic strands of their plots more separate than they are in Gaskell's earlier text.

Louisa converts Mr. Gradgrind away from utilitarianism. Her actions teach him not to prostitute others, not to treat them as property. But that personal and emotional conversion replaces any form of economic change in the novel. The story of Harthouse's attempted seduction of Louisa appears to occupy such a prominent place in *Hard Times* both because it appears to provide a symbolic resolution to the economic problems of the narrative and also because it is staged as a theatrical spectacle. Harthouse's pursuit of Louisa is presented through the voyeurism of Mrs. Sparsit who becomes an avid spectator to the process of seduction. She observes Louisa, in the words of Jacqueline Rose, with a "relentless and punishing scrutiny," in the course of which the whole concept of a woman's sexual "fall" becomes reified: "Much watching of Louisa, and much consequent observation of her impenetrable demeanour, which keenly whetted and sharpened Mrs. Sparsit's edge, must have given her as it were a lift, in the way of inspiration. She erected in her mind a mighty Staircase, with a dark pit of shame and ruin at the bottom; and down those stairs, from day to day and hour to hour, she saw Louisa coming" (2.10.188). Mrs. Sparsit's overwhelming desire to watch leads her not only to fantasize about Louisa's undoing but also to want literally to witness it. Like Greg and Acton who, as they contend, write about prostitution despite their sense of revulsion, Mrs. Sparsit proceeds "heedless of long grass and briers, of worms, snails, and slugs, and all the creeping things that be" (2.11.196) to spy on a secret meeting between Harthouse and Louisa. Assuming Louisa to have given in to Harthouse's seduction at the end of that meeting, Mrs. Sparsit is described as "exult[ing] hugely. The figure had plunged down the precipice, and she felt herself, as it were, attending on the body" (2.11.199). Through the figure of Mrs. Sparsit, *Hard Times* represents the way that, as Rose has argued, the body of the "fallen" woman can become a central, spectacular focus drawing all the viewer's attention.

In *Mary Barton*, the heroine becomes a theatrical spectacle in the courtroom scene where everyone crowds in to hear a story of seduction and betrayal and to look at the woman who attracted the attention of Harry Carson, the mill owner's son. Both Mary's story and her body become public property in this scene. Yet, rather than simply allowing the story of Carson's attempted seduction of

Mary to distract attention away from the economic issues raised earlier in *Mary Barton*, Gaskell foregrounds the moment when the Victorian audience and legal system misread a crime because they *want* to look at erotic rather than economic motives. In *Mary Barton*, a single scapegoat like Mrs. Sparsit does not bear the burden of the general social desire to scrutinize the "fallen" woman. Instead, in Gaskell's novel, the whole of Victorian society is characterized as wanting to look at Mary. It is not just old Mr. Carson who wants to see the "fatal Helen" who brought about his son's death but everyone in the novel, including its narrator, who, though avowedly not present in the courtroom at the time, eagerly conveys an eyewitness's description of Mary's physical appearance. Gaskell emphasizes that in looking at Mary's body and fantasizing about Harry Carson's pursuit of her, the audience in the courtroom, the lawyers, the police, and the judges, all turn their eyes away from thinking about the workers as the potential murderers of Harry Carson. Because we, as readers of Gaskell's novel, know before the trial scene that John Barton actually committed the murder, we are excruciatingly conscious of the fact that Victorian society is *not* looking at its own economic problems. Later in *Mary Barton* when Job Legh is asked why, knowing all the facts, he never suspected that John Barton was the murderer, he provides an explanation that could be read as a gloss for the whole trial scene: " 'But still, you see, one's often blind to many a thing that lies right under one's nose, till it's pointed out. And till I heard what John Barton had to say yon night, I could not have seen what reason he had for doing it; while in the case of Jem, any one who looked at Mary Barton might have seen a cause for jealousy, clear enough' " (37.455).

In the end of both *Hard Times* and *Mary Barton*, when an erotic plot moves into the foreground to mask economic crimes, guilt remains securely located in the obscured economic realm. Though Louisa Gradgrind and Mary Barton become public spectacles, neither is literally guilty; both resist their seducers by refusing at the last minute to fall. But at the moment when both heroines are freed from the literal threat of sexual seduction and betrayal, they begin to be characterized figuratively as "fallen" women. In *Hard Times*, when Louisa has refused Harthouse and returned home to her father, she is represented as "fallen," both because of her literal position and her description of herself. After she throws herself into her father's arms: "He tightened his hold in time to prevent her sinking on the floor, but she cried out in a terrible voice, "I shall die if you hold me! Let me *fall* upon the ground!" And he laid her down there, and saw the pride of his heart and the triumph of his system lying, an insensible heap, at his feet" (2.12.204, emphasis added). Similarly, in *Mary Barton*, once Harry Carson is killed and Mary Barton is no longer threatened with sexual violence, she immediately begins to be characterized in terms that associate her with the figure of the "fallen" woman. She leaves Manchester, locking her home behind her, and thus emerges from the safety of the domestic sphere to go to Liverpool to search for an alibi for Jem. She begins to walk the streets of a strange city and to be characterized as if she were a professional streetwalker. As the wife of the sailor, who finally "saves" Mary when she is abandoned on the pier says: " 'Perhaps . . . thou'rt a bad one; I almost misdoubt thee, thou'rt so pretty. Well-a-well! it's the bad ones as have the broken hearts, sure enough . . . it's the sinful as bear the bitter, bitter grief in their crushed hearts, poor souls' " (31.377). Because they are not literally guilty, Louisa and Mary are safe objects for the Victorian viewers' attention, providing an outlet for fascination with sexual scandal and at the same time proving themselves to be "pure" in the end. Their status as women, who are figuratively but not literally "fallen," means they can function with particular effectiveness to screen or veil the economic plots of the novels in which they appear.

North and South, the Gaskell's novel which followed *Hard Times* in *Household Words*, reveals most clearly what it is like to be a woman in the position of having to cover over economic or class conflicts. This novel is narrated from the perspective of Margaret Hale, who embodies the contradictory middle-class feelings of sympathy for the workers and anxiety about what they threaten. Gaskell represents that double impulse within Margaret perhaps most apparently in the scene of the riot at Thornton's mill. In that scene, Margaret's sympathy leads her to insist that Thornton, the mill owner, confront the workers directly and hear their grievances. Her subsequent anxiety about what the workers in their rage will do to their employer leads her to go out to protect Thornton. This scene and a later scene where Margaret accompanies her brother to the train station and plays a similarly protective role, function in *North and South* as vignettes.[35] They show in microcosm how midcentury anxieties about economic ambiguities or class conflicts were displaced by fascination with the image of an improperly public woman. Though Margaret Hale, compared to the other heroines discussed in this chapter, is the least directly connected to any form of seduction or sexual betrayal, she is nevertheless characterized as a "fallen" woman when she enters the public sphere.[36] In *North and South*, Gaskell shows why mid-Victorian rhetoric was so interested in dramatizing the figure of the "fallen" woman as well as how that dramatization limited women who sought to take any kind of public social action.

The scene of the riot at Thornton's mill is structured as a virtual tableau vivant where Gaskell represents the ideological relation between the economic and the erotic through the relative positioning of her characters. It is also the scene, of any in the various social novels considered in this chapter, that contains the most direct depiction of class conflict. In it, we see the workers angrily attack their employer's mill and the employer come out of his stronghold to face them. But when the possibility of a direct attack by workers on the mill owner erupts, Margaret Hale interposes herself between the two sides, making "her body into a shield" and forcing Thornton to "shelter behind a woman" (22.234–35). Struck by a stone thrown by one of the strikers and rendered unconscious, Margaret literally "falls," and Thornton holds her body out to the crowd, deriding them with the shameful spectacle of what their violence has effected. With this injury to an "inno-

35. In analyzing the interaction between public and private in the novel, Catherine Gallagher also discusses the riot scene and the scene at the train station as parallel (Gallagher, *The Industrial Reformation of English Fiction*, 172–76).

36. While Margaret Hale is herself innocent, Gaskell did contemplate including in *North and South* (which she was then thinking of titling *Margaret Hale*) the figure of what she called a wayward girl: "I have half wondered whether another character might not be introduced into Margaret,—Mrs Thornton, the mother, to have taken as a sort of humble companion & young housekeeper the \orphan/ daughter of an old friend in humble, retired country life on the borders of Lancashire,—& this girl to be in love with Mr Thornton in a kind of passionate despairing way,—but both jealous of Margaret, & yet angry that she gives Mr Thornton pain—I know the kind of wild wayward character that grows up in lonesome places" ("To John Forster, [23 April 1854]," letter 191, in *Letters*, 281).

cent" woman, the guilt which had previously been shared by both master and men is suddenly placed entirely on the shoulders of the workers, as Thornton makes clear in his speech to them: " 'You fall—you hundreds—on one man; and when a woman comes before you, to ask you for your own sakes to be reasonable creatures, your cowardly wrath falls upon her! You do well!' They were silent while he spoke. They were watching, open-eyed and open-mouthed, the thread of dark-red blood . . . " (22.235). With its repetition of the word fall, Thornton's speech suggests that when the attack on the mill becomes an attack on Margaret, economic conflicts are being rewritten in terms of the story of women's sexual transgressions; in rioting—in striking for their rights—the workers are now defined as having "fallen." As this passage moves from Thornton's comments to the workers' gaze, it also displays how the theatrical presentation of a literally fallen woman makes her into a kind of heraldic emblem. Margaret's bleeding and unconscious body becomes the visual focus of the scene, deflecting both the workers and the mill owner from their anger over economic issues which initially motivated the conflict at the mill.

The iconography of the scene in front of the mill further invites the novel's readers to interpret it in terms of an extremely familiar, mythic version of the story of the "fallen" woman. A tableau in which a beautiful woman stands with a single male protector and confronts an angry mob that threatens to stone her inevitably evokes the story of Mary Magdalene, an identification Victorian readers would easily have made. Yet, in the confrontation with the workers, Thornton is the one who first appears to occupy the position of the Magdalene, since he is the one they wish to stone. In contrast, Margaret stands, Christ-like, seeking the crowd's forgiveness for him. With the actual stoning and its aftermath, however, the guilt shifts not only from the master to the workers but also figuratively from Thornton to Margaret, whose bleeding body now makes her a kind of symbolic Magdalene. Gaskell's use of the Magdalene imagery to depict a woman who acts for the social good rather than sexually emphasizes the representational dilemma she confronts as a novelist. Although Margaret does, in fact, succeed in defusing the riot and moving the workers to return home before they can be injured by the soldiers Thornton has summoned to quiet the riot, as a woman in the public sphere, her actions cannot be interpreted or represented in terms of any rhetoric other than that associated with "fallen" women and prostitution.[37]

The scenes following the riot show how quickly Margaret's public actions are interpreted in terms of narratives of sexual impropriety. Immediately after Margaret is struck down, Thornton leaves her in the care of his sister and her maid, both of whom read the heroine's act of going to Thornton's aid as a gesture of "exposing" herself in public. In her semiconscious state, Margaret overhears one of the servants describe how another " 'saw Miss Hale with her arms about master's neck, hugging him before all the people.' " Thornton's sister responds, " 'I dare say, she'd give her eyes if he'd marry her,—which he never will, I can tell her. But I don't believe she'd be so bold and forward as to put her arms round his neck' " (22.239). Mrs. Thornton will later describe Margaret as so "compromised" by what happened during the riot that Thornton must marry her. Thornton himself proposes to Margaret because he, like the other characters in the novel, misreads her gesture of throwing her arms around him as an expression of erotic or romantic feelings rather than political or social concern. Even during the riot, Thornton is distracted from the aggressive anger he feels toward his workers because he remembers the feel of Margaret's unconscious body in his arms, "every nerve in his body thrilling at the thought of her" (22.237). When Margaret herself dwells retrospectively on her own actions in front of the mill and on the comments others make about them, she exclaims: " 'I, who hate scenes—I, who have despised people for showing emotion—who have thought them wanting in self-control—I went down and must needs throw myself into the mêlée, like a romantic fool! . . . it is no wonder those people thought I was in love with him, after disgracing myself in that way. . . . Oh, how low I am fallen that they should say that of me!' " (23.247).[38] While she goes on to insist

37. Gaskell's novels, which strongly influenced Josephine Butler, the founder of the Ladies National Association, suggest one of the reasons that association formed and became active in its campaign against the Contagious Diseases Acts. If, in the Victorian era, women's public actions were always constituted in terms that made them seem analogous to prostitution, then, in a sense, one of the few arenas where it was possible for women to become publicly active was precisely in defense of prostitutes.

38. Catherine Gallagher cites both this passage from Gaskell and the earlier

that she is pure before God, her exclamation suggests that having acted and been discussed in that public way makes her feel like a "fallen" woman. As the narrator later explains, Margaret is tormented by the consciousness of having been a spectacle and experiences "a deep sense of shame that she should thus be the object of universal regard—a sense of shame so acute that it seemed as if she would fain have burrowed into the earth to hide herself, and yet she could not escape out of that unwinking glare of many eyes" (23.249).[39]

In the later scene where Margaret accompanies her brother to the train station in order to protect him, she is similarly characterized as making a public spectacle of herself and described in terms that make her sound like a sexually transgressive woman. Initially, when persuading her father that she should be allowed to go to the station, Margaret asserts that she is not afraid of returning home alone at night because, as she puts it, "'I am getting very brave and very hard. It is a well-lighted road all the way home, if it should be dark. But I was out last week much later' " (32.330). This statement reminds the reader how frequently Margaret walks the city streets in the novel, an activity that leads to her involvement with the working classes and could also easily suggest streetwalking in its professional sense. When she arrives at the station, Margaret insists that she be the one to buy the ticket so that her brother will not be seen and identified. By making a shield of herself, as she did in the scene of the riot at the mill, Margaret once again finds that she has become a public spectacle; she is the object of the "impertinent stare[s]" of "some idle-looking men [who] were lounging about with the stationmaster" (32.331–32). Earlier in the scene, she had already found herself the object of the male gaze when, standing in the darkness and bidding her brother farewell,

description of Louisa falling in *Hard Times* in the course of discussing the linkage between public and private in both novels (Gallagher, *Industrial Reformation of English Fiction*, 172–73, 156–57).

39. The descriptions of Margaret's feelings in *North and South* should remind us of Gaskell's description of what it was like for her to publish *Ruth* and feel members of the congregation seeing her as an "improper" woman. (See my discussion of Gaskell's comments in Chapter 3.) By the end of *North and South*, we have come to understand the midcentury economic motivations that made the image of the improperly public woman so inescapable for Gaskell in her economic dealings with Dickens.

she became aware of Mr. Thornton riding by and watching her publicly embrace an apparent stranger.

As with the riot scene, other characters in the novel again cannot avoid interpreting Margaret's actions in terms of familiar Victorian narratives about public women and impropriety. Mrs. Thornton eventually confronts Margaret and accuses her of "gallivanting with a young man in the dusk" (38.390). Thornton himself begins to think of Margaret as split between purity and sexuality; in his imagination, she becomes both Una and Duessa (40.411). He finds himself

> haunted by the remembrance of the handsome young man, with whom she stood in an attitude of such familiar confidence . . . At that late hour, so far from home! It took a great moral effort to galvanize his trust—erstwhile so perfect—in Margaret's pure and exquisite maidenliness, into life; as soon as the effort ceased, his trust dropped down dead and powerless: and all sorts of wild fancies chased each other like dreams through his mind. (33.339)

When Margaret finally lies about having been at the station in order to continue to protect her brother, she describes her own actions in the following terms: "Trusting to herself, she had fallen. It was a just consequence of her sin, that all excuses for it, all temptation to it, should remain forever unknown to the person in whose opinion it had sunk her lowest" (48.502). Knowing that Thornton will recognize her as a liar because he has seen her at the station, Margaret finds her relationship to him abruptly changed; "she suddenly found herself at his feet, and was strangely distressed at her fall" (35.356).[40]

What lies hidden behind the erotic spectacle of Margaret at the train station is not a representation of the conflict between masters and men but a figure who embodies the contradictory middle-class feelings about that conflict. The person Margaret shields at the train station, her brother Frederick Hale, is a curiously murky figure

40. Though Thornton knows Margaret has lied about being at the train station, he uses his position as a magistrate to cover up her lie during the inquest into Leonards's death. This is the moment at which Margaret's position in North and South comes closest to being like that of Jemima Bradshaw in Ruth and Louisa Gradgrind in Hard Times. It is as if, by lying and allowing that lie to be concealed, she sells her honor to Thornton in order to protect her brother.

in *North and South*. The few descriptions given of him and his actions suggest that he should be linked, at least figuratively, to the aimless and appropriative brothers in *Ruth* and *Hard Times*. When the newspapers call Frederick a "traitor of the blackest dye" (14.153), that phrase might remind us of Tom Gradgrind disguised as a blackamoor. Moreover, when Hale playfully tells his sister that his philosophy of life is "a sort of parody on the maxim of 'Get money, my son, honestly, if you can; but get money' "(30.315), he sounds as if he could be Tom or Richard Bradshaw characterizing their fathers' business advice in terms that make that advice sound like an invitation to steal. Later Hale is characterized as taking pleasure in a "stolen visit" home because "it has had all the charm which the Frenchwoman attributed to forbidden pleasures" and as liking, when he was a child, to steal apples because, as Margaret says, " 'some one had told you that stolen fruit tasted sweetest, which you took au pied de la lettre, and off went a-robbing' " (31.323). This imagery associates him both with stealing and, through the use of French and the biblical reference to stealing apples, with sexuality and the fall.

But the "crimes" Frederick Hale actually commits in *North and South* are more ambiguous than stealing, forgery, or embezzlement. The reason that Margaret must protect him at the train station and that he has been described as a traitor is that he has been condemned in the English courts as a mutineer. That initial "crime" of mutiny, a rebellion against his superiors, could be read as resembling the actions of the workers who riot in protest against Thornton at his mill. As Catherine Gallagher notes: "The incident at Thornton's mill and her brother's mutiny involve similar ethical issues for Margaret. In the first incident, she believes that Thornton is exercising his authority in an unreasonable and even brutal manner. . . . The same hatred of imperious authority leads her to justify her brother's mutiny."[41] By representing Frederick Hale as a mutineer rather than a thief, Gaskell seems to be trying to resist the impulse to transfer guilt from masters to workers. She does not immediately represent Hale's action as negative or criminal. She does not translate the gesture of fighting back against tyranny into the gesture of taking something that belongs to someone else.

41. Gallagher, *The Industrial Reformation of English Fiction*, 174.

Readers, however, never receive a full account of the mutiny in *North and South* and thus are never able to determine whether Hale's actions are heroic or not. At the train station, his actions lead to the fall and eventual death of Leonards, a drunken sailor who served under Hale and who wishes to turn him in for mutiny. Yet once again, the novel is strangely unclear about what actually happens between the two men at the station, and, as a result, we never know how guilty Frederick is. Hale is thus defined both as someone who rebels against those above him and as someone who allows those below him to *fall* to their death. He seems to represent both the workers' resistant actions toward the masters and the masters' negligent actions toward the workers. The ambiguities or blurriness of his actions, the mixture of questionable heroism with questionable guilt, represents, I would argue, the middle-class ambivalence about its own attitudes toward the conflict between classes. *North and South* suggests that it is this ambivalence which is being covered over by the spectacle of the figuratively "fallen" woman.

The problem that critics, especially materialist critics, have with *North and South* and even *Mary Barton* is their sense that Gaskell attempts to address the question of the working classes but finally fails to do so. As Catherine Gallagher says of *Mary Barton*, it is a novel where, though Gaskell "does not find a narrative form that satisfactorily *reveals* the reality of working-class life, she does identify several conventional genres that *hide* the reality."[42] This statement brilliantly describes the structure of Gaskell's novel, and its language echoes the terms used by critics from Raymond Williams onward, who are sympathetic to Gaskell's "attempts" to depict class conflict but at the same time imply that ideally one would want her to have been able to "reveal" more. The logic of these critiques of Gaskell, which imply that working-class life is a "reality" that needs to be "exposed," is characteristic of the kind of logic used in mid-nineteenth-century discussions of prostitution. As Rose notes, Greg and Acton represent their own work in writing about prostitution as an act of lifting the veil to expose the reality of the scarred face it hides. This emphasis on gestures of "exposure" reappears throughout the work of critics writing about fictional representations of prostitution. Peter Brooks, for example,

42. Ibid., 67, emphasis added.

asserts that it might be possible "to trace a kind of progressive unveiling of the erotic body in the nineteenth-century novel."[43]

Laurie Langbauer has pointed out how such comments tend to essentialize and reify the body of the woman and has noted how similar comments are made by materialist feminists, who "emphasize the body—the prostitute's body—because they argue that insisting on it might *uncover* an important hidden essence, the necessity of material and economic factors to the construction of reality."[44] Even when Catherine Gallagher emphasizes the metaphorical linkage of professional writing with prostitution, she ends up praising a gesture of exposure by arguing that such a linkage was useful to George Eliot because it allowed her to "*expos[e]* the unnaturalness of the commercial literary economy—its severance from 'real wants.' "[45] Rhetoric in which critics talk about "exposing" the real wants, or in Williams's case the authenticity, of working-class life replicates the logic of mid-nineteenth-century discussions of prostitution which by associating workers with prostitutes created an arena in which both could be defined as objects or property. What is interesting about *Mary Barton* and *North and South* is that Gaskell does *not* pull back the veil to "reveal" the reality of working-class life.

Such a gesture would, besides reifying the working classes, also mean dismissing the figure of the improperly public woman as nothing more than a veil. Williams implicitly makes exactly this gesture when he dismisses the whole foregrounding of Mary Barton's story at the end of Gaskell's novel as being "of little lasting interest."[46] But Gaskell also does not simply allow the figure of the "fallen" woman to veil the economic conflicts raised in her novels as, I would argue, happens in the end of Dickens's *Hard Times*. Instead, both *Mary Barton* and *North and South* contain scenes where Gaskell dramatizes the moment when the figure of the improperly public woman deflects the viewers' attention away from economic

43. Brooks, *Reading for Plot*, 143.
44. Langbauer, *Women and Romance*, 109, emphasis added. Langbauer's "An Early Romance: The Ideology of the Body in Mary Wollstonecraft's Writing" provides an extended discussion of the way writing about prostitution seems to necessitate the rhetorical gesture of exposing the woman's body (ibid., 108–26).
45. Gallagher, "George Eliot and *Daniel Deronda*," 47, emphasis added.
46. Williams, *Culture and Society*, 89.

concerns. In foregrounding these scenes, Gaskell does not reify the working classes but represents an ideological network in which middle-class attitudes toward the working classes are intertwined with a specific definition of femininity. I would agree with Raymond Williams's assertion that the story and characterizations in *Mary Barton* are "characteristic of the structure of feeling within which [Gaskell] was working."[47] But unlike Williams, I read the structures of feeling represented in Gaskell's novels as having to do not only with questions of class but also with questions of gender and the way in which the two interconnect.

In Chapters 2 and 4, I have examined novels written at midcentury, all of which show a fascination with questions of class difference, of what the possibility of social mobility might mean. But as one moves from the Brontë novels to the novels of Dickens and Gaskell, one feels a growing sense of anxiety about what changes in class structure might engender. The overall movement from Shelley and the Brontës to Gaskell and Dickens, that is, from the first half of the nineteenth century to the second, has been a movement from a sense that the economic realm was expanding, either in the arena of production or of the empire, to a sense of anxiety about potential conflicts of interest. As one moves from Mary Shelley's *Frankenstein*, Emily Brontë's *Wuthering Heights*, and Charlotte Brontë's *Jane Eyre* to Elizabeth Gaskell's novels, one also notices a shift in emphasis in the way models of gender difference are used. While the earlier novels, written in a period of greater economic confidence, deal primarily with the definition of masculinity that was foregrounded at the moment in which Shelley or the Brontës were writing, the later novels, written at a period of greater economic anxiety, emphasize the definition of femininity that was foregrounded at the moment Gaskell was writing. In 1870, when George Eliot wrote Book II of *Middlemarch*, anxieties about the collapse of social structures, which Matthew Arnold and others defined as anarchy, were part of the intellectual climate of the times and were once again linked to a specific definition of femininity. If, in the case of Elizabeth Gaskell, we see the constraints that arise from the negative image of the public or "fallen" woman, in the

47. Ibid.

case of George Eliot, we see how the definition of women as excluded from the public realm of culture and scholarship can itself become negative—a definition of femininity as fragmented or biologically broken.

5

"High Art and Science Always Require the Whole Man": Culture and Menstruation in *Middlemarch*

> WOMAN is the subject which for some time back our benevolence has been disposed to take in hand, fitfully and piecemeal. We have been grieved, startled, shocked, perplexed, baffled; still, with our usual activity, we have been long at work, beating about the bush, flying at this symptom, attacking that fragment, relieving this distress, denouncing that abomination.
> —W. R. Greg, "Why Are Women Redundant?"

As one moves from the midcentury novels of the Brontës, Dickens, and Gaskell to George Eliot's *Middlemarch*, written in 1870, questions of class difference begin to be dealt with not in terms of property-owning but of access to education or to what Matthew Arnold calls "culture."[1] *Middlemarch* resembles Dickens's and Gaskell's novels of the mid-1850s in being written in a climate of anxiety about the collapse of social hierarchies. In the late nineteenth century, that anxiety was expressed as a fear of anarchy, a fear that civilization might collapse into fragments.[2] Arnold's title *Culture and Anarchy* identifies what liberal intellectuals of that time period defined as the antidote to anxieties about political unrest: an ideal of culture that was designed to deal with the class inequities of the 1840s and 1850s by redistributing knowledge as opposed to wealth. The new educational systems of the 1860s and 70s were intended

---

1. For an extended discussion of George Eliot's relation to the liberal intellectual traditions of the 1860s and 70s see Daniel Cottom, *Social Figures: George Eliot, Social History, and Literary Representation* (1987).

2. When George Eliot was writing Book 2 of *Middlemarch*, she may have been particularly sensitive to the possibility of anarchic uprisings which destroyed monuments of culture. That was the historical moment of the reign of the Commune in Paris and the toppling of the Vendome Column. For a discussion of artistic responses to the political disruptions in Paris in 1870–71, see Neil Hertz, "Medusa's Head: Male Hysteria under Political Pressure," in *The End of the Line: Essays on Psychoanalysis and the Sublime* (1986), 161–91.

to make culture accessible to everyone regardless of their " 'accidents' of birth, class, and history."[3] While this new concept of education might sound as if it would level social differences, in fact, the cultural antidote to anarchy was always emphatically characterized, as George Henry Lewes puts it, as *"high* art and science."[4] This emphasis on a hierarchy within culture itself implicitly positioned some individuals as incapable of understanding the "high" culture that was apparently open to all. In the late nineteenth century, the territory defined as excluded from culture was, as we shall see, associated with both "the mob" and femininity.[5]

Late nineteenth-century anxieties about anarchy could be and were translated into anxieties about literary style, particularly the style of realist writers such as George Eliot. As the following quotation suggests, contemporaries could read the systematic attention to detail that was characteristic of realism as an expression of the kind of anarchic fragmentation generally feared during the period. Baudelaire writes: "An artist with a perfect sense of form but one accustomed to relying above all on his memory and his imagination will find himself at the mercy of a riot of details all clamouring for justice with the fury of a mob in love with absolute equality. . . . The more our artist turns an impartial eye on detail, the greater is the state of anarchy."[6] Eliot's extreme dependence on detail was one of the stylistic traits critics almost invariably noted in reviewing her novels.[7] Henry James, for example, in an 1873 review for *Galaxy*, asserts that *"Middlemarch* is a treasure-house of details, but it

3. Cottom, *Social Figures*, 5.

4. George Henry Lewes, "Unsigned Review," from the *Edinburgh Review*, in Allott, *The Brontës: The Critical Heritage*, 161.

5. For a discussion of how George Eliot was frustrated by the way her gender positioned her as excluded from Arnoldian definitions of culture, see Deirdre David, *Intellectual Women and Victorian Patriarchy: Harriet Martineau, Elizabeth Barrett Browning, George Eliot* (1987). David shows how "the conflict between female desire for cultural autonomy and male intellectual authority" (187) leads repeatedly in Eliot's novels to the frustration of that female desire.

6. Charles Baudelaire, *The Painter of Modern Life and Other Essays*, trans. and ed. Jonathan Mayne (1964), 16, cited in Naomi Schor, *Readings in Detail: Aesthetics and the Feminine* (1987), 21.

7. For a general discussion of the use of detail in Eliot's novels and its relation to the way femininity is constructed, see Laurie Langbauer, "Recycling Patriarchy's Garbage: George Eliot's Pessimism and the Problem of a Site for Feminism," in *Women and Romance*, 197–216.

is an indifferent whole."[8] In Eliot's case, the excessive use of detail was explicitly associated with femininity and was opposed to a more masculine sense of wholeness. In an earlier unsigned review in *The Nation*, James describes Eliot as having "a certain masculine comprehensiveness," but also as being "a feminine—a delightfully feminine—writer." For James, this means that her writing exhibits "exquisitely good taste on a *small* scale, the absence of taste on a *large*" and, in a phrase, that evokes a sense of fragmentation even as it denies it, "the *unbroken* current of feeling and, we may add, of expression, which distinguish the feminine mind."[9]

James's opposition between comprehensiveness and detail, or between large and small, is a version, I would argue, of the Arnoldian opposition between cultural wholeness and the fragmentation of anarchy. James's comments suggest that that opposition, so crucial to late nineteenth-century discussions of art and education, was intertwined with a model of gender difference that defines masculinity as whole, full, or coherent, and femininity as, in the words of W. R. Greg, "only a fragment of a thing."[10] Eliot confronted the definition of femininity as fragmentary much closer to home and much earlier in her career than in Greg's articles on redundant women or Henry James's reviews of her novels. In 1850, two years before George Henry Lewes met George Eliot and seven years before she published her first fiction, he made the following comments in the course of evaluating Charlotte Brontë's novels for the *Edinburgh Review*:

> The grand function of woman, it must always be recollected, is, and ever must be, Maternity . . . consequently for twenty years of the best years of their lives—those very years in which men either rear the grand fabric or lay the solid foundations of their fame and fortune— women are mainly occupied by the cares, the duties, the enjoyments and the sufferings of maternity. During large parts of these years, too, their bodily health is generally so broken and precarious as to incapacitate them for any strenuous exertion. . . . how could such oc-

8. Henry James, "Unsigned review," from *Galaxy*, in *George Eliot: The Critical Heritage*, ed. David Carroll (1971), 353.

9. Henry James, "Unsigned review," from the *Nation*, in ibid., 277, emphasis added.

10. William Rathbone Greg, "Why Are Women Redundant?," *National Review* 14 (April 1862): 435.

cupations consort with the intense and unremitting studies which seared the eyeballs of Milton . . . ? High art and science always require the *whole* man.[11]

This passage dramatically illustrates the model of gender difference that made Eliot's position as a woman writer and a liberal intellectual virtually contradictory. The definition of femininity as broken and incapacitated meant that, as a woman, George Eliot was conceived to be incapable of participating in the ideal of "high" culture which, as a liberal thinker, she espoused. In order to enter the realm of literary scholarship where fame and fortune are built, Eliot had to construct a full-fledged masculine persona for herself which was so powerful that it persists to this day.

The fact that, among its many uses, this Victorian model of gender difference functioned to keep women writers in their place is suggested by the context in which Lewes articulated it so vehemently. He was reviewing *Shirley*, a review that Charlotte Brontë described as so "brutal and savage" it left her "cold and sick."[12] Brontë was shocked by Lewes's comments, in part, because he had responded extremely favorably to her previous novel, *Jane Eyre*. But in moving from *Jane Eyre* to *Shirley*, Brontë had shifted from writing about her own and other women's personal experiences to writing about politics and history. Lewes responded to Brontë's shift in subject matter by defining it as a transgression into masculine territory. He condemned her later novel for what he called its "over-masculine vigour" and characterized Brontë as a woman who, in the words of Schiller on Madame de Stael's *Corinne*, " 'steps out of her sex—without elevating herself above it.' "[13] The terms

11. George Henry Lewes, "Unsigned review," from the *Edinburgh Review*, in Allott, *The Brontës: The Critical Heritage*, 161. This passage was of enough importance to Lewes that he used it again two years later in "The Lady Novelists," *Westminster Review* 58 (1852): 129–41. The terms of Lewes's discussion—its references to being able to build or erect something, its anxiety about fragmentation, its final allusion to blindness—may seem a quite startlingly Freudian evocation and denial of castration anxiety. I would read Freud's own insistence on associating masculinity with wholeness and femininity with fragmentation as an inherent aspect of late Victorian thinking about gender.

12. "To W. S. Williams, 10 January 1850," cited in Allott, *The Brontës: The Critical Heritage*, 160.

13. Lewes, "Unsigned review," from the *Edinburgh Review*, in Allott, *The Brontës: The Critical Heritage*, 163, 169.

of Lewes's final critical judgement of Brontë suggest that the definition of femininity as broken or fragmented, which he introduces early in his essay, allows him to define women as naturally excluded from the realm of history and politics, or, as he puts it, from the realm of "high art and science." Lewes's argument that women's biology—their broken bodily health—incapacitated them for strenuous intellectual exertion was characteristic of the arguments that were being made in late nineteenth-century debates in both England and America about whether women should have access to higher education. A number of writers argued that menstruation as well as child-bearing rendered women unfit for higher learning. As James MacGrigor Allan put it in an address given to the Anthropological Society of London in 1869, the year Eliot began *Middlemarch*:

> Although the duration of the menstrual period differs greatly according to race, temperament, and health, it will be within the mark to state that women are unwell, from this cause, on the average two days in the month, or say one month in the year. At such times, women are unfit for any great mental or physical labour. They suffer under a languour and depression which disqualify them for thought or action. . . . In intellectual labour, man has surpassed, does now, and always will surpass woman, for the obvious reason that nature does not periodically interrupt his thought and application.[14]

To understand why definitions of femininity as biologically limited proliferated at the same time that liberal intellectuals were advocating a new ideal of culture, I want to look closely at two texts: chapter 20 of *Middlemarch*, where Eliot depicts Dorothea confronting Casaubon and Rome, and "Dickens in Relation to Criticism," George Henry Lewes's posthumous critical evaluation of

14. James MacGrigor Allan, *Anthropological Review* 7 (1869): 118–19, cited in Elaine Showalter and English Showalter, "Victorian Women and Menstruation," in *Suffer and Be Still: Women and the Victorian Age*, ed. Martha Vicinus (1973), 40. The Showalters' article is particularly helpful in relation to *Middlemarch* since it discusses the way that debates about women and menstruation escalated in the later half of the century—particularly in the years immediately after the publication of *Middlemarch*—in both England and America. For another article which provides good general background on Victorian attitudes toward menstruation, see Sally Shuttleworth, "Female Circulation: Medical Discourse and Popular Advertising in the Mid-Victorian Era," in *Body/Politics: Women and the Discourses of Science*, ed. Mary Jacobus, Evelyn Fox Keller, and Sally Shuttleworth (1990), 47–69.

Dickens, written on the occasion of the publication of Forster's *Life of Dickens*. These two works literally came out of the same context (both were written in the Eliot-Lewes household), and both were produced at almost exactly the same time (Book 2 of *Middlemarch* and Lewes's review of Dickens both appeared in print in February 1872). The two texts also contain a number of similar images. But, while Eliot, in the Rome section of *Middlemarch*, challenges the model of gender difference that opposes masculine wholeness to feminine fragmentation, in "Dickens in Relation to Criticism," Lewes uses that model of gender difference at an almost subliminal level to define Dickens as feminine and fragmented and therefore, as a "low" or popular writer whose characters appeal only to "un-cultivated" readers. Both Eliot and Lewes are interested in a realm that is defined as outside "high" culture, but while Eliot seeks to resist being enclosed in that realm, Lewes seeks to position Dickens within it. Together Eliot's novel and Lewes's essay allow us to see how an apparently essentialist or biological definition of femininity was strategically useful in the late nineteenth-century intellectual privileging of "high" culture.

Rome was the perfect arena for Eliot to stage a female spectator's confrontation with a concept of cultural wholeness that implicitly excluded her. Late nineteenth-century intellectuals viewed Rome, in the words of the narrator of *Middlemarch*, as the "city of visible history," the embodiment of the classical heritage which made up Western civilization. That classical culture was, however, clearly defined as patriarchal, as Eliot emphasizes in *Middlemarch* when she describes Latin and Greek, the languages Dorothea wants to learn from Casaubon, as "those provinces of masculine knowledge [which] seemed to her a standing-ground from which all truth could be seen more truly" (*MM* 1.7.47). Eliot dramatizes the moment in which an individual suddenly attains a perspective from which the fragments he sees around him suddenly make sense in *Romola*, when she portrays Baldassare suddenly regaining his ability to read the Greek letters which an hour before had seemed like hieroglyphics. Using images that recur in her description of Dorothea in Rome, Eliot characterizes Baldassare's recovered ability to understand his surroundings in the following manner:

That city, which had been a weary labyrinth, was material that he could subdue to his purposes now: his mind glanced through its affairs with flashing conjecture; he was once more a man who knew cities, whose sense of vision was instructed with large experience, and who felt the keen delight of holding all things in the grasp of language. Nouns! Images!—his mind rushed through its wealth without pausing, like one who enters on a great inheritance. [15]

In this moment, Baldassare experiences what James calls masculine comprehensiveness; he is able to hold everything together within the grasp of his imagination and enter into his cultural inheritance. But the word inheritance, combined with the previous reference to wealth, suggests that culture itself is here being conceived as a kind of property. And, as in Chapter 4, where we saw that under laissez-faire capitalism property-owning was only apparently open to all, in this instance the term inheritance, with its patrilineal associations, suggests that cultural wealth is also open to some and closed to others.

Freud's accounts of the fantasies and anxieties he had about entering Rome provide a paradigmatic account of what it feels like first to be excluded from and then included within one's cultural heritage. In his dreams, Freud experienced a sense of wanting desperately to go to Rome but also a fear that something would block or prevent his entry into that city. [16] For him, the city's significance was encapsulated in Michelangelo's statue of the patriarch Moses, which stands in Rome and, in Freud's eyes, structurally stood for both the classical culture that produced it and his own Jewish heritage. But when Freud first sees the statue he finds himself moved by it without understanding why. [17] His resultant

15. George Eliot, *Romola*, ed. Andrew Saunders (1980), bk. 8, chap. 38, p. 406. My attention was called to this scene from *Romola* and this passage through Neil Hertz's use of it in "Recognizing Casaubon," *The End of the Line*, 75–96. Hertz reads the moment in *Romola* and Dorothea's confrontation with Rome as instances of the sublime. For a discussion of what I perceive as the limitations of Hertz's approach, see the introduction.

16. For Freud's discussions of his dreams of Rome, see Sigmund Freud, *The Interpretation of Dreams*, trans. James Strachey (1965), 226–30, 358–59, 477–78.

17. Freud's description of his response to Michelangelo's Moses seems a particularly appropriate gloss to the Rome section of *Middlemarch* since Freud characterizes his initial difficulty as a kind of "intellectual bewilderment" (Sigmund Freud, "The Moses of Michelangelo" [1914], in *Character and Culture*, ed. Philip Rieff [1963], 81). Dorothea responds similarly to the art works of Rome, those "long vistas of white forms. . . . Forms both pale and glowing [which] took possession of her young sense" (*MM* 2.20.144).

sense of confusion and doubt make him feel as if he is excluded from the patriarchal culture the statue represents. As he writes:

> How often have I mounted the steep steps of the unlovely Courso Cavour to the lonely place where the deserted church stands, and have essayed to support the angry scorn of the hero's glance! Sometimes I have crept cautiously out of the half-gloom of the interior as though I myself belonged to the mob upon whom his eye is turned— the mob which can hold fast no conviction, which has neither faith nor patience and which rejoices when it has regained its illusory idols.[18]

Here Freud feels as if he is part of the rebellious and unruly mob, whose actions threaten to level hierarchies.[19] His sense of being excluded from culture leaves him feeling not only part of the anarchic masses but also, as Coppélia Kahn has pointed out, feminized: "The statue that bends an angry glance on him is his masculine ego ideal, and the childish, fickle mob that Moses found worshipping the golden calf when he descended from the mountain is the weak, 'womanish' part of himself that Freud feared giving in to. The passage springs from memories of self-reproaches arising from his fear of not being man enough for the great task he had set himself."[20] Freud's initial feeling of uncertainty is, however, followed by a return of the power to interpret. Like the passage from *Romola* in which Baldassare recovers from his feelings of confusion and is suddenly able to hold all things within the grasp of language, Freud is able to look at even the smallest detail of the statue, such as the positioning of a few hairs in Moses's beard, and pull those fragments together into a single comprehen-

18. Freud, "The Moses of Michelangelo," in *Character and Culture*, 82–83.

19. For Freud, the image of Rome is also associated with a patricidal impulse that becomes revolutionary when his dreams take on a political edge. See Carl Schorske, "Politics and Patricide in Freud's *Interpretation of Dreams*," in *Fin-de-Siècle Vienna* (1980), 181–207. "The Moses of Michelangelo," published in 1914, points indirectly toward contemporary political revolutions when Freud mentions "a Russian art-connoisseur, Ivan Lermolieff, [who] had caused a revolution in the art galleries of Europe..." (Freud, "The Moses of Michelangelo," in *Character and Culture*, 91).

20. Coppélia Kahn, "The Hand That Rocks the Cradle," in *The (M)other Tongue: Essays in Psychoanalytic Interpretation*, ed. Shirley Nelson Garner, Claire Kahane, and Madelon Sprengnether (1985), 86.

sive reading of Michelangelo's representation of the Jewish patriarch.[21] Freud's encounter with Michelangelo's Moses, in which he experiences first a sense of anxiety about the leveling of social hierarchies, which is then allayed by his subsequent ability to enter into his cultural inheritance, is paradigmatic of the way in which Rome functioned in the late Victorian political unconscious.

However, when George Eliot sets out in *Middlemarch* to depict a *female* figure confronting the "city of visible history," she herself confronts the insistent characterization of culture, as represented by Rome, as a patriarchal institution that excluded the two intertwined concepts of the mob and femininity. In describing Dorothea's experience of Rome in chapter 20 of *Middlemarch* Eliot therefore draws on literary models that show female rather than male figures that are associated with Rome: Charles Dickens's *Little Dorrit* and Charlotte Brontë's *Jane Eyre*. In Dickens's novel, Little Dorrit is shown with her father in Rome following his release from debtors' prison. In Brontë's novel, Jane's first angry response to her tormentor, John Reed, is made possible by her reading of Goldsmith's *History of Rome*. In both novels, Rome is associated with the relation between a female figure and a male figure who could be thought of as representing patriarchal authority—in Dickens's novel, a father, in Brontë's, a son who is the unofficial head of an otherwise all-female household. Both novels also use the interaction between genders to articulate a model of class relations that reflects the social unrest of the period in which they were written, the late 1840s and early 1850s. In *Jane Eyre*, a novel written and published during the height of the Chartist disturbances, Jane's initial rebellion against John Reed and her description of him as a tyrant are characterized in terms that make them analogous to working-class rebellions. In contrast, in *Little Dorrit*, Little Dorrit's dutiful work in support of her father is characterized in terms that make it analogous to working-class support of the structures above it. George Eliot draws on these two politically opposite texts in

21. Throughout the essay, Freud repeatedly praises those who seek to bring fragments or pieces together. He cites an art connoisseur who was able to distinguish originals from fakes by paying attention to those details of the work that appear most trivial and reading them for signs of the artist's overall style. Later, he praises Pope Julius II, for whose tomb Michelangelo designed the statue of Moses, for attempting to unite the fragmentary states of Italy.

constructing *her* version of an encounter between a female figure and an emblem of patriarchal authority in Rome.

In *Little Dorrit*, Dickens's idealized and altruistic heroine functions as a counterrevolutionary figure. The traces of revolution that lurk around the edges of Dickens's novel are enacted perhaps most directly in the comic scene where Pancks leaps over his employer, the Patriarch, and cuts his long hair. In a novel that opens in Marseilles, a city identified with the French Revolution, and begins by referring to the guillotine as the "national razor," Pancks's gesture inevitably suggests decapitation and political revolution. However, Little Dorrit, the figure who stands at the heart of the novel, counters any revolutionary impulses Dickens may invoke by remaining uncritically supportive of patriarchal structures, as represented first by her father, Mr. Dorrit, the Father of the Marshalsea, and later by Arthur Clennam.[22] In both cases, it is Little Dorrit's work that maintains the paternal image and keeps it from falling apart.[23] That work in support of the patriarchy is so idealized in Dickens's novel that Lionel Trilling can accurately de-

22. Dickens's *Little Dorrit* shows how the son's potentially revolutionary anger against the father could be countered by a feminine position in which the daughter works to support or maintain patriarchal wholeness. As Forster's *Life of Dickens* allowed Victorian readers to understand, in *Little Dorrit*, as in other novels such as *David Copperfield*, Dickens rewrote his own childhood experience of having his family confined to debtors' prison. This was the period during his childhood when Dickens was angriest at his father, and *Little Dorrit* reflects that anger, in part, through its gallery of negative paternal figures. In *Little Dorrit*, Dickens defuses his potentially dangerous revolutionary anger against the father by rewriting himself as Little Dorrit, the figure in that novel who stands in the familial position closest to the one Dickens himself occupied when his family was sent to prison. Like Dickens, she is the only member of her family not imprisoned and therefore, the one who must work to support the others. But unlike Dickens, Little Dorrit never displays the slightest traces of resentment about what she must do. As Mary Jacobus explains in a slightly different context, " 'A hero is someone who has had the courage to rebel against his father and has in the end victoriously overcome him.' The antithesis of such a hero . . . can only be a woman or a patient Griselda" (Mary Jacobus, "The Law of/and Gender: Genre Theory and the *Prelude*," *Diacritics* 14 [Winter 1984]: 54).

23. A number of critics have pointed out that Little Dorrit's position as supporter of patriarchal wholeness means that she is less of an ideal figure than the novel's characterization of her suggests since she is implicated in maintaining the oppressive system the novel criticizes. See Janice M. Carlisle, "*Little Dorrit*: Necessary Fictions," *Studies in the Novel* 7 (1975): 195–214; Dianne F. Sadoff, "Storytelling and the Figure of the Father in *Little Dorrit*," *PMLA* 95 (1980): 332–47; Elaine Showalter, "Guilt, Authority and the Shadows of *Little Dorrit*," *Nineteenth-Century Fiction* 34 (1979): 20–40.

scribe Little Dorrit as "the Beatrice of the Comedy, the paraclete in female form . . . the child of the parable, the negation of the social will."[24] For George Eliot, it is precisely the extreme idealism of such figures as Little Dorrit that reveals and also undermines the conservative argument Dickens is implicitly making about class relations. As Eliot comments in "The Natural History of German Life," Dickens is the "one great novelist who is gifted with the utmost power of rendering the external traits of our town population," but he also becomes "as transcendent in his unreality as he was a moment before in his artistic truthfulness."[25] She concludes that:

> but for the precious salt of his humour . . . his preternaturally virtuous poor children and artisans, his melodramatic boatmen and courtezans, would be as noxious as Eugène Sue's idealized proletaires in encouraging the miserable fallacy that . . . the working-classes are in a condition to enter at once into a millennial state of *altruism*, wherein everyone is caring for everyone else, and no one for himself.[26]

The phrases Eliot uses in this passage to criticize Dickens—transcendent unreality, preternaturally virtuous, a millennial state of altruism—describe exactly those qualities which, as Trilling's comments make clear, Dickens's novel celebrates in Little Dorrit. Read as a criticism of *Little Dorrit*, Eliot's comments in "The Natural History of German Life" suggest that Dickens's image of an idealized daughter supporting her father with unquestioning devotion and hard but invisible work articulates a middle-class fantasy of the working classes devoting themselves wholeheartedly and without complaint to shoring up a crumbling patriarchal system.

Diametrically opposed to this representation of Little Dorrit in Dickens's novel, Jane Eyre at the opening of Brontë's novel, is represented in a position not of support but of rebellion. When John Reed attempts to exercise his patriarchal authority by reappropriating the book Jane is reading and throwing it at her, Jane

24. Lionel Trilling, *The Opposing Self* (1959), 56.

25. George Eliot, "The Natural History of German Life," in *The Essays of George Eliot*, ed. Thomas Pinney (1963), 271. Eliot wrote "The Natural History of German Life" while *Little Dorrit* was appearing serially. She refers to Mrs. Plornish in the course of both praising and criticizing Dickens's representations of working-class figures.

26. Ibid., 271–72.

retaliates violently and characterizes her action in terms that define it as a gesture of revolution:[27]

> "Wicked and cruel boy!" I said. "You are like a murderer—you are like a slave-driver—you are like the Roman emperors!"
>
> I had read Goldsmith's *History of Rome*, and had formed my opinion of Nero, Caligula, &c. Also I had drawn parallels in silence, which I never thought thus to have declared out loud.
>
> "What, what!" he cried. "Did she say that to me? Did you hear her, Eliza and Georgiana? Won't I tell Mama? but first—"
>
> He ran headlong at me: I felt him grasp my hair and my shoulder: he had closed with a desperate thing. I really saw in him a tyrant: a murderer. I felt a drop or two of blood from my head trickle down my neck, and was sensible of somewhat pungent suffering: these sensations for the time predominated over fear, and I received him in frantic sort. I don't very well know what I did with my hands, but he called me "Rat! rat!" and bellowed out aloud. (*JE* 1:43)

While Jane resists her oppressor physically, her references to Rome identify her actions not just as an expression of personal anger against John Reed but as part of what John Brenkman describes as

> the discontinuous heritage of revolt—the symbolizations and representations of those who have been vanquished in the social struggles of the past. Slaves, peasants, and workers as well as women and oppressed peoples have developed cultural practices and traditions in which can be read their resistance to domination and their historically defeated attempts to oppose injustice and oppression.[28]

27. The Marxist-Feminist Literature Collective's reading of the Brontë novels would suggest that Charlotte Brontë can embody such fierce rebelliousness in her female protagonist in part because there is no strong masculine figure representing patriarchal authority in the novel. As the Collective notes about all the Brontë novels: "The bourgeois kinship structure of the period, predicated on the exchange of women, is . . . evaded. None of the heroines have fathers present to give them away in marriage. . . . in all these texts the devised absence of the father represents a triple evasion of . . . class structure, kinship structure and Oedipal socialisation. Its consequences are that there is no father from whom the bourgeois woman can inherit property, no father to exchange her in marriage, and no father to create the conditions for typical Oedipal socialisation" (The Marxist-Feminist Literature Collective, "Women's Writing: *Jane Eyre, Shirley, Villette, Aurora Leigh*," *Ideology and Consciousness* [Spring 1978], 1:29–30).

28. John Brenkman, *Culture and Domination* (1987), 230.

The particular images Jane uses—of emperors and slaves, of Nero and Caligula—allow us to hear in her rebellious speech echoes of the rhetoric of late eighteenth and early nineteenth-century working-class and dissenting writers. One finds, for example, rhetoric similar to Jane's in the religious dissident Alexander Kilham's 1795 pamphlet, *The Progress of Liberty*, where he asserts, "We detest the conduct of persecuting Neros, and all the bloody actions of the great Whore of Babylon."[29] Similar imagery appears in William Cobbett's 1821 article in the *Political Register*, where he writes, "I most firmly believed when I was a boy, that the Pope was a prodigious woman, dressed in a dreadful robe, which had been made red by being dipped in the blood of Protestants."[30]

The images Kilham and Cobbett use, of tyrannous female figures associated with blood and dressed in red robes, are also evoked indirectly in *Jane Eyre*, not in the scene of Jane's rebellion but in the scene immediately following where Jane is confined to a room swathed in scarlet draperies. Both Kilham's and Cobbett's scarlet women and Brontë's red-room should, I think, be read as associated with the image of menstruation. As Elaine Showalter has argued about Brontë's novel:

> With its deadly and bloody connotations, its Freudian wealth of secret compartments, wardrobes, drawers, and jewel chest, the red-room has strong associations with the adult female body; Mrs. Reed, of course, is a widow in her prime. Jane's ritual imprisonment here, and the subsequent episodes of ostracism at Gateshead, where she is forbidden to eat, play, or socialize with other members of the family, is an adolescent rite of passage that has curious anthropological affinities to the menarchal ceremonies of Eskimo or South Sea Island tribes.[31]

I would suggest that in *Jane Eyre*, the red-room represents not Jane's literal menstruation but rather, the way in which the idea of menstruation was used during the Victorian period to confine or limit

29. Alexander Kilham, *The Progress of Liberty amongst the People Called Methodists* (1793), cited in E. P. Thompson, *The Making of the English Working Class* (1966), 44.
30. William Cobbett, *Political Register*, 13 January 1821, cited in Thompson, *The Making of the English Working Classes*, 36n.
31. Elaine Showalter, *A Literature of Their Own: British Women Novelists from Brontë to Lessing* (1977), 114–15.

any rebellious impulses women might have by defining femininity as biologically incapacitated. Cobbett's and Kilham's association of bloody women with tyranny is characteristic of the way that menstruation was conceived to act on women. As Sally Shuttleworth comments, nineteenth-century advertisements emphasized "woman's subjection to the tyrannous processes of the menstrual cycle."[32]

The difference between the way Cobbett and Kilham use the image of the bloody or tyrannously menstruating woman and the way that same image works in *Jane Eyre* suggests the problems raised by this definition of femininity for women writers like Brontë or George Eliot. When male writers such as Cobbett and Kilham articulate a position of rebellion, they do so by opposing themselves to a bloody or negative female figure who represents tyranny. When Jane Eyre articulates a similarly rebellious position, she finds herself defined *as* the negative, menstruating woman. No matter what the masculine position is, even if it is the rebellious position associated with what we might call anarchy, it still opposes itself to an image of femininity defined as biologically incapacitated. Conversely, no matter what political position femininity embodies—whether, as in the case of Little Dorrit, it is conservative, representing the support of the patriarchal order, or, as in the case of Jane Eyre, it is radical, representing rebellion against that order—the female figure is always positioned outside the realm of patriarchal culture. It is this peculiarly persistent model of gender difference that Eliot resists in the Rome section of *Middlemarch* by using *Little Dorrit* to deconstruct the definition of masculinity as whole, full, or coherent, and *Jane Eyre* to refuse the definition of femininity as fragmented, broken or biologically incapacitated.[33]

Eliot's depiction of Dorothea's relation to Casaubon in the early chapters of *Middlemarch* resembles Dickens's depiction of Little Dorrit. Wanting to think of herself as one of Milton's dutiful daughters,

32. Sally Shuttleworth, "Female Circulation," 48.
33. *Little Dorrit* and *Jane Eyre* are two of a number of texts Eliot alludes to in the Rome section of her novel. The scene in *Villette*, for example, where Lucy Snowe contemplates the picture of Cleopatra in the art gallery is echoed in the scene in *Middlemarch* where Will Ladislaw first sees Dorothea Brooke in a Vatican art gallery contemplating "the reclining Ariadne, then called the Cleopatra, [which] lies in the marble voluptuousness of her beauty, the drapery folding around her with a petal-like ease and tenderness" (2.19.140).

Dorothea feels an almost religious desire to throw "herself, met-
aphorically at Mr. Casaubon's feet, and kiss his unfashionable
shoelaces as if he were a Protestant Pope" (1.5.37). Such sentiments
suggest her resemblance to Dickens's heroine who, in her complete
worship of her father, indeed acts as a kind of Dorrit-thea.[34] Eliot
was herself familiar with the position of dutiful daughterly devotion
from her own professional life where, as Gilbert and Gubar note,
she elevated her older male colleagues to the status of "fatherly
gods" and performed work for them that was both crucial but also
completely invisible.[35] On the *Westminster Review*, for example,
Eliot occupied a position remarkably similar to the one Dickens
represents through the figure of Little Dorrit:[36] "Despite her pro-
longed work, her name did not even appear in her edition of David
Friedrich Strauss's *The Life of Jesus* (1846). As Gordon Haight explains, 'She was quite willing to let Chapman pose as chief editor
[of the *Westminster Review*] while she did the real work without
public acknowledgement.' "[37]

34. There are a number of structural similarities between *Middlemarch* and *Little
Dorrit*. In describing the genesis of these novels, both authors explain that they
thought first of a story about social ills—for Dickens the story of Arthur Clennam
and the Circumlocution Office, for Eliot the story of Lydgate and the medical
profession—and subsequently of a story about a woman—Little Dorrit and Dorothea. Thus both authors began their novels with the woman's story, only later
connecting it to the story of social ills. In the preface to his novel, Dickens uses
two images to explain the resultant double narrative structure of *Little Dorrit*; it is
like both a piece of weaving and a journey where travellers unknowingly converge.
In *Middlemarch*, Eliot uses similar imagery to describe the joining of Dorothea's story
with Lydgate's; it is like "unravelling certain human lots, and seeing how they were
woven and interwoven" (2.15.105) and like "the stealthy convergence of human
lots" (1.11.70). For a detailed discussion of the genesis of *Little Dorrit* and *Middlemarch*, see Paul D. Herring, "Dickens's Monthly Number Plans for *Little Dorrit*,"
Modern Philology 64 (1966–67): 22–63; Jerome Beaty, "*Middlemarch*" *from Notebook to
Novel: A Study in George Eliot's Method*, Illinois Studies in Language and Literature
47 (1960).
    35. Gilbert and Gubar, *Madwoman*, 450–51.
    36. Eliot's own irony makes it difficult to identify precisely what her attitude
was towards the devoted stance of the "dutiful daughter." When, for example, she
notes that she asked to be called " 'Deutera, which *means* second and *sounds* a little
like daughter' in relation to a particularly unimpressive Dr. Brabant" (ibid.), it is
hard to know whether to read that comment as serious or tongue in cheek. Similarly
in *Middlemarch*, at the same moment that Dorothea's devotion to Casaubon seems
to be celebrated, Casaubon himself is constructed in such a way that that devotion
seems ridiculous.
    37. Ibid., 450–51.

In the Rome section of *Middlemarch*, however, Eliot invokes *Little Dorrit* not to perpetuate the model of gender difference that defines femininity as dutiful devotion to an emblem of masculine authority but to represent the collapse of that adoring attitude on the part of Dorothea. The Rome scenes in *Little Dorrit* were particularly useful to Eliot because they represent a moment of contradiction in Dickens's novel. While, on the one hand, Dickens's conservative impulses lead him to represent Little Dorrit as consistently and uncritically supportive of paternal authority, on the other hand, he wants to represent change or reform in those patriarchal structures. He does so by showing the collapse of old, negative or idle paternal figures and institutions such as Mr. Dorrit, the Patriarch, Mr. Merdle, and the Circumlocution Office which are then replaced by the avatars of a new industrious paternalism, Arthur Clennam, Daniel Doyce, and the Works. In order for reform to come about there must be a moment when the old system is falling to pieces and the new one has not yet replaced it. In *Little Dorrit*, that transition takes place when the Dorrits are in Rome; at that point in the novel, Mr. Dorrit goes mad and dies while, at the same time, back in London, Mr. Merdle's financial empire collapses, he commits suicide, and Arthur Clennam is committed to debtors' prison. Appropriately, the collapse of the old paternal order occurs at the moment when Little Dorrit, the figure of support, is no longer working for her father and has not yet begun to work for Arthur Clennam. At the critical juncture when Little Dorrit finds herself idle among the ruins of Rome, the novel almost allows the daughter to recognize that the paternal image she supported was never inherently whole or coherent but something her own work maintained. It is the possibility of such a recognition on Little Dorrit's part that Eliot capitalizes on in her depiction of Dorothea's changing perception of Casaubon in the Rome scenes of *Middlemarch*.

Reminiscent of the scene in the middle of Dickens's novel where Little Dorrit finds herself in Rome after being released from the Marshalsea prison, in chapter 20 of *Middlemarch*, Dorothea finds herself, for the first time, outside the narrow limits of Middlemarch provincial life and in the "city of visible history." Both Dickens's and Eliot's heroines experience this sudden widening of their horizons as presenting them with a vista which seems almost beyond comprehension. Little Dorrit sees the ruins of old Rome. The ruins of the vast old Amphitheatre, of the old Temples, of the old commemorative Arches, of the old trodden highways, of the old tombs, [which] besides being what they were, to her were ruins of the old Marshalsea—ruins of her own old life— ruins of the faces and forms that of old peopled it—ruins of its loves, hopes, cares, and joys. Two ruined spheres of action and suffering were before the solitary girl often sitting on some broken fragment. [38]

For Dorothea, Rome is a place of "stupendous fragmentariness" filled with "the grandest ruins" and "gigantic broken revelations" (*MM* 20.143–4). Both novels juxtapose these scenes in which daughter figures confront the ruins of Rome with scenes in which father figures are having their portraits painted. While both Mr. Dorrit and Mr. Casaubon assume that the resultant portrait will convey a sense of their consequence, in both cases, the portrait-painting scene actually reveals the male figure to be pompous, ridiculous, and self-inflated. The juxtaposition of these two scenes suggests that in the Rome sections of both novels what is collapsing or falling to ruins is the image of patriarchal authority that both Little Dorrit and Dorothea have previously maintained—Dickens's heroine through her physical labor, Eliot's through her adoring attitude. [39]

While Dickens never follows up on the natural consequences of the collapse of the paternal image in *Little Dorrit* by showing his heroine becoming critical of her father, [40] in *Middlemarch*, Eliot

38. Charles Dickens, *Little Dorrit* (1967), bk. 2, chap. 15, p. 671.

39. The juxtaposition of these two scenes could also be read in Lacanian terms as representing the juncture at which the narcissistically invested image of the self as a coherent whole is exposed as a fantasy and falls to pieces. But both *Little Dorrit* and *Middlemarch* depict this collapse taking place across the boundary of gender difference. While the masculine position has been the locus of the "whole" or full self not only for the father figure but also for the feminine figure who worked to support him, the feminine is now potentially the locus from which it would be possible to recognize the collapse of that fantasy of wholeness. In Lacan's retelling of the mirror stage, it is always the mother who holds the child up to the mirror in which he (perhaps he or she) sees an image of himself as whole. Lacan also encodes the feminine as supporting or making possible that first imaginary sense of the wholeness of the self.

40. Indeed Dickens emphasizes that there is absolutely no change in Little Dorrit's devoted attitude over the course of his novel by showing her dedicating herself to serve Arthur Clennam in exactly the same way and exactly the same place (the same imprisoning room in the Marshalsea) that she served her father.

shows Dorothea seeing Casaubon in an entirely new light. Appropriately, Eliot uses the images which, in Dickens's novel, convey the mental breakdown and death of Mr. Dorrit to convey in her novel the breakdown or "death" of Dorothea's fantasy that Casaubon will function for her as a scholarly Milton or a fatherly god. In *Little Dorrit*, Mr. Dorrit finally goes mad in the middle of one of his lavish parties and believes himself to be back in the Marshalsea. In that moment, as the narrator describes, "the broad stairs of his Roman palace were contracted . . . to the narrow stairs of his London prison."[41] In *Middlemarch*, this image of Rome contracting into a labyrinthine prison becomes a figure for the change in Dorothea's perception of Casaubon. She looks at him and feels "with a stifling depression, that the large vistas and wide fresh air which she had dreamed of finding in her husband's mind were replaced by anterooms and winding passages which seemed to lead nowither" (2.20.145). This is an image that bears enough importance for Eliot that she repeats it, describing Dorothea as "gradually ceasing to expect with her former delightful confidence that she should see any wide opening where she followed him. Poor Mr Casaubon himself was lost among small closets and winding stairs" (2.20.146–47). These images suggest that instead of the widening of possibilities that one expected Dorothea and Little Dorrit to experience as they moved from Middlemarch or the Marshalsea to Rome, there is a narrowing down, a return to the imprisoning environment which they have apparently left behind. But in both novels, that return is inscribed not in the female spectator or in Rome but in the male figure who theoretically promised access to the wider world—in Casaubon's case, the world of scholarship and history. In representing Dorothea's suddenly changed perception of Casaubon in Rome, Eliot dramatizes the moment when a female figure looks at a male and ceases to see him as the embodiment of cultural wholeness. In that moment, Dorothea is shown recognizing that the masculine perspective does not guarantee whole, full, or coherent vision.[42]

41. Dickens, *Little Dorrit*, 2.19.710.
42. In representing Dorothea coming to this understanding, Eliot anticipates the position of a contemporary feminist critic like Cora Kaplan who writes "In the early stages of thinking about women and writing I had, in common with other feminists, talked mostly about the ways in which women were denied access to something I

The difficulty, however, for the woman writer in representing this moment when the fantasy of masculine wholeness collapses is that the resultant fragmentation will simply be projected back onto the feminine position. In an 1872 review of the first four books of *Middlemarch*, for example, Richard Holt Hutton characterizes the Rome scenes and the whole of the early plot involving Dorothea and Casaubon as "the breaking in pieces of poor Dorothea's effort after an ideal work."[43] Hutton associates the fragmentation of the Rome scenes with Dorothea rather than with Casaubon. Eliot engages the danger of representing the feminine position in this traditional way when she depicts Dorothea confronting not Casaubon but Rome whose "vast wreck of ambitious ideals . . . at first jarred her as with an electric shock, and then urged themselves on her with that ache belonging to a glut of confused ideas which check the flow of emotion" (2.20.144). This is the kind of experience that Freud has when he faces Michelangelo's Moses and feels himself "being moved by a thing without knowing why I am thus affected and what it is that affects me."[44] The difficulty for Eliot in representing a female spectator in that kind of confused position is, as we saw in Freud's essay, that the position itself is inherently defined as feminine. In depicting Dorothea as overwhelmed by the "deep impressions" Rome makes on her, the danger for Eliot is that her heroine's incomprehension will simply be read as confirmation that she lacks what James called "masculine comprehensiveness." As Mr. Brooke asserts early in *Middlemarch*, "There is a

---

have called 'full' subjectivity. While any term so abstract evokes more meaning than it can possibly contain in a given context, what I was working towards was a description of a position within culture where women could, without impediment, exist as speaking subjects. I now think that this way of posing the question of writing/speaking and subjectivity is misleading. It assumes, for instance, that *men* write from a realized and realizable autonomy in which they are, in fact, not fantasy, the conscious, constant and triumphant sources of the meanings they produce" (Kaplan, *Sea Changes*, 225).

43. Richard Holt Hutton, unsigned reviews, from the *Spectator*, in Carroll, *George Eliot: The Critical Heritage*, 311. Hutton goes on to complain about George Eliot's resolution of Dorothea's story through the figure of Will Ladislaw in terms that continue to articulate an opposition between wholeness and fragmentation. He asserts that "Will Ladislaw is altogether uninteresting . . . but for very fine fragments of political remark. . . . He is petulant, small, and made up of spurts of character, without any wholeness and largeness" (ibid., 311).

44. Freud, "The Moses of Michelangelo," 81.

lightness about the feminine mind" such that "deep studies, classics, mathematics, that kind of thing, are too taxing for a woman" (1.7.48). In depicting Dorothea confronted with Rome, Eliot invokes and also resists the definition of woman as inherently, even biologically, incapable of understanding Rome and the patriarchal culture it represents by invoking the red-room scene from Charlotte Brontë's *Jane Eyre*.

In the red-room scene in Brontë's novel, as in the Rome scene in Eliot's, a heroine has been prevented from gaining access to culture. Jane wants to read, and her book is taken away from her. Dorothea wants to learn classical languages and instead confronts a city she does not have the intellectual tools to understand. The sense of frustration each of these heroines experiences is described in terms that evoke the definition of women as rendered biologically unfit for higher learning because of menstruation. In *Jane Eyre*, Jane responds to first being confined to the red-room by exclaiming: "Superstition was with me at that moment: but it was not yet her hour for complete victory: my blood was still warm; the mood of the revolted slave was still bracing me with its bitter vigour; I had to stem a rapid rush of retrospective thought before I quailed to the dismal present" (2.46). Eliot picks up a series of terms from this paragraph—superstition, warm blood, the dismal or sordid present—and uses them to describe the impression Rome first makes on Dorothea. She sees it as "ruins and basilicas, palaces and colossi, set in the midst of a sordid present, where all that was living and warm-blooded seemed sunk in the deep degeneracy of a superstition divorced from reverence" (2.20.143).[45] This sentence

45. Q. D. Leavis's reading of this moment in *Middlemarch* suggests that the imagery from Brontë's *Jane Eyre* with its echoes of the rhetoric of religious dissidents such as Kilham might have been useful to Eliot because of her interest in religious controversy. Leavis reminds readers that *Middlemarch* is set in 1832, three years after the Catholic Emancipation Act, and then goes on to read the Rome scenes in terms of anti-Catholic feeling. She writes: "The honeymoon is in Rome, contrived to set up the obligatory Catholic-Protestant opposition. Dorothea, as a strong-minded young lady of the age, is an ardent Evangelical and as the product of a narrow Puritanical education (in Switzerland) is profoundly shocked by Rome, with its sordid present, sunk in the 'deep degeneracy of a superstition divorced from reverence.' But this is all, for Roman Catholics were not felt to be a menace to the Church of England at this date and criticism was directed at Evangelicals. For while the Catholics were pitied for their superstitious religion, and Dissenters were socially contemptible and their religion ridiculous, the Evangelicals were the real threat. It

opens the long passage in chapter 20 of *Middlemarch* where Eliot conveys Dorothea's experience of Rome as a collection of fragments. That experience culminates with Dorothea's hallucinatory vision of St. Peter's with "the red drapery which was being hung for Christmas spreading itself everywhere like a disease of the retina" (2.20.144). This image also recalls Jane's imprisonment in a room hung with scarlet draperies in which she has an hallucinatory vision that will stay with her the rest of her life. The imagery of warm blood and red draperies in both novels implies that Jane and Dorothea are confined by a superstitious definition of themselves as bloody or menstruating and therefore biologically incapable of comprehending the "higher" learning they seek.[46]

In *Middlemarch*, however, Eliot resists this limiting definition of femininity by invoking but also changing the terms of *Jane Eyre* as she invokes but also changes the terms of Dickens's *Little Dorrit* in order to resist the association of masculinity with wholeness. As we have seen, both Dickens and Brontë, in novels written in light of the political unrest of the late 1840s, use models of gender difference to articulate relations between classes: Little Dorrit *works* to support her father, Jane Eyre *rebels* against John Reed's tyranny. But in *Middlemarch*, a novel of the 1870s, those earlier political

---

is characteristic of George Eliot's large-minded intellect that she shows the historic Rome, even of a 'degenerate present,' able to impress Dorothea with this spectacle of human achievement as exhibited in art and religious history, which seems to culminate in St. Peter's and to make her realize the inadequacy of her narrow Protestant conception of life and man; and the rest of the novel works this out" (Leavis, *Collected Essays*, 3 vols., ed. G. Singh [1989], 3:134).

46. In *Literary Women*, Ellen Moers discusses the image of the "Red Deeps" in *The Mill on the Floss* in terms similar to the ones I use here to talk about Eliot's use of the red-room scene from *Jane Eyre*. Laurie Langbauer has pointed out the dangers of such readings. She cites a number of Victorian reviewers who criticized Eliot for depicting women's sexuality, in figures such as Hetty Sorrell in *Adam Bede* and Maggie Tulliver in her response to Stephen Guest in *The Mill on the Floss*, with "an almost obstetric accuracy of detail" (from the *Examiner*, quoted in Carroll, *George Eliot: The Critical Heritage*, 11). Langbauer also notes how frequently modern critics return to reading George Eliot in terms of the body, citing Ellen Moers and the current critical debates on Daniel Deronda's circumcision (Langbauer, *Women and Romance*, 214–15n.). As she puts it, "Woman's association with detail quickly becomes her reduction to anatomical detail" (ibid., 214). I am arguing that, in the Rome sections of *Middlemarch*, Eliot dramatizes the dangers of the anatomical readings of women prevalent in the mid-nineteenth century and also begins to deconstruct them.

conflicts are rewritten in aesthetic or cultural terms. Thus while in Dickens's novel, Little Dorrit cannot stop working for her father because that gesture would represent social collapse, in Eliot's novel, Dorothea is devoted to Casaubon because he embodies an ideal of "high" culture. Dorothea's intellectual stance can therefore change without threatening political upheaval, as it does when she learns to see Casaubon in a new light. In alluding to *Jane Eyre* in *Middlemarch*, Eliot similarly rewrites the terms of Brontë's depictions of the early confrontations between Jane and the Reeds so that they involve Dorothea's confrontation with an image of culture as opposed to direct antagonism between individuals. In *Jane Eyre*, it is Jane who feels a sense of superstition, whose warm blood is roused and who feels caught in the dismal present. In the parallel passage from *Middlemarch*, these qualities are no longer associated with the female spectator, Dorothea, but with what she sees, Rome itself. It is the ruins and basilicas that are associated with the lack of warm blood, St. Peter's that is hung with scarlet draperies. Through a slight shift in emphasis in her representations, Eliot refuses to link images of fragmentation to a female figure and ground them in her biology. Instead, she associates fragmentation with the city which I have been arguing embodies the Victorian ideal of patriarchal culture. The Rome scenes in *Middlemarch* are disconcerting because in them, in order to resist the seemingly unbreakable linkage between femininity and fragmentation, Eliot represents culture itself not as a seamless whole but as a heterogeneous construct made up of myriad pieces.

If chapter 20 of *Middlemarch* shows Eliot resisting a traditional model of gender difference by translating class relations into conflicts over culture, George Henry Lewes's essay "Dickens in Relation to Criticism" shows how the privileging of "high" over "low" culture can be used to articulate what is implicitly a class difference. Lewes's essay restages the kind of encounter which, as I have been arguing, was repeatedly articulated through nineteenth-century accounts of visiting Rome, an encounter between patriarchal culture and those who appear to be outside it. Unlike Freud or Dorothea Brooke in Rome, however, George Henry Lewes positions himself from the beginning of his essay as inside the realm of high art and culture; he is effectively the patriarch addressing Dickens who stands where Freud does when he looks at the statue of Moses, with the mob in love with absolute equality. For Lewes, Dickens's imagination threatens to level artistic hierarchies because it appeals to readers from such a wide range of class and educational backgrounds. In his essay, Lewes moves to defuse the power of the Dickensian imagination by positioning it as absolutely outside the realm of high culture. He does so by defining Dickens as feminine, using a series of images that Eliot uses in *Middlemarch* to describe Dorothea as excluded from the realm of history and knowledge represented by Rome. Once Dickens is defined as feminine and therefore naturally incapable of strenuous intellectual efforts, Lewes can emphasize the absolute difference between "high" and "low" or popular culture, in essence, between his own position as a critic and Dickens's as a novelist. In reasserting this literary hierarchy, Lewes also emphasizes class difference by defining readers who take uncritical pleasure in Dickens's work as less cultivated, hence of a different class, than those whose "noble emotions" allow them to appreciate "high" art and culture.[47]

"Dickens in Relation to Criticism" opens with Lewes differentiating himself from elitist critics who have looked down on Dickens's work. In contrast, Lewes insists on paying tribute to the power of the Dickensian imagination. He praises the sensual immediacy of the characters in Dickens's novels, and, in a rather strange image, asserts that Dickens imagined those characters with such extraordinary clarity and detail because he envisioned them in the same way that one has a hallucination. He saw them, in Lewes's words, as one "hears voices, and sees objects, with the distinctness of direct perception."[48] Those characters then com-

47. The confrontation between Lewes and Dickens staged in "Dickens in Relation to Criticism" reproduces the schism that Marxist historians such as Tom Nairn and Perry Anderson have shown to be crucial to the shifting class structure of nineteenth-century Britain. As Terry Lovell explains, Nairn and Anderson argue that the British industrial bourgeoisie failed to "produce a compelling ideology on which to build its hegemony." Instead, "close links" formed "between the British literary intelligentsia and the still surviving anachronistic ruling elite." As a result, "English literary criticism . . . came to occupy the place left absent at the heart of bourgeois culture" (Terry Lovell, *Consuming Fiction* [1987], 2–3). In his essay, Lewes speaks as a member of the British literary intelligentsia and as a voice of the ruling elite in order to put Dickens—a potentially powerful voice of bourgeois ideology—in his place.

48. George Henry Lewes, "Dickens in Relation to Criticism," in *The Dickens Critics*, ed. George Ford and Lauriat Lane, Jr. (1972), 59.

pelled responses from such a wide variety of readers because "the vividness of their presentation triumphed over reflection."[49] For Lewes, Dickens himself represents "an almost unique example of a mind of singular force in which, so to speak, sensations never passed into ideas."[50] The language in all of these descriptions of Dickens echoes the wording of the passage that comes at the end of chapter 21 of *Middlemarch* where Dorothea, after the collapse of her fantasies about Casaubon as a scholarly god, sees him with almost hallucinatory clarity as her equal. As the narrator explains, Dorothea is suddenly able to "conceive with that distinctness which is no longer reflection but feeling—an idea wrought back to the directness of sense, like the solidity of objects—that he had an equivalent centre of self, whence the lights and shadows must always fall with a certain difference" (2.21.157). This is the uncanny moment in *Middlemarch* when the hierarchy between masculine and feminine and between scholarship and ignorance appears to collapse. In acknowledging the power of the Dickensian imagination, Lewes also allows for the possibility of the collapse of the artistic hierarchy which separates high culture from low.

Having granted the potentially anarchic power of Dickens's imagination, Lewes proceeds to limit that power by defining it as feminine, thereby reasserting traditional hierarchies. As the essay goes on, Dickens is described as speaking "the *mother-tongue* of the heart" and as setting "in motion the secret springs of sympathy by touching the *domestic* affections."[51] At the height of his praise, Lewes asserts that Dickens "only touched common life, but he touched it to 'fine issues.' "[52] This final phrase is the same one that Eliot uses in the Finale of *Middlemarch* to describe Dorothea going down into the common life, where "her finely touched spirit had still its fine issues" (Finale 611). As Mary Jacobus has noted, when this passage first appeared in the 1871–72 edition of *Middlemarch*, it replaced an earlier passage which describes Dorothea's actions as

the mixed result of young and noble impulse struggling under prosaic conditions. Among the many remarks passed on her mistakes, it was

49. Ibid., 61.
50. Ibid., 69.
51. Ibid., 62, 63, emphasis added.
52. Ibid., 68.

never said in the neighborhood of Middlemarch that such mistakes could not have happened if the society into which she was born had not smiled on . . . modes of education which make a woman's knowledge another name for motley ignorance—on rules of conduct which are in flat contradiction with its own loudly asserted beliefs. While this is the social air in which mortals begin to breathe, there will be collisions such as those in Dorothea's life, where great feelings will take the aspect of error, and great faith the aspect of illusion."[53]

The earlier passage foregrounds the limitations of women's education which I have been arguing underlie much of Eliot's depiction of Dorothea in Rome. Both it and the passage that replaced it emphasize that, at the end of *Middlemarch*, Dorothea's power is limited.[54] Unlike Saint Theresa, Dorothea will be excluded from the public life of social reform; she will be relegated to the traditional feminine sphere of influence where her actions will have an incalculably diffusive effect on those around her. As the narrator states in the concluding paragraph of Eliot's novel, Dorothea's fine acts will remain "unhistoric" (Finale 611).

To define Dickens as feminine is to exclude him, as Dorothea is excluded in the Rome scenes and at the end of *Middlemarch*, from the realm of history. As Lewes's essay moves toward its close, those qualities that were initially signs of the power of Dickens's imagination become signs of its limitations. The emotional intensity initially conveyed through the analogy with hallucination is now read as a sign not of the triumph of feeling but of the "marked absence of the reflective tendency" in Dickens.[55] Even more damningly, from Lewes's point of view, there is "no indication of the past life of humanity having ever occupied him."[56] Now characterized as appealing to those "to whom all the refinements of Art and Literature are as meaningless hieroglyphs,"[57] Dickens is here firmly positioned outside the realm of "high" culture. This de-

53. Cited in Mary Jacobus, *Reading Woman: Essays in Feminist Criticism* (1986), 36.
54. Eliot's use of less explicitly gender specific language in the later version of *Middlemarch* seems to me effective because it allows us to see that the limiting mid-Victorian definition of femininity was a cultural construct that could be applied to male as well as female figures.
55. Lewes, "Dickens in Relation to Criticism," 69.
56. Ibid.
57. Ibid., 68.

scription of Dickens might remind us of the passage from *Romola* where Baldassare is able to decipher the letters of the Greek alphabet that a minute before had seemed meaningless. The pleasure Baldassare feels in being able to enter into a cultural inheritance, represented by a knowledge of classics and history, is what Lewes's essay defines Dickens and his readers as lacking. It is at this point in "Dickens in Relation to Criticism" that Lewes's tone becomes most elitist. In imagery that suggests not only the class hierarchies of England but also the racial and cultural hierarchies of the empire, Lewes now asserts that Dickens's characters move his readers in the same way that a "waxwork figure, or a wooden Scotchman at the door of a tobacconist" would move a *"savage"* but that they have no appeal for the "cultivated" reader of "exquisite" taste and *"noble"* emotions. [58]

The personal anecdotes which Lewes tells about Dickens at the end of "Dickens in Relation to Criticism" reinforce the connection between Dickens's exclusion from the realm of history and his feminization. Lewes concludes his critical evaluation of Dickens by asserting that "he never was and never would have been a student." [59] This statement defines Dickens as limited not because his class background prevented him from becoming a scholar but because he is inherently incapable of scholarship. After making this statement, Lewes immediately confirms his own assertion by relating a story about his horror at first seeing Dickens's library and discovering that it contained only unread presentation copies of three-volume novels. Lewes then describes a later meeting when Dickens showed himself to be more serious about social issues but still "remained outside philosophy, science and the higher literature." [60] Here Lewes is positioning Dickens as definitively excluded from the realm of "high art and science" which, he argues in his review of Charlotte Brontë, "require the whole man." Not surprisingly, Lewes goes on to associate Dickens with broken women as opposed to whole men in the last anecdote he tells at the end of "Dickens in Relation to Criticism."

That final anecdote reinforces the essay's overall "feminization"

58. Ibid., 67, emphasis added.
59. Ibid., 69.
60. Ibid., 70.

of Dickens by emphasizing his almost morbid sensitivity to women and characterizing that sensitivity as itself feminine.[61] It is a story Dickens told shortly before his death about the power of his dreams, a story Lewes retells virtually without commentary: "One night after one of his public readings, he dreamt that he was in a room where everyone was dressed in scarlet. (The probable origin of this was the mass of scarlet opera-cloaks worn by the ladies among the audience, having left a sort of *afterglow* on his retina)."[62] In his dream, Dickens stumbles against a woman named Miss Napier. Two days later, at another reading, he met an unknown woman in a scarlet opera cloak whose name turned out to be Napier. Like the image of hallucination invoked early in Lewes's essay, this anecdote links Dickens's imaginative powers to the uncanny or the supernatural. But I am interested less in what Dickens intended the anecdote to convey than in the parenthetical comment Lewes introduces into the middle of Dickens's story. The language of that comment echoes the passage in *Middlemarch* where Eliot describes Dorothea's hallucinatory vision of St. Peter's which "in certain states of dull forlornness [she] all her life continued to see . . . [with] the red drapery which was being hung for Christmas spreading itself everywhere like a disease of the retina" (2.20.144).

This is the section of *Middlemarch* that, I have argued, is most explicitly associated, through allusions to Brontë's red-room scene, with the definition of women as incapable of participating in higher education because of biological differences such as menstruation. Once one hears the echo of *Middlemarch* in Lewes's final anecdote one also notices that other echoes of Eliot's novel in Lewes's essay can be read as suggesting menstruation. The word "issue" noted earlier as part of Lewes's simultaneous praise and feminization of Dickens is repeatedly used in biblical language to denote both childbirth and menstruation, as in the following passage: "And if a woman have an issue, and her issue in her flesh be blood, she

61. Between the anecdote about Dickens's library and the story of his dream, Lewes refers briefly to Dickens's fascination with his sister-in-law and his frustrated desire to be buried in the same catacomb with her. This is clearly another story which emphasizes, quite literally, Dickens's morbid identification with women.
62. Lewes, "Dickens in Relation to Criticism," 72–73.

shall be put apart seven days.''[63] The specific phrase in which that term is used in Lewes's essay and in *Middlemarch*, "touch'd to fine issues," comes from *Measure for Measure*, where it had early been read as a reference to the biblical story "of the 'woman with an issue of blood,' who came up secretly behind Jesus to touch his garment because she believed it would make her whole; and Jesus knew she was there because 'he felt the virtue go out of him.' "[64] (This is, of course, the perfect parable to illustrate the anxiety that feminine biological brokenness would in some way impair or destroy masculine wholeness.) In "Dickens in Relation to Criticism," the subliminal textual pattern suggesting menstruation works to reinforce Lewes's characterization of Dickens and his readers as naturally or inherently incapable of participating in "high" culture; it allows Lewes to associate Dickens with the territory in which women, because of their reproductive physiology, were defined as unfit for higher education. Lewes's essay brilliantly demonstrates how the image of feminine fragmentation, evidently grounded in women's biology, was an extremely useful discursive position in arguments about culture, an arena that has apparently nothing to do with gender difference.

Because, as critics, we have been trained in a system that perpetuates the Arnoldian ideal of "high" culture, it is difficult not to reinscribe the pattern that privileges an ideal of cultural wholeness in our critical readings and, in the process, exclude or denigrate anarchic feminine fragmentation. One can see, for example, how Neil Hertz's brilliant and persuasive reading of chapter 20 of *Middlemarch*, in "Recognizing Casaubon," ends up unintentionally replicating the movement of Lewes's essay. Hertz begins by acknowledging the power of Eliot's and also implicitly of Dorothea's imagination. He initially characterizes the scene in which Dorothea looks at Casaubon and conceives of him as having an equivalent center of self as "an epitome of the moral imagination

63. Leviticus 15:19, cited in Elaine and English Showalter, "Victorian Women and Menstruation," 38.

64. Meredith Skura cites this reading of the phrase "fine issues" and notes that it was first articulated in Sir Walter Whitier's 1794 volume, *A Specimen Commentary on Shakespeare* (Skura, *The Literary Uses of the Psychoanalytic Process* [1981], 262n.).

at work."[65] Yet he also finds such scenes in which, as he explains, there is an expansion of the female character and a corresponding contraction of the male to be peculiarly unsettling. Having acknowledged the uneasiness caused by such moments of leveling, Hertz proceeds to analyze Dorothea's confrontation with the "stupendous fragmentariness" of Rome in a way that reinscribes more traditional hierarchies. He argues that Dorothea

> has been shown attempting to come to terms not simply with her husband, but with the heterogeneous assault of Rome, with a collection of signs that may be summed up in a verbal formulation (e.g. "all this vast wreck of ambitious ideals") but which neither Dorothea nor the author is in a position to render as a totality. . . . The plurality of unmasterable fragments is converted into a repetitive series of painful tokens. This is a dark sublimity, beyond the pleasure principle for Dorothea, and sufficiently at odds with the values of Victorian humanism to be distressing to George Eliot as well. The later paragraph, in which Dorothea recognizes Casaubon, may be read as, quite literally, a domestication of the anxiety associated with the earlier moment.[66]

When Hertz asserts that neither Dorothea nor Eliot is in a position to render the ruins of Rome a totality, he reiterates, without introducing the question of gender, the Victorian assumption that masculinity would be the only position from which such totalization would be possible.

The implicit gendering of the ability to pull the pieces of Rome together into a coherent whole becomes explicit when Hertz describes the ruins, in Dorothea's vision of them, as "unmasterable fragments." Once the possibility of "mastery" has been evoked, Hertz can return to the gesture Dorothea makes when she looks at Casaubon and sees him as her equivalent and read it not as a sign of the general power of Eliot's and Dorothea's imaginations but as a gesture of "domestication." We might remember here Lewes's strategy of redefining the Dickensian imagination as touching the "domestic affections." Once Hertz has implicitly reintroduced gender hierarchies into his argument, he can do so explicitly.

65. Hertz, *The End of the Line*, 83.
66. Ibid., 91–92.

The final analogue he cites for Eliot's description of Dorothea in Rome is a passage from the *Essay Concerning Human Understanding* in which, as Hertz explains, "Locke praises the aptness with which the human senses are scaled to man's position in the hierarchy of creatures."[67] Here we have a reference to hierarchy in a sentence where the term "human" is equated with and replaced by the not-so-universal term "man." Hertz's use of the term human echoes his earlier reference to the values of Victorian humanism. And, while I would agree with Hertz that Eliot is at odds with the values of Victorian humanism in her depiction of Rome as fragmented, Hertz himself carefully reinscribes those values in his final invocation of Locke.

The problem with the late Victorian concept of culture is, as this essay has repeatedly demonstrated, that while it purports to be open to all, it must, in fact, always define a territory that it excludes. As a woman writer, George Eliot was inevitably sensitive to such exclusions because, as we have seen, the excluded territory was defined through images of feminine debility. The gesture of resistance Eliot makes in the Rome scenes, to depict culture itself as a collection of heterogeneous parts rather than as a whole, anticipates current critical impulses to seize the term culture and redefine it so that it signifies not a single Culture but myriad cultures. *Outside the Pale* is poised between the nineteenth-century and the modern definitions of culture. On the one hand, it has traced a series of exclusions of femininity that culminate, in the case of George Eliot, in the exclusion of femininity from the Arnoldian concept of culture. At the same time, however, each of these chapters has read these exclusions as taking place within what modern criticism has taught us to call culture, a field of diverse, competing, and interdependent discourses. In that field, as one discourse becomes dominant another is inevitably represented as repressed or denied. In this book, I have read a series of novels produced over the course of the nineteenth century by positioning them within the discursive field in which they were written. In each case, I have attempted to resist Victorian humanism's insistence on hierarchy by seeking to analyze rather than reinscribe the relative positioning of dominant and repressed discourses.

67. Ibid., 95.

Conclusion: Products, Simians, Prostitutes, and Menstruating Women: What Do They Have in Common?

> The monster in the text is not woman, or the woman writer; rather, it is this repressed vacillation of gender or the instability of identity—the ambiguity of subjectivity itself which returns to wreak havoc on consciousness, on hierarchy, and on unitary schemes designed to repress the otherness of femininity.
> —Mary Jacobus, *Reading Woman*

Each of the five women authors I have considered found herself unable to participate fully in the literary institutions and practices of the time period because of a construction of femininity that defined women as excluded from culture. The gestures of exclusion each woman writer experienced in the literary establishment were, moreover, not separate from but part and parcel of the overall Victorian symbolic economy as it was articulated at the moment she was writing. The interconnection between literary and other discourses meant that when authors such as Shelley, the Brontës, Gaskell, and Eliot wrote from a position defined as excluded or repressed, their novels foregrounded the contradictions inherent in the definition of masculinity that excluded them and also in the economic, social, and political positions articulated through that model of gender difference. Each chapter of *Outside the Pale* has foregrounded an image of what Victorian society defined as monstrously negative, an image, in W. R. Greg's words, of what was for them "out of the pale of humanity."[1] In each case, these images—of monstrous products, the simianized Irish, prostitutes, and menstruating women—were associated, either directly or indirectly, with the repressed otherness of femininity and also with the social, political, and economic issues that were being repressed at the moment the woman was writing. The novels these women

1. Greg, "Prostitution," 450.

writers produced were unsettling because, in giving shape to what nineteenth-century society sought to deny or exclude, they threatened, in the words of Mary Jacobus, to wreak havoc on hierarchy. In the case of Shelley, the Brontës, Gaskell, and Eliot, the monstrous figures their novels make visible threatened to disrupt nineteenth-century social, literary, and economic institutions, which purported to be universal or all-inclusive, by showing precisely what those institutions excluded.

In the case of Mary Shelley, a limiting definition of femininity positioned her as excluded from being able to enact the role of the Romantic poet. The irony inherent in Shelley's sense of exclusion is that, in developing the whole concept of the poetic imagination, the Romantics used the language of the common "man" because they wanted to emphasize that the imaginative power they celebrated was open to all. The association of femininity with the material which is implicit in their discussions of abstraction and spirituality marks the gap where something is excluded or denied in their apparently all-inclusive position. When Mary Shelley writes *Frankenstein*, she makes the materiality the Romantics repressed visible in the figure of the monster. In so doing, she shows that while the Romantic poets conceived their emphasis on abstraction as a counter to the excessive materialism of their time, as Coleridge makes clear in his political writings, they, in fact, replicated the gesture which made that materialism possible. As Marx has shown, commodities can be valued beyond the arena in which they are used—can be fetishized—only if their material or manufactured nature is denied or ignored. Shelley's novel shows how early capitalist fantasies of the unlimited power of production necessitated a denial that worked at first mainly at a conceptual level, a denial of the materiality inherent in production, but which would lead, as we saw in the novels written at midcentury, to a denial of those who were part of the process of manufacturing, the working classes.

Emily and Charlotte Brontë experienced themselves as excluded from the kinds of narratives of upward mobility that were enacted by their father and encoded in the stories of Heathcliff and Rochester. As with the Romantic belief in the power of the poetic imagination, the fantasy of the self-made man was compelling to mid-Victorian audiences because it was articulated as open to all.

Midcentury class inequities could be tolerated if it was possible to believe that everyone could potentially overcome the limits of their situation and make themselves into something better. Such fantasies of unlimited opportunities were, as I have argued, integrally linked to the expansion of the British empire. If one could not find a way to redress one's grievances at home, one could fantasize that it would be possible to do so abroad. (Witness the number of literary figures from *Mary Barton* to *Great Expectations* who emigrate in order to acquire wealth and/or class status.) Again, however, the way in which femininity is excluded from this fantasy marks the fact that the narrative of upward mobility, which is apparently open to all, is, in fact, closed to some. The mid-Victorian fantasy of class elevation was closed to those, like the simianized Irish, who must, in the logic of imperialism, remain in the position of the colonized or dominated. It was the desire to dominate implicit in the narrative of the self-made man which Victorian audiences did not want to see and which the Brontës made visible in their novels by depicting Heathcliff and Rochester in terms of midcentury stereotypes of racial difference.

Like the Brontës, Elizabeth Gaskell found herself excluded from the realm of the marketplace, in this case, the professional literary marketplace where figures such as Dickens exercised their power as editors and publishers. Similar to the narrative of the self-made man, the literary marketplace was defined as an arena where everyone could potentially achieve fame and fortune or make a name for themselves. When Dickens asked writers to contribute to his periodicals, he was implicitly inviting them to think of their own work as valuable property. Once again, however, the definition of femininity that is foregrounded in Gaskell's interactions with Dickens marks the way in which the apparently all-inclusive literary marketplace was exclusive. The splitting of femininity into a negative public and a proper private image meant that a mid-Victorian woman could not fully participate in the market economy because to do so would make her an improperly public woman who resembled the prostitute. In being asked to write for *Household Words*, Gaskell is invited to think of herself as a property owner but finds instead, in the course of her editorial dealings with Dickens, that she is defined as property and that even her stories do not remain under her control. This definition of the individual as property, which was foregrounded not only in contemporary discussions of prostitution but also in characterizations of workers as prostituted, is what midcentury Victorian society wanted both to assert and deny. Laissez-faire economic philosophy invited everyone to become property owners while, at the same time, defining some as ineligible to achieve that status.

George Eliot confronted a definition of women as biologically incapable of higher education and therefore found herself unable to function as a full-fledged advocate or disciple of "culture." The irony here, as I have argued, is that the ideal of culture, developed by Arnold, Lewes and others, was expressly designed to be open to all. This model of culture was conceived in economic terms; it is culture thought of as property, as the references to cultural inheritances or heritage suggest. Here we have the moment when class inequities were apparently going to be resolved by a redistribution of cultural wealth. Once again, however, the definition of femininity that emerges during that time period marks a gap or contradiction in that apparently all-inclusive definition of culture by showing that it was, in fact, exclusive. The culture celebrated by Lewes, Arnold, and others is emphatically defined as "high" culture, a term that implies that there are some who will not be able to understand it. Those excluded from culture were defined not as incapacitated because of their background or experience, but as naturally or inherently incapable of higher studies. This natural inability to comprehend "high" culture was articulated through the figure of the menstruating woman whose tyrannous biological processes were defined as controlling her intellectual life. The territory associated with this monstrously debilitated feminine figure, a territory conceived as absolutely excluded from culture, made it possible to define the ideal of "culture" as open to all while practically keeping it closed to some.

All four of the disruptive images foregrounded in *Outside the Pale*—monstrous products, the simianized Irish, prostitutes, and menstruating women—are associated both with the repressed otherness of femininity and with the economic, social, and political issues the dominant culture sought to repress. The first two images—the monster as an emblem of the materiality inherent in the process of production and Heathcliff and Rochester as emblems of the colonial subtext of narratives of upward mobility—foreground the cultural issues that were being debated and repressed at the time *Frankenstein*, *Wuthering Heights*, and *Jane Eyre* were written. In Chapters 1 and 2, those images, which raise issues of production and imperialism, are connected to definitions of femininity as excluded, to Shelley's sense of being defined as material, to the Brontës' sense of being positioned, in Forçade's words, outside "the political, colonial and mercantile activities of the English people."[2] The second two images—of "fallen" women who are improperly public, wayward, or deviant, and of women defined as biologically broken and incapable of strenuous mental activity— foreground a definition of femininity as a monstrous or excluded territory. In Chapters 3, 4, and 5, these images of the repressed otherness of femininity are connected to the economic and social issues that were also being repressed at the time Gaskell and Dickens were writing and Eliot wrote *Middlemarch*; the image of the prostitute is linked to questions about the working class and property owning, the image of the menstruating woman to questions of who had access to "high" culture. In the epigraph to my introduction, I cited Cora Kaplan, who argues that "to understand how ... two categories ... are articulated together transforms our analysis of each of them."[3] In the readings performed in this book, I have worked to map out the connection between two excluded territories, one having to do with a definition of gender difference, the other with repressed economic, political, racial, and social issues. Ideally, the process of exploring that interconnection transforms our understanding of particular models of gender difference, of the political, economic, and social issues associated with those models of gender difference, and of the nineteenth-century fictional texts, where those two discursive systems are articulated together.

2. Forçade, "Review," from *Revue des deux mondes*, in Allott, *The Brontës: The Critical Heritage*, 102.

3. Kaplan, *Sea Changes*, 149.

Works Cited

Acton, William. *A Practical Treatise on Diseases of the Urinary and Generative Organs*. London: Churchill, 1851.

——. *Prostitution*. Ed. Peter Fryer. New York: Frederick A. Praeger, 1969.

——. "Review of *A Short Account of the London Magdalene Hospital* and *De la prostitution dans la Ville de Paris* Par A. J. B. Parent-Duchâtelet." *Quarterly Review* 83 (September 1848): 359–76.

Alcoff, Linda. "Cultural Feminism versus Post-Structuralism: The Identity Crisis in Feminist Theory." *Signs* 13.3 (1988): 405–36.

Allott, Miriam, ed. *The Brontës: The Critical Heritage*. London: Routledge and Kegan Paul, 1974.

Anderson, Perry. *Lineages of the Absolutist State*. London: Verso, 1979.

Baldick, Chris. *In Frankenstein's Shadow: Myth, Monstrosity, and Nineteenth-Century Writing*. Oxford: Clarendon Press, 1987.

Beaty, Jerome. *"Middlemarch" from Notebook to Novel: A Study of George Eliot's Method*. Illinois Studies in Language and Literature 47. Urbana: University of Illinois Press, 1960.

Bhabha, Homi. "Of Mimicry and Man: The Ambivalence of Colonial Discourse." *October* 28 (Spring 1984): 125–33.

——. "The Other Question: Difference, Discrimination and the Discourse of Colonialism." In *Literature, Politics, Theory: Papers from the Essex Conference 1976–84*. Ed. Frances Barker et al., 148–72. London: Methuen, 1986.

Boas, Franz. *Race, Language, and Culture*. New York: The Free Press, 1940.

Brenkman, John. *Culture and Domination*. Ithaca: Cornell University Press, 1987.

Brontë, Charlotte. *Jane Eyre*. New York: Penguin, 1966.

——. *Shirley*. Ed. Andrew Hook and Judith Hook. New York: Penguin, 1974.

Brontë, Emily. *Wuthering Heights*. 3d, rev. ed. Ed. William M. Sale Jr. and Richard J. Dunn. New York: W. W. Norton, 1990.

Brooks, Peter. " 'Godlike Science-Unhallowed Arts': Language, Nature, and Monstrosity." In *The Endurance of Frankenstein: Essays on Mary Shelley's Novel*. Ed. George Levine and U. C. Knoepflmacher, 205–20. Berkeley: University of California Press, 1979.

——. *Reading for Plot: Design and Intention in Narrative*. New York: Alfred A. Knopf, 1984.

Butler, Josephine. *An Autobiographical Memoir*. Ed. George W. Johnson and Lucy A. Johnson. Bristol: J. W. Arrowsmith, 1915.

Cannon, John. *The Road to Haworth: The Story of the Brontës' Irish Ancestry*. London: Weidenfeld and Nicholson, 1980.

Carlisle, Janice M. "*Little Dorrit*: Necessary Fictions." *Studies in the Novel* 7 (1975): 195–214.

Carroll, David, ed. *George Eliot: The Critical Heritage*. London: Routledge and Kegan Paul, 1971.

Collin, Dorothy W. "The Composition of Mrs. Gaskell's *North and South*." *Bulletin of the John Rylands Library Manchester* 54 (August 1971): 67–93.

Cottom, Daniel. *Social Figures: George Eliot, Social History, and Literary Representation*. Minneapolis: University of Minnesota Press, 1987.

Curtis, L. Perry, Jr. *Anglo-Saxons and Celts: A Study of Anti-Irish Prejudice in Victorian England*. Studies in British History and Culture, Vol. 2. Bridgeport: University of Bridgeport Press, 1968.

——. *Apes and Angels: The Irishman in Victorian Caricature*. Washington, D.C.: The Smithsonian Institution Press, 1971.

Cvetkovich, Ann. "Ghostlier Determinations: The Economy of Sensation and *The Woman in White*." *Novel* (Fall 1989): 24–43.

David, Deirdre. *Intellectual Women and Victorian Patriarchy: Harriet Martineau, Elizabeth Barrett Browning, George Eliot*. Ithaca: Cornell University Press, 1987.

Davidoff, Leonore. "Class and Gender in Victorian England: The Diaries of Arthur J. Munby and Hannah Cullwick." *Feminist Studies* 5 (Spring 1979): 86–141.

de Lauretis, Teresa. *Alice Doesn't: Feminism, Semiotics, Cinema*. Bloomington: Indiana University Press, 1984.

——. *Technologies of Gender: Essays on Theory, Film, and Fiction*. Bloomington: Indiana University Press, 1987.

Deleuze, Gilles. *Foucault*. Minneapolis: University of Minnesota Press, 1988.

Deleuze, Gilles, and Félix Guattari. *Anti-Oedipus: Capitalism and Schizophrenia*. Minneapolis: University of Minnesota Press, 1983.

de Man, Paul. "The Rhetoric of Temporality." In *Interpretation: Theory and Practice*. Ed. Charles S. Singleton, 173–209. Baltimore: Johns Hopkins University Press, 1969.

Dickens, Charles. *Bleak House*. Ed. Norman Page. New York: Penguin, 1971.

——. *David Copperfield*. Ed. Trevor Blount. New York: Penguin, 1956.

——. *The Dickens Letters*. Ed. Madeline House and Graham Storey et al. 6 vols. to date. Oxford: Clarendon Press: 1965–.

——. *Hard Times*. New York: Bantam, 1964.

——. "A Home for Homeless Women." *Household Words* 7 (23 April 1853): 169–75.

——. *Little Dorrit*. New York: Penguin, 1967.

——. "Untitled." *Household Words* 17 (June 1858): 601.

Eagleton, Terry. *Myths of Power: A Marxist Study of the Brontës*. New York: Barnes and Noble Books, 1975.

Eliot, George. *The Essays of George Eliot*. Ed. Thomas Pinney. London: Routledge and Kegan Paul, 1963.

——. *Middlemarch*. Ed. Gordon S. Haight. Boston: Houghton Mifflin, 1956.

——. *Romola*. Ed. Andrew Sanders. New York: Penguin, 1980.

Ellis, Kate. "Monsters in the Garden: Mary Shelley and the Bourgeois Family." In *The Endurance of Frankenstein: Essays on Mary Shelley's Novel*. Ed. George Levine and U. C. Knoepflmacher, 123–43. Berkeley: University of California Press, 1979.

Ford, George and Lauriat Lane, Jr., eds. *The Dickens Critics*. Westport, Conn.: The Greenwood Press, 1972.

Foucault, Michel. *The History of Sexuality*. Vol I: *An Introduction*. Trans. Robert Hurley. New York: Random House, 1980.

Freud, Sigmund. *The Interpretation of Dreams*. Trans. James Strachey. New York: Avon Books, 1965.

——. "The Moses of Michelangelo." In *Character and Culture*. Ed. Philip Rieff, 80–106. New York: Macmillan, 1963.

Fuss, Diana. *Essentially Speaking: Feminism, Nature, and Difference*. New York: Routledge, 1989.

Gaines, Jane. "White Privilege and Looking Relations: Race and Gender in Feminist Film Theory." In *Issues in Feminist Film Criticism*. Ed. Patricia Ehrens, 197–214. Bloomington: Indiana University Press, 1990.

Gallagher, Catherine. "The Body versus the Social Body in the Works of Thomas Malthus and Henry Mayhew." *Representations* 14 (Spring 1986): 83–106.

——. "George Eliot and *Daniel Deronda*: The Prostitute and the Jewish Question." In *Sex, Politics, and Science in the Nineteenth-Century Novel*, Selected Papers from the English Institute, 1983–84, n.s. 10. Ed. Ruth Bernard Yeazell, 39–62. Baltimore: Johns Hopkins University Press, 1986.

——. *The Industrial Reformation of English Fiction: Social Discourse and Narrative Form 1832–1867*. Chicago: University of Chicago Press, 1985.

Gaskell, Elizabeth. *The Letters of Mrs. Gaskell*. Ed. J. A. V. Chapple and Arthur Pollard. Cambridge: Harvard University Press, 1967.

——. *The Life of Charlotte Brontë*. Ed. Winifred Gérin. London: The Folio Society, 1971.

——. *Mary Barton: A Tale of Manchester Life*. Ed. Stephen Gill. New York: Penguin, 1970.

——. *North and South*. Ed. Dorothy Collin. New York: Penguin, 1970.

——. *Ruth*. Ed. Alan Shelston. New York: Oxford University Press, 1985.

Gérin, Winifred. *Elizabeth Gaskell: A Biography*. Oxford: Clarendon Press, 1976.

——. *Emily Brontë: A Biography*. Oxford: Clarendon Press, 1971.

Gilbert, Sandra, and Susan Gubar. *The Madwoman in the Attic: The Woman Writer and the Nineteenth-Century Literary Imagination*. New Haven: Yale University Press, 1979.

Gilman, Sander. *Difference and Pathology: Stereotypes of Sexuality, Race, and Madness*. Ithaca: Cornell University Press, 1985.

Greg, William Rathbone. "The False Morality of Lady Novelists." *National Review* 7 (1869): 144–67.

——. "Prostitution." *Westminster Review* 53 (1850): 448–506.

——. "Why Are Women Redundant?" *National Review* 14 (April 1862): 434–60.

Grubb, Gerald G. "Dickens's Editorial Methods." *Studies in Philology* 40 (1943): 79–100.

——. "Dickens's Influence as an Editor." *Studies in Philology* 42 (1945): 811–23.

——. "Dickens's Pattern of Weekly Serialization." *ELH* 9 (June 1942): 141–56.

——. "The Editorial Policies of Charles Dickens." *PMLA* 58 (December 1943): 1110–24.

Hechter, Michael. *Internal Colonialism: The Celtic Fringe in British National Development, 1536–1966*. Berkeley: University of California Press, 1976.

Helsinger, Elizabeth, Robin Lauterbach Sheets, and William Veeder, eds. *The Woman Question: Society and Literature in Britain and America 1837–1883*. 3 vols. Chicago: University of Chicago Press, 1983.

Herring, Paul D. "Dickens's Monthly Number Plans for *Little Dorrit*," *Modern Philology* 64 (1966–67): 22–63.

Hertz, Neil. *The End of the Line: Essays on Psychoanalysis and the Sublime*. New York: Columbia University Press, 1985.

Hindess, Barry, and Paul Hirst. *Pre-Capitalist Modes of Production*. London: Routledge and Kegan Paul, 1975.

Homans, Margaret. *Bearing the Word: Language and Female Experience in Nineteenth-Century Women's Writing*. Chicago: University of Chicago Press, 1986.

——. *Women Writers and Poetic Identity: Dorothy Wordsworth, Emily Brontë, and Emily Dickinson*. Princeton: Princeton University Press, 1980.

Hopkins, Annette B. "Dickens and Mrs. Gaskell." *Huntington Library Quarterly* 9 (August 1946): 357–85.

——. *Elizabeth Gaskell: Her Life and Works*. London: John Lehmann, 1952.

Irigaray, Luce. *This Sex Which Is Not One*. Trans. Catherine Porter with Carolyn Burke. Ithaca: Cornell University Press, 1985.

Jacobus, Mary. "The Law of/and Gender: Genre Theory and *The Prelude*." *Diacritics* 14 (Winter 1984): 47–57.

——. *Reading Woman: Essays in Feminist Criticism*. New York: Columbia University Press, 1986.

Jameson, Fredric. *The Political Unconscious: Narrative as a Socially Symbolic Act*. Ithaca: Cornell University Press, 1981.

JanMohamed, Abdul. "The Economy of Manichean Allegory: The Function of Racial Difference in Colonialist Literature." *Critical Inquiry* 12.1 (1985): 59–87.

Johnson, Barbara. *A World of Difference*. Baltimore: Johns Hopkins University Press, 1987.

Johnson, Edgar. *Charles Dickens: His Tragedy and Triumph*. New York: Simon and Schuster, 1952.

Kahn, Coppélia. "The Hand That Rocks the Cradle: Recent Gender Theories and Their Implications." In *The (M)other Tongue: Essays in Feminist Psychoanalytic Interpretation*. Ed. Shirley Nelson Garner, Claire Kahane, and Madelon Sprengnether, 72–89. Ithaca: Cornell University Press, 1985.

Kamuf, Peggy. "Replacing Feminist Criticism." In *Conflicts in Feminism*. Ed. Marianne Hirsch and Evelyn Fox Keller, 105–11. New York: Routledge, 1990.

Kamuf, Peggy, and Nancy K. Miller. "Parisian Letters: Between Feminism and Deconstruction." In *Conflicts in Feminism*. Ed. Marianne Hirsch and Evelyn Fox Keller, 121–33. New York: Routledge, 1990.

Kaplan, Cora. *Sea Changes: Essays on Culture and Feminism*. London: Verso, 1986.

Kaplan, Fred. *Dickens: A Biography*. New York: William Morrow, 1989.

Kavanaugh, James. *Emily Brontë*. Oxford: Basil Blackwell, 1985.

Kestner, Joseph A. *Mythology and Misogyny: The Social Discourse of Nineteenth-Century British Classical-Subject Painting*. Madison: University of Wisconsin Press, 1989.

Kiely, Robert. *The Romantic Novel in England*. Cambridge: Harvard University Press, 1972.

Kra, Pauline. "The Role of the Harem in Imitations of Montesquieu's *Lettres persanes*." *Studies in Voltaire and the Eighteenth Century* 182 (1979): 272–83.

Kristeva, Julia. *Powers of Horror: An Essay in Abjection*. Trans. Leon S. Roudiez. New York: Columbia University Press, 1982.

Langbauer, Laurie. "Dickens's Streetwalkers: Women and the Form of Romance." *ELH* 53 (1986): 411–31.

——. *Women and Romance: The Consolations of Gender in the English Novel*. Ithaca: Cornell University Press, 1990.

Leavis, Q. D. *Collected Essays*. 3 vols. Ed. G. Singh. Cambridge: Cambridge University Press, 1989.

Lehmann, Rudolph C. *Dickens as Editor*. London: Sturgis and Walton, 1912.

Levine, George. *The Realistic Imagination: English Fiction from Frankenstein to Lady Chatterley*. Chicago: University of Chicago Press, 1981.

Lewes, George Henry. "The Lady Novelists." *Westminster Review* 58 (1852): 129–41.

Lovell, Terry. *Consuming Fiction*. London: Verso, 1987.

Macherey, Pierre. *A Theory of Literary Production*. London: Routledge and Kegan Paul, 1978.

McMurtry, John. *The Structure of Marx's World View*. Princeton: Princeton University Press, 1978.

Mani, Lata. "Contentious Traditions: The Debate on *Sati* in Colonial India." In *Recasting Women: Essays in Colonial History*. Ed. Kumkum Sangari and Sudesh Vaid, 88–126. New Delhi: Kali for Women, 1989.

Marx, Karl. *The Portable Karl Marx*. Ed Eugene Kamenka. New York: Penguin, 1984.

———. *Selected Writings*. Ed. David McLellan. Oxford: Oxford University Press, 1977.

Marxist Feminist Literature Collective. "Women's Writing: *Jane Eyre, Shirley, Villette, Aurora Leigh*." *Ideology and Consciousness* 1 (Spring 1978): 27–48.

Mellor, Anne. *Mary Shelley: Her Life, Her Fiction, Her Monsters*. New York: Methuen, 1988.

Meredith, George. *Diana of the Crossways*. Ed. Arthur Symons. NewYork: Modern Library, n.d.

Miller, David A. *The Novel and the Police*. Berkeley: University of California Press, 1988.

Miller, Nancy K. "The Text's Heroine: A Feminist Critic and Her Fictions." In *Conflicts in Feminism*. Ed. Marianne Hirsch and Evelyn Fox Keller, 112–20. New York: Routledge, 1990.

Miyoshi, Masao. *The Divided Self: A Perspective on the Literature of the Victorians*. New York: New York University Press, 1969.

Moers, Ellen. "*Bleak House*: The Agitating Women." *The Dickensian* 69 (January 1973): 13–24.

———. *Literary Women: The Great Writers*. New York: Doubleday, 1976.

Moretti, Franco. *Signs Taken for Wonders: Essays in the Sociology of Literary Forms*. London: Verso, 1983.

O'Brien, Mary. *The Politics of Reproduction*. London: Routledge and Kegan Paul, 1981.

O'Flinn, Paul. "Production and Reproduction: The Case of *Frankenstein*." In *Popular Fictions: Essays in Literature and History*. Ed. Peter Humm et al., 196–221. London: Methuen, 1986.

Parry, Benita. "Problems in Current Theories of Colonial Discourse." *Oxford Literary Review* 9.1–2 (1987): 27–58.

Poovey, Mary. *The Proper Lady and the Woman Writer: Ideology as Style in the Works of Mary Wollstonecraft, Mary Shelley, and Jane Austen*. Chicago: University of Chicago Press, 1974. ˙

———. "Speaking of the Body: Mid-Victorian Constructions of Female Desire." In *Body/Politics: Women and the Discourses of Science*. Ed. Mary Jacobus, Evelyn Fox Keller, and Sally Shuttleworth, 29–46. New York: Routledge, 1990.

———. *Uneven Developments: The Ideological Work of Gender in Mid-Victorian England*. Chicago: University of Chicago Press, 1988.

Radhakrishnan, R. "Ethnic Identity and Post-Structuralist Differance." *Cultural Critique* 6 (1987): 199–220.

Rose, Jacqueline. *Sexuality in the Field of Vision.* London: Verso, 1986.

Sadoff, Dianne F. "Storytelling and the Figure of the Father in *Little Dorrit*." *PMLA* 95 (1980): 332–47.

Said, Edward. *Orientalism.* New York: Vintage, 1979.

Scarry, Elaine. *The Body in Pain: The Making and Unmaking of the World.* Oxford: Oxford University Press, 1985.

Schor, Hilary. "The Plot of the Beautiful Ignoramus: *Ruth* and the Tradition of the Fallen Woman." In *Sex and Death in Victorian Literature.* Ed. Regina Barreca, 158–77. Bloomington: Indiana University Press, 1990.

Schor, Naomi. *Readings in Detail: Aesthetics and the Feminine.* New York: Methuen, 1987.

Schorske, Carl E. *Fin-de-Siècle Vienna.* New York: Random House, 1980.

Scott, Joan. "Gender: A Useful Category of Historical Analysis." In *Coming to Terms: Feminism, Theory, Politics.* Ed. Elizabeth Weed, 81–100. New York: Routledge, 1989.

Shelley, Mary. *Frankenstein.* New York: Signet, 1965.

——. *Frankenstein: The 1818 Text.* Ed. James Reiger. Chicago: University of Chicago Press, 1974.

——. *The Journals of Mary Shelley.* 2 vols. Ed. Paula R. Feldman and Diana Scott-Kilvert. Oxford: Clarendon Press, 1987.

——. *The Letters of Mary Wollstonecraft Shelley.* 3 vols. Ed. Betty T. Bennett. Baltimore: Johns Hopkins University Press, 1980–88.

Shelley, Percy. *The Poetical Works.* Ed. Edward Dowden. New York: Thomas Y. Crowell, 1893.

——. *The Letters of Percy Bysshe Shelley.* 2 vols. Ed. Frederick L. Jones. Oxford: Clarendon Press, 1964.

Showalter, Elaine. "Guilt, Authority, and the Shadows of *Little Dorrit*." *Nineteenth-Century Fiction* 34 (1979): 20–40.

——. *A Literature of Their Own.* Princeton: Princeton University Press, 1976.

Showalter, Elaine, and English Showalter. "Victorian Women and Menstruation." In *Suffer and Be Still: Women in the Victorian Age.* Ed. Martha Vicinus, 38–44. Bloomington: University of Indiana Press, 1972.

Shuttleworth, Sally. "Female Circulation: Medical Discourse and Popular Advertising in the Mid-Victorian Era." In *Body/Politics: Women and the Discourses of Science.* Ed. Mary Jacobus, Evelyn Fox Keller, and Sally Shuttleworth, 47–68. New York: Routledge, 1990.

Skura, Meredith. *The Literary Uses of the Psychoanalytic Process.* New Haven: Yale University Press, 1981.

Spivak, Gayatri. "Three Women's Texts and a Critique of Imperialism." In *"Race," Writing, and Difference.* Ed. Henry Louis Gates, Jr., 262–80. Chicago: University of Chicago Press, 1986.

Sterrenburg, Lee. "Mary Shelley's Monster: Politics and Psyche in *Frankenstein*." In *The Endurance of Frankenstein: Essays on Mary Shelley's Novel.*

Ed. George Levine and U. C. Knoepflmacher, 143–71. Berkeley: University of California Press, 1979.

Sutherland, J. A. *Victorian Novelists and Publishers*. Chicago: University of Chicago Press, 1976.

Thompson, E. P. *The Making of the English Working Class*. New York: Vintage, 1966.

Tillotson, Kathleen. *Novels of the Eighteen-Forties*. Oxford: Clarendon Press, 1954.

Trilling, Lionel. *The Opposing Self*. New York: Viking Press, 1959.

Van Ghent, Dorothy. *The English Novel: Form and Function*. New York: Harper and Row, 1953.

Veeder, William. *Mary Shelley and Frankenstein: The Fate of Androgyny*. Chicago: University of Chicago Press, 1986.

Walkowitz, Judith. *Prostitution and Victorian Society: Women, Class, and the State*. Cambridge: Cambridge University Press, 1980.

Weigle, Marta. *Creation and Procreation: Feminist Reflections on Mythologies of Cosmogony and Parturition*. Philadelphia: University of Pennsylvania Press, 1989.

Williams, Raymond. *Culture and Society, 1780–1950*. New York: Columbia University Press, 1958.

——. *Politics and Letters: Interviews with "New Left Review"*. London: NLB, 1979.

Winnifrith, Tom. *A New Life of Charlotte Brontë*. London: Macmillan Press, 1988.

Wittfogel, Karl. *Oriental Despotism*. New Haven: Yale University Press, 1957.

Wollstonecraft, Mary. *A Vindication of the Rights of Women*. Ed. Charles W. Hagelman, Jr. New York: W. W. Norton and Co., 1967.

Woolf, Virginia. *A Room of One's Own*. New York: Harcourt, Brace and World, 1929.

Zonana, Joyce. "They Will Prove the Truth of My Tale: Safie's Letters and the Feminist Core of Mary Shelley's *Frankenstein*." *Journal of Narrative Technique* 21 (Spring 1991): 170–84.

Index

Reading Women Writing

A SERIES EDITED BY

Shari Benstock and Celeste Schenck

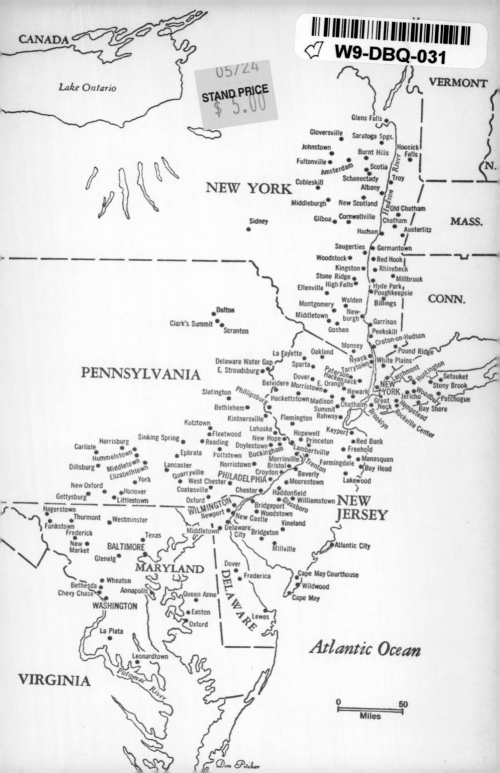

CANADA

Lake Ontario

VERMONT

N.

NEW YORK

Glens Falls
Gloversville
Saratoga Spgs.
Johnstown
Burnt Hills
Hoosick Falls
Fultonville
Amsterdam
Scotia
Troy
Cobleskill
Schenectady
Albany
Middleburgh
New Scotland
Old Chatham
Gilboa
Cornwallville
Chatham
Sidney
Hudson
Austerlitz

MASS.

Saugerties
Germantown
Woodstock
Red Hook
Kingston
Rhinebeck
Stone Ridge
Millbrook
High Falls
Hyde Park
Ellenville
Poughkeepsie
Montgomery
Walden
Billings
Middletown
Newburgh
Garrison
Goshen
Peekskill
Monsey
Croton-on-Hudson
La Fayette
Oakland
Pound Ridge
Delaware Water Gap
Sparta
Nyack
White Plains
E. Stroudsburg
Dover
Paterson
Larchmont
Huntington
Belvidere
Morristown
Hackensack
Setauket
Slatington
Phillipsburg
E. Orange
Stony Brook
Hackettstown
Newark
Woodbul
Patchogue
Bethlehem
Madison
NEW YORK
Jericho
Bay Shore
Kintnersville
Summit
Great Neck
Hempstead
Flemington
Rahway
Brooklyn
Rockville Center
Kutztown
Lahaska
Keyport
Harrisburg
Fleetwood
New Hope
Hopewell
Red Bank
Carlisle
Sinking Spring
Reading
Doylestown
Princeton
Freehold
Hummelstown
Ephrata
Pottstown
Buckingham
Lambertville
Farmingdale
Manasquan
Dillsburg
Middletown
Lancaster
Norristown
Morrisville
Trenton
Bay Head
Elizabethtown
Quarryville
Bristol
Beverly
New Oxford
York
West Chester
Croydon
Moorestown
Lakewood
Hanover
Coatesville
PHILADELPHIA
Gettysburg
Littlestown
Chester
Haddonfield
Williamstown
Hagerstown
Oxford
WILMINGTON
Bridgeport
Glassboro
NEW JERSEY
Thurmont
Westminster
Newport
Woodstown
Funkstown
Texas
New Castle
Vineland
Frederick
Middletown
Delaware City
New Market
BALTIMORE
Bridgeton
Glenelg
Millville
Atlantic City
MARYLAND
Dover
Bethesda
Wheaton
Frederica
Cape May Courthouse
Chevy Chase
Annapolis
Wildwood
WASHINGTON
Queen Anne
Cape May
Easton
Oxford
DELAWARE
Lewes
La Plata

Atlantic Ocean

PENNSYLVANIA

CONN.

Hudson River

Leonardtown

Potomac River

VIRGINIA

0   50
Miles

Don Pitcher

CLARK'S SUMMIT

Dalton
Clark's Summit
Scranton

HITTING THE
Antiques Trail

HITTING THE
Antiques Trail

By
Ann Kilborn Cole

DAVID McKAY COMPANY, INC.
New York

Contents

Introduction

THE old adage that farther fields seem greener would certainly appear to hold in the world of antiques. More and more collectors are going forth, usually by car, to see what other areas of the country have to offer that they cannot get at home. Perhaps they have covered the shops in their own neighborhood regularly, or perhaps they live where there are no shops—if such a thing is possible. Or perhaps they want to find different things that are regional. Sometimes they set out on a true antiques safari and at other times they include their searching with business or pleasure trips. But one thing is sure, that few cars set forth on a trip, if only for a day, without one rider at least on the lookout for that provocative sign, ANTIQUES.

Some enthusiasts more in the know than others know where to go, but many more do not. Vaguely they think of New England as the mecca for the antiques pilgrim, or of Pennsylvania as being plummy with Pennsylvania Dutch primitives. The South with its heritage of fine living must, they argue, have treasures worth investigating. But there is much more to the picture of antique shopping than these generalities.

I have written this book, consequently, as a sort of survey for the uninitiated. My intention is to spot the parts of the country where antiques flourish, to set the localities where there are concentrations of shops, to discuss prices, methods of selling, and in fact to give a sort of capsule view of this very big business as it exists at its starting point, the eastern part of the country. I have tried to gather as far as possible the names of dealers along the way with their specialties, hours, seasons, etc. Thus if you are on the march, let's say for a tin pie safe, a Sheffield epergne, or a rare doll to add to your collection, I hope by consulting this book you will know where to head or where to stop.

I have set myself the limit of the eastern seaboard for two reasons: first of all a survey of the entire country could not be covered in one book, at least not thoroughly; second, it is the seaboard, the home of the original colonies, where the antiques started to put on age and where, supposedly, they can still be found in the greatest numbers. There are, of course, across the whole country spots where the antiques of the region flourish, where settlers from foreign parts brought over and made their own special wares, but in the Midwest and far West you are going to find much of the same sort of thing as in the eastern portion of the country, either brought there by the covered wagons of the pioneers or the station wagons and trucks of the dealers who have gone East for supplies.

To get the true picture of the antiques business as of today and what it has to offer its buying public I did my own traveling, more than sixty-five hundred miles of it, from the tip of Maine to the foot of Florida. Much of what I dimly knew or suspected turned out to be true, but I wanted facts, and facts I got, many of them surprising. I found, first of all, a tremendous business, much larger than I had expected. In the span of a generation the antiques business has stepped right up into the ranks of "big business" with all kinds of side lines and allied businesses.

I found, too, that the whole pattern of the antiques shop is changing. No longer do small, intimate places crammed with true antiques from local sources (any piece of which you covet) dominate the highways. Now, because of the dwindling sources of true antiques, many a shop is apt to be anything from a gift shop or a decorating shop to what we could in truth call simply a secondhand shop. Dealers are often forced to buy and sell things that I feel sure they are secretly ashamed of. If you establish a business today without a backlog of good stock, or sufficient capital to pay high prices from the sources available for good things—usually other dealers or sales— it takes almost superhuman effort. Yet it is being done every day. More and more people are getting into the act. Wholesalers supply them with enough to fill a small shop and they are off on a new business venture. Hopeful young couples with a feeling for old things open up their houses while they supplement the shop takings with another line of work. Women who want or have to find some income without leaving home feel an antiques business is just about right. Whether all these newcomers will survive or not will depend upon their business acumen, locality, patience, and instinct for finding the right things. While I salute their courage I would prefer to give them a few years before I considered them seriously as established businesses. I have come upon too many empty shops where the proprietors have fled, given up, died, or moved away.

I have found much wholesale dealing in antiques, shops that cater exclusively to other dealers and retail shops that admit that 50 per cent of their business is done with other dealers. "Dealers welcome" is a common note in most shop ads. So much seems to pass from shop to shop in the trade that you wonder when it finally comes to rest in private hands. Certainly this way of doing business must up the ultimate retail price to the private buyer.

One of my findings is that the antiques shop does not seem to depend so much upon the transient or road business as it once did. Now you find shops open only by appointment, meaning that the proprietor has probably had his fill of "lookers" and wants to spend his time only on those seriously intent upon buying. He is probably able to prosper on his regular customers. We might say that the antiques-buying public has brought this on itself by using the shops only for window-shopping or as museums.

Other shops prefer to do their business by mail, either wholly or partly, as this does not keep them tied to long hours in a shop. Still others do a great part of their business at antiques shows, going from one to another up and down the country. There is a new hierarchy of show promoters who do nothing but manage shows, and each seems to have his own "stable" of exhibitors who go on the road with him.

From all of this I have drawn this conclusion, that the antiques business is a rather casual one, conducted like no other, spotty in returns, and too often most unbusinesslike in its conduct. The truly successful shops run like any good retail business, where the proprietor gives his full time and energy, are few and far between. But that they do exist is heartening to know and a cause for rejoicing when you ring that bell or enter that front door.

Because I am hoping that the dealers as well as the buyers will share this book I have undertaken to point out a few but telling places where they are falling short in their selling methods. I did my traveling not as a professional but as a casual buyer, and I took pains to put myself into the boots of the buyer on the road looking for good things generally or perhaps a few things in particular.

Out of all my experiences I have come to the conclusion that there is still an antiques business of stature in this country, that it is thriving, and that if you know where to go and are willing to pay stiff prices you can still find good things. I have also found out that in spite of the plaint, "It is getting harder every day to find things," the dealers are optimistic. All except one very serious and very young man who looked me in the eye and asked dolefully, "What do you think is going to happen to the antiques business five years from now?" I tried to be just as serious when I answered him, saying, "I don't think we have to worry too much. Remember there are just as many antiques around as there always have been, aside from some small loss from breakage and deterioration. But they are changing hands. Some dealers may have to go out of business, the inefficient ones perhaps or the unscrupulous ones. There may not be enough good antiques in the market to keep the new dealers busy who are rushing into the business. But the flow of antiques will go on. Old people are still dying off, old homes are still being cleaned out, famous collections are being broken up, museums overcrowded are cleaning house. Antiques are still around and probably will be for a good many years. The dealers will just have to work a little harder to find them—and they will have to pay more to get them."

One of the truest things that I think I heard on my travels was a remark from a dealer whose stock was still outstanding. "If you want to do business these days," he said, "you must make up your mind to pay high prices for the good things. It isn't like it used to be when you could be sure of doubling your money or doing even better. Nobody makes money like that any more. But I tell you when I find a rare piece I buy it no matter what the price. I know I'll never regret it, and if I can afford to hold on to it I won't lose."

So that's the way it looks from where I sit. The stuff is still around, perhaps not quite in the open profusion it once was or at the same prices. It is scattered over greater areas and you have to know where to look for it. I hope this book with its findings will help you to do so.

Happy hunting!

HITTING THE
Antiques Trail

CHAPTER 1.

Getting Ready

IT IS ONE thing to plan an antiques-hunting trip and another to carry it off with profit. If you are setting out on other business or for pleasure, the chances are not so great. At least you have seen the country, stayed at a few good motels, had perhaps some good meals with different food at outstanding restaurants, met some interesting fellow travelers, and come home refreshed even if the back of the car is not jammed with a deacon's bench, a tin weathervane, and cartons of glass and china, or with Junior perched on an old wagon seat for the homeward part of the trip.

But to take a trip with antiques the first object one should have some definite returns. Mileage and food and shelter cost money. You can't do it in comfort for much less than $15.00 a day for a car and one person. And so it behooves the seeker after antiques on the road to know as much about the business as possible before he starts out. There are ways of doing this. One of the best ways is to read the various magazines devoted to antiques. There are five of them, *Antiques, Spinning Wheel, The Antiques Journal, Hobbies,* and *The Antique Dealer* for the trade. There is also a monthly paper, *The Antique Trader.* All of these have dealer listings by states and towns not too inclusive but at least suggestive. Here you will find the ads of the more aggressive dealers in the country. You can make your own list or consult the back pages of this book—that is what they are for. It is too bad that there is not in this country, as there is in England, a full directory of antiques dealers. Once a year the Tantivy Press brings out a new edition of the *Antiques Yearbook*. It sells for ten shillings sixpence—about $1.50 in our money, and would seem to be about as complete as possible, listing most of the dealers—admitting that there may be some who do not want to be included—besides suggesting tours to certain spots rich in antiques, lists of museums, shows, allied businesses such as packers, refinishers, etc., and gems of general information—all in all, a fine job. It is also full of ads and fine photos. Every knowledgeable buyer of antiques who goes to the British Isles carries one under his arm.

The nearest thing to the British *Antiques Yearbook* over here is *Mastai's Classified Directory of American Art and Antique Dealers,* a fine job listing dealers by states and towns, which is revised every year. But it is an expensive book and to be really useful should be replaced every year or so, as the business changes so rapidly. Moreover, it does not always give full addresses nor does it signify the kind of goods sold nor the hours or days when a shop is open. However, for anyone doing a lot of antiques shopping away from home it could prove invaluable.

There is another small directory, a subscription affair, which is also at the moment incomplete but a step in the right direction. Perhaps our business over here is still too new and fluid to make an over-all directory possible. Shops come and go fast. On the other side the antiques business is old and respected with centuries of material to feed it. Many family businesses in the British Isles have continued through several generations. There are many new ones, of course, grown up out of the brisk trade with American tourists and dealers. But that is not the point. Antiques is a business of stature far removed from the junk shop and worthy of recording and tapping.

But here you can get only a partial picture of what goes on in the antiques world. You can do better if you want to combine an antiques informational or sight-seeing trip with your buying—a very good idea—for the museums and old houses are listed town by town in the AAA tour books with hours, days open, price of admission, and so on. This is very helpful. My AAA book did me a good turn when I was in North Carolina. I had planned to see the new Tryon Palace restoration in New Bern as I went through that afternoon. I assumed it would be open until five, and I was not hurrying until it occurred to me that perhaps I should consult my tour book. To my surprise I found the closing hour was four, so I stepped on the gas and made it in time to take the last tour before the closing hour.

Another way to find dealers in any vicinity in which you might find yourself is to consult the yellow pages of the telephone book. Almost every town of any size has a commercial listing section like this. Unfortunately all the dealers do not take advantage of it, but enough do to give you a starting point. Too, you generally have no way of telling the kind or quality of the shops listed. But query the dealers as you go. Most of them you will find cooperative, especially if they do not have what you are looking for. They know the trade in their area better than any listing, and certainly better than the gas-station boy who fills up your car. This listing is a good way to find the specialists, the man who sells guns, the woman who has buttons or dolls, the dealer who goes in for old books or Civil War items. While a dealer may list himself as selling a "general line," a good term covering almost anything and everything, he usually has some favorite item which he features.

Choosing a companion for the trip is another matter to decide upon before you start out. Of course a trip can be done alone—and often better than with the wrong friend, but the road can get very lonesome and driving monotonous without a rider in the other seat. Naturally, it is only common sense to share your trip with someone who enjoys antiques as much as you do. It is expecting too much to ask a friend to mark time or hang around bored to the teeth while you spend time in an antiques shop. Just about the moment when you and the dealer are coming to terms or he is about to bring out a rare piece from some hidden reserve you become aware of the friend filing her nails outside in the car or pacing restlessly up and down the sidewalk. Your conscience gives a lurch and you cut your visit short to go out and apologize for the delay. No matter how much she may remonstrate, "But I don't mind, really," or how clear you have made it that you are taking the trip primarily for the business of buying antiques you will not be comfortable. I know, it's happened to me. So try to pick someone who will go all the way with you and, if possible, an enthusiast who has wants of her own to look for.

When it comes to going with the family it is a different matter. The desires of the family will come first, but at least you can insist upon having it your way part of the time. It takes a lot of doing to make Dad stop when you see an ANTIQUES sign ahead. In fact, he seems to step on the gas instead of slowing up. The best of men will do this. There is one good way to get around this difficulty. Get him interested in collecting something himself. This is not too hard to do if you introduce him to the right things. Once a man has more than a bowing acquaintance with some particular antique item he stops at nothing. He becomes far more fanatical than his mate. He may get impatient in the glass and china shops but promise him a visit to a dealer in primitives or guns or coins or military prints, and family togetherness is not imperiled.

Of course the way you plan your trip will depend upon how serious you are about picking up antiques and how much buying you intend to do. If it is just a question of "browsing" as you go, a knickknack here, a souvenir spoon there, a cute little match holder or an adorable little workbox in that pile of junk, it won't matter where you stop. But if you are serious in finding just the right things for your American décor, an early dressing table or a painted fan or a piece for your Actress glass collection, you should have the right localities in mind. Don't expect to find Pennsylvania Dutch pieces in New England—though occasionally you'll come upon a piece or two in the shops of Yankee dealers who have been down country on a buying spree. If you want marine items, whaling pieces, old maps, ship models, scrimshaw, etc., you will head for the New England coast. That is where you'll find the China trade stuff, too. Hudson River pieces should be found close to that region. But one of the things to keep in mind is that today antiques get around just the way people do. You'll find tin pie safes usually considered Pennsylvania pieces—though some will not agree with this—in Maryland and Virginia and Sandwich lamps as far south as Florida. However, one thing to remember is that when you do find a piece out of its native locale it is going to cost more as it means that it has passed through more than one dealer's hands and transportation costs have added to the total.

Another thing that needs to be decided before you start out is the question of money. How much are you prepared to spend? If you are a compulsive buyer—and how many of us are!—it might be well to put yourself on a budget. This is particularly true if it is not your own money you are spending. Each time Dad's hand goes into his pocket or wallet it goes in more slowly and finally does not go in at all. Have it out with him before you go. Announce that you mean to buy certain things and how far can you go? It will stave off a lot of problems along the way.

One of the first rules in this uncertain game of antiques buying is this: if you have doubts, wait. Nobody is forcing you to buy at every shop you visit. There is a difference between looking for something you really want and "just looking" idly. Any dealer can tell the difference. Things do not sell so quickly that you can't return and pick up a doubtful choice later. There's nothing like "sleeping on it" when you are out to make an important purchase. Better to retrace your steps than make a bad buy on impulse. Often all you need is a few minutes away from the shop and the dealer, and time to think about it or talk it over with family or friend. Go off and have lunch and weigh it pro and con. Or visit another shop in the vicinity. You may find something you want more, or the same piece cheaper, or—this does happen—so much of the same thing that now you are sure the first piece was a reproduction, after all. This was brought home to me in Virginia. I saw a Stippled Star goblet, and as this is not too common a pattern I picked it up to examine it. The dealer was honest, or seemed to be, when he said, "I really don't know. It came in with some other old things." But I had my doubts. I put it back on the shelf. Not an hour later I went into a shop where Stippled Star goblets were lined up on a window shelf—and in all colors. Then I knew. They were being reproduced until they multiplied like guinea pigs.

The best way to carry money is to buy traveler's checks. They can be cashed almost anywhere. So this is the safest way to pay for your antiques. It is far better than carrying too much cash or too little and having to ask a dealer to take a check. I have been surprised at the number of dealers who *will* take checks. The few times I have had to use a check I have asked first, "Will you take a check? I know it is asking a lot of you, and I will not feel offended if you say no." They probably feel it is worth the gamble to make a sale, especially if the amount is not too large.

There is another matter to take into consideration before you start out—luggage. If you plan to bring your antiques home with you—and you should if possible, to save transportation costs—you are going to need all the room you can make in the car itself and in the trunk. So luggage should be kept to the minimum or shifted to a luggage rack installed on the top of the car. Private buyers are not apt to pick up enough to make a trailer necessary, but a little rented carryall like this can transport quite a lot of cumbersome furniture, which will do away with the cost of crating and shipping. Don't forget to throw plenty of old quilts and blankets and rope in the back of your car before you start out. This equipment is always in my trunk, so I am ready for anything wherever I go. Of course the ideal car for antiquing is the station wagon. Many dealers depend upon nothing larger for their own shopping. So fill it up with gas and get out your maps and let's get started on what can be for the antiques enthusiast the most exciting way to spend a vacation.

CHAPTER 2.

Where the Antiques
Shops Are

IT IS NO exaggeration to say that practically every main highway in this country has its quota of antiques shops as well as many secondary roads, dirt roads, and lanes. But naturally they are few and far between in some areas and clustered like grapes on a stem in others. The big cities are full of them, so are the small towns. Visiting the city shops with heavy traffic, parking difficulties, and ignorance of the city streets and addresses makes it hard on the tourist. If you want to do the shops in places such as New York, Boston, Philadelphia, Baltimore, Washington, Richmond, or Atlanta, it is a good idea to make a one-time thing of it, visit the city expressly for the purpose of antiquing, and plan to stay put there for a few days at a central hotel. Then you can put up your car, study your city map, walk, or take taxis or busses and enjoy what these city shops have to offer in more or less comfort. Some people do not mind city driving and are willing to use their own cars for the purpose of getting around, but it takes doing even in the smaller towns, where parking and traffic difficulties are just as bad. It is one thing to sail through a town on a well-marked route number but another to find parking space near a shop you may have on your list, or sometimes even to find the shop.

Perhaps this is why so many shops aimed at the tourist trade have taken to the outskirts, even to the open country. Usually they pick roads where tourists pass if there is a choice of location to be made. If a shop is in a home, it is apt to be anywhere, or if it does not depend upon transient trade it can hide up almost any lane. For such places you do not need more beforehand information than a sign or an arrow inviting you to stop.

As far as the concentration of shops go there are many well-known spots where you can cover half-a-dozen shops in a morning. Why these places have developed it is often hard to tell. Perhaps the success and reputation of one big dealer have attracted others. Dealers will tell you that far from taking business away from each other several shops in one neighborhood increase business all around. Hennicker, New Hampshire, is such a place, as is New Hope, Pennsylvania. It may be because the particular section was already rich in antiques or perhaps a museum or historical mansion attracting antiques-minded visitors consequently attracted the antiques shops too. At any rate, it is a good idea to head for these concentrations if only to save time.

So, East, West, North, South you set your sights, and map in hand go forth on a new adventure. Your direction will naturally vary with the season. You are not apt to go far North in the winter even if you do not mind winter driving. Many New England shops close for the winter months, except perhaps those in winter sports areas. Many dealers like to take this time to catch up with their personal affairs, to stock up their shops in readiness for the next season's buying, or to take a well-earned vacation. Many have two shops, a winter shop and a summer shop, and divide their time between the two. Through the Middle Atlantic states you are more apt to find shops open all year although in the worst winter weather they may take time off for days or weeks at a time. In the South the reverse is true. Many shops in Florida do not open until November.

The question arises as to whether it is sensible to go after antiques in vacation areas in the season. There are two answers to that. One is that prices usually rise during the height of vacation buying and you are not apt to get bargains at this time, if there are such things as antiques bargains any more. But, on the other hand, you will find the shops full of goods during the season in resort areas. Over and over I have had dealers apologize to me at the end of the season for the appearance of their shops. "The summer has cleaned me out," they will say, "and I haven't had a chance to get new stock." Of course this holds true only when the season has been a good one. A rainy summer up North or a cold winter down South will play havoc with a resort antiques business. In which case the buyer gains. Usually two good times to buy are just before the season starts and just after it closes, before June 15 and after Labor Day in New England and before November 1 and in late March down South. Then the dealers are looking for cash to buy stock for the oncoming season or else to get as much cash out of what is left in their shops before the winter or the summer sets in. Choice may not be so good but prices will be better. One dealer admitted to me that she always raised her prices at the beginning of the summer in upper New York although she did a year-round business. "It isn't because I am trying to defraud people, but from experience I know the summer trade that goes up and down this road to the camps and the mountains is different. They are on the whole bargainers and chiselers. They always want a discount. So I get ready for them with prices I can shave without an argument."

Another dealer told me she always put away her good things for the summer. "The summer transient trade does not appreciate them," she said. "When the serious buyers appear, I can always get them out of hiding."

What she admitted was repeated in another way by a Maine dealer whose shop lay along a well-traveled highway to the coast. At first sight it looked junky, the kind of place where many people stop with the mistaken idea that this is where you get the bargains. Evidently it was angling for the tourist trade with its oxbows and crocks and run-of-the-mill crockery outside. Inside, it was even worse, a real tourist trap with walls covered with plates of no particular age or value and shelves crowded with cups and saucers of the same kind. But when I persevered and dug into the interior I discovered a row of china closets all locked and all full of fine pieces of china and glass. "Why, you have a Meigh apostle pitcher!" I exclaimed to the dealer who, housewifely in a printed apron, hovered nearby. Her face lighted up. "At last," she said, "here is somebody who knows!" Then she went on to explain the rest of her shop. "I don't like to sell these plates and things for antiques," she said. "But I have to keep them for the tourists. People go into antiques shops nowadays for souvenirs, for something to take home, and this is about all they know or can afford to buy. I can sell any of these cups and saucers for a couple of dollars and they think they are getting an antique— something old. Of course they are old, but not that old. I have to do it because I need this trade to keep the place going." Later on she led me to the "back room" where there was a good stock of Maine primitives to look over.

So it would seem that the quality of the shops in a district depends very much upon the type of buyers who pass the door. Certain vacation areas are going to attract those with more ready money than antiques sense. Raiding the antiques shops to such resorters is all part of the vacation picture. They will pay more for the same sort of thing they could get at home if they went looking for it. Fortunately this is not necessarily true of all summer buyers up North or winter buyers down South, but it is something for the serious buyer to keep in mind and to steer him off the beaten track.

CHAPTER 3.

Dealers You Will Meet

AT HOME you probably have a pleasant relationship, perhaps even a warm friendship, with a number of your local dealers especially if you are a more or less regular customer. You have weeded out those whom you have reason to distrust or whose ways of doing business you do not like. But on the road you are at the mercy of each new dealer you approach and it will be up to you to assess them for honesty, knowledge, and fairness. This will not always be easy to do. You will have to rely upon your judgment of people generally and upon your experience in buying antiques.

I always get annoyed at the criticism of dishonesty against dealers as a whole. True, much of it is deserved. The antiques business, by its very nature, offers opportunities for all kinds of sharp bargaining and dishonest dealing. But, like the apples in the barrel where one bad one will contaminate the whole barrelful, so a few dishonest dealers will give the whole business a bad name. Personally, I have come across very few whom I would not trust. But I have heard stories, plenty of them, and many I am inclined to doubt. Often they are heard about the big dealers whose very survival depends upon honest business practices, and usually the story comes from someone who in his own opinion has been "gypped." But has he? Most criticisms aimed at dealers come from those who do not know the workings of the antiques business. Usually they concern prices.

No one ever thinks he gets enough from a dealer when he sells off an old piece. He expects to get the retail going price for his antique item, leaving no margin for profit, overhead, and other expenses for the dealer who buys it. Or often the story is only hearsay that gets better—or worse—in the telling. It may, perhaps, be prompted by professional jealousy though not so often as one might believe. Often a dealer is accused of dishonesty when it is a case of ignorance. Canny dealers will beware of claiming age or genuineness for something they are not sure of for just this reason. But there are dealers who are afraid to admit a doubt, and equivocate by saying they bought it for old. No good, enduring business is built on half-tone honesty like this. That is why I am more apt to trust the dealer who has been in the business for some years. If he has survived years of dealing with the public in spite of all rumors and groundless or vicious stories, if he has outlived his mistakes or learned to own up to them, if he stands back of his goods, he must be reliable. Otherwise he would not have been able to hold on to his good, buying customers over the years.

These older, established dealers in the antiques business want to keep it honest and legitimate. I heard of one area this summer where the dealers were trying to form an association for their mutual benefit. At a preliminary meeting it was decided that no one should be admitted to the organization who was selling reproductions—that is as old pieces—or otherwise misrepresenting goods. Things went well until somehow a dealer was admitted who was known to do both these things. He was a friend of some of the dealer members and a schism evolved. The organizer of the association dropped out and so did most of the others. The organization went by the board. Because, of course, it is one thing to know that a man is dishonest and another to have to prove it publicly—perhaps to the detriment of the whole trade in the area. Local jealousies and private feuds make organizations of this kind difficult, and it is too bad because some genuine stamp of approval would be appreciated by the buying public.

So when you are on the road and dealing with people you do not know you will have to take the bad with the good. There is one association that stands for high standards in the business, The Art and Antique Dealers' League of America. But its membership is very limited. Usually a member displays his membership on his card or sign or stationery. But the names represent only a very small percentage of the hundreds of dealers in the country. No doubt there are many who would like to belong to it but who would find the cost prohibitive or the qualifications too stiff. But membership in state and local associations could be a warrant of substantial and reliable business dealings. I am not always sure that it is. And it is not always representative of the area, either. Often older dealers in a community for one reason or another refuse to join an association, whereas the newcomers, with their reputations still to be made, usually do. A lot of good could be done for the business as a whole by something constructive along these lines with emphasis on a code of selling ethics which would dispel the doubts of the buying public. The thing, of course, boils down to who is going to be the judge and arbiter in each case. There are problems in this sort of organizing but they are not insurmountable.

You will not have been upon the road long before you discover that shops can be classified in several ways, first as to the kind of material they sell. At the top of the list of wayside shops come the fine, long-established businesses who handle the very best, the rarest, the genuine museum-type antiques of which a greater part if not all are American. Very often such businesses are housed in homes which are in themselves antiques and perfect settings for the pieces displayed in them. The reputations of these shops are national. Often they are open only by appointment, and a few are, as one southern gentleman said to me, "a bit long in the nose," meaning what many of us would call "snooty." But in general I would say that they welcome the average buyer if he is sincerely on the trail of something special. They are not the "browsing" shops, but there is no reason why the seeker of good antiques should not put such shops on his list. Don't let their elegance or the superior knowledge of the proprietor intimidate you. You may be able to tell him something. And don't apologize if you walk out without purchasing anything.

A few short looks around may convince you that you will not find anything in your price range in this milieu, but don't give up. State your wants. You may get a surprise. I was looking around in one very beautiful New York State shop where I saw a number of things I would have liked to have owned but which were way beyond my pocketbook. Reluctantly I turned my back on a Merry Man plate I coveted and was preparing to leave when I spied a small metal bottle ticket—or a wine label as it is called in this country. Now old labels of any kind are rare. I idly turned the tag and saw the price—50 cents. I could not believe my eyes. But I saw it was a crude thing, of some kind of white metal, probably not made for display but for the cellar. However, it was interesting in its way and I was glad to pay for it and take it along.

No good dealer can afford to be highhanded with any customer who comes into his shop or house. He can't tell from appearances what he may be turning away. One of the country's top dealers in Connecticut with a long history of buying and selling behind her emphasizes this fact. "You think you can size up people, but you never know. I try to be nice to everybody even when they only ring the bell to use my bathroom," she told me with a laugh. "Appearances can be deceiving in this business as well as in many others. They may dress shabbily purposely—oh, yes, they do—or they may be buying for somebody else. They must like good things or they wouldn't bother to come in and look around."

What irks these dealers most are the out-and-out "lookers," those who come in with no intention of buying at all either now or in the future, those whose curiosity is greater than their knowledge of antiques or who use the shop like a museum. A man in St. Augustine with a shop along the elegant lines of a decorating business featuring costly imported pieces is situated right on one of the narrow streets of that part of the city frequented by tourists. He told me that so many sight-seers wandered in off the sidewalk and remained to scoff at his prices and the pieces and even to insult him with their ignorant remarks that he had to put up a rope across the doorway if he wanted to keep his doors open. Of course this is an exception, but it holds true to some extent in almost all the better shops. You can understand why they indicate *By appointment only.* So if antiquing is just a lark to you and not a serious business, keep away from this class of shop.

The next type is what I call the good run-of-the-mill shop where you can find almost anything, good, bad, indifferent, old, and not-so-old. It carries what is known as a *general line* which can embrace furniture, glass, china, silver, metals, primitives, and so on, anything the owner can get with a genuine antique value. Stocks vary considerably in quality in this type of shop. Some have very high-class items, in others the stock is mixed. But usually you can find something that appeals to you. They have been in business long enough to have a good working capital and backlog of true antiques to which they do not have to add haphazardly. This is what I call the true American antiques shop, the kind you've been visiting for years and that you will meet anywhere. You are just as apt to pick up an Empire sofa here as a mustache cup, an old weather vane as a Gibson-girl plate.

These shops are not second-rate by any means. They have high standards even if they do not cater to the Queen Anne or Dr. Wall Worcester class of buyers. They are the standbys of the business. In this class are specialists who either combine a specialty with a general line of goods or devote their whole business to it. There are also specialists in the first category of high-class shops who deal in rare items for advanced collectors, things such as prints, oriental import china, Wedgwood, very early glass, and silver, for instance. But collectors of items on a less rarefied scale or the so-called beginning collectors will have no trouble finding shops that specialize in primitives, country furniture, buttons, dolls, lamps, pressed glass, political items, pewter, ephemera (paper items), country-store items, toys, banks, and so on. When the shops specify this on their cards or ads or signs it means usually that the preponderance of their goods is along their chosen line or that they have enough of one kind of thing to mention it.

Prices in this second class of shops are not low either. Nor will you be able to catch a dealer out with something he does not know enough about to price correctly. These dealers are well informed, especially if they have been about it for years. There are few bargains except perhaps in items which cannot be sold in a certain community. And even these dealers from other areas will relieve him of. You won't find many "sleepers" in this class of shop but you will find the unusual item very often, especially if the stock has come from old houses in the neighborhood. When a dealer goes farther afield to buy or buys in quantity, he is going to invest more in sure-fire sellers. So all in all this kind of shop is the happy hunting ground for the average buyer who will mark it *** or ** or * as he sees fit.

Now you come down to a third type of shop which sometimes deserves its name of antiques shop and sometimes does not. Nobody is criticizing it as a *business,* but as an antiques shop it often leaves much to be desired. The trade calls such dealers "cup and saucer" dealers. It is the shop that goes in for "old things" but not too old. It is selling what it can get, the late pieces that date no earlier than 1890 perhaps and were used through the early 1900s maybe only as late as thirty years ago and well within the memory of the shopper. It trades on nostalgia. Here and there among the late china and glass and bric-a-brac you might find a good piece. But these shops sell and make money because so much of the buying public has no education in antiques and thinks just because a thing is "old" it has value. Much of the china they display is German or Austrian of the later nineteenth century, the pieces that were sold as wedding presents in the jewelry stores of 1890 to 1910, the late unclassified patterns of pressed glass, the late Victorian knickknacks off the mantels and whatnots, little washstands of grained oak, plated silver, even early Woolworth. In a locality where good antiques are very scarce they flourish.

Now many of such dealers are well aware of what they have—and have not. To many it may be a first step toward a better business. The stuff fills the shop and keeps it filled until it can be replaced with better things. Usually these are recent businesses entered into by a woman who turns her sunporch into a shop and is happy with small pickings. Sometimes they are shops that have deteriorated. I know two such that I have been visiting for years, places where I could be sure of finding something good or unusual. I was disappointed, almost shocked, this summer when I revisited them and saw the quality of the stock they were reduced to selling. I could not accept the excuse that "it is getting so hard to find things," when a shop one mile down the road could still turn up interesting, buyable antiques. I am sure the answer lies in the fact that these dealers will not pay the current high prices to get good things. They are usually long-time dealers who have been used to picking up bargains at sales or from private homes at prices where they could double their money. Those days are gone. Too many people today know the value of the old things they own. Nobody gets a bargain at a sale any more because there is always someone to bid who knows what he is bidding for. Eager-beaver private bidders will outbid the dealers often extravagantly. Many dealers tell me they feel it is wasted time to go to sales today. Yet this is where the good old things come out of hiding. And so because they are afraid to spend the money, or perhaps do not have the capital to invest, they buy the obvious stuff, the things that used to go to the secondhand man or the rummage sales.

Perhaps these dealers don't care. They are making money, aren't they? Why should they beat their brains out and squander gas and time looking for better things? But if they are dealers dedicated to the business with a real love for good things, no matter how routine their business can become, they won't feel this way. I was amused at one very proper old gentleman who was showing me through his beautifully furnished rooms where every piece was worth a place in a museum. We paused at one table where he said apologetically, "These are some of my odds and ends which I have priced for popular buying. One has to have them, you know." I looked at his "odds and ends," which were much better than the usual run of things you find in the average shop, and laughed. "I wish more dealers handled 'odds and ends' of this sort," I said. "The trash one meets today is unbelievable."

He raised his gray eyebrows, smiled, and shrugged. "But they sell," he said. "I wish I had to pay the income tax that some of those people do."

I left him arranging his New England glass pieces on a window shelf and I could not feel sorry for him. He was working with what he liked even though he did not perhaps make a sale a day.

There is a natural resentment in the trade itself about this third class of dealer. One young woman whose home in a New England village was a joy to behold, whose cupboards and shelves held fine things—but not too fine for the average buyer—put it this way: "If only those shops did not call themselves antiques dealers. It isn't fair to those of us who have put a lot of time, study, and money into our businesses to be classed with the shops that sell pure trash. There should be some way of rating dealers in this country."

Well, that would take some doing. After all, who is to say what is trash and what is antique? Right here I think I should say that my tastes are not by any means highbrow. I love the fine things and I am glad that certain shops can survive and that many people can afford to buy them. But I also like the not-so-fine or rare things that have age enough to give them importance, that have interest, history, fine workmanship. I have often said I would like to own one piece of various things, a Hester Bateman silver piece, for instance, a Stiegel or Amelung flask, a lacy Sandwich plate, a Nicholas Lutz signed bowl, a Waterford compote, a Gaudy Dutch teapot, a Chester County spice cabinet, a St. Louis paperweight, a Chelsea figurine, a canary mug, a Battersea enamel box, a Willard banjo clock, a primitive portrait, or a Sheraton inlaid sewing table. But my wants are far from being filled. Instead, I can be happy with an unusual iron trivet, a green-leaf dessert set (Wedgwood, pre-1890), a painted tin knife box, some amusing figural bottles, a rare ironstone plate marked Classical Antiquities series of 1849, a "Ladies' Companion" leather etui or sewing kit, a small Russian tin teabox, a heavenly-blue Paris Exposition souvenir bottle, and so on—things that can be picked up in any good shop but which I would never call trash. Of course it is argued that today's trash may be tomorrow's treasure. But this can be true only if there is some intrinsic value in the piece other than age.

To be quite fair this third class of dealer often tries to be honest. Perhaps he will call himself by a name that sets the tone of his business more exactly, *The Browsing Shop,* for instance, or *The Then and Now Shop,* or *Grandma's Attic,* or *Yesterday's Treasures,* studiously avoiding the word antique. This is a step in the right direction and one to be recommended. You can't afford to pass up these shops entirely. If you have the time to browse and poke they can be fascinating picking, and here is where you will find a lot of the small items people collect these days. And you may possibly find a "sleeper," a good piece that has not been recognized.

The fourth source for the antiques shopper is the out-and-out junk shop or secondhand store. In other days many an antiques business started from such beginnings. But not so much today. The former junkman is far outnumbered by the informed, discerning dealer, who may even have studied for his calling. One woman down South with a very nice display, of which perhaps half were antiques, and good ones, told me proudly that her daughter was studying antiques in college, preparatory to taking over the business when she came out.

But the junk shops still thrive. You see the signs everywhere, ANTIQUES AND USED FURNITURE, as you drive along. If you are tempted to go in and look you'll probably be disappointed. Too many people have been there looking before you. The junk shops are combed regularly by the pickers and antiques dealers. Junkmen have become so antique-conscious that they know the good things instinctively and sell them off to dealers who can get better prices than the junk shop can. A "sleeper" does not stay here too long. Someone is going to find it. But of course there may be a few antiques on hand, and if you want to get your hands dirty and have plenty of time you may pick up something of value. A man I know who made a business trip recently did just this. A collector of military items, he took a look around the town where he was staying overnight, and finding little decided there was nothing there. Near his hotel was a dusty secondhand shop into which he wandered as he was leaving. Again he found nothing until he spied way back in a dark case a medal in its original box. His heart leaped. It was a rare one. Like most canny collectors he showed no excitement but asked to see it with several other things. "What's this medal? Do you know?" he asked the dealer. The man admitted he did not, but he was canny enough to sense a sale. My friend had to pay $5.00 for it, probably a big profit for the dealer, but as he said, he almost ran back to his hotel for fear the dealer might wake up and change his mind. It was only one of three known to be in existence. Of course it was his knowledge that paid off in his favor.

And now we get back to the subject of reliability which knows no boundaries of classification and affects all dealers, top and bottom of the list. You can find dishonest dealers among the best shops if you can believe the stories. The big fakes put over on the public make exciting reading and hearing. You hear about ersatz furniture assembled from many old pieces, furniture added to or taken away from, new windsor chairs left out in the salt air for six months to "age"; touched up, painted over and forged paintings; silver or pewter with old hallmarks that have been soldered into newer pieces, and so on. It even makes good TV viewing. But again these are the exceptions, and I don't feel that repeating them helps the antiques business as a whole. It makes people afraid to buy. But these dramatic stories do not affect the average buyer too much. It takes time and money to produce a fake good enough to fool a seasoned buyer, hence the big forgeries will occur in the high-priced brackets. It is said that there is hardly a collection that does not have—or has had—in it one bogus piece.

What the average buyer has to look out for are the reproductions now so rampant in almost every popular collectible, rebuilt pieces (even in the so-called country furniture), where little of the original wood is left and where the dealer says reassuringly, "It's all old wood," false stories on age, origin, or authenticity put forth by dealers who don't know or don't care. One of the things the buyer must consider is the price. Is it fair or dreamed up at the moment because of his evident enthusiasm?

I am not alone in decrying the habit of many dealers of not pricing their goods or using a cipher on the tag which they can translate at will. They run the risk of being suspected of letting the price fit the customer though this may not always be true. I've asked dealers about this habit and I have got various answers. One says she does it to protect herself against other dealers who come to do comparative shopping or who ask for too much of a discount. As a rule dealers extend the courtesy of a dealer discount to other dealers. This runs usually 10 per cent to 20 per cent or more, depending on what and how much they buy. If the retail price is displayed and it is already kept low enough to entice the private buyer, the dealer discount will bring it too low for any profit to the original seller. One dealer admits she marks up her pieces with this in mind, high enough to take care of a dealer discount, and then stands ready to reduce them to normal if need be for the private buyer when he comes along. The hitch here, of course, is that the dealer buyer knows prices as well as she does and won't play ball her way. A dealer I know well refused to allow a dealer discount to anyone. "I am not after that kind of business," she says. "I'd rather keep my prices low for everybody," she adds, and she does. But this custom of giving a discount does present a problem for dealers which many solve by not showing the asking retail price.

One dealer told me something I had not considered. When I asked why some of her pieces were priced and others not she said, "I can't put a price on the things I buy locally. People are funny, and when I buy from them they are in the next day to see what I am asking for what they have parted with. They think I am a robber if I have a $7.50 price on something I bought from them for $5.00."

I feel one reason for withholding prices is a sort of snobbishness, a relic of the days when nice people did not talk about money, or how much things cost. "Why discuss price?" such shops seem to say. "If it is something you want, the price should be no consideration." However, no matter how much money you may have, price is always a consideration. Collectors, no matter how well heeled they may be, are canny buyers. What the lack of a tag really does is to allow a bargaining leeway, especially if the piece is in the higher brackets with hundreds of dollars involved. Nobody expects to pay the first price asked on a thing of this magnitude any more than he would think of paying the first price asked on a piece of real estate. He may lose out by bargaining, but the dealer will not. He knows where he can stop, and can decide whether to make the sale at a lower price or wait for the next customer.

So there are probably legitimate reasons why some dealers do not price their goods. However, I still say the average buyer respects a tag that says unequivocally what the price is. Usually I walk out of a shop or away from a booth at an antiques show where pieces aren't priced. I don't want to have to call the dealer's attention and ask a question every time I spot a piece I like. As my funds are limited, the price makes all the difference between my buying and not buying. So I am forced to ask, "How much is this?" "What are you asking for that?" until it gets embarrassing. When the dealer shifts from foot to foot and looks bored, I waste no pity on him. I can shop in half the time when I can read the price tags.

Pricing goods is often an uncertain business for the dealer. If he has nothing to go by he has to guess at the worth and what the market will bring. I've spoken to dealers who have not priced an article because they are unfamiliar with it and don't know what to ask. Price guides of various kinds have tended to set the norm, and while prices in various parts of the country will vary they offer a range that gives a dealer some idea. But the most sensible way is to figure the price from the cost. One dealer shrugs her shoulders philosophically as she says, "I don't go by what other people ask. I price according to what I have had to pay for a piece. I'm content to make a fair profit. Sometimes I undersell the market this way, and sometimes I get stuck with it or have to take a loss. But I feel it is a fair way to do business in this business that has no rules." She is not an exception. Many dealers price in this way, but many others prefer to follow the market more closely.

Illustrative of this very thing is the story of my Sandwich perfume bottles. I saw them in a shop where I have bought things for some years, and I fell in love with them at sight. I did not know then what kind of glass they were, though I felt they were good. They were of a clear apple green and perfect. I bought them for $20.00 and sat on my conscience to do it. Later I kept asking questions about them and finally found out they were Sandwich. I knew then I had made a good buy. This year I revisited the shop. Mrs. X, who is a friendly and very responsible dealer, greeted me with "You got a good buy on those green perfume bottles two years ago, didn't you? They were Sandwich, you know. I saw a pair last week and they were priced at $65.00." Feeling a bit guilty though without reason, I smiled and said yes, I had found out about them. I was sorry if she had regretted the sale. She passed it off philosophically. "I didn't know they were Sandwich either," she said, "but I don't regret it. I made a good profit. I can't complain. And after all, that was some time ago. I probably couldn't have sold them for that much then, and I certainly wouldn't have held on to them."

In many shops you will find dealers who are willing to shave a price if you are interested, or if they need a cash sale badly enough at the moment. I don't like to contest a price with a dealer, especially if I know him and respect him. It's a bad habit. Many get angry, and

I don't blame them. In principle I don't trust a dealer whose prices are not stable. But there are reasons for this price-shaving, too. A New York dealer told me why. "There's a certain clientele that drops in here that I recognize the minute they come in the door. They always want special prices for everything. They like to think they have found a bargain. Now while I don't mind cutting a price occasionally when I know a customer is serious or for someone who has given me a lot of business or perhaps wants it badly and can't afford it, I don't make a practice of it. I don't like to be held up and argued with. I price as fairly as I can, and I hope my goods are worth what I ask for them. Customers who try to beat me down wouldn't do it in another kind of store. So when I see these gals coming I take off the tags. They get what they pay for whichever way they do it."

There are some shops, however, where you feel that things are priced high so that they can be reduced. If this is your conclusion, it does no harm to ask the leading question, "Is this the best price you can make on this plate?" If the answer is a firm yes, let it go at that and don't press it any further. I try to be courteous about this kind of dealing. If I find prices too high, I sometimes say so but not accusingly. "This plate is beyond my pocketbook, I'm sorry to say," I may remark. "I like it and I'd buy it if it were cheaper but I am not questioning your price." Sometimes the dealer relents and I get the plate, other times it stays there. But I can't bludgeon the dealer even though I feel his prices are out of line.

Reliability concerns more things than fair pricing. There is that big question of reproductions. Why will dealers handle them at all? Even when they are quite honest about them, it does something to your feeling of respect for fair dealing when you pick up piece after piece and are told, "That's not old. That's new." It seems to water down the value of the rest of the stock. What genuine daisy-and-button butter dish is going to look its worth when there is a long row of new daisy-and-button tumblers close by? When you see so much milk glass of new origin around how can you get excited over a few old pieces in the locked cupboard? That, to my mind, does a lot of harm to the antiques business, more than the selling of the new pieces as old. Much of the value and part of the charm of antiques are the fact that they do not exist in abundance. It is bad enough when a dealer keeps her reproductions separate from her old things, as some do, but when they mix them up—well, one can't help but wonder if antiquity is not allowed to rub off, as it were, on the new pieces.

When you are traveling and visiting many shops you are more apt to recognize the reproductions when they show up. They have a habit of turning up too frequently. I'm very leery of a certain little blue glass hat which I've seen everywhere I go. I can't believe they are all genuine. Yet if they are reproductions, they are good ones. I hope I shall have a chance someday soon actually to compare an old one with a new one. If buying reproductions worries you, there is one answer: know your subject well so you can recognize the new from the old. Keep abreast with all the literature on it, articles in the magazines, books that expose the facts and list the reproductions being made. Of course they can't keep up with the fakes completely, but they help. Another thing is to go to the gift shops and look at and examine the new pieces that want to look like antiques. For all the reproductions do not land in the antiques shops. Most of them were never intended to be fakes. Another way is to study the catalogues that supply the gift shops or mail-order business with this pseudo-Americana. While many of these reproductions are easily recognizable as such, some are very good and hard to spot. But with a little practice and experience it can be done.

Another evidence of reliability—or unreliability—is the way a dealer discusses a restored piece. If he is honest, he will say, "That is all original except the brasses and one foot," or "That is a married piece," meaning parts of two similar pieces put together, as in the lower and upper parts of a cupboard. The result may be quite beautiful and to the uninitiated may seem perfectly mated, but it should not be sold as an entirely original piece. The price should reflect that it was made up from old pieces. Sometimes very nice pieces are made from old wood, are beautifully pegged, and as exact in detail as an authentic piece. For your purpose they may do as well as an original but you should be told what they are and pay accordingly. Authorities say that if more than 40 per cent of the piece is new or added it should not be called an antique at all. However, if a fine old piece has been liberally mended, new feet or a new drawer added, a split side replaced, an arm recarved, new splats inserted, it may still have an appeal that is not to be passed up. Half an antique may satisfy you more than none at all. But again the price should reflect this substitution. For resale purposes you should be able to get your money out of it.

Beware of the dealer who is a little too glib with his information about the age or authenticity of a piece. It takes the weight of authority to pass judgment on old pieces with certainty. Even the experts make mistakes. Hence the qualifying terms such as Stiegel-type or Lutz-type or Duncan Phyfe period. I was reminded of this when I asked to see a certain Bachman piece in a big museum—Bachman being the name of a Lancaster, Pennsylvania, family of craftsmen who made fine furniture in the Philadelphia style for several generations. The hostess led me to it but she said, "We've changed our minds about this being absolutely Bachman. There is not enough documentation. It could be a Philadelphia piece. So we are now saying 'a Philadelphia-style piece.'"

So if the experts can make mistakes how can the dealers always be so sure? Take this sort of conversation: "I know this goes back to 1840. The old lady who sold it to me was almost ninety and she remembers it on her grandmother's table when she was a girl. It was a wedding present, her grandmother said." Now this might be true, but the memory of old ladies is not always reliable and family history can get garbled along the way. So take such stories with a grain of salt. Some dealers have a stock answer when you ask where a piece has come from. "Right out of an old house not three miles from here," they will say, and not even with tongue in cheek. But the honest ones—and thank goodness there are many of them!—will tell you that they got it from another dealer or with a lot of junk from an old house, or at a sale, or bought it from a picker who came by with a carful of antique pieces. Some of the more imaginative dishonest ones will attribute ownership to some famous person or will quote book, chapter, and page where it has been pictured or described if they feel you don't know about such things.

By all of which I do not mean to say that the dealers are not informed about antiques. In fact, I am always amazed at the amount of knowledge a dealer can accumulate in a few years of handling old things. But I am also amazed at how little many of them know beyond the things they are handling, their popularity, market price, and availability. I can't imagine trying to run an antiques shop without a library of standard books for reference. But how often do you see a row of books in a shop or get any indication that there might be a shelfful in the house? When I do see a shelf or two of good books on antiques in a shop my respect for that dealer and her knowledge rises quickly. One very good dealer I used to know before she retired had a library I envied. When she or her husband bought an important piece, they would get out the books to research everything they could gather about it. When she displayed that piece in her shop, you knew you were getting the whole story and that she was not just talking through her hat. One dealer I met on my travels down South had a card on everything she displayed on which were written date, origin, maker, purpose of the piece, etc. You trusted her.

One of the best evidences of reliability is the willingness of the dealer to stand back of his wares and his word. You can't help but respect him who says, "To my knowledge it is old. I bought it for old. I have looked it up in the books. So I'll guarantee it, and if you find out that I am wrong I'll buy it back." The dealer runs a chance here of the buyer's accepting another dealer's word over his, but such a guarantee is worth it to establish business integrity.

There is one thing I do want to say about the antiques business generally. In spite of the fact that more people are getting into it it is attracting more people of substance, good taste, and education. Where, years ago, one had little choice between the scholarly antiquarian and the ignorant junkman, now it is a highly acceptable way of making a living for people whose social status is as good— perhaps better—than yours or mine.

CHAPTER 4.

𝕳𝖔𝖜 𝖙𝖔 𝕾𝖎𝖟𝖊 𝖀𝖕 𝖆 𝕾𝖍𝖔𝖕

IF YOU stopped at every shop along the highway where an antiques sign was displayed you wouldn't get far in a day's driving, especially along those main-traveled roads where shops abound. That is why some kind of guide is necessary. However, no guide is complete, and there are many wayside shops that will reward the time spent in them. The question is how to know the good shops where your time will not be wasted.

After driving thousands of miles and popping in and out of hundreds of shops, I have developed a sort of instinct about them based on their appearance first on the outside and then on the inside. I'm not always right, but my guessing percentage is high—high enough to pass on a word of advice to dealers: remember that the first impression of your shop is its outside appearance. It is what makes people stop. It can be as assuring as a good handshake. It should in some way indicate the kind and quality of the goods sold there. For instance, I always feel doubtful about the shop that displays rows of crocks, wagon wheels, broken-down furniture, and tables full of bric-a-brac. It sets the shop as being very low grade, close to a junk shop even though the sign may say ANTIQUES. Possibly inside it might have better things, an unimportant general line spiked here and there with a few buyable pieces, but if I am in a hurry I won't stop and take the chance of having to poke through a lot of useless stuff to find one thing I might buy.

I've probably passed up some good opportunities because I have misjudged shops from their exteriors. One I would have passed by except that I had the name on my list; it had been reported to me as worth looking into. It was on a main highway, but I had trouble finding it because the sign had blown down. When I finally spotted it I almost drove on because it was such an unimposing frame house, almost shabby, with a row of chamber pots full of marigolds on the porch railing. But then I got a glimpse of richly colored glass at the windows and I drove in. Inside, I found a courteous, informed dealer and rooms full of fine glass with an outstanding collection of old lamps. I would certainly have missed something if I had driven on.

Now it isn't necessary for a shop to be dressed up to attract attention, although often a few well-chosen pieces will make the cars slow down and stop. But it should look businesslike and inviting. And there is no reason in the world why an antiques shop should be dark and dusty and ill kept. I believe a lot of dealers think that this is what the public that passes on four wheels goes in for, that the wagon wheels and oxyokes and china washbowls and pitchers spell antiques for them. To the uninitiated they may be the symbols of antiquity. They may even be suspicious of the shop that shines and is in some kind of order. Old things, they argue, should look grimy. Or they believe, with no basis in fact, that this is the kind of place where you will get a bargain. Far from it. I have seen some of the most outlandish prices in such shops. I know of one where the owner, a shrewd Pennsylvania Dutchman, prices with no reason at all. His stock is 75 per cent junk. He buys out whole houses, is the man at the country sale who used to be called the "penny" man who takes what nobody else will bid for. But he has some good pieces if you can recognize them and find them as you wade through his sheds and barns. But he prices outrageously high with no concern for value or market price. He probably gets it from those who know no better, though he will come down when he finds out that you are on to him.

I've seen a chipped gray stoneware cuspidor with blue decorations priced at $2.00 which finally went for 25 cents. If you were riding along the road and did not know his habits, you would think, "Look at this place! This is where you get the bargains."

Just because a business is in a barn or a shed does not signify good pickings either. Often a dealer keeps his junk in the barn and his good things in his house with good reason. It is very easy to lose things by theft in the antiques business, and an owner with no help cannot be out in his shop at all times. Hence the better things are kept where he can keep an eye on them. But barns make fine places to display primitives, large pieces of furniture, and the like. They do give a certain quaint and rustic appeal. One of the nicest shops I visited this summer is housed in a New England barn. There the old timbers set off the tastefully arranged Queen Anne and Chippendale, the pewter and Sheffield plate which hobnob with Historic Blue china and red pottery in the pine cupboards. No one, except perhaps a very few favored friends and customers, is admitted to the house. This man and his wife apparently cherish their privacy.

But many dealers do not. As many shops are part of the house as not. Often the antiques overflow the family living quarters. Many dealers seem to like to live with the things they sell. A story is told about one dealer who was giving a luncheon for her club when a customer appeared. He was after the beautiful dropleaf table at which the ladies were just attacking their chicken salad. He had spotted the table the day before and had come back to pack it in his station wagon and take it back to New York. So the ladies were asked to pick up their plates and gather on the side porch while the table was dismantled and two smaller ones out of stock assembled. Nobody seemed to mind. They were used to such things when they went to Sarah's house. But it was fun, as her décor was always changing and you might sip tea from Old Chelsea one day and coffee from Wedgwood the next.

Often it is impossible to spot the antiques businesses that are conducted in private homes. If you look carefully you may get a glimpse of glass or china on the window sills, and if you can read the neat little sign on the drive you decide that it must be open for business. Will you go in or won't you? I have heard many people say that they do not like to have to go to a front door and ring a bell to be admitted to a private home where antiques are sold. They feel uncomfortable, as if they were transgressing or that it puts too much importance on their call. They feel that by invading the owner's privacy they are more or less obliged to buy something. I don't feel this way. If this is the way a dealer chooses to do business, then he should be ready to receive anyone, buyers, the curious, or what have you. If he does not want transients ringing his doorbell, he can prevent it by not putting out a sign or can specify business only by appointment. Or he can just not answer the bell!

This is a point, however, for dealers to remember if they do want the trade from the road. Often a special entrance at the side with the word, SHOP, ANTIQUES, or ENTRANCE will overcome any hesitancy on the part of the caller. If the door is left open or unlocked, it is a further invitation to walk in. I've been surprised on several occasions at the carelessness of dealers who leave their shops untended. One morning I walked around a small garage with the doors wide open for ten minutes waiting for the proprietor to appear. The TV was going merrily in the kitchen. Maybe the owner was on the telephone for her usual morning talk. I could have walked off with many dollars' worth of small items before I finally went back to my car and drove off.

So don't be intimidated by the antiques business that is conducted in the home, not if you are looking for something special or are in the mood or have the money to buy what appeals to you.

Once you are inside the shop, how can you value it and how soon? If you have been in many shops it should not take long. I have become such an adept at this thing that now I can practically glance over the shelves and tables and come up with a pretty fair estimate in a few minutes. But then it is my business. If I am uncertain, I do a bit of delving. I start looking for the things I am most familiar with and often base my evaluation on what I find in those categories. For instance, a very few seconds looking over a shelf or two of pressed glass will determine if the patterns are old, are the ones wanted, or are of the very late, often unnamed, varieties. This does not mean that I condemn a shop that does not carry the things I know or want. But it is a beginning, especially if I am trying to judge the price range of the shop. After I have priced half-a-dozen pieces of various kinds and compared them in my mind with what I know is the average going price I can judge better whether this is a high-priced shop or not. How often you hear the remark, "Yes, she has nice things but she is terribly high in price." But perhaps the shop under fire is not high priced for the quality of the goods. All ironstone, for instance, does not cost the same. You may get a bed warmer in one shop for $25.00 and have to pay $35.00 in another, but the latter one could be older, more beautifully chased, and with a different handle.

The way a shop is kept means a lot to me. I've dwelt on this earlier in the book. I am not one of the dust-and-cobwebs sorority. Brass that is shining, furniture that is polished, and glassware that gleams do not lessen in value. I feel that things that are beautiful in themselves should be kept that way. It means that someone cares about them, and if the dealer loves the things he sells that is a big point in his favor. How often you have heard a dealer say with real warmth, "I hate to part with this, I like it so much. But business is business, and I can't afford to keep it. Maybe I'm not a good businesswoman but I find myself buying the things I like and then hating to sell them." I'd trust a dealer like that.

Naturally it takes a lot of work to keep a shop that is crammed full of small things clean and shining. But a lot of spit and polish is not necessary, merely a normal amount of cleanliness will do. And order of a sort. Why can't all the pressed glass be kept together? Why can't the primitives be gathered in one corner? It will save both the dealer's time in the end and that of the customers who might not be the browsing type. The wonder of it all is how dealers really know what they have in the mish-mash of some shops. Yet they do, even if they have to look ten minutes to find a pansy majolica butter pat that "was right here yesterday." A certain order or appearance of order works in favor of the dealer, proclaiming that he is a person with an orderly mind and consequently a person with a good business sense.

It would be a shame to condemn a shop entirely on the lack of order and cleanliness. Some of the best buys I have ever made have come from places that were neither clean nor orderly. But in each case I have had the time to poke around and move mountains of chairs and bring down dust upon my head.

Maybe this is the place to tell a story that has a political overtone. A few years ago friends of mine sent me an SOS by phone. They simply had to find some kind of unusual tin container that they could pack with their product, which they were publicizing and which would be presented to President Eisenhower and televised. Did I know of anything? It should be old. I racked my brains, called up a number of friendly dealers in search of a piece of old tole of the right size and shape. There seemed to be nothing in the market at the moment. So I got out the car and drove up the road fifteen miles to the man who has everything—if you can find it. When I specified my want he shook his head. He had nothing. But somehow I couldn't take his no for an answer. I started looking myself, climbing up rickety stairs to his lofts, putting down one foot after another carefully among the old china basins, broken slates, busted lanterns, and piles of old clothes and quilts. I wished I had a geiger counter. Then I struck it, almost putting my foot through it, a beautiful three-cornered box for a military hat, of fine old tin with a handle for carrying. It even had the owner's name and town on it. These are rarities. I bought it immediately. It couldn't have been better. My friends took it to a pair of young artists who do very fine tin decorating. They painted the old tin very skillfully so that it could be a showpiece for the President's Gettysburg home when the contents were "all," as the Dutch say. The point is that by persevering

I found a treasure, but I doubt if I would have done it except that it was almost a national emergency.

Certainly order in a shop can give the buyer a quicker estimate of the kind of stock the shop carries. You don't have to linger if you don't like it. I was rather amusingly reminded of this this summer when I dropped into an attractive-looking shop along a Rhode Island highway. A quick look at the inside of the shop and the proprietor assured me there was nothing here to interest me, either for my purpose or the purpose of this book. Things were nice in a sort of elegant, decorative way but not too old. The owner had an arty appearance as if she had dressed for the role. I murmured a few polite remarks and was about to step out when an old man, very neat in appearance and looking as if he had a fat wallet in his hip pocket, walked in. He had been driven up in a car with a uniformed chauffeur. He stood stock-still among the cut glass and Haviland and Japanese lacquer and asked in a loud voice. "Do you have a bean pot?"

The owner looked annoyed and turned her back, murmuring something I could not hear. She was almost rude. I smiled to myself at the idea of anyone believing a bean pot could have been hiding behind a tapestry wall piece, but I did think she could have been nicer about it. Apparently the old man had not heard her. He waited, then he said, "Well, aren't you going to look for one?" This time she turned on him to say, "I told you I don't have any. You should know that."

The old man turned away looking honestly disappointed. Perhaps he was not very discerning; perhaps he thought that any place displaying the sign ANTIQUES should have a bean pot. But bean pots are not necessarily antique, and he might have done better to look for one in a hardware store. Added to this was a piece of news that my traveling companion passed on to me. She had stayed behind when I went into the shop to do something to her hair and face and had seen the old man and his chauffeur drive up. They both remained in the car, however, as if they were waiting for something, probably for me to come out. Then tired of outsitting them she went in to join me. The old man followed a few minutes later. So now I began to wonder. Had the old man really wanted a bean pot? Or was it a ruse of some kind? My mind tuned to fiction began to smell a story. We tossed it around for some miles after we rode away, but finally I dismissed it as a fantasy and put it down merely as an example of the way some people shop in antique shops, expecting the most unusual things to turn up in the most unusual places, and being disappointed when they don't. But sizing up a shop from its wares is a habit that will save a lot of time, also embarrassing questions and perhaps rude answers.

The kind of shop you enter can be judged very quickly, I believe, by the personality of the owner himself. Now I concede that standing about all day waiting for the "lookers" to stop looking or the undecided to come to a decision, and then ending up selling a dollar glass salt or with no sale at all, is not conducive to developing a warm, outgoing personality. Yet many dealers seem to achieve it. They have learned to accept the unpleasant as well as the pleasant part of their work because they like it or like people. To many otherwise house-bound persons a business like this brings the world to their door. Others have learned to put themselves out just because it is good business. A few overdo it. I like to be welcomed genially and courteously but not overwhelmed or fawned upon. I don't like to be called *dearie*. I don't want to be sold against my will, nor do I want to be treated as if I were the little woman who isn't there. I don't want to be talked to so incessantly that my mind is diverted from what I am looking for. Yet all these things happen when dealers get the wrong idea of how to sell. Genuine interest and sincerity should dictate the face that the dealer shows his buying public. The happy medium where you are greeted with a simple smile and a good morning or afternoon goes over big. It seems scarcely believable, but sometimes you are not greeted. Dealers have sat at a desk and never even looked up from their books, they have dusted or unpacked cartons without a word of greeting. You practically have to hit them between the eyes with some sign that you are a real buyer before you can get their attention. But the others, how wonderful it is to walk into a shop and be greeted in a pleasant way, asked politely if you have anything special in mind, invited to look as long as you please, and be attended when you need attention but not hovered over! I don't even mind if a dealer is grumpy if he answers my questions and is not rude. He may be worrying about his taxes or have a sick child in the house. Or he may be having "wife trouble," as in the case of one unforgivably rude dealer I encountered.

Happily these dealers are few and far between. I have found many friendly ones whom I would like to know better. I have drunk coffee with them and discussed everything from politics to grandchildren. I've been consulted on prices, taken into their holy-of-holies to see their private collections, told trade secrets, and even given small things I have admired. In other words, I have been treated like a real person by a real person. I remember stopping one day in a shop at the end of a day and apologizing to the dealer who looked tired and distrait. She admitted she had been trying to get herself together for a weekend trip to see her daughter. She hadn't even had time to wash her hair—and every woman knows what a hardship that is. "It's been a busy day," she said wearily. "Twelve people have come in and gone out without buying; only one sale for two dollars." Even before I told her my story and my reason for calling on her she insisted upon my staying and seeing her things, perhaps because she sensed my interest and appreciated my desire not to impose on her. But maybe it was just her hard-earned affability with everyone. At any rate I ended up looking over her extensive button collection, picking up bits of trade gossip, and being refreshed with a glass of ice-cold ginger ale. I have met her again at city shows, and there, too, in the middle of utter confusion she has been just as friendly under different but equally trying circumstances. Here is a woman who has realized what the role of a successful dealer should be.

Very often the discourtesy that a client encounters in a shop is because of the bad habits of the buying public. It is astounding what offenses an otherwise well-mannered, considerate person can commit when he goes into a crowded shop to buy antiques. As I have said, his very attitude can set up a defense in the salesperson. So many go into a shop with suspicion showing in every movement. "I am not going to be gypped if I can help it," his gestures seem to say. If he is not suspicious, he is at least cautious, moving with seeming unconcern, afraid to show enthusiasm, giving what he is most interested in only a passing glance.

Then there are the sotto-voce remarks intended for the dealer to overhear. "Will you look at that? My mother had one of those for years—and now they call it antique!" Or, "We gave away my grandmother's pickle caster to the cleaning woman, and here it is marked $30.00. Wow!" Or, "I sold a box of old marbles just like those not long ago for $1.00. And now look, $5.00 for just one! Robbery!" Or, "Sort of a junky place, isn't it? Let's get out."

One of the worst sins to commit in an antiques shop is what the trade calls "lid-lifting." It's a bad habit we all can fall into. It tells us nothing to lift the lid of every tureen or sugarbowl we pass. Unless we are genuinely interested and looking for nicks or inside cracks it is better to keep hands off. But there seem to be some people who must handle everything. They will pick up and examine the piece even when they have no interest in it. They will work mechanical things that should be handled gently. A man will slip out his penknife and scrape away the paint on a piece of furniture to examine the wood. They are taking a chance.

Shops take care of this business of damage and breaking in various ways. Many put up a cute little sign saying, "If you break it it's yours." But I feel very strongly that, sign or no sign, if a customer does break something even of little value he should offer to pay for it whether the dealer demands it or not. Most dealers expect this and it is up to the dealer to determine what to do. He may set a price that will at least cover his loss, or he may demand the full retail price. There is nothing the customer can do about it but pay. Some people may argue that the dealer should be insured against breakage.

This is not practical. Not only is it extremely costly, but with a dealer's stock switching almost daily it would be impossible to pinpoint individual pieces. Most dealers I have questioned say that insurance is far beyond their means. There may be individual cases where some high-priced article is insured, but this hardly concerns the casual buyer.

But breakage often is not the customer's fault. Some shops are so crammed with goods that it is hard to pass between the tables or get near the shelves without danger of knocking something down. Many a customer feels like the proverbial bull in the china shop in such places. This, I feel, is the dealer's responsibility. However, when a careless customer sweeps through a shop, coat swinging open or a shoulder bag bouncing around, it becomes the buyer's responsibility also. One thing that could reduce a lot of damage would be the proper tagging of items so that the prices are not hidden and will not have to be sought by turning the article upside down or by peering into its innards.

Another annoyance is the person who takes children into a shop. The best-behaved child is a hazard in a place crowded with china and glass even if he is old enough to appreciate it. I don't think a dealer should be asked to put up with it. Some dealers are frank about not admitting children—or animals. Others woo children with lollipops or toys to stay put in a safe spot. Older children who do appreciate what they see around them should be taught the good principles of looking. If they want to examine something, they should ask to do so.

Dealers hold their breaths when customers start tapping glass to get the bell tone. There is a way of doing this that should be left to the dealer. One who has been in the business many years, long enough to know all the tricks and hazards of the trade, unlocked one closet in which she had many pieces of old glass and cut glass. "I have to keep them where they can't be handled, and I'll show you why. See this beautiful bowl, a signed Hawkes piece. It was perfect when I bought it. Now look at the nicks. They have all been made by the heavy rings on the fingers of the 'tappers,' as I call them. I'll lose money on this piece because I've had to reduce the price."

Just because of these things I hesitate to pick up anything valuable and breakable. If I want to feel it for texture, to hold it up to the light to feel it for chipped edges, or look for cracks, I ask the dealer to get it off the shelf or from the back of the table. I had my lesson once when I was putting a lovely piece of Canton china back into a cupboard. The cupboard was painted light blue, shelves and all, and what I hadn't realized was that the shelf had a scalloped front. I set the piece on what I thought was the front edge of the shelf but was empty space. It crashed down and broke, taking with it a fine cup and saucer underneath.

So if you happen upon a surly dealer, examine your own behavior. Furtiveness and distrust and showing off what you know will throw any dealer off. She either gets hardened to the point of rudeness or philosophic to the point of indifference. Can you blame her—or him? All in all, I believe the women dealers come off better. As a sex we are supposed to have more patience and endurance, which is what an antiques dealer needs in abundance.

Many people express embarrassment when they leave a shop without buying. Certainly nobody expects to buy in every shop he visits. There are times, however, when you have taken up a lot of the dealer's time, looking at everything, asking questions, discussing antiques generally, when a small token purchase can be the courteous thing. Dealers recognize this feeling and are apt to keep a table full of small things just for this purpose. They may not even be old, greeting cards, perhaps, or hostess items, or local products. I think it is a good idea, and I usually take advantage of it. Not much money is expended but it makes everyone feel better.

CHAPTER 5.

Where the Antiques Come From

WHEN you have been in a dozen or more shops in one day and passed up maybe a dozen more you are bound to ask yourself, as I do continually, "Where does it all come from?" Can there possibly be enough old articles still in good condition coming out of the attics and cellars or being gradually released by families that are dying out to fill the shops up and down the whole nation? To hear the dealers talk there isn't. Everywhere you hear sighs and groans. Finding good antiques with the prestige of age upon them is like prospecting for gold. Yet the shops continue to flourish, new ones start up, old ones still bulge with items of more or less antiquity. I have never seen a cleaned-out shop yet no matter how much the owner apologizes for its emptiness. So antiques of some kind must still be available.

But they are harder to get because they must be spread over many more shops these days. There may be 300 shops in a state that used to have perhaps 50. But where do the antiques come from? Ideally they still come out of the old homes which for some reason or another are forced to dispose of their heirlooms. In my work as a newspaper antiques columnist, there isn't a week when I do not get at least one letter from an older person who says her children or grandchildren do not want old things, so how can she get rid of her possessions now? Or perhaps she needs the money to aid a sick

44

husband or to add to her social security. Unfortunately what she has may not be enough to do her much good. She reads the papers and magazines and has an exaggerated idea of what antiques bring. If what she has is not very valuable, I try to encourage her to give it away to someone who will appreciate it. But these are the things, the bits of old glass and china, the Lincoln rocker, the iron toys, the brise fan, the Paisley shawl, the crimping iron, the china doll, all the things the dealers want and which get into circulation when she finally decides to let go. A good dealer usually knows where the good things are in his locality and will often make periodic visits to see how close to the selling point the owner is. It sounds ghoulish, but it can be done with finesse and understanding.

I said this was the ideal situation. It occurs frequently enough to keep the stock flowing, but not enough to keep all the shops filled. More and more dealers have had to compromise. They have had to stretch their concept of antiques to include things of much more recent origin, with dates reaching into the early 1900s, perhaps even as late as thirty years ago—as, for instance, Quimper china or Wallace Nutting prints. Strictly speaking, these are not antiques, but they are old enough to have a certain charm, usually nostalgic, and if they have any beauty or value at all are worth saving, for they will in time become antiques. These are the things that many beginning collectors seek. In fact, it is the collectors who support the antiques business generally, whether it is for early Strawberry soft paste china or a late Touraine dinner set. Some shops simply augment their stock with these late pieces, but others are almost entirely stocked with them. Such shops actually are not dealing in antiques in the precise sense, but in old pieces, interesting, quaint, or unusual items. This sort of shop has its place and is not to be dismissed as unimportant. You'll find here many familiar things, the cut glass perhaps that is back in such favor that it is moving into the best shops. This glass flourished in what is known as its Brilliant Period, about which we are most familiar, from 1880 to 1910 or even longer. This has become so important a seller that the antiques shops are finding it hard to stock. Yet it is eighty years old at its earliest and scarcely fifty years at its latest. Many of us can remember when it was used—but only for high occasions. It was the "Sunday" glass of our mothers and grandmothers at the time when people had Sunday clothes. I can remember Sunday suppers at home when we had "company" and a gorgeous cut-glass bowl was always filled with topaz canned quinces to go with the 1-2-3-4 cake for dessert. It was too precious and took too much time to wash and polish oneself—this was never left to the maid—for daily use. No detergents then. It was expensive for its day, too. Then came the turn against it, probably about the time when the domestic problem became acute and the housewife had more things to do than wash cut glass. People gave it to the rummage shop or to the cleaning woman (as I did in 1930—a whole barrelful of it). This is one of those come-lately antiques that perhaps had a good reason for being collected. It can never be made again. It would cost too much today to produce, even if the artisans skilled enough to do it could be found.

The oddity or not-so-new shop is the place to look for the carnival glass or taffeta glass, as it is sometimes called, the poor man's Tiffany of the 1900's. It was giveaway glass as prizes at carnivals—hence the name, or was used as premiums with baking powder, which gives it another name, Baking Powder Glass. It was a cheap, inferior version of the popular iridescent glass made to sell when Tiffany, Quezal, Aurene, etc., were flourishing. It is not beautiful glass, only occasionally, and many dealers scorn it and will not handle it, but collectors go for it. It is not even as old as cut glass. Novelty stores sold it until very recent years. Then why is it such a popular item in some shops? Perhaps because it is still not very costly and there is plenty of it. It helps to fill the shops.

Silver deposit glass is another late comer you will find in these shops. It was made around the early 1900's, is pretty but not important from an antique viewpoint, and still not costly.

Haviland china is a big seller in the late antiques market. While the Haviland family began its operations in Limoges, France, as early as 1842, most of the china on the market today is of much later date. It was the wedding china of the turn of the century and was made in America from 1936 on. It is still beautiful china and will probably never go out of date for those who like a delicate table setting.

Also on the china tables you'll find the Austrian and German pieces which were the wedding presents of the 1890's and 1900's, with much gold and flowers, marked or unmarked, maybe with only the name of the importer. These were sold in the jewelry and silver shops of the times, and were considered quite elegant. Among these may be a sprinkling of the Royal Bayreuth tomato, lobster, or tapestry pieces. There are sure to be pieces of hand-painted china here done on American Lenox ware or imported Limoges. Some will be professionally painted and quite beautiful but even the amateurish items done by Aunt Emma with pale wild roses and forget-me-nots will sell. Buffalo pottery's Deldare ware from 1908 on is being bought up. So are the Gibson-girl plates, the Rose O'Neill pieces (made in Germany), and the Sunbonnet Babies, not to mention late souvenir plates or the calendar plates up to 1929. On the china shelves and tables will be found Japanese Noritake cups and saucers, late Willowware, fish sets, bone dishes, butter pats from late Victorian tables, and ring trees, dresser bottles, and trays of the same period.

In some shops the late-Victorian furniture overshadows period pieces or even country pine. You may have to settle for an atrocious grained-oak washstand, a brass bed, wicker porch furniture, or ice-cream-parlor chairs, many of which the decorators, in their search for the quaint, have taken to their hearts. Silver will be of the plated variety—odd pieces, perhaps cookie jars, pickle jars, condiment sets, bride's baskets, all of glass in plated silver frames. There will be plenty of souvenir spoons which the collector will pick over for the rarer or more valuable ones. There will be twentieth-century Schoenhut toys (made by the famous Philadelphia firm of toymakers from 1872 on), magic lanterns and slides, late tole transfer on tin containers, wooden potato mashers, tin nutmeg graters, yellowware pudding molds, many only recently discarded from modern kitchens.

All these things are what many dealers have been forced to rely upon to fill their stocks.

Now other dealers prefer to fill up with gift items, distinctive modern pieces that will go with antiques. Often such a shop is very attractive and if you know exactly what you are looking for, may yield some good old things, though there won't be so many of them. Again I don't think the dedicated dealers like to do this. One admitted this recently with a sigh. Her reputation of years has been built on old pieces and good ones. But she pointed to a table full of what looked like old silver. "It's new, but it follows the old lines. I've had to put in a few things like this to take care of my young buyers. They don't have the money to pay for my old things but I like to keep them coming. Someday they may be able to afford the fine old things I sell."

Closely akin to the gift-and-antiques shop is the one that goes in for "decorating items." Here, again, they mix the old with the new. Sometimes they are out-and-out decorators using antiques when they can find them and fit them into modern schemes, good reproductions when they can't. I am more and more impressed with the way in which modern decorators have learned to use old pieces to advantage without going entirely traditional. They, too, are good supporters of the antiques business. But in many shops the term "decorative items" is apt to mean usable antiques for the home rather than the sort you would buy to fill collections. Again such shops have their place in the picture, and without them many good antiques might not see the light of day.

Last are the importers who go abroad to find things to fill their shops. Many of them would rather do this than to fill up with trash and junk. At least what they get is fairly sure of being good in its way, although many are sending back reproductions such as brass chestnut roasters, Staffordshire dogs, and Dutch modern pewter. It has come to the point where a shop that does not sell some imports is an exception rather than the rule. This is particularly true in parts of the country where native antiques are scarce. It is true in the city shops that go in more for elegance than for primitives.

Feeling differs among the dealers about selling imports from England and the Continent. Some are quite proud of their wares. Others like to give the impression that they are still sellers of Americana. One dealer who has a long history back of her brags that her stock is still 95 per cent American. On the other hand, the young salesman in a very elegant shop down South answered my question about imports versus American pieces by taking me to a side hall where he pointed disparagingly to a highboy and said, "This is the only American piece we have. New England, of course."

In talking about importations one thing must be remembered—that much of our so-called Americana was originally imported from the mother countries, particularly England, before we began to make our own good pieces. All the fine English china and porcelain, such as Bow and Chelsea, Wedgwood, Spode, and Worcester, came into this country in the early days. So why draw the line now? The pieces are just the same as those that adorned the old tea tables and cupboards. This is true of many other wares, silver and Sheffield, brass, pewter, and so on. Any collection of Americana is sure to include pieces not made in this country. Staffordshire can be as American as Pennsylvania Dutch fractur. Much of the early china was made expressly for export to this country. For many years America did not have fine china of its own to compete with the imports. In fact, imported wares were held in higher esteem than the few varieties that were made here, as, for instance, Tucker china, which did its best to look like French imported ware.

We were not much better off in brass. Many of the early fireplace equipment pieces, the andirons, scuttles, tools, candlesticks, etc., came from England. So why not add to them now? In glass we were better off. While we did not have the fine cut work of the English and Irish factories we did have good blown and etched glass as early as Stiegel, Wistar, and Ammelung. Even in the art glass field of the late 1800s we were close on the heels of such craftsmen as Webb,

Northwood, and others. So a signed Webb piece is not out of place standing beside a Mount Washington peachblow vase or a threaded bowl by Nicholas Lutz of Sandwich fame.

So it is all in how you look at it. If you yearn for a Leeds or Lowestoft piece, you no longer have to go to England to purchase it. But if you want a tea set of our own Tucker china you may have to travel more miles to find it.

We are so closely wedded to English pieces in this country that it is often hard to tell when a piece actually came in. While it was required by the McKinley Act to impress the name of the country of origin after 1891 on all imported wares, many old pieces brought over by individuals now will not have the name of the country on it. In a recent TV show—Dave Garroway's, to be exact—a brass tavern tobacco box to be used at a bar was displayed as part of an exhibit recently sent over to this country for some kind of British publicity. It was most ingenious. When a coin was dropped in a slot, it released the lid to the tobacco compartment. Now I had just seen such a box down in the Old Salem, North Carolina, restoration (in fact, I had photographed it for an article when it was still in Pennsylvania), and there is another one in Williamsburg. Two hundred years stood between the importation of these pieces yet we call the two American and the last one English.

We still have not covered all the ways in which the old things reach the shops. I have spoken about the ways the heirs dispose of the contents of an old house, calling in the dealers to bid on them. Things are also brought to dealers, and many of them profit from this way of disposing of antiques. But they do not like to buy unless they know the seller or something about him. They do not want to be caught with stolen property.

Then there are the sales, private, country, and city auctions. Through them, many antiques get on the market, but for the dealers they are not what they used to be. Occasionally the time, weather, lack of publicity, or some other factor may play into the dealer's hands, but too often the individual bidder keeps the prices too high for a healthy profit. "Look at that woman," a dealer whispered to me at a show not long ago. "I've been trying to sell her a lovely finished bench table in my shop for weeks and here she goes and buys that second-rate made-up piece for more than I was asking. People have an idea that anything at a sale is cheap. I find I can't give up the time any more for these sales. They used to be attended by knowledgeable people. Now they're crowded with suburban women who have spare time and money—and no real information about antiques values. I may stand around all day trying to pick up one or two pieces at a price that's fair. But too often now the amateurs step in and bid items up way beyond their value."

At one big auction house, where whole collections are sold after being advertised, prices go so high that most dealers give up. It is the collectors who as a rule support such sales and fight for pieces which may have been off the market for years.

There are many dealers who cannot take the time nor do not have the opportunity to go looking for stock. This is especially true if it is a one-man business. So they must depend upon what comes to them. They buy from other dealers either in their shops or at antiques shows, or from "pickers," those men or women who make a business of nosing out the antiques of an area and taking them around to their dealer clients. The dealer likes to know his picker. He does not want to have dubious goods foisted upon him. Often these pickers have occupations that get them into the homes where they can spot the old pieces and perhaps buy them. They are people such as meter readers, insurance men, etc. But picking is a business in itself, because a picker, too, has to be informed as to the age and value of what he is buying. Some dealers now even have pickers abroad to whom they write their wants.

Among the dealers are many who are wholesalers who do nothing but sell to other dealers. Where do *they* get their stuff? From the same sources as the retail dealer only in a larger way. They might be called specialists in buying as well as selling. One very well-known wholesaler in Pennsylvania whose goods fill up the trucks that travel

South and West takes periodic trips to England and the Continent sending back vanloads of goods for which he knows there is a big demand. He will have dozens of grandfather clocks, some in prime condition, some needing repairs, as well as clock parts, faces, pendulums, works, cases, etc. He will have cartons full of brass candlesticks, single and in pairs and of all periods, Staffordshire dogs by the dozen, scales of all kinds, a dozen epergnes always in stock to choose from, platters as plentiful as pancakes, brass and copper kettles, bed warmers, trivets, andirons, fireplace fenders, tilt-top tables, washbasins and pitchers, colored glass, figurines, lavabos, vases, tiles, all in bewildering abundance. Until a few years ago his stock was predominantly American, but now his native pieces are getting scarcer. In his home are housed his private collections of American pieces from which he will not part.

I have heard it said that many dealers hold back on some of their good pieces with the feeling that prices will continue to rise and their profits increase with the years. This may be so of those who deal in high-priced items, but I doubt if it holds true to much extent with the average dealer who must keep his shop stocked and can't afford to keep anything under cover.

The amazing thing about this dealer-to-dealer business is how far it will go. At an antiques sale, where dealers mill around from booth to booth, a piece may pass from one hand to another several times, each time at a profit, if only a small one. Naturally this practice tends to keep prices high. The dealer discount may be only 10 per cent—it can be more—but if it is taken three times on one piece it has upped the original price almost 30 per cent before it reaches the private buyer. There are, of course, good reasons why dealers buy from each other. As I have said, it saves them time and gas and effort nosing out the things for themselves. They may not make more than 10 per cent but it puts something in the shop for selling. At an antiques fair, where there can be anywhere from ten to fifty dealers, this kind of buying works out even better.

Now what is one dealer's bête noire can be another dealer's quick sale. They all know their clientele and what their clients are looking for. They have their specialties. A woman who goes in for prints may pick up some good buys from another dealer who can't sell prints or who may not know much about them. A dealer has a client who is looking for a certain kind of small washstand. She finds it at another dealer's, takes her 10 per cent, puts it on again, plus perhaps a bit more and turns it over quickly.

So that is the way it goes. It is one reason why antiques travel around as much as the American public itself. They tell me that the carnival glass and the cut glass are going to Texas where there is a great demand for them. The South comes North for its primitives. Today anyone in the antiques business has a bigger problem in buying material than in selling it. Of course there is always a certain percentage of stuff in almost any shop that hangs around for a long time and may represent quite a bit of invested funds. But most dealers do not worry about it. If they need cash, they may stage a one-day sale to get rid of the dead wood, or they may feel that it is good filler to keep the shop from looking empty. But the canny dealer knows he must keep his stock moving, not only to keep the money coming in and funds fluid, but to give his shop a "new look." When customers come in and see the same old things, visit after visit, they begin to believe that the shop is not doing business. After all, there is nothing that succeeds like success. Of course the customer on the road will not meet this situation. It is all fresh to him, and among the previously unwanted stuff he may find just what he is looking for. Consequently, he should be welcomed by the dealers.

The question often arises, what do dealers really make these days? Is there a living in it? For many, yes. But it takes a lot of doing and capital as it does for any business. Percentages of profit can vary from 10 per cent or 12 per cent in a year to more than 25 per cent, but it is the volume that counts. Many small antiques businesses conducted in the home probably bring in small pickings. But the overhead is practically nothing. It will give a single woman or a housewife something interesting to do and brings the world to her door. She may be willing to let it stop there, expanding and improving her stock as she can without a strain upon capital. Other shops do better, sometimes supporting two people, partners or a husband and a wife. A two-man business is a good thing, as it gives one a chance to go out and buy and the other to stay home and keep shop. It is a comfortable way of life if the proprietors dwell with the business and are content to live simply. If they want to build it up—and many do—they can take it in easy steps.

Many businesses start with a private collection which has been gathered up over the years, and, while representing some cash investment, is nothing compared to the capital needed to start a new business right now. I know of a thriving "small antiques" business, mostly glass and china, which started with the owners' private collection of glass that had threatened to overflow the home. It has proved a good nucleus for other things, and the knowledge gained by the collectors over the years gives the shop authority and reliability.

There are many businesses that have been inherited and thrive because they have a well-established name back of them and a backlog of good stock. These going businesses often support a whole family. There is an interesting story of a popular, busy shop in Maine which began as a sort of "white elephant" outlet many years ago. A woman in her middle years then began to buy up and sell the pieces her friends wanted to get rid of. Some were antiques. She got involved in cleaning out old attics and barns and cellars, taking anything and everything. Her house and barns bulged with unclassified stuff. Then she got too old to keep on. Arthritis took over. She gave the business to a favorite nephew, a prosperous businessman who accepted it with reservations and gave it to his wife to turn over as quickly as possible. But to his surprise business got brisker and brisker. The antiquers found out about it in their search for items that had once been trash. Now the nephew is retired and both he and his wife tend shop, which is always crowded, while Aunt Min rocks quietly on the lawn and looks on, well pleased with the gold mine she had prospected.

"Don't you get tired?" I asked this rather distinguished-looking man as he wrapped up a small perfume bottle for me.

"Of course," he said, "but I've never had so much fun in my life."

I think he meant it. Looked at in this way the antiques business can be fun, and I really think that many people involved in it get more fun than money out of it and are willing to keep it that way. Fortunately for the antiques buyer these shops line the highways and spot the towns and make pleasant shopping along the road.

CHAPTER 6.

The Ways Antiques Are Sold

WHILE there are thousands of shops that sell retail across the nation, there are many that do not rely on this type of doing business. The tendency seems to be to make selling easier. There is no doubt that it is a grueling business. Even the well-established, thriving dealers will tell you that some days not one person will enter the shop and yet it has to be kept open and attended on the chance that business will come in the door. Weather makes a difference here, too, as it does in many other lines. Many dealers alleviate this condition by cutting down the hours or days when they keep open. Now if you are familiar with their habits you can shop accordingly, but if you are a stranger passing along the road you can be disappointed. A dealer runs a chance when he closes the shop for a dash to the post office or the market. I've seen signs on doors, "Back in ten minutes," and have waited half an hour only to drive away without being able to visit the shop. There is no telling what I might have bought if the door had been open.

Sometimes the shops do not even put signs on the door. One morning I started out bright and early to canvass the shops along a certain well-traveled road to Connecticut. I rapped on doors of four shops and got no answer. The places were deserted. Then I began to get suspicious. Sure enough, on inquiry in the village I found there was an antiques show going on a few miles away. I figured that most of the absentees were either exhibiting or visiting there. By that time I had to be on my way so I missed out on looking over the stock of four good dealers. If they had indicated on their doors that they were at the sale I would have been saved a lot of trouble and might have made time to visit the show myself. I suppose they assumed that everyone knew about the show and would understand where they were. But they forgot the transient business that went past their doors. Maybe business from the road is spotty and maybe it is trying to give attention to the casual looker who takes up your time and buys nothing. But it is a natural hazard of the occupation. The antiques business is not the only one that has to put up with such uncertainties. Service with a smile is one of the biggest assets that any man or woman can equip himself with, and in the long run it pays off. Every good businessman knows that you can't overlook the small buyer or the almost-buyer. I always remember an axiom that a bond salesman told me once passed on to him by a canny old customer: "Never neglect your smallest buyer," he said. "Someday he may be your largest buyer or lead you to a big sale." So I do think it behooves the owners of antiques shops to remember this and keep open when they say they will be open, and give some consideration to the strangers who drop in if only to look.

Of course this applies more closely to the retail shop that expects and perhaps relies upon transient business. Otherwise, why would they advertise their shops with signs along the way? Which brings up another thing about which dealers are particularly unbusiness-like—*signs*. Dealers, please, if you are going to have an outdoor sign, make it a big one! Presumably everyone who approaches your shop will be coming by car. So it should be big enough and bold enough to be read in time to give the driver a chance to slow up. And it should be easily read from either direction. I've whizzed by many a shop which did not announce itself properly and because turning back on the highway or making a sudden shift to the other side of the road in the middle of heavy traffic was a chore, I've kept on. It is all very well to have an artistic sign in script or Old English lettering hanging from a post at the door or driveway, but it does the autoist no good unless you have prepared him for it. There is nothing like an arrow with bold black letters announcing ANTIQUES ahead and giving the distance, too.

Again there is the matter of parking. It can be a problem but one the proprietor should put every effort into solving. Usually it is illegal to park along the road and often dangerous, and so the alternative is to drive into a driveway or alleyway as quickly as possible. Now if the right entrance is not indicated, one gets into the driveway for the next house. It can be very confusing. This placing of signs takes a lot of planning and imagination and is of much more importance than many dealers seem to think. The local people who know may have no trouble, but stopping should be made easy for the traveling stranger.

Town shops have parking problems, too. If they lie on a busy street, they should take some means so that the autoist can get at them without too much trouble. It may mean renting space in a parking lot, or displaying directions for reaching a back alley, anything that will lure the motorist to stop instead of driving on as I have done only too often.

If I seem to have digressed to point up dealer failings it is in the cause of better business habits, as they will affect the buyer on the road for whom this book is primarily intended. They are all things I have experienced personally and I feel this is the place to bring them to the dealers' attention.

Now to get back to other ways of doing business in antiques, we must consider those who sell by mail. Many augment their shop business this way, getting out a mimeographed circular every so often listing items they feel their clients might be interested in. This is a very satisfactory way of reaching customers, and if well conducted is a good way to shop. It entails a lot of paper work but as one dealer says, it can be done sitting down. A straight mail-order business is no help to the antiquer on the road, but one that combines it with retail selling can be of real service to the transient buyer. If you like what you see in such a shop, you can have your name put on the mailing list for later purchasing.

Another digression from the "open shop" way of doing business is by appointment only. This is apt to happen when a business has progressed to the point where it has a good clientele of regular customers, or perhaps where it specializes sharply or deals in high-priced items that do not interest the average buyer. These businesses feel, and rightly, that if a buyer takes the time and makes the effort to make an appointment to see their wares that a sale is more likely than it would be from a casual dropper-in. If the business will stand such a method of doing business, it is probably a good one from the seller's viewpoint. It takes the drudgery out of selling. It does not work out so well for the buyer on the road. It does not appeal to me. Perhaps because I am not primarily a serious collector. I am more of an impulsive buyer. When I see something I like I buy it if I can afford it. I believe there are many like me. And certainly for those of us who take to the road to do our antique-buying, appointments are difficult to arrange. But it would be foolish to dismiss these shops entirely. Often a phone call an hour or even a few minutes ahead is enough to set up a meeting. And often, too, a ring of the doorbell will gain you admittance if the dealer is home and feels you are serious.

Now there are some dealers who have no shops at all, who do business through the antiques shows. They travel from one to another, sometimes covering hundreds of miles. They are well known and their contacts in the various towns and cities seek them out. Of course they do not have the room to display all their wares. Some must be left at home, but they can be publicized and called upon if necessary. They are not hampered by a shop that must be kept open whether they are home to attend it or not. One dealer whom I met recently in a busy resort town in New England solves this absentee problem very nicely. Her delightful little hole-in-the-wall shop on a picturesque street is jammed with pewter—her specialty—and other small antiques for the summer season. Then, in autumn, she packs up, goes South, takes off for a month's rest, and then works her way North again, stopping at shows along the way. I don't know how the over-all profits from such a business would compare with a year-round open shop, but certainly it is a way of catching the resort trade during a short season and keeping in circulation the rest of the year. Other dealers manage the same problem with two shops, a summer one and a winter one.

One point the traveler should remember is to watch for the antiques shows along the way. There are so many these days that you cannot drive many miles without bumping into one in progress. Some are just small local shows, others may attract dealers from quite a distance. It might be a good idea to carry a list of shows with you. All the magazines dealing with antiques list them for months ahead. Or stop at a local post office and inquire if one is going on.

There is a new kind of sale that is making itself felt in regions where antiques flourish. This is the one-day sale or mart in the open or under cover. A number of dealers will get together and bring their stuff to a certain spot and sell informally, often right out of their station wagons. A stop at such a show, if it coincides with your driving schedule, is bound to be interesting.

Here and there on your travels you are going to come up against some clever ways that progressive dealers use to promote business. An unusual piece displayed on the lawn in front of the shop is always an invitation to come in and look further and usually indicates an interesting shop. It may be an old sleigh, a covered wagon, a carriage, a carousel horse, a spinning wheel, or even a gypsy wagon. It slows you down and arouses curiosity. It can be a good gimmick if it is done well and followed up with good merchandise. Signs can be interesting, too. I remember a large one along the front of an old railroad station that had been turned into a shop. The place was called the Railroad Shop and had a large choo-choo painted under the lettering. A shop called the Rocking Chair has a real rocking chair swinging in the breeze. One of the smartest selling gimmicks I know of is a big blackboard at the side of the big doors opening on a large red barn where some of the finest and most selective antiques are sold. As one would never expect to come upon a Queen Anne wing chair or a Willard clock or a set of King's Rose china in a barn like this, the canny owners list their outstanding treasures with the prices on the big slate. Before you step into the barn you know what to expect. This is a striking example of a dealer who has put thought into selling good things.

Another way in which a dealer can call attention to his business is with the name. Many do not bother, feeling that the name of the owner is enough. Certainly it is more dignified than the playful tags you meet along the way. I think the tendency is away from this "cuteness," however. The day of the Shoppe is over and dealers seem to be taking pains to find names that are distinctive as well as enticing. Many of them take the date of the house, the 1670 Tavern, the 1804 House, etc. It sets the place back into the years when supposedly their merchandise originated. Many describe the house in other ways, the Blue Shutters, the White Barn, the Red Barn, Ice Pond Farm, the Château, Lilac Cottage, the Old Stone House, the Mill, the Pink House, the Old Gothic House, the Old Toll Gate, Eleven Oaks, and so on. Some use a symbol, derived perhaps from an old inn sign such as the Stagecoach, the Whaling Schooner, the King's Crown, the Gargoyle. Many are alluring because they make you stop and ask yourself why, things such as the Red Velvet Shop, the Empty Bottle, the Four Winds, the Blue Pacific, the Witch Pot, the Lamplighter, Pig and Saddle, etc. Still more borrow from the trade, such as the Corner Cupboard—there are three of these that I know of—Spinning Wheel, Betty Lamp, Whatnot, Oxbow, Copper Lantern, Toby Shop, and on and on. Others come closer to the main idea of the shops with names such as the Dickerin' Shop, Plunder Shop, Lucretia's Loot, the Attic, Memory Lane, Keepsake, Potpourri, Hobby House, Family Heirlooms, etc. One could go on indefinitely, and a list of shop names would make good reading if nothing else. Who thought them up and why? Silly though some may be, you won't forget them, and that perhaps is the test.

And so the traveler on the road looking for antiques must keep in mind that he is dealing with a business of many angles and thus is apt to come up with many situations disappointing as well as pleasing. Don't condemn the whole business of selling antiques because three dealers in a row have been rude or not at home when they should be. The fourth will probably turn out to be so friendly and knowing that you will want to linger a long time and return again and again. For every shop that is slipshod, badly run, indifferent, or discourteous, I can name five that are just the opposite. For antiques is a big business and the selling of them takes not only knowledge but a keen business acumen. More and more dealers are awakening to this fact and are acting accordingly.

CHAPTER 7.

The Antiquing Trail

AS I HAVE said earlier in this book, I have based my facts and opinions of the antiques business on my own experience. For years I have been making many trips by car around the country either for vacation purposes or to visit friends at a distance, and almost always I have combined my tripping with antiquing as I traveled. But to make this book as immediate as tomorrow I determined to cover the ground by car this year with antiques only in mind. I went into the shops not only to buy but to look, to assess, to ask questions. While I took the well-traveled roads, the arteries which the average tourist would hit in his trips up and down the eastern seaboard, I did go off on tangents when it seemed worth while to do so. I armed myself with lists culled from magazines and other pieces of information, catalogues of the big antiques shows, member lists of associations, names given to me by friends or other dealers or remembered from previous trips. I took my maps, state by state, and marked the spots where there were antiques shops. In this way it was easy to find them as I drove and to aim for localities where there seemed to be a concentration of them.

As I live in Pennsylvania, forty miles west of Philadelphia, and it was July, I decided to head north to hit the vacation time in New England. While the turnpikes are the quickest method of travel for getting to Maine, I avoided them because I wanted to drive along the main roads and go through the towns where the shops lie. You can't antique on a turnpike. Besides, I enjoy the old roads more. I like the variety they offer, the opportunity to slow up for towns and to relax, to eat your lunch from a basket under a wayside tree, to stop at a turnout and view the landscape, in other words, to take your time, which is the only way to make a long trip endurable. Moreover, except for speed limits, most of the main roads are as good for driving as the turnpikes.

My first trip North I was accompanied by a friend, as interested in antiques as I am, though not professionally so. We got out of Pennsylvania by way of the Northeast Extension of the Pennsylvania Turnpike to the Lehighton Exchange, then east on Route 22 through Stroudsburg and up Route 209 to Matamoras on the Delaware River, across the bridge to Port Jervis, and across the state heading toward Peekskill and the bridge across the Hudson.

I did not stop in Pennsylvania because those shops could be covered later, but in this mid-eastern area of New York State my map was spotted with red dots signifying antiques shops. This is a big vacation area for New Yorkers and I felt as long as we were in no great rush it would be well to stop off at as many places as we could. So we left Route 209 temporarily to go east toward Goshen where several shops were listed. Visits there all rewarded the effort. We stopped at a small town called Slate Hill where a modest front-porch house surprised us with its treasures. It was here we were shown the most unique Rockingham tea and coffee set I have ever seen. It was of dark brown pottery with raised motifs in color, but the most surprising part was the finial on the top of the coffeepot, a miniature coffeepot itself. It looked as if it were one of those one-of-a-kind pieces that some imaginative potter had done, tongue in cheek.

It was near Goshen, on a broad sweep of road, that I was welcomed heartily by a woman dealer with a large barn full of everything. She knew my two previous books well, in fact she said she used my collector's book "like a Bible." Very heart-warming words! Here it was that I saw another unusual item, a large Majolica plate with raised decorations of greenery with a coiled snake in the center, realistic enough to make you shudder. I have seen two more since, but then it was new to me. The dealer had not put a price on it yet because she was waiting to see exactly what it was. She thought it was French. I think she was right. Her specialty was old paintings of the Hudson River school which she said were in great demand. I was interested in her personally, because she had come into the business when left a widow with two small daughters and she had had to find something she could do at home. That was twenty years ago. Her small business has bloomed into a successful venture. This is the kind of thing that puts life into a pursuit like mine. With a touch of human interest the inanimate bits of the past seem to take on life. What matters as much as what they are is why they were gathered together and how.

There are several good dealers in and around Middletown, New York. One, just off the main road, on a sort of by-pass, is a small store that at first sight would seem unpromising. Downstairs were the usual small things, lots of china and glass, a few good pieces among them, but when the dealer insisted on taking me upstairs I was impressed. Here were some fine Hudson Valley pieces, furniture and paintings with oddments not seen in my part of the country. This dealer had been associated with antiques for years, her mother had been a confirmed collector and her sister an artist. So I listened carefully to what she told me about her things. I felt sure she knew her subject.

After a few more stops we headed over to Ellenville, where I had the name of a dealer who specialized in buttons. Now I don't know too much about buttons, only in a general way, because I have never collected them, but it was here that I realized what such a hobby could mean—and cost. The dealer confessed that she had practically gone into debt to buy up a famous collection which had just been thrown on the market. She had not yet had time to classify it, but in spite of the fact that she was getting ready to go off for the weekend, she took time out to show me some of her best boards or cards. Here it was I saw a dozen French enamel picture buttons, each one as exquisitely executed as any brooch or snuffbox. They were valued, as I remember, in the neighborhood of $1,000 for the card. She also showed me another set of twelve English buttons of silver each one etched with a different balloon-ascension scene. This, too, was valued around $1,000. As I looked around the rooms overflowing with buttons like the sands of the sea from boxes and drawers and cases, I wondered how this dealer could keep her head and her patience. But it was evident she did. I would be willing to bet that if a customer with a special button want came in and asked for it the dealer would be able to put her fingers on it in a few seconds.

Next across to Peekskill and good old Route 202, one of the longest and most meandering routes in the eastern part of the country. A motel for the night was a layover on the west side of the Hudson. What a boon these motels are, especially when you are not aiming for the big city hotels! In all my thousands of miles of driving I have yet to find one that was not clean or moderately comfortable. Some were even sumptuous. And always a private bath to refresh the weary traveler. Occasionally in some sections off the through roads they were simple in their appointments, but never primitive, nothing like the "cabins" we once knew when they were new and novel. I was to discover one thing about motels. For two people they are moderate in price, no more than a good hotel, but for the lone traveler they can be expensive. There is little reduction made for one person, especially in the season when a motel owner can expect to have a full house every night. In the season also, especially near a weekend, I found it better to phone ahead for a reservation. These motels are the essence of comfort, always plenty of hot water, ice cubes in a bucket or out of a machine, reading matter beside the bed recent enough to be interesting, good reading lamps with high-power bulbs, air conditioners or heaters which you can turn on or off at will, carpeted floors, plenty of hangers and closet room, good mirrors, easy chairs, your car within a yard from your door, no tipping, and often an adjoining restaurant. God bless the motels, say I, and every other traveler on the road!

Next day we got an early start and headed east for Route 7 and Ridgefield, Connecticut. Here are several shops, but I particularly wanted to visit one of the top, much-advertised ones known to all antiques buyers. It is owned and operated by a gracious woman in the business for many years, following her mother before her. Her whole house, a beautiful Connecticut home setting a bit above the highway, is her shop. She is the dealer who said with pride that her stock was 95 per cent American. She had not yet had to rely upon imports brought over in the last ship. When I asked her how she managed to keep such fine things in stock, she told me that many things were brought *to* her for sale. People knew her reputation. She carried high-class items and got good prices for them and could afford to pay well for what she bought. She also told me that she bought back pieces that she or her mother had sold many years before. She was at the moment elated at a secretary an old lady had finally decided to part with, one the dealer's mother had sold her in the early days of the shop. Today she had been able to give the owner more than she paid for it originally and would still make a profit because of the rise in prices.

It was here over coffee around a William-and-Mary gateleg table that we met a Hyde Park dealer whose specialty is early paintings and Americana. He seemed unusually interested in my account of the book I was working on and felt it was much needed if only to list the specialties of the dealers up and down the country.

Next door along this Connecticut road was another dealer I did not want to miss because his specialty is hooked rugs and also twin beds which he makes out of old ones. But unfortunately he was not home and I missed seeing the fine things which I had heard that he had.

Up now on famous Route 7. Along this main highway which runs many miles north from Norwalk, through Connecticut, Massachusetts, Vermont, and into Canada lie the shops, sometimes close together, sometimes spread for miles. It has been called "the antiquing highway." From it, sorties can be made to Hartford, Holyoke, Greenfield, Brattleboro on east-west cross-country roads also with their quota of shops. Around Sharon, Salisbury, Falls Village, Canaan, we drove into a rich settlement of shops. Unfortunately that was the morning when many were away at a local antiques show, but we caught a few home and found here the kind of shops that a discriminating buyer likes.

At Sharon I looked up among other names on my list a shop in a quiet street where a lovely lady in dressing gown and pin curls answered my ring. She apologized that she had just washed her hair (that was the day when everyone seemed to be washing her hair— it must have been the time of the moon!). Her shop was in the basement of her house, small but crammed with nice things, though she explained she kept her best pieces upstairs. It was here my friend found her first two pieces of Diamond Band or Portland Band glass which she collects. This is such a rare pattern that she felt as if she had struck oil. I found this dealer both interesting and interested. Later she went to the trouble of mailing me a clipping from a magazine about a piece I owned and had been talking to her about.

At Lakeville an attractive shop along the highway, though not on my list, suggested a stop. We were not sorry we drove in. Here again we found a dealer who had been in the business for years, and though his stock was not large, owing to a physical condition which forced him to limit his activities, we found it very interesting and spent some time with him listening to his stories. I found a lovely old "spaghetti" creamware bowl there which I have yet completely to identify, and a bunch of huge old keys which I intend to make into a door knocker.

From here we headed west for a few miles over to Millerton on Route 22, a New York main road paralleling Route 7 all the way north and a favorite of mine on my trips to Vermont, because of lighter traffic and expanse of scenery with the Vermont hills to the

right. There was a dealer at Millerton I wanted to catch. I found
her home and was rewarded with seeing her fine display of lamps
which were her specialty. Of particular note were a pair of lavender
opaque glass lamps of Sandwich origin and an unusual miniature
lamp or night lamp in the shape of a turtle about which I wrote to a
collecting friend of mine. It was here I found what I'd been looking
for for some time, a glass reservoir to replace a broken one for an
old lamp with an iron base and a porcelain standard. It was so
exactly right in size and pattern that I felt it was worth the miles I
had driven out of my way to see this shop.

Back to Route 7 again with stops at Salisbury and Canaan. At
Ashley Falls, just over the border in Massachusetts, we found a shop
newly moved into an inviting spot at a busy crossroads. While most
of the business was confined to the big barn, the house and fenced
patio had been furnished in primitives, an inspiration to any home-
owner with a yen for early-American décor. It was evident that the
proprietors, both men, had a feeling for the unusual. They told me
they did a lot of business with museums. Here I felt that, in spite of
the quality of the items, prices were reasonable. And it was here
that I threw caution to the winds and bought a pair of pewter
molds, beautiful things shaped like bunches of asparagus and designed most probably for jellies or puddings. They had an English
registry mark which pegged the date as 1868, but they had been
bought in the neighborhood from an estate that was being settled. I
was practically the first visitor to see them, as the acquisition was so
new they had not yet been priced. I quieted my conscience by promising myself that I was buying them for my son who has an old
inn and likes unusual pieces for décor. So now they sit serenely
on a pine fireplace shelf, but he swears when asparagus time comes
he is going to turn out the handsomest pair of mousses in them
you ever saw.

A few more stops and on to Great Barrington and to Stockbridge
for a late lunch. They were just opening a gift shop at the Red Lion
Inn where we ate. This is a very old hostelry well known to many

generations of vacationers. There we almost missed a big opportunity when we decided to pass up the new gift shop. But it turned out when we took a brief peep into the shop that they were selling off with their new gifts a whole roomful of pieces recently cleaned out of the attics and storerooms of the inn. It was all good Americana from as early as the 1830s. Many of the pieces were nicked, cracked, with broken handles and missing lids, but there were plenty in good condition. An appraiser had set the prices and they were reasonable. Needless to say my friend and I went haywire and bought and bought. We came away with some lovely blue Canton plates, an early ironstone fruit bowl, a Portobello pitcher, some Wedgwood calendar tiles, an iron swivel toaster for the fireplace, among other things. The back of the car was beginning to pile up, but we went off happy with our treasures.

In the town of Stockbridge we found other antiques businesses, one well known nationally housed in one of the lovely old New England white-painted dwellings under the elms. This was one of the places where you walked up and rang the bell. When you were ushered into the wide hall, you felt as if you should get out your calling card. Elegance was the word here with plenty of American pieces and all authentic. One item to remember was a pair of painted Sheraton chairs with the original upholstery still bright and intact. Although I had announced that we were not buyers only seekers of information, the gentleman owner was as courteous as if we were about to settle for a $3,000 highboy. He, too, expressed the opinion that one could never afford to be rude to anyone and told the story of a shabby man who had been back to the shop six times but had never bought anything. On the seventh visit, however, he made a purchase of tremendous importance and staggering price. When we left, we filled our lungs with fresh air and came down to earth after breathing the rare atmosphere of that lovely, museum-like home.

That afternoon we went back to Route 22 to pick up a few near-lying points I had marked on my map. One was at Austerlitz, where I found a well-advertised business hiding behind the barrier of the small local post office. The postmistress, whose son it was who had the business, explained that her few rooms housed only part of it, he had more in his own home a short distance away. I was surprised at the quality of the things gathered in these simple rooms, but when I heard that the son had begun this business at an early age, continued through college, and was also an auctioneer, I could see how he had such a fund of information about antiques, as well as knowing what to buy and where.

Another short detour in the rain this day took us to the shop of a well-known dealer, whom I had met at the New York shows, to see her fine collection of coronation items in which she specializes. Unfortunately she was away at a show, but a very new and charming young daughter-in-law just arrived from Germany with her G.I. husband did the hostess act for us in perfect English. It was most interesting to talk to this pretty girl and get her reactions. I think she was still a bit surprised at what we call antiques over here. At home, she said, old things were taken as a matter of course.

Straight up through the rain now to Hoosick Falls, where the business begun by the famous authority on American glass, George McKearin, now deceased, is still being conducted by his daughter. Though much of his glass has been distributed among the museums, there are still many fine things to be seen in the shop which is housed in a small house in the garden on a shady New England side street.

From here east to Bennington and an end-of-the-day visit to the museum to take a second look at the famous pottery, also some new additions to the glass galleries. A cup of coffee with Mrs. Green, the gracious assistant to Mr. Barrett, the curator, who was not there at the time, put a cheerful and restful period to what had been a hard day.

Choosing a motel in that part of the country is like spending the proverbial penny in the candy store. The choice is wide and bewildering. We made a good choice and after doing the Bennington shops the next morning set out east toward Brattleboro on Route 9.

Here is another famous antiquing trail to be remembered. It goes across the two states of Vermont and New Hampshire and into the foot of Maine. It was liberally spotted with red dots on my map. Though occasionally we whizzed by places that did not look too promising, we found a number of good shops that day, including places in Brattleboro and Keene and the concentration area of Henniker, Hillsboro, and Hopkinton. Here we found plenty of Americana with only a sprinkling of imported pieces. I was impressed with the very old house of one young woman who led us through beautifully decorated rooms with painted shelves full of fine china, not shoplike at all. It was delightful, the more so when she took us to still another room which had not been touched because it had on the walls the original stenciling done in the primitive New England manner. While I would not go so far as to say that proper surroundings and décor are a necessity for conducting a good antiques business, it does help to see things set against the background in which they were first used.

At Concord we kept east on Route 9 because we were heading for Maine and a house party near Kennebunkport. We left the rich coast area, dotted with spots on my map, for day sorties from our cottage on Cape Porpoise. This time the car was full each day with three other enthusiasts, two of whom regaled us along the way with stories of the things "Mama" used to have and which they'd thrown away. All along here, on Route 1, are the famous shops of vacationland, of Rye Beach, Portsmouth, York Harbor and York Beach, Ogunquit, Kennebunk and Kennebunkport, Portland, Brunswick, Bath, Boothbay Harbor, Damariscotta, Thomaston, and Rockland. I felt this year that Maine prices were not as high as might be expected from a resort area. But I was told that it had been a cool and rainy summer and this was probably reflected in the prices.

One shop known for many years fascinated me. It was housed in an old gabled mansion of twenty-two rooms, all full of antiques of all kinds, periods, and condition, There were china, glass, furniture, primitives. One room, for instance, was entirely devoted to plates among which could be found many good ones. Here I picked up a Bible-sized Victorian book box probably destined for a library table with a drawer that pulled out where the edges of the pages would have been. I fortunately "saw it first," because after I'd bought it everyone in our party wanted it. Our hostess was in seventh heaven because she recognized the rose pattern in her Minton china and was able to buy very reasonably two cups and saucers to match her set at home. It was hard to tear ourselves away from this abundance of antiquity under one roof. I learned later that the original owner who had amassed this huge stock over the years was dead and that the place was being run by a famous corporation. Why, I don't know, unless perhaps it might have belonged to someone in the family of the concern. It is going to take years to sell off that tremendous stock, but perhaps it will be bought out intact.

In the several days' time before we set out for home via the turnpikes we were able to cover many local shops pinpointed on my map. At one very small shop that specialized in pewter and open only for the summer I came across another of those odd things which make canvassing the shops a constantly occurring adventure. This time it was a French pewter piece shaped like a sabot or boot and beautifully wrought and chased. It was originally a vessel to serve wine from, utterly impractical today, but un unforgettable piece of value to the collector. Say Ogunquit to me and the picture of that lovely pewter piece will always pop up. In fact, my whole map is spotted with memories like this. "Yes," I'll say, "I remember that place. That was where I saw the blue glass chamber pot that was supposed to have belonged to Empress Eugénie." Or, "It was in that little village where I saw the first and only Majolica mustache cup I've ever come across."

New England Revisited

I paid my second visit to New England in August when I set out alone, this time with the prospect of a stopover in Vermont with friends soon to leave for California—and incidentally to sell antiques out there. Following my usual way up from Pennsylvania, I cut over through Connecticut and mid-Massachusetts, catching some shops I had missed on the first trip North. Up Route 5 this time to Brattle-boro again. This is another main south-and-north artery paralleling Route 7 along the Connecticut River. Just south of Brattleboro I found a shop which I had seen many times in the ads. I didn't have much trouble finding it. Never have I seen a place so well marked. Signs plastered the place. You couldn't miss it. It looked like a well-stocked junk shop but I was soon to reverse my opinion. The owner had had the place a long time as had his father before him. I gathered from his conversation that some years back he would have had more important pieces to display, but now, like so many others, he was reduced to selling what he could get. He was specializing in coins and guns but if you knew what to look for you could find among the stuff from the old houses he cleared out an unusual piece of china or glass or other Americana.

Now I turned north on Route 5, shuttling back and forth over the river to catch both Vermont and New Hampshire dealers. There were many places where I was tempted to linger, among them a well-known dealer in dolls and dollhouses. An hour spent there brought home to me why dolls have always fascinated collectors and why so many dealers specialize in them. Also why there are so many small doll museums scattered throughout the country. One could make a Doll Tour and not have to drive many miles between stops.

In a small town of Wetherfield Bow—what a lovely name! It sounds like an English village—I had a nice conversation with a dealer who had been in the business only five years but was making a very good showing. The thing that interested me most here was her husband's collection of distillery glasses, which she took me into the house to see. These are the small tumblers put out by the liquor distillers as ads with the names usually etched on them. I'd never seen them before. She assured me they were inexpensive and not too uncommon, but I must admit I have never seen another one yet in my travels.

A fine place at Ascutney I had to cross off my list because it was up for sale and the owner did not know what was going to happen to the business. I hope she decided to stay in her lovely white barn because she had many beautiful things.

At Hartland I came upon the wayside shop of a dealer who had been in business many years and was not too pleased at the turn it had taken. We batted words and opinions around for a long time until some paying visitors came in to look at his fine American pieces. He allowed as how the good wayside antiques shop would soon be no more, that there were too many people in the business, that there were too many antiques shows and too many museums all eating up the supply for the dealers who used to sell them. I've heard these things said by others, and I admit that there is some truth in them—but not the whole truth.

I had timed this trip so I could catch two Vermont shows on my way North, the one at Woodstock particularly. I must admit that I was disappointed. It may have been larger and more imposing in other years, but I didn't find what I was looking for—a lot of Vermont dealers all in one place to be visited in a few hours. But what it lacked in size it did make up for in quality. Among the twelve dealers who had taken space in the big room of the modern community house I found many good things and met some fine people. I was able to examine firsthand the pieces of a dealer who advertises lighting fixtures as her specialty. I also met the energetic dealer who has been primarily responsible for gathering both the New Hampshire dealers and the Vermont dealers into their respective associations which both seem fairly inclusive. But I missed the Vermont dealers themselves. The people I met with one exception were mostly from New Hampshire, Massachusetts, and New York.

I came away with a somewhat changed concept of antiques shows. I know that many dealers travel regularly from show to show—almost like the old vaudeville circuits—many spending more time away from home and the home shop than in it. I also felt that it was the large city shows that attracted them. But this and several others I attended in the vacation areas gave me new ideas. I decided that if you want to catch the smaller dealers of a locality in one spot, aim for the local, less important shows sponsored by the woman's club, a church group, or some local charity.

This was confirmed in my mind when I got to Newbury, up Route 5, passing through Lyme, Orford, and Haverill, all spotted on my map. At Newbury a show called *The Cracker Barrel* was in progress. It was part of some kind of summer festival held on the village green, including an art show and other exhibits. Here the local dealers were about half and half divided between Vermont and New Hampshire across the river. The material exhibited was all good with New England pieces such as Bennington, American pewter, hooked rugs, prints, etc., in abundance.

Another motel that night, and across Vermont through Barre— the marble city. I would have liked to have stopped to visit the exhibit there but I had to remind myself that my business was antiques not marble. Then through Montpelier, the capital, and west on Route 2, the big east-west highway that goes from Burlington on the west to the tip of Maine. It was raining again that day and traveling was not made easy by construction work going on for a big interstate highway. But I was familiar with this part of the country from other trips and I detoured down to Starksboro for a visit to a favorite dealer where I have always found good antiques— and reasonable. I picked up a few things, a small white Staffordshire deer, a quaint old cigar case, and a lovely old trivet in a pattern I had never seen before. I by-passed Shelburne and the Museum that day because of the weather and landed at my host's in time for a warm reception and a good dinner.

Again I made sorties from the lovely Vermont farmhouse, so tastefully restored, to places which they knew and where they had bought. They were on a buying spree to augment their stock of antiques which they were taking with them to California and hoped to sell out there. We stopped off in my favorite shop in their village where I asked questions and got good answers about Vermont dealers generally. These two—both man and wife—are unusually well informed. They were certainly not pessimistic about the antiques business. That good things could still be found was dramatically proved when we stepped inside the door. Both my host and I made a beeline for a legitimate Puritan Bible box standing on a chair. It was of dark oak, deeply carved with the original iron hasps and hinges. Among the apothecary bottles, the Mary Gregory glass, the late Spode plates, it looked as out of place as a doughboy in tomorrow's Memorial Day parade. The owner explained that he had just bought it when it came up at a sale where a collection was being broken up. I was so happy when my friend said with no hesitation, "Sold!" I knew it would go to California with them, a striking example of the way antiques get around these days.

One novelty I picked up in a Burlington shop given over mostly to glass was a pair of old glass insulator cups that had been used on electric poles. I'd seen them before in aqua and green but these were the most beautiful amethyst you could imagine. They were threaded for screwing on the wooden arms, and the glass was heavy and bubbly. I don't know where they were made but I certainly mean to find out. They are on my window shelf now, picking up the winter sunshine and sending out a soul-satisfying blast of pure color. Several people have suggested ways of using them, but I am satisfied to leave them where they are, pure pools of beauty and nothing more.

Monday morning I started out early to cross to Maine on Route 2. I wanted to catch the New Hampshire shops in the northern part of the state in the White Mountain district. This is another vacation area and was heavily spotted on my map. It was a good day, clear and cool. The mountains were never lovelier. I kept on Route 2 with detours for Whitefield, Littleton, and Bethlehem. At Littleton I almost missed one of the nicest shops in the region because I had not spotted it on my map. But the sign was big and I turned back to park in front of what was an old inn right on the highway. The shop was housed in the barns and the inn, which once had been a prosperous farmhouse in the family of the owner's wife. I arrived at coffee-break time and shared a cup and some good conversation with the genial proprietor and his attractive wife in a large room gleaming with copper and brass, silver, and Sheffield plate. Later I was taken for a tour of the inn, every room, bedrooms and all, furnished with genuine antiques refinished and adapted for comfortable modern living. The pieces were for sale and were replaced when sold. This dealer had a way with old furniture, making it into usable pieces without destroying lines or functions, except when necessary. I was entranced with a small bedroom writing table made from an old melodeon with the keyboard set upright across the back in a sort of decorative frieze.

On Route 2 on the way to Bethlehem I stopped at another attractive shop, this one on my map. It was low and red-roofed, set beside a small stream. Most of the pieces were china, glass, and what they call "small antiques," but all were very well chosen. The proprietors were hospitable and I spent some time there. Here I picked up another piece of Diamond Band glass for my friend and an amethyst Sandwich bowl at a price I could afford.

Over to Twin Mountain in the heart of the mountains, and back to Route 2 again. I made a few more stops along the way, but one place I wanted particularly to visit because of its reputation I could not find. I had been told it was just off the highway, but the owner apparently did not believe in signs—or perhaps droppers-in—and so I missed it. It was along here that I almost passed the big, shabby schoolhouse which I mentioned in another chapter. But I am glad I stopped because among the plethora of plates and cups and saucers, I found an amusing old paperweight with tinsel background, a ceramic ointment box from a Philadelphia chemist more than one hundred years old, a transfer mug, and a stoppered bottle that had once held Dutch gin.

Bangor was my stopping place for the next three days, where an old friend with a house like a museum insisted upon my staying. I had often gone antiquing with her in the old days, and again I knew many of the dealers in northern Maine. I was fortunate enough to be there when the Ellsworth Antique Show was on and spent a worth-while afternoon talking to old friends and new. There were quite a few local Maine dealers here as well as big ones from out of town, because this show so close to Bar Harbor has the reputation of being one of the big summer shows. Again I picked up another piece of Diamond Band glass and a beautiful little carved wooden box with a sifter top which the dealer thought had been made for nutmeg.

And now I was ready to go down the coast toward Rockland, where I had left off on my first trip. This is another area that I know well, and I took a leisurely drive down Route 1, stopping to renew contacts as I went. At Hampden one of my favorite dealers brought out a painted plank chair with decoration still fairly discernible and with the label of the maker still under the seat. It had been made in Maine in 1848. "If I can get it in the trunk, I'll take it," I told the dealer who once had sold me the only slag flask I had ever seen. Of course we got it in, and along it went to Pennsylvania and a new home.

One of the most satisfactory calls I made along the way was at a place I had often passed but never visited. It was a huge farmhouse standing high along the road near Winterport. Now today I had a good reason for pulling into the steep drive. I was received at the kitchen door by an elderly man in overalls who called his wife, a cherubic little woman whose business it was. It did not take her long to absorb my story. She led me with great pride around to see her treasures—and treasures they were, representing a lifetime of buying and selling. I would like to have seen that business in its heyday, for even now, in 1960, there was enough fine stuff to stock three good wayside shops. And how she loved her things! Just as I was leaving she led me away from admiring a beautiful carved-back sofa of Duncan Phyfe period with the ends representing the heads of birds—swans, I think—to what looked like a low primitive bench or box on legs. "Have you ever seen a baby's bathtub in Staffordshire?" she asked as she raised the lid. Sure enough, there it was, a small blue-and-white china tub roughly shaped like a figure 8 and embedded into the frame of the box like a pea in the pod. A museum piece, she called it, and I agreed.

Searsport and Belfast have quite a few shops. I stopped in several and found good things in all. In one where the owner was a good friend of my recent hostess I lingered for some time looking over her very large collection of all kinds of Americana. No imports here. I spotted several pieces of what I can only describe as "bubble glass," though I am sure if it once had a name it was not that. I have been fascinated with it and its history for some time. It comes in various colors and sizes but basically it is a piece with three solid balls of glass at the base and a fourth ball on top for a paperweight. Often the fourth ball is replaced with an inkwell or a vase. Some time ago I found a collection of it not far from home in Pennsylvania, which the owner had been building up for years. He did not know what it was nor where it had been made though he had bought one piece from a man in south Jersey and another had come from Germany. From time to time I have seen it at antiques shows but nobody else seemed to know what it was either.

I began to dig for information but got nowhere. I even showed a photograph of it to Mr. McKearin while he was still living but he could only say that he thought it might have been made in a New England glass factory. Corning Museum could not seem to trace it either. Then when I was in Europe this past summer I picked up two pairs of vases in it, one pair a delightful clear vaseline color, in a shop in the Pantiles at Tunbridge Wells, and the other a rainbow-prismed clear glass in white with sterling-silver rims in a Shepherd's Market shop, in London. Both called it bubble glass, and from the hallmark on the silver I knew it was of English origin.

Next I saw it in Ellenville, New York, and when I asked the owner she said it was "Corning, of course." And now here before me in Searsport, Maine, were two handsome pieces of it, one in ruby, the other a rich blue, the four balls almost as large as tennis balls. "What is it?" I asked the owner. "Why, Sandwich, of course," she said. So there I was, no wiser. Perhaps all the answers were right. Sometime I may get the true story, but it points up one of the fascinating aspects of a trip like mine, the things you see, the things you learn, even when you don't buy.

Camden, another vacation spot, has some good shops of more than local repute. As I had already covered the coast as far as Rockland, I cut inland and caught up a few rewarding shops that were spotted through Maine, getting down into New Hampshire again through Sanford and Rochester. I was aiming for the Concord Show, another big one and full of both local and foreign dealers. I had already met so many of them at other shows that I did not spend too much time there, enticing though the exhibits were. I wanted to get on down to Massachusetts which I sampled generously—it would have been impossible to have covered my map, which had broken out in a rash of dots like measles especially around Boston and its suburbs. But again I had met many of these names at the New York shows and what I did see convinced me that the Hub of the Commonwealth was indeed rich with relics of the past. Here is good hunting and should take in the north shore including Salem and neighboring towns as well as the south shore down to the Cape. The Cape itself I left for another trip, as it was the height of the summer season and I knew it would be overcrowded.

Over to Northampton and Holyoke via Route 5 again, and pausing a few minutes in Old Deerfield Village which I had seen a few years ago. It's well worth a visit if you are going that way. Down into Connecticut, picking up a few mid-state shops around Hartford. One thing I noticed was that the nearer I got to home, like the old mare, the less I felt like stopping. But when I did stop I made my visits more selective. Across the Hudson this time to Poughkeepsie, stopping to see a dealer whose interest in this book has been very keen and who has been of great help to me in tracking down the names for my list. I was surprised, though perhaps I shouldn't have been, at how often the dealers cooperated. I found the ones I met generally helpful and interested. Apparently one touch of antiquity makes the whole world kin.

On the way to Poughkeepsie I stopped off in Millbrook where there are several good shops, one very well known nationally and a member of the Art and Antique Dealers' League of America. It was well worth the visit even though the owner herself was not at home. It had a New York City look—a thing I noted more and more as we got nearer to that city—very sophisticated and expensive but also very authentic, with many fine imported pieces as well as top Americana.

Home now by the turnpikes where there was no temptation to stop until I pulled into my own garage, tired but with a feeling of deep satisfaction at what I had accomplished.

Cape Cod

I am glad I left this part of New England for a separate trip because I had never been out on the Cape before and there was much to see. The day after Labor Day I started out with the same antiques-loving friend who had gone to Maine with me. We went up the coast, this time using the Connecticut Turnpike part way to save time. Our first main stop was Newport, where we stayed that night and took the morning off to visit the shops and several old houses. The shops in Newport have some fine things many of which have come out of the old mansions which are now closed or given over to institutions. What an affluent society must have gathered there in the old days! Such elegance! One dealer told me there is still some entertaining being done on a large scale. He had one customer who comes in to buy china, glass, and other table settings but will take nothing less than four dozen of any one thing, as this apparently is the scale of his entertaining. In another shop were evidences of the grand oriental pieces that these big houses used in their décor—rugs, wall-pieces, statuary, etc.

Still along the coast to New Bedford and a stop at the Whaling

Museum there on Johnny Cake Hill—what a lovely name! The few shops in this town naturally went in heavily for marine and whaling items. A stop at Falmouth, and then out the south shore of the Cape finding a great succession of shops, through Santuit, Osterville, Hyannis, Dennisport, Harwichport, Chatham, and Orleans. Missing any one would have been a tragedy. I was impressed by the quality of the antiques displayed in them although it was the end of their season and most of the shops were "picking up the pieces" after a busy summer. Besides plenty of fine primitive Americana, there is a touch of distinction in what they offer, things such as fine porcelains, Sandwich glass, of course, and period furniture. The Cape has two kinds of clientele, the well-heeled owners of the summer places there and the tourists who swarm over the roads in the season. I must say I did not find too much "junk" aimed at the tourist trade. There seemed to be a certain dignity in even the smaller shops. At one shop in particular where we spent a morning I found a man and his wife who to me represented the best in every way, their shop stocked with good seasoned antiques and primitives, fine glass and china, themselves as dedicated and informed as any dealers anywhere. They answered my questions about business on the Cape generally and I felt I had got a bird's-eye view of that area.

At Hyannis we inquired about the boat trips to Nantucket but found the schedule and the time involved did not fit our plans. I was sorry, but resolved to do it another time.

We stayed at the tip of the Cape at Provincetown that night and I must say we were disappointed at its commercialism which even with the season over asserted itself on every hand. So back the next morning, this time on 6A, covering the shops along the north shore and shuttling back and forth occasionally to catch a few in the middle. In one shop in particular we did some buying because the prices were so reasonable. More Diamond Band glass for my friend here. We eyed a pair of signed Nicholas Lutz bowls at such a respectable price we almost weakened, but went on. Now I'm sorry.

Sandwich was our main objective that day with its Glass Museum now in its second year. What an experience! To see the big selection of the finest pieces all under one roof, cases and cases of sparkling lacy glass, windows with glass shelves and glassed in like cases holding rows of colored glass against the light, other cases of pressed glass and miniature pieces, other oddments of Sandwich history, was like sitting down to a banquet. We visited the shops in Sandwich before we went back to West Falmouth to spend the night with an insistent friend before setting out for home.

We went home by way of Providence this time, using the turnpikes to get us home that night. We were glad we did. The next day a hurricane struck all along the route we had left behind.

The South

It was October when I decided to devote several weeks to penetrating the South on my program of investigation. This time I had to go alone. It was not my first time to drive South and I knew the territory and roads fairly well. But I decided to go over through Delaware instead of through Washington, as I was not too familiar with the dealers in Delaware outside of Wilmington. I must admit I did not find many. I had remembered one shop in New Castle when I had gone there for an Open House Day. It was gone, but I found a new one, well worth a trip to that historic town. The two proprietors had recently moved East from the Midwest and the stock they brought with them was outstanding. To me this shop represented how happily good Americana and imported decorative items could be mixed for any décor. For instance, they showed me an elaborate knitted afghan with raised wool flowers all in the gayest colors. It was in fairly good condition, but what would one do with it? I got the answer when I met the two young men at a city antiques show. They had actually cut out the best of the coverlet and framed it for a wallpiece of decided distinction.

It was here that I saw a unique piece, a dining table about seven feet long in mahogany Queen-Anne style but with two rounded drop leaves. Opened, it made a large and impressive oval table; closed, it could stand against a wall as a serving piece. It was a very de-luxe translation, you might say, of the convenient harvest table. Here, too, I saw another oddity, a windsor chair made of steel, though painted to resemble wood. Only nine of them had been made, probably for an institution, the owners told me. Here, too, I saw some carved wood pieces—very much in demand now for wallpieces. These had been made from the top of a pilaster on some old building, cleaned down, cut in half to make a pair of wall ornaments. I put down this shop on my list as a must.

Down to Dover by Route 40, the Dupont Highway, with few stops. Scarcely anything here to report except one shop where I had a good talk with the proprietor who followed my Sunday newspaper feature regularly. "Oh, so you're the girl to blame," he said when I told him who I was. "Every time you write about something I get a rush for it, sell out, and wish I had more." I told him many dealers told me the same thing. His stuff was better than I had expected from the outside but very high in price. This was the first sign of the rise in the mercury of the price thermometer which stayed high all the way down South. That day I traced down several shops where owners were not home, or had moved, or were selling out, or were too low in stock to mention. It was disappointing.

I crossed the Potomac at the Bay Bridge and went down through Maryland on Route 301. I had visited many of the shops along the Eastern Shore during Maryland Open House Days so kept on to Fredericksburg. There I met a dealer who took pleasure in showing me her things, but I was hard put to hide my disappointment at the quality of them and the prices. But she did have a specialty, my first meeting with it in the South—Civil War items. Anything, anything at all relating to the war was welcome, she said. Like all the rest, she was getting ready for the surge in business brought on by the coming Centennial on the War in January 1961. I found the South full of such things, prints, uniform buttons, epaulets, caps, insignia, flags, documents, etc. This dealer was generous enough to give me the names of several good dealers in the vicinity and over toward Culpeper, but as I was turned south I decided to leave them for my return trip.

Down on Route 301 toward Richmond, with a few stops along the way, notably one at Hanover Court House a few miles north of the city. Here I fell in love with another fine shop run by two dedicated gentlemen. I compared it mentally with the shop I had visited in New Castle, another happy communion between fine Americana and imports such as Chelsea figures, Spode, etc. The owners pointed with pride to a real Virginia piece, a small tilt-top table with inlay, explaining how hard it now was to find native pieces like this. That day I formed an opinion which may be wrong, but it is my own. I believe that men dealers are far more serious than women, and perhaps show better taste. It may be just that their businesses are vocations, not side lines, or maybe it is because men are not afraid to spend money for what they want. They seem to go at it with more vigor and in a larger way.

Richmond is rich with shops. I could not cover many of them. It would be several days' work in itself. I took time to go to the Valentine Museum to see some of the exhibits I had been reading about. I was disappointed. It was the end of the week, Friday afternoon, people were busy, and many of the things I had read about I found were under cover. This happens quite often in museums that do not have the room to show all their treasures, I know. Some things especially attracted me—a case of Staffordshire animals that had been collected by the novelist, the late Ellen Glasgow; a room of costumes showed what the well-dressed mother of other years wore during her pregnancy. Unbelievable!

From Richmond I went east to Williamsburg, not my first trip there, fortunately, because I was not able to stay. It was Homecoming Week for William and Mary College, and there was not a single lodging left in the town. Threading my way through a web of traffic as heavy as Times Square, I finally got out and over to Yorktown where I spent the night. From there I covered shops along the Bay, Gloucester, Hampton, Virginia Beach, and Norfolk, and then inland to Suffolk and south on Route 32 to Edenton. I went out of my way to include Elizabeth City where I had spotted several places. I found one which had been practically blown away by Donna, the hurricane. Fortunately their summer shop at Nag's Head had been left intact. They were rebuilding the antiques shop which was connected with a thriving business in authentic reproductions, mostly pine and maple. This is quite a thing in the South, especially through North Carolina.

Still south on Route 17 to New Bern, where I took the tour through the newly restored Tryon Palace, a beautiful red-brick building with room after room full of antiques of the period that could have been there originally. This has been quite a project, as only one of the wings of the original palace was still standing when the restoration began, but like Williamsburg it has been faithfully reconstructed from old plans and papers. There are two good dealers in Bern with the sort of things you'd expect in a town like this.

Down Route 17 along the coast through Wilmington and Myrtle Beach with few stops—it was Sunday—until I reached Charleston. I set out early Monday morning through the streets of this town which I have often visited. Up and down Church Street and King Street I went on foot, in and out of beckoning doors, finding beautiful things. A lot of imports here, silver, objets d'art, porcelains, and period furniture. I made one purchase, an interesting plate from a set of sixteen, a French faïence piece with the history carefully written on the back.

Like a lot of the South, Charleston likes its things elegant. But I am sure—in fact, I know—that what lies within the old houses that stand tall and stately behind their garden doors and balconies is of far more importance than anything shown in the shops. Here in Charleston is one of the big shops of the country, known to all who do any buying in antiques. Here Americana flourishes as well as imported things. It is not a fine shop in the elegant sense of the word, but it is full from basement to top floor with unusual things and collectors' items. For instance, I counted at least twenty lavabos as

I wandered around the rooms unescorted. They were in every conceivable material—china, brass, stoneware, tin, and from many countries. A large case of fine paperweights, French and American, faced shelves of apothecary jars and albarellos. A series of Staffordshire cottages and pastel burners occupied a shelf above another of banks. There were lusters and metals and boxes of Civil War items through which two Middle West dealers were poking avidly as I passed. One room upstairs was given over entirely to prints. There were Audubons in large folio size, a whole series of military prints, *Vanity Fair* caricatures, and so on. It was here I stumbled over a chair over which was thrown an old rug, an amusing home-made hooked one. I learned it was called a Magic Rug, for in the center of the pattern was a ring where one stood—presumably a child—and facing a certain way could read the magic inscription hooked into the border. I suppose others of these have been made, but it was the first and only one I had ever seen.

Savannah was the next stop. The afternoon when I arrived it was too hot for anything to make much sense. It is not easy to park in Savannah, but once I had found a place I decided to leave the car and walk. There are some fine shops in this old city which is so typically southern. I felt here again the elegance which the South seems to prefer in its old things. In one of the better shops I lingered not only for the air conditioning but because the owner was so pleasant and helpful. This shop leaned to the decorative side of the business and it showed only imported things. One thing that caught my fancy was a basket full of silver, Sheffield and glass door plates brought over from England where they had been used on swinging doors in the old mansions. They were of great variety and quite beautiful with etching, openwork, and *repoussé*. When I asked what they were being sold for, the dealer said for the same purpose, to protect doors from fingerprints. Some were being used as switch plates.

Another very large business in Savannah, I found, was given over to imports, too, only here I saw more Continental pieces. I have heard that this dealer family has recently bought out a whole ninety-room château in Italy and will have to move to accommodate new stock.

Because it was so hot I kept down the coast, picking up Route A1A along the beaches where cool breezes were a relief. I did not go into Jacksonville, though I knew there were several good shops there. But I did linger at St. Augustine. There are enough shops here to keep one busy for some time. They vary from the elegant decorating establishments to the modest "cup-and-saucer" type. Here I found a doll specialist who not only sells her dolls and miniatures but makes dolls as well, molding the heads in bisque and china. I spent an hour with her in her new home and shop which she was readying for an early opening.

A motel that night at Marineland with the ocean pounding just beyond my window and more cool breezes to ease the stress of the day. Because I had been warned by several dealers that most of the shops farther south in Palm Beach, Fort Lauderdale, and Miami, would not yet be open for the season. I turned inland at Daytona to catch the many dealers with which the map of Florida is spotted. I had picked up the membership lists of two different associations and was surprised at the number of shops in Florida and also that many of them did a year-round business. Asked where they got their stock, they told me that much of it came to them from residents who had brought it South with them when they came to Florida to end their days. Others admitted they went North or bought from northern dealers. Certainly this state has few native antiques. Many of the shops are winter outlets for northern dealers who move or distribute their stock as the seasons change.

While there are a few outstanding shops in Florida they are as a rule the hit-or-miss variety that sells what it can get. One of the finest collections of art glass I have ever seen in one shop I found along the highway outside of St. Augustine. This dealer knows her trade and is in communication with many collectors all over the country. On the west coast in Tampa is another dealer whose summer shop is in Massachusetts, and whose listings are more like a museum than a shop. He seems to go in for things such as fine enamels, jewelry, and Fabergé. These are only two, but I did find others. The tourist going South for the winter will with patience be able to pick up some nice pieces if he is willing to pay the higher prices. The southern dealers do not like to be reminded that their prices are high, naturally. But it is not their fault. The fact that most of their antiques have to be brought in from other than local sources adds to the cost.

Through Florida, then, hitting the towns such as Orlando, Winter Park, Ocala, De Land, Silver Springs, Lake Wales, Lakeland, Tampa (not St. Petersburg), and back to Lake City to start North into Georgia where the hot weather broke that afternoon after a heavy rainstorm.

There are not many wayside shops in Georgia. They are clustered in and near the cities, Macon, Columbus, and Atlanta. I stopped off at two towns, Barnesville and Griffin, spotted on my map. In the first I found a fine business in a lovely house full of such distinctive pieces as mahogany banquet tables, portraits, imported items, an occasional old southern piece, and some unique things such as a high-backed chair with eagle carving at the back, reminiscent of New England and Samuel McIntire of Salem. At the second shop along the main highway I felt I was back home because I recognized so many pieces which I felt sure had come from a wholesale dealer in my neighborhood. I was not surprised when the friendly older woman, who said she was the mother of the owner, told me her son was up North buying.

I planned to stay in the heart of Atlanta that night so I would have no difficulty in reaching the city dealers there. I felt I should cover them rather closely, as they seemed to represent the core of Georgia's antique business. After I had learned to distinguish between Peachtree Street N.E. and Peachtree N.W. I made progress. Here, if I had not suspected it before, was spread out the whole elaborate and pretentious antiques business of the South. Elegance is the word. And to get it most of the dealers have to import it. Crystal chandeliers, French ormolu, Italian credenzas with painted bodies and marble tops. Chelsea figures, Worcester tea sets, armoires, and gilt mirrors all in such profusion they made me gasp—yes, gasp—at what the fine homes of Atlanta and other Georgian homes must be like and the money they represented. In one of the best shops which I sought out first I was met at the door by a neatly uniformed colored maid who handed me over to a young assistant from upstairs who showed me through a succession of rooms of the proportions of a museum. Though I had made it plain I had not come in to buy, he was most courteous, not "long in the nose," as I had been warned I might find this shop. When the subject of Doughty birds came up I happened to confess I knew about them but had never seen one. He took the trouble to go up to a storeroom and bring one down for me to look at, all packed up in its special case. These are the beautiful colored ceramic birds of various species created by a modern sculptor and much in demand. They are expensive but right in every way to consort with the finest Meissen and Chelsea.

Farther out on Peachtree Street I went into another establishment similar to this first one. The owner here was a personable young man with whom I felt on familiar footing, as we had covered much the same territory in England this past summer. I was even able to give him the names of a few shops he had missed. I felt I could ask him a question which bothered me: what had happened to all the fine antiques that the South must have once possessed? Books have been written about the treasures of the South, but where were they— outside of museums? First of all, he said that many were still tightly held by the old families. Pride ran high here, and what was left was highly cherished. Museums had absorbed much, also restorations. Much had been destroyed by the War, meaning the Civil War, of course, and much had been taken North by the Union troops. Much, too, had been given away to the servants who had not valued them enough to preserve them. I suppose this is true. I remembered one southern trip I made when I included the Natchez Pilgrimage and went through some of the old houses. I had been surprised to find the furnishings more Victorian than anything earlier. These pieces are still available, but where are the early ones?

In one small shop on Peachtree Street with no claim to elegance I found a dealer who had some very nice pieces of early-American glass, though most of her shop was given over to small antiques of lesser importance. Still, there was evidence of good taste if not of age. Here I bought a curious dumbbell-shaped bottle of weathered aqua glass which the dealer said had been picked up on the beach beyond Savannah. Someone had brought in a whole boxful of them. She thought they were old rum bottles off a ship and washed in by the sea dear knows how long ago. Maybe, maybe not. At any rate, it is interesting.

From Atlanta I decided to return North inland through the mountains. Again I was fairly familiar with the resort areas around Highlands, Asheville, Hendersonville, etc., having spent summer weeks in the locality. I also knew Blowing Rock and Lenoir, having toured—not as an actress, but a sort of chaperon—one summer with Bob Porterfield's Barter Theatre troups in that section. This whole part of the country is beautiful driving, but tedious, with serpentine roads that are hard on the braking foot as you round one curve after another. I aimed for a motel at Brevard that night and almost missed out because of the weekend traffic. I think everyone had come out to see the autumn colors in the mountains that week. I finally found shelter in a very clean little cottage-type hostelry, but it was cold in spite of the electric heater.

There are some shops scattered around this North Carolina region but not in great numbers. Asheville has a few good ones. Unfortunately I hit that part of the state on Sunday and found many shops closed. I checked and found that the Old Salem restoration at Winston-Salem was open so I spent the afternoon there. It was well worth while. This is another Williamsburg in its way, with many of the old buildings still standing. In 1776 the Moravians, a religious sect, followers of John (or Jan) Hus, settled the region and planned the town as an ideal community. They made many of their own things, particularly pottery, brick, and tiles. I was interested in the tall tile stoves that I saw in several of the houses, similar to the ceramic stoves of middle Europe. Five of the houses are open in the quiet village where some private families still live and where several antiques shops—closed, of course—seem to prosper. The Salem Academy and College, a thriving institution, occupies several of the old houses built in the late 1700's.

I had been tempted to go North by way of the Blue Ridge and the Skyline Drive, a scenic extravaganza in any season. But it had turned so cold and windy I decided to keep east of the mountains in Virginia—and I was glad I did. Even so, I was practically blown back to Pennsylvania with winds of forty-five miles an hour and got home to find there had been snow—in October!

But I was able to stop along the way at some of the Virginia and Maryland places I had missed on the way down. I particularly wanted to find out what there was in Charlottesville, home of the University of Virginia and so close to Monticello, Jefferson's home. I found several good shops, and while there was still that touch of southern elegance discernible I could begin to detect the antique quality we value in the North. After all, didn't the Pennsylvania settlers go down the Shenandoah Valley taking their belongings with them? Up through Culpeper I went, looking up some of the dealers I had heard about in Fredericksburg on the way South. Then to Middleburg, where one of the top dealers of the country has her fine shop filled with period pieces. Through Leesburg into Maryland and to Frederick and from there to cut over by way of Taneytown to say hello to my good friends at *Spinning Wheel* magazine, where I checked on some names on my list. Then to Hanover and York, the home of some of the best in Pennsylvania Dutch and east on the Lincoln Highway home.

I have not mentioned much about New York or Pennsylvania or New Jersey because being close to home they had already provided much information about the state of the antiques business in those areas. I grew up in Pennsylvania and got my first taste for antiques and antiques buying at the country sales around Bucks and Chester counties many years ago when one could still get a nice camphor glass tumbler for ten cents. Short trips in these states have resulted in many dealer friends whom I meet again and again at shows and with whom I have been able to compare notes. Particularly is this so of New Jersey. Here is a state that is not associated with antiquity in the public mind, yet it is rich in history and full of old native things. You may not find much Wistar or South Jersey glass around any more—most of it has been gathered up by the museums, but you'll find real Americana, fine pieces from the Quaker homes close to Philadelphia and almost as many primitives as in New England. Upper New Jersey is more apt to reflect the elegance of the New York shops with many importations, but you'll find every kind of shop in this state. In fact when I think of New Jersey I think of the antiques shop every buyer dreams about, along a small road or in a small town, scattered rather than concentrated in the cities and full of buyable things. A tour through New Jersey on the way to its shore resorts will not be disappointing.

There is one thing I'd like to suggest to those who take to the road for antiques: don't miss the museums, restorations, and such along the way. There is nothing that educates one more in the subject of antiques than to see them in their natural habitat or in authentic collections. Here you'll see things you'll never or perhaps only rarely meet in the shops, and on the other hand you'll come across many things the shops display, which later you will recognize and identify with pride.

You can either plan your trip to take in some of the high spots along the way, or using the AAA tour books as I have mentioned earlier in this book, check the things to be seen and visited as you go. Let's say you are heading north from New York. We won't talk about Manhattan or Brooklyn and the many museums there—that is another story. But it might be well to take a trip out through Long Island both for the shops of which there are many and to see certain exhibits there such as the Suffolk County Whaling Museum at Sag

Harbor for relics of the whaling industry. The Suffolk Museum at Stony Brook has a Carriage House where you can see not only the collection of old carriages, wagons, and sleds but reproductions of an old cobbler's shop and a country store of a hundred years ago. Close to Stony Brook at Setauket is a typical salt-box house of the early 1700's called the Thompson House, which has been restored and equipped with the furnishings of the period. It is the head-quarters for the Society for the Preservation of Long Island Antiquities. At East Hampton make it a point to stop at "Home, Sweet Home," where the composer John Howard Payne was born, and examine the furnishings of the period 1791–1852. At Southampton there is another whaling exhibit at the Historical Museum and a showing of old cars and engines in working order at the Long Island Automotive Museum there.

But let's say you are starting up through eastern New York along both sides of the Hudson—a territory that this book covers. You may want to stop off in Yonkers to see the Phillipse Manor Hall, one of the earliest of the Hudson Valley colonial dwellings. Or make a stop at Tarrytown to go through Sunnyside, the home of Washington Irving from 1835 to 1859, furnished in the period. At Croton-on-Hudson on the east side of the river lies Van Courtlandt Manor, another restored late seventeenth-century house with all the appropriate household items and furnishings. Kingston, a Dutch trading post, has interesting old buildings with antiques of the area to be seen in the Senate House and Museum. Albany, too, has some fine old houses, notably the Schuyler Mansion and the Olcott-Ten Broeck house furnished in the Federal period. If you are coming into New York State from the west you will not want to miss the famous Corning Glass Museum near Elmira or another museum at Montour Falls, where there is a collection of political campaign items for the connoisseur. At Watkins Glen close by you will find Yankee Village on the site of the 150-year-old village of Irelandville. Many antiques are to be found in the various buildings, the 1838 manor house, church, schoolhouse, country store, and ice-cream parlor. You may want to keep on to Goshen and take a look at the Hall of Fame of the Trotter with its Currier and Ives prints and other memorials of the development of the Standard-bred horse. In the same region west of the Hudson is Monroe, where the old museum village of Smith's Clove is situated. This is another educational restoration of thirty buildings including an apothecary's shop, stove museum, clock shop, country store, gun museum, and so on.

West of Albany lies Cooperstown, the site of another ambitious village restoration in the Farmer's Museum area of the baseball memorial project. East of Albany is a place called Sand Lake where there is a Doll Museum with a collection of over eleven hundred dolls of all ages and countries. Keeping on through New York State to reach Vermont, be sure and spend some time at Old Chatham, where the Shaker Museum, housed in big barns, gives a vivid picture of the simple life and crafts as well as the ingenuity of this Shaker sect. There you'll see the real Shaker furniture, which perhaps you have only read about.

And now you'll probably turn east to Vermont and at Bennington find your way to the Bennington Historical Society's Museum, one of the finest New England has to offer with its collections of the famous Bennington stoneware, Rockingham, and Parian, as well as a lot of glass, furniture, silver, costumes, and uniforms. Continuing north on famous Route 7 you'll hit Middlebury and the Sheldon Museum with authentic furnishings and tools typical of Vermont village life of about 1829. Just south of Burlington the Shelburne Museum looms on your left, the spacious village recreation area with its lake steamer, covered bridge, and many buildings housing some of the finest collections of antiques in the country.

In all of New England you are going to be faced by dozens of restored houses as you drive along through historic countryside. If you stop at all of them, you will have no time to shop, particularly if you add visits to the many historical-society buildings. But there are of course notable exhibits it would be foolish to miss. In Concord, New Hampshire, you will certainly stop at the Historical

Society's Museum to see New Hampshire furniture and portraits. At Franklin is the home of Daniel Webster and at Hillsboro the Franklin Pierce Homestead. At Manchester, south of Concord, you have the Currier Gallery of Art, which in addition to its art has displays of glass, silver, furniture, and hooked rugs. Peterborough is a must if you are coming east from Bennington and Brattleboro, for there is situated the Goyette Museum of Americana, an opportunity to view an extensive array of dolls, furniture, glass, china, "horseless carriages," and fire apparatus—all housed in shops along a typical village street. In New Hampshire, Portsmouth is the town to linger in for its examples of early architecture. But beyond the portals of some of these houses are furnishings and items of the period. Now you will probably keep on into Maine, and here again you will find open houses, at Wiscasset, Thomaston, York, Camden, Ellsworth, South Berwick, Portland, and Kittery, to name a few. There is a good Historical Society Museum at Brunswick showing regional Americana, guns, costumes, tools, and furniture. At Searsport the Penobscot Marine Museum will attract the masculine contingent of your party.

Coming down from Maine you will linger in Massachusetts if you can tear yourself away from the shops. A trip out to the Cape is a must, and there you'll visit the Crocker Tavern at Barnstable with its eighteenth-century antiques, the Falmouth Historical Society's house showing the old wallpaper as a background for whaling items and ship models, the recently opened home of the Sandwich Historical Society with its fabulous collection of Sandwich glass. If you go over to Nantucket you will be sure to see the Whaling Museum there and some fine old houses with their period furnishings open to the public.

Back on the mainland you'll find more whaling exhibits at Gloucester and New Bedford. At Gloucester are some fine houses, among them that famous house Beaufort, a museum in itself with its many period rooms. The city of Boston has so many places of antique interest it can't be taken in, in a short time. Plan to give it plenty of time or pass it up in favor of surrounding places of antiquity such as Salem with its wonderful houses, its examples of Samuel McIntyre carvings, its Essex Institute, where some of the finest collections are housed. You'll want to stop at the Wayside Inn at South Sudbury and the houses in Concord and Lexington. At Waltham, the clock city, there is the Franklin Dennison collection of watches at the Waltham Precision Instrument Company's plant, some of the watches four hundred years old. From Worcester's Antiquarian Society's treasures you may want to veer north a few miles to find the Princeton Museum of Antique Autos, which has on view besides autos, steam engines, circus wagons, baby carriages, etc.

Of course Sturbridge Village is on your map, and time spent in the reconstructed village with its many buildings and displays of old glass, home furnishings, pottery, general store items, and all the rest will be well worth while. Another Massachusetts restoration should not be missed—Old Deerfield on Route 5, a place of great charm and full of interest to the collector of antiques.

Connecticut seems to have more than its share of old homes and historic exhibits. But it has several fine museums too that should not be missed, notably the American Clock and Watch Museum at Bristol, the Avery Memorial of the Athenaeum of Hartford, the Colt collection in the State Library of that city, and the Winchester Gun Museum in New Haven.

If you hit Rhode Island, look for restored houses in East Greenwich, Johnston, Newport (particularly the Hunter House, which stages special exhibitions of Americana), Providence, Saunderstown (Gilbert Stuart's birthplace), and Saylesville (the Eleazar Arnold House, 1687).

The scene changes when you get down to Pennsylvania; no more whaling exhibits, or clock factories (except the Hamilton at Lancaster), but plenty of exhibits of Pennsylvania Dutch primitives and mores. To find these go to Reading to the Historical Society there and the Reading Public Museum and Art Gallery, the lobby of the Hotel Brunswick in Lancaster, the Landis Valley Farm Museum started by the late Carl Dreppard near Lancaster, to the Schwenk-

felder Library at Pennsburg (for their Bible and fractur collections) ,
to the Hershey Museum in the Chocolate Town where you can see
truly authentic Stiegel glass as well as Gaudy Dutch and other native
wares, to the famous Titus Geesey rooms of the Philadelphia
Museum of Art, to the Public Library of Philadelphia's Main
Branch for the famous Henry S. Borneman collection of fractur.
One can find very old things in Pennsylvania that are not Pennsyl-
vania Dutch in origin, and to see them you should visit the Moravian
Museum at Lititz, the Doylestown Historical Society's home in
Doylestown for old tools and implements up to 1830, the Washington
Memorial Museum at Valley Forge, the Chester County Historical
Society at West Chester, Pennsylvania, the Franklin Institute in
Philadelphia, the Atwater Kent Museum in Philadelphia, and of
course the Art Museum there, the William Penn restoration, Penns-
bury Manor, at Morrisville, the Ephrata Cloisters, the Fort Hunter
Museum near Harrisburg, the 1710 House near West Chester, the
Whitefield House in Nazareth (for Moravian relics) , Hopewell
Furnace to see the workings of an old forge and furnace and the
sumptuous mansion of the ironmaster now in process of restoration
and furnishing, Gettysburg's National Museum, which houses one
of the largest collections of Civil War relics in the world.

New Jersey is not as rich in historical exhibits as some of the
other states but it does have its fine old homes and several historical
societies like those in Trenton, Freehold, Haddonfield, Cape May
Court House, Morristown, Salem, Middletown, New Brunswick, and
Hackensack, which have preserved the native antiques for visitors to
see. One restoration is in progress, the Batsto area in the Wharton
tract in South Jersey, scene of the old New Jersey ironworks. It was
here that the first Mason jars were made.

In Delaware besides the State Museum at Dover and a very fine
old house at Lewes, the Zwaanendael House of Dutch Renaissance
architecture, full of colonial antiques, the outstanding place to visit
is the famous Dupont Winterthur Museum. Here you can spend a
whole day in the rooms, which number over one hundred, but

arrangements must be made ahead of time. There is one town, New Castle, which opens its houses once a year, usually in May.

The best time to see Maryland is also during its Open House Days in the spring, a three-day affair, when many of the fine old Eastern Shore houses are thrown open to the public. Here you can see more antiques at home than in most museums. Annapolis has its fine houses, some of which are always open to the public. Baltimore, like the other cities, should be given plenty of time for its museums and houses. Don't forget the Peale Museum with its portraits by that famous artist.

Like the antiques shops, the museums dwindle in number as you penetrate the South. Virginia has its Mount Vernon, Monticello, and its star restoration, Williamsburg. There's an old apothecary shop exhibit at Fredericksburg as well as the one in Alexandria. The Mariner's Museum at Newport News is worth visiting for more than its collection of miniature carved ships. In Richmond are several museums, the Virginia Museum of Fine Arts, where the famous Pratt collection of Russian Easter Eggs can be seen, the Confederate Museum with its wealth of war relics, and the Valentine Museum with its rotating exhibitions of costumes, jewelry, fans, figurines, china, etc. At Stratford Hall, the home of Robert E. Lee is open to the public; the furnishings date from 1800.

There are plenty of things to see in the South, beautiful gardens, wild-life preserves, museums of natural history, and historic monuments, but not too many repositories of antiques. One of the finest things North Carolina has to offer is the newly restored Tryon Palace at New Bern, where every room is authentically furnished with fine colonial items. In Old Salem just outside Winston-Salem is another recent restoration of the Wachovian settlement of the Moravians begun in the late 1700's. Raleigh has its Hall of History with collections of glass, furniture, and costumes as well as other exhibits covering the first English settlements in America. One North Carolina oddity that attracts visitors is the Tweetsie Railroad, the restoration of an old narrow-gauge line near Blowing Rock. It boasts a general store and a saloon of the 1880's.

Most of South Carolina's Americana is centered in Charleston. Here are some of the most gracious houses of the South, many open to the public, and a museum with collections of glass, textiles, crafts, and implements used in early South Carolina days.

Georgia gives the traveler very little reason to stop except for an occasional old church, house, or battleground. There is a museum of the Historical Society in Atlanta.

Florida, rich in sunshine and golden fruit, has very little to offer either except the famous hobby museum in St. Augustine imported from Chicago by O. C. Lightner. But a full day can be spent here viewing the innumerable collections of Americana, which run the gamut from pocket match boxes to cut glass. Rooms are given up to such things as parasols and umbrellas, aprons, dolls, buttons, locks and keys, jewelry, badges, Rogers groups, musical instruments, cigar-store items, etc. Hardly a collectible is neglected. In St. Augustine also is the Old Spanish Treasury, a *coquina* house furnished as it was a century ago. On Lake Worth you'll find James Melton's collection of antique automobiles in his Autorama, which also exhibits things like mechanical toys, dolls, baby carriages, music boxes, and trains. At Sarasota, the circus city, there is the Circus Hall of Fame to lure collectors of circusiana and in the Museum of the Circus the McManus magic collection. In this city also is a Music Box Arcade connected with Horn's Cars of Yesterday. Antique automobiles as well as horse-drawn vehicles have been given display prestige at the Carriage Cavalcade in Silver Springs.

That about hits the high spots you will find traveling the eastern seaboard as I did. When I counted up my mileage for the several trips I made in the course of the year I found I had done over 6,800 miles. Summing up my findings, I would say that for quality and quantity of Americana go to New England—to Vermont, New Hampshire, Maine, Massachusetts, Rhode Island, and Connecticut in that order. For still more Americana of a different kind look into

New York, Pennsylvania, New Jersey, Maryland, and Virginia. Don't go South primarily for antiques. Shops are too far apart and have few pieces of local importance. Your choice is limited to fine imported items, the same as you could find on Fifty-seventh Street in New York, or stuff brought down from the North. No primitives to speak of. When I spoke to one dealer about this she summed it up with a few words. "Primitives? I can't sell them even if I could find them. What I buy and sell are just the pretty things for the home." When you do strike a shop with a variety of good authentic antiques it is more than likely to be an extension of the shop of a northern dealer gone South for the winter.

For prices I think you'll find Vermont the cheapest, at least when I was there. For the number of shops scattered throughout the state New Hampshire and New Jersey seem to share the honors. For a consistently good quality in a small area the prize goes to Cape Cod. Long Island is full of dealers who seem to repeat what New York City has to offer, more sophisticated than homely in quality. Rhode Island and Delaware, both small states with historical beginnings, for some reason are not particularly rich in dealers except in the cities, but Pennsylvania is overrun with them especially in the Dutch country of York, Lancaster, and Reading and around New Hope, Bucks County, where New Yorkers have sought the country life. Maryland and Virginia, both below the Mason-Dixon Line, have a good supply of shops with stocks similar to what you find farther north.

Of course there will be plenty of exceptions to these general statements cropping up, and I know there will be some who may not agree with my findings. That is to be expected. One swallow does not make a summer, and one survey even to the extent of mine cannot uncover all the facts. But one thing I know my readers will agree on is the fact that there is nothing more exciting than to set forth on a search for the rare, the unusual, the missing item for your collection, the unexpected piece for your home—in short, for antiques generally. Every shop is a new adventure, every road promises the possibility of a real find, every lane with its crooked sign beckons you on, every piece tucked so carefully in the back of the car is a triumph, a treasure rescued from the sea of oblivion.

And the unpacking when you get home! You spread them out for a private showing among your antiques-minded friends. "I got this tray in a shop where the proprietor's hands shook so much I was afraid to see him handle his china." Or "I love this teapot, don't you? Of course it has a slight crack, but I know it's real old Ridgeway." Or "I'm so glad I went back for this lamp. It's supposed to be Sandwich. I wasn't sure until I saw one just like it on Cape Cod." And so on and so on. A story for each piece, a memory, a newly made friend. Half the fun of traveling, they say, is what you bring back, the souvenirs, which for years will remind you of the trip and its experiences. But how much better than pine pillows and funny hats and plastic dolls are the pieces of lasting value you have bought at the little antiques shops along the way!

So fill up the car with gas, man it with a friendly crew, get out the maps, and tuck this book in the glove compartment for quick and ready reference. I hope it proves helpful to all of you who are setting forth on the antiques trail this year.

Again I say, happy hunting, and the best of loot!

Directory of Antiques Dealers

This list of dealers in the sixteen states along the eastern seaboard, arranged geographically from north to south, is intended to be helpful and suggestive rather than comprehensive. It does not pretend to cover all the dealers in this part of the country, which would be a stupendous job. It has been compiled from various sources, particularly from personal contact with the dealers, also from names provided by other dealers. Other names have come from show promotors, from antiques show exhibitor lists, from lists of various associations, local and state, from ads in the magazines—in short, from every source where a name has made itself known through some kind of advertising or publicity. If names have been left out, I am sorry.

MAINE

Auburn

Fairview Antiques, Marshall Avenue. Mr. and Mrs. Ralph Matthews. Glass, china, etc. Open all year.

Mabel F. Lamb, 128 Hampton Street. Off Route 12. General antiques, lamps and lampshades. By appointment.

Tedna's Antiques, 63 Hillcrest Street. Ted and Edna Paul. (Mr. and Mrs. Theodore Paul.) Early pine.

Augusta

McLaughlin's Antiques, Western Avenue. End of Maine Turnpike. General line.

Bangor

Samuel Stern, 416 Hancock Street. General line. Appointment suggested.

Bath

C. N. Flood, 619 High Street. Large general line, twenty-two rooms full.

Bethel

Bea Brown's Antique Shop, Main Street, opposite post office. Open June, July, and August.

Boothbay Harbor

The Little Barn, Commercial Street. Mrs. Shirley Andrews, Miss Leslie Perkins, and Robert C. Brown. Fine general line. Open June 15 to September 15. Closed Sundays.

Bowdoinham

The Old Glass Shop, Upper Main Street, nine miles north of Brunswick. Norman and Daisy Nye. Early American glass, specializing in glass cup plates.

Brunswick

Smith's Antique Shop, 4 South Street. Specializing in dolls, toys, Valentines, primitives, and advertising cards. Appointment suggested.

Barbara Giles, Antiques, 76 Pleasant Street. General line. Open all year.

Camden

W. J. French, 10 High Street, Route 1. Early New England furniture, glass, etc. Open in summer. By appointment after Labor Day.

Lillian B. Schueler, Route 1. Choice china, glass, and American furniture.

Cape Porpoise

Witch-Pot Antiques. Helen I. Pack. General line.

Coopers Mills

Ed Howe. Powder flasks, guns, swords, old books.

Damariscotta Mills

Owl's Nest Antiques, Route 213. Mrs. Janette MacMurray. Collectors' items, glass, china, early pine, maple, cherry, and mahogany furniture. Open all year.

Dixfield

Ione Harlow, 1820 House. Early furniture, glass, china, pewter, hooked rugs, primitives.

Douglas Hill—Sebago

Glass Basket Antiques. Dorothy-Lee Jones. Choice blown, Sandwich, Victorian, English, and French glass and porcelain.

Dover-Foxcroft

Robert G. Hall, 9 Essex Street. Associate, Urban B. McNaughton. Fine general line of American antiques.

Claude and Grace Jenkins, 56 West Main Street. Furniture, glass, china, copper, brass, primitives.

East Boothbay
> The Trade Shop, Route 96. Harriet and Peter Jones. Everything and lots of it.

East Otisfield
> Mr. and Mrs. Philip A. Tetu. Route 121 on Lake Thompson. General line from Maine homes. Open June to Labor Day. Also at Lewiston.

Eliot
> The Yankee Trader, Route 101, five and a half miles from Route 1 in Kittery. General line specializing in clocks in running order.

Ellsworth
> Merrill's Antiques, Route 2. Mrs. Grace C. Merrill, Mrs. Ada M. Goodwin. Glass, china, bric-a-brac.
> Red Barn Antiques, Route 230. Calista Sterling. Good general line.

Falmouth
> Reiche's Antiques, 67 Allen Avenue Extension. Good general line.
> Blue Cradle Antiques, 99 Blackstrap Road, six miles from Portland via Washington Avenue. The Henry Springers. By appointment only.

Falmouth Foreside
> Getchell's Antiques, Shore Road, Route 88, one mile from Route 1 Turnpike Exit.
> Pollyanna Shop, 301 Foreside Avenue (Route 88). General line.
> Aileen's Antiques, Junction Routes 1 and 88. 2 Providence Avenue. Aileen C. and Richard M. Wilkins. Cut glass, colored glass, china.

Gardiner
> Morrell's Antiques, 106 Highland Avenue. Hazel I. Morrell. Glass, china, bric-a-brac. Open all year.
> May C. Lawrence, 144 Brunswick Avenue. General line.

Gorham
> Greenleaf's Antiques, Fort Hill Road, Route 114. Coins, iron toys, banks, glass, china, furniture. Open all year.
> Lord's Antiques, Beech Ridge Road, North Scarboro. Specializing in pattern glass, coins, jewelry, china, art glass.
> Mrs. Lincoln L. Cleaves, Church Street. General line. Open May to October.

Hampden
> Mrs. Horace J. Chesley, Route 1. General line.

Kennebunk Lower Village
> The Forge, Mrs. Mabel T. Littlefield. A summer shop. Small antiques.

Kennebunkport

Old Eagle Book Shop, Main and Elm Streets. Mr. and Mrs. Copelin Day. Old books and some small antiques.

Pig and Saddle. Summer shop of Boston Shop. Curios and antiques.

Anna Benjamin. Specializes in lamps, clocks, Early American furniture, primitives, and collectors' items.

Kittery

Albert H. Eveleth, 14 Government Street. General line and specializing in guns. Open after April 1, Monday through Friday, also some weekends.

Monmouth

Antiquesmart, Philip Tetu and Randall Young. Wednesdays and Saturdays.

Naples Village

Goldthwaites' Antiques, Route 302. Mr. and Mrs. Earl Goldthwaite. General line of authentic antiques.

Newcastle

Maine Antiques, Route 1. Myrtle Gascoigne. Early pine, period pieces, paintings, bric-a-brac, rugs. Open after July 4.

Northeast Harbor

Hill Antique Galleries, from Ellsworth and Mt. Desert Island on Route 198. Jewelry, period pieces, clocks, mirrors. Open May 1 to December 1.

North Edgecomb

Jack Partridge. Early American furniture.

North Gorham

Three Monks Antiques. Two miles from Boody's Store at North Windham, just off the River Road. Large general line.

Ogunquit

The Matthews. Shore Road. Mr. and Mrs. George D. Matthews. China, glass, small furniture, specialty pewter. Summer only.

Orland

The King's Cupboard, Route 1. Mr. and Mrs. Samuel King. General line and collectors' items.

Pemaquid Point

Lighthouse Antiques, Route 130. Roy W. Gillespie. Glass, china, primitives, nautical items. Open all year.

Perry

The Red Sleigh Antiques, Route 1. Mrs. Walter Pottle and Miss Mary E. Hilton. Glass and small antiques. Open June 1 to October 1.

Pittsfield

Mr. and Mrs. W. T. Kenniston, Route 2. General line, much china. Open
Sundays.

Portland

F. O. Bailey Co., Inc., 72 Free Street. Large warehouse of items.

Albert H. Chelsey, 1064 Westbrook Street opposite airport. China and
glass.

Miss Jean DeLand Miller, 12 Bancroft Street. Hand decorating and
refinishing.

Olde Gothic House, 86 Spring Street. Near art museum. Good general
line.

Mrs. Ethel Carle, 12 Lightfoot Street. Glass, china, bric-a-brac, and
jewelry.

Addievilla J. Nielsen, 1442 Washington Street. Glass, china, and
bric-a-brac.

Longfellow Antique Shop, 86 Portland Street opposite post office.
Specializing in lamps.

Presque Isle

Ann's Antique Shop, 160 State Street. General line. Country-store items.

Raymond

A Point of View, Route 85. Florence Paine. Glass, china, bric-a-brac,
lamps, and small furniture.

Readfield

The 1804 House, twelve miles west of Augusta on Route 17. Mrs. Arthur
J. Fenton. General line.

Reeds Ferry

Mansion House Antiques, Anna M. Dybeck.

Rockland

Rubenstein's, Route 1. Large selection of everything.

Round Pond Harbor

Red House Antiques, on Route 32. George W. Dietz. Old and new pieces,
American and imported.

Sail-Ho Antiques, Route 32. Mr. and Mrs. Robert L. Foster. Also at
Newcastle. Furniture, glass, and china, early and Victorian.

Rumford

Goddard's Antiques. On Route 2 near town. General line.

Saco

Little Horse Antique Shop, Route 1. Bill and Thelma Howell. General
line; lamps a specialty.

Salisbury Cove

Dwight Minnich. Fine prints.

Sanford

Horse Shoe Drive Antiques, Route 109. Lower Main Street. Maud DuBois. General line.

Searsport

The Treasure House, Route 1. Liela M. and Merton F. Banks. Fine general line.

Leonard's Antiques, Route 1. General line; colored, pattern and art glass. Open daily all year.

Bob's Antiques, Route 1. General line. Fine lamp selection.

Stonington

The Tin Pedlar's Shop, Luella E. Frazier. Decorating and restoring done on trays and other tole. Lamps made. Reverse painting on glass. By appointment only.

Thomaston

Weaver's Antiques, 20 Erin Street. Lawrence S. and Evelyn D. General line. Open all year.

Topsham

Elizabeth C. White, 36 Main Street. China, glass, furniture, dolls, quilts, and painted portraits. Open all year.

Turner Center

Turner Center Antique Shop. Large general line.

Wayne

The Country Squire Shop, on Androscoggin Lake. Gladys and Henry Waitt. Good browsing shop. Castor bottles a specialty.

Wayne, North Wayne

Lonefeather Antiques, on Lovejoy Pond. Mary Sundin. Large general line.

Wells

The Edith E. Cooke Shop, Route 1. Edith E. Cooke, Don Marsh Jordan, and Robert R. James. Fine general line; lamps, paperweights, and imports.

Gray Gardens Antiques, Route 9. Mrs. Myrtle Gray. General line with accent on dolls and buttons.

Toby House, Route 1. Small summer shop of New York dealers. Small antiques.

Westbrook

Roosevelt Trail Antique Shop, Pride's Corner, 865 Bridgton Road,

Route 302. Wealtha M. Young. General line. Open May 15 to
October 1.

Winterport

Mrs. Elmer H. Clements, Route 1. Fine line of early glass, china, furniture, and rugs.

Wiscasset

The Mad Welshman's Antiques, Middle Street, left from Route 1. Ship
paintings, marine items, folk art, painted furniture, cabinet furniture.
Open all year.

Lilac Cottage on-the-Green, Route 1. Alice R. Adams. Fine period
furniture, porcelains, clocks, pewter, old silver, paintings, and marine
items.

York

Dickerin' Shop, South Side Road. William J. L. Roop. General line plus
paperweights, guns, and silver.

York Beach

Florence Leggett, 104 Broadway. General line specializing in buttons,
jewelry, and rare collectors' items.

York Corners

Sawyer's Antiques, Junction Routes 1 and 1A. E. S. Laughton. General
line plus music boxes, books, and marine items. Open May to October.

NEW HAMPSHIRE

Alstead

Edith F. Provost, Summer Street. Glass, china, and small antiques. Open
evenings and weekends.

Alton

Hill's Antiques, Main Street. Pattern and colored glass and china.

Amherst

The Carriage Shed, Route 101 going toward Manchester, on road beyond
Horace Greeley restaurant. Gladys Pestana and Arlene Smith. General
line. Open all year.

Bedford

The Holbrooks, 117 South River Road, Route 3 opposite Manchester
Country Club. Doris and Griggs Holbrook. General line.

Bow

Verna H. Morrell. On Route 3A, river road, four miles south of Concord. General line.

Bradford

Twin Cradle Antiques, Main Street, Route 103. Lee and Bertha Allen. Bric-a-brac and furniture. Open May to October.

Bristol

Rustiques for Antiques, Route 3A, Lake Street. The Friendsons. Primitives, weather vanes, wrought iron, glass, china, pine and maple furniture. Open April 1 to November 1.

Canaan

The Plunder Shop, Route 4. Robert W. Tyrrell. Guns, glass, china, and furniture.

Candia

Helen B. Thurber, Route 107A. General line, specializing in braided rugs. Open April 1 to November 1. Rest of year by appointment.

The What-Not Shop, Route 107A. Alice G. Hall and Jennie B. Amazeen. General line; small antiques. Open May 1 to November 1.

Center Harbor

Helen Halpern Antiques, Huston's Corners between Center Harbor and Moultonboro. Small antiques. Open daily and Sunday, June to September.

Vick Antiques, Route 25 at the Sutton Place between Moultonboro and Meredith. Mary Ragland. Distinctive silver, brass, china, pewter, colored glass. Open June to October.

Charlestown

Mrs. Eleanor Sawyer. Opposite Shell station, no sign. Imports, pottery, porcelains, glass, etc. Open all year.

Charlestown (North)

Finette Sullivan. Route 12. General line; rare colored glass.

Chester

The One Horse Shay, Raymond Road, Route 102. Beatrice H. Stone. General line including early fireplace items and lighting devices.

Chocorua

Lucky Acres Antiques, Route 16. Ralph Chamberlain. General line including guns, primitives, and oddities. Open all year.

Concord

House of Baldwin, 6 North State Street. General line including jewelry and silver. Open all year.

Grace Casey Gallery of Antiques, N. H. Highway Hotel on traffic circle junction Routes 2, 202, and 9. Collectors' items and decorative objects.

Kay-Winn Shop, 30½ State Street. Winnie Morrison. Glass, china, dolls, and lamps.

Margaret W. Kimball, 160 Broadway, corner of Wiggin Street. General line including tinware and jewelry. Open all year.

The Little Shop Antiques, 1 State Street. Beulah Voute. General line including tin and woodenware. Open all year.

Mary's Antiques, 9 East Side Drive, just off Routes 202, 4, and 9. Mary Vigeant. General line; china and bric-a-brac. Open all year.

Wing's Antique Shop, 101 Manchester Street, Route 3, one and a half miles south of Concord. General line. Open all year.

Contoocook

Barberry Hedge Antiques, Maple Street. Nellie and Ronald Daniels. General line.

Conway (North)

The Gralyn Antique Shop, Pearly C. and Robert A. Goldberg. Early American pieces. Open all year.

Croydon Flat

Jane's Cabin, four and a half miles north of Newport, one mile off Route 10. Jane Chworowsky. General line. Open June to October.

Deering

The Studio, Hayfields, Mrs. Ruth Hicks Wolf. Restoration of authentic designs on furniture, toleware, walls, and floors. Mirror and clock glasses.

Derry

Chickie's Antiques, Island Pond Road. Mrs. Henry A. Weber. General line. Open all year.

House O' Pine Antiques, Eden Street, off Birch Street. Pearla M. Cross. Small selection of fine pieces. Appointment suggested.

The Village Green Antiques, 10 South Main Street. On Route 28 by-pass. Dorothea Reebenacker. China and glass. Open all year.

Dover

Hanson's Antique Place, 831 Central Avenue, Route 16. Early glass, china, rugs, furniture. Open May 1 to end of October.

Picket Fence Antiques, two miles out on Broadway turn right on Rollins Road—Clements Road, Rollinsford next left. Marjorie L. Norton. Pattern glass and rose bowls. Open all year.

Dunbarton

Old Settler Antiques, seven miles west of Concord on Route 13. The Newells. General line. Open all year every day except Sundays.

Durham

Wheelwright Antique Shop, Route 125, one mile south of Route 4. H.

Jean Swett. General line, specializing in art glass, pattern glass, and china. Open May 15 to October 15.

Alex Danoff. Fine porcelains and unusual items.

Effingham

Lord's Hall at Lord's Hill, Route 153. Carlton and Marguerite Earle. Early American and later antiques. Open June through October.

Enfield Center

The What-Not Shop, Route 4A. Florence B. Emerson. China, glass, and bric-a-brac. Small pieces of furniture. Open all year.

Epsom

The Flaxwheel. Route 28 south of Epsom traffic circle. General line. Early pine furniture. Open all year.

Exeter

Edwin M. C. French, Jr., 34 Main Street, Route 101. Early American pieces.

Higgins Antiques, Shady Lane off High Street. Ruth Higgins Charles. China, glass, dolls, prints, and small furniture.

Fitzwilliam

Country Antiques, on the common. Virginia F. Smith. Iron, brass, copper, pewter, pine, cherry, and maple pieces.

Cranberry House Antiques, Junction Routes 12 and 119. General line. Open April 1 to December 31.

Davis Homestead. On old Route 12. Early pieces. Open all year.

The Mountain Shop, Reba E. Greene. General line.

Rockhollow Antiques, A. C. Stephens. Early American pieces and general line.

The Tack Room. Junction Routes 12 and 119.

Franklin

Cobwebs and Dust Antique Shop, 309 North Main Street, Route 3A. Mrs. Elizabeth N. Rowell. General line plus rugs, pewter, music boxes, kitchen utensils, etc. Open all year.

Longfellow's Antique Shop, Gardner C. Longfellow. General line.

May L. Wood, 19 West Bow Street back of Elks Club. China, art glass, colored glass cruets, bric-a-brac. Open all year.

Franklin (West)

The Duchess Antique Shop, 607 South Main Street, Route 3. Verna R. Rowell. General line.

Gilmanton

Sign of the Eagle, Frank Bigelow. General line.

Gilmanton Corner
 Trudell's Antique Shop, Edith and Edmund A. Trudell. General line
 and bric-a-brac.

Gilmanton Iron Works
 Sara A. Sexton. General line including pine furniture in the rough and
 finished; lift-top commodes. Open May to October.

Goffstown
 The 1810 House, 5 South Mast Street. Mary E. Jones. General line but
 mostly glass and china.

Greenland
 Oxbow Antique Shop, Old Portsmouth-Exeter Road. Dorothy and
 Anthony Vendetti. General line. Open all year.
 Robinson's Old Lantern Shop, Route 101, Portsmouth-Exeter Road.
 Sheldon and Eva Robinson. General line, lanterns. Handmade repro-
 ductions of lighting fixtures. Open all year.

Hampstead
 The Copper Pot Antiques, Old Stage Road, Route 121. Muriel Kalil.
 General line; buttons and post cards. Open March 20 to December 20.

Hancock
 The Flaxwheel Shop, Norway Hill Route 123 off Route 202 by-pass.
 Maybelle D. Wood. General line. Open all year.
 Ivy Shop, opposite John Hancock House. Marion Manning. Glass, china,
 furniture, bric-a-brac, and dolls.
 Otto Laxy and Kenneth Johnson. Summer shop of these Boston dealers.
 Specializing in pattern glass.

Hanover
 Marie Louise Antiques, Lyme Road, three miles from Dartmouth College.
 Glass, china, furniture. Specializes in art glass. Open all year, no
 evenings, every day.

Henniker
 James and Evelyn Wilcoxin, Routes 9 and 202. New England antiques.
 Mink Hill Farms, Mrs. Ladd. General line, fine china and glass.
 Antiques-at-the-Oaks, Marion T. Nelson. General line. Open all year.

Hillsboro
 George's Antiques, Routes 202 and 9. Country pieces.
 Georgiana's Antiques, Route 149, one fourth mile from square. Georgiana
 M. Giles. Early pine and maple, glass, china. Open all year.
 E. Kurtzner's Antique Jewelry. Near Sylvania plant on Routes 202
 and 9. Open all year.

Hillsboro Center

Olde Dunbar House, Ralph Currier Stuart. Americana and imports.

The Well Sweep Antique Shop, Edith Nelson Withington. General line of decorative antiques. Open April 1 to December 1.

Hollis

The Bargain Barn, Depot Road. Marian and Harold Farnum. General line.

Hollis Village Antique Shop, Monument Square. Harriet Carter. General line. Open April 20 to December 20. Rest of the year by appointment.

Hooksett

Sprague's, on Route 3, seven miles north of Manchester. Guns, swords and accessories, furniture, and primitives. Open all year.

Hopkinton

C. A. Van Rensselaer, Jr. In village next to Hopkinton Inn. Prints, paintings, hardware, and Americana. Open all year.

Anderson's Towne House, South Road, in village just off Route 202. New England furniture, accessories, lamps, botany print shades. Open daily all year.

Intervale

The Thomas Cottage, on Route 16, three miles north of North Conway. Grace Thomas. Small antiques.

Jaffrey

Red Sleigh Antiques, Howard Hill Road near ball park. Doris Gill. General line. April 1 to December 1. Rest of the year by appointment.

Keene

Stage Coach Antiques, Route 12, five miles south of Keene. The McKanes. General line. Open all year.

Kingston

Herbert H. Dyer, junction Routes 125, 107, and 111. General line. Open all year.

Kingston (East)

Howard S. Webster, on Route 107, half mile west of depot. General line. Open all year.

Laconia

The Gables Antique Shop, 112 Court Street, Route 3. Early American and Victorian frames, glass, china, and furniture.

Dorothy V. Randlett, on Route 106, Prescott Hill. General line. By appointment.

Scott's Antique Shop and Guest House, 127 Court Street, Route 3. Early Americana. Open all year.

Lebanon (West)

Thomas McCondach and Son. Junction Routes 4 and 10. Large stock. General line. Open all year.

Littleton

Brookside Antiques, on the Bethlehem Road. Ann and Harry Wright. Clocks, furniture, and collectors' items in glass and china. Always open.

Beal's Barn Antiques, on Route 2 at Beal House. The Gradys. Mirrors, Currier & Ives prints, pewter, silver, brass, furniture (especially beds).

Londonderry

Arun-dell Antiques, on Route 128, Monmouth Road. Mary C. Carll. General line; pattern and colored glass. Open all year.

1752 House, on Route 128. Don and Florence Kidder. General line. Open all year.

Lyme

Fenno's, on Route 10 opposite school. Jess and Sally Fenno. Furniture, china, glass, some from John Fenno house now at Old Sturbridge Village, Massachusetts. Open all year.

The Foxes. China, glass, Early American furniture.

Manchester

Amy's Antiques, 151 Goffstown Road. Amelia Mansur. China, glass, and rugs. Open all year.

Ann Chickering, 451 Beacon Street. General line and books. Open all year, every day, except Sundays.

Lion D'or Antiques, 253 Lake Avenue. Ellen Turner and Phil Leclerc. Early American, decorative furniture and paintings. New shop. Open all year.

Manchester (West)

Richter's Antique Shop, 187 Varney Street, Route 114A. General line and buttons. Open all year.

Marlow

Mandana's Antiques, on Route 10. The Loverens. General line; primitives and bric-a-brac. Open April to January 1.

Melvin Village

May Whitehead, Lake Winnipesaukee, opposite village church on Route 109 between Wolfeboro and Moultonboro. General line; collectors' items. Open May 31 to October 12.

Meredith

Bickford's Antique Shop, Highland Street opposite Congregational Church. Chester C. Bickford. General line.

The Carriage House, Main Street next to old high school. Hope Lincoln and Alzora Hale Eldridge. Prints, books, decorative accessories, china, and furniture. Open July 1 to September 15.

Ripley's Antiques. Laconia Road, Route 3. Early Americana. Open all year.

Milford

Centurywood Antiques, on Route 101 between Milford and Wilton. Harry and Celia Melendy. General line. Open April through November.

Olde Country House, 22 Union Square. Americana exclusively. Open after 1 P.M. all year.

The Woodshed, 66 Nashua Street. General line. Tin, iron, woodenware, books, and post cards.

Milton Mills

Kippy's Antiques, Main Street, two miles off Route 16. F. E. Carswell. General line; dolls, clocks, coins. Open all year.

Mont Vernon

Old Red Barn, in village, Route 13 between Milford and New Boston. Alice London Bailey. General line.

New Boston

Beulah's Antiques, Box Elder Farm, Clark Hill Road. Beulah M. Hayes. General line; hooked and braided rugs.

Harold A. Todd, River Road. Early New England pieces. Open all year.

Newbury

The Little Shop, on Route 103B at railroad crossing. Elizabeth Sheldon. General line. Open May to October. In winter, Acton Center, Massachusetts, on Route 27.

Province House, on traffic circle on 103A at Park entrance. Jack G. Sweeney. General line. Open all year.

New Ipswich

Arthur and Ramona Hovgaard, Peterborough Road, Routes 123 and 124. General line. Open all year.

New London

The Curious Shop, Route 11. Vivian Cox and Sylvia Sharpe. General line, American and imported. Open all year.

Laurids Lauridsen Antiques, one mile from Route 11 on Knights Hill. Specializing in Early American furniture, rough and finished.

Newport

Yetman's Shop, 141 South Main Street. Large general line. Open all year.

North Haverhill

Maples Antique Shop, on Route 10, four miles south of Woodsville.

Grace C. Woodward. General line. Open June 1 to October 12. In winter, 134 Oliver Street, Malden, Massachusetts.

Northwood

The Open Door, on Route 4 near Route 152. Mrs. Blanche L. Holmes. Small antiques. Open June 15 to Labor Day.

Northwood Ridge

Red Sleigh Antiques. Beatrice G. Lowrie. General line. Open March to December 1.

Nottingham

Olsen's Carriage Shed, on Route 156 off Routes 101 and 152. General line. Open May 1 to December 1.

Orford

Brass Kettle Antiques, on Route 25A. Furniture a specialty.

Ossipee

Stage Coach House, junction Routes 16 and 28. Eleanor H. Ballard. General line. Open May 30 to October 30.

Pelham

Hartley's Barn, Mammoth Road, Route 128, ten miles north of Lowell. Silver and old jewelry specialties. Closed Mondays and evenings. Open May to December.

Pembroke

The Tavern, Route 3, six miles south of Concord. Gordon and Priscilla Davison. General line and bric-a-brac. Open all year.

Penacook

The Four Winds, 98 Borough Road, one half mile west of Routes 3 and 4. Edna N. Smith. General line.

Peterborough

Brackett House, at the junction of Routes 101 and 123, one fourth mile off Route 202. Marshall Parks. New England antiques, Sheffield plate, paintings, paneling, mantels, stoves.

Strawberry Hill, Elm Street opposite Goyette Museum. Eva and Richard Day. General line including dolls, paintings, and oriental items. Open March 15 to November 15.

Pike

David's Corner, Main Street, Route 25. David Goldfeller. Open May 15 to September 10. New York address, 1664 York Avenue, New York 28.

Plymouth

The 1820 House, Routes 3A and 25, a half mile west of common. Ivanetta Morrison. General line. Open all year.

Plymouth (West)

The Uriah Pike Place, now located at the Old Turnpike School Route 3A, one mile south of circle. Howard T. Oedel. Primitives, small furniture, decorative pieces. Open July 1 to September 1.

Portsmouth

Long Meadow Inn Antiques, Mary F. Hartnett. General line. Early American pieces. Open March 15 to December 15.

Richard Mills, 3 Richards Avenue. Books, prints, marine items, local Americana.

Raymond

Gladacres Antiques, north of town, Deerfield Road, one mile off Route 101. Gladys Beebe. General line. Open May 15 to November 1.

Rindge

Barrett's Antiques, on Route 202. Edith and Ernest Barrett. Early American pieces. Open April to January 1.

Rochester

Lincoln's Antiques, 35 Prospect Street off Portland Street. Eunice I. Lincoln. General line. Open all year.

Rumney Depot

This'n That Antiques, Route 25 West. Mrs. Earle E. Andrews. General line and primitives. Open June to October.

Rumney Village

Nelson's Antiques, Stinson Lake Road. John and Kay Nelson. General line; guns.

Rye

Merrymeeting Antiques, Central Road. George C. Duquenne. Period furniture, glass, and china.

Rye Center

Ye Olde Parsonage Antique Shop and Inn. Early American pieces.

Rye (West)

Jo-Hen Antiques, Washington Road. Joan and Henry Walker. General line. Open all year.

Sanbornton

Gazalea Antiques, on Route 127, six miles north of Franklin. George and Grace Phillips. Bric-a-brac, glass, china. Open all year.

Wiggins Brothers, Route 3B. Early American pieces, paintings, and decorative items.

South Kingston

The Hawlands Shop, Route 25, eight miles from Haverhill, Massachusetts.

Mailing address, Plaistow, New Hampshire. Oriental art, jade, ivories, bronzes, jewelry, bric-a-brac. General line. Open daily all year.

South Newbury

The Roberts, new shop of seasoned collectors. Clocks a specialty.

Stoddard

The Andersons, Route 123 between Routes 9 and 10. Bertha and Robins Anderson. General line and bric-a-brac. Open all year.

Sunapee (South)

Hazel's Antique Shop, on Route 103 between State Park and Newport. Hazel Russell. General line, Staffordshire. Open May 30 to October 15.

Sutton (South)

Estelle S. Smith, on Route 114 between New London and Bradford. General line. Open all year.

Tamworth

Harry F. Damon. Specializing in Early American furniture.

Tilton

W. P. Hopkinson's Antiques, 144 Main Street. General line; country furniture. Open all year.

Jeannette Corkrey's Antiques, Route 3, Franklin Road. Early American items.

High Hope Farm, Route 3 three miles north of Tilton. Barbara Bird and Jerre Elliott. Lamps, primitives, early New Hampshire furniture, hand weaving. Open all year.

Tuftonboro Corner

The Corner Shop, six miles west of Ossipee, nine miles north of Wolfeboro. General line. Open all year.

Twin Mountain

Wynn Lodge, Route 3. Hilda B. Wynn. General line. Early items and jewelry. Open June to November. In winter, 40 Dracut Street, Dorchester, Massachusetts.

Wakefield

Gage Hill Farm, just off Route 16. Elsie and Herbert Johnson. General line; braided rugs. Open all year.

Warner

Robert Graham Chase. Primitives, furniture, and oil paintings.

Warren

Old Glass Shop Antiques, on Route 25, south of Morse Museum. O. F. Mertsch, Jr. Early collectibles in soft paste, Lowestoft, needlework pictures, glass, Bennington primitives, and small furniture. Open all year.

Weare
    Elizabeth Stokes. Eighteenth-century furniture, soft paste, porcelain, accessories and New Hampshire and Maine hooked rugs. Open all year.
Wentworth
    Louise Hackethal, on Routes 25 and 118. Early items. Open May to November.
    The Granite Post, Routes 25 and 118. Primitives, china, and furniture. Open all year.
Whitefield
    The Carriage Room Antiques, on Route 116. Paul M. Fitzmorris. General line; collectors' items.
Wilton (West)
    Brooksmeet Antique Shop, just off Route 101. L. R. and S. J. Frye. General line. Open all year. Closed Saturdays except by appointment.
Wolfeboro
    Birch Road Antiques, Route 28. Cecil M. Swift. General line. Open March through December.
    The Doe Studio, North Main Street, Route 109. General line and bric-a-brac. Open May 30 to October 12.
    Sadie A. Hutchins Antiques, Center Street, Route 28. General line locally collected.
    Marden's Antiques, Elm Street, Route 109A. Ruby K. Marden. General line.
    Miss Marie A. Robbins, 64 North Main Street, Route 109. Small antiques and primitives. Open July and August. By appointment in June and September.
Woodstock (North)
    Bonnie View Antiques, on Route 3. The Parlees. General line specializing in colored glass and china. Open June 15 to October 15.

VERMONT

Arlington
    Whimsy Antiques, Harriette G. Miller. Fine collectors' items. Summers only. By appointment.
    Marjorie Berge, one mile south of Arlington Village on Route 7. Glass, china, lamps, and unusual items. Open all year.
Arlington (East)
    Ice Pond Farm Antiques, one and a half miles east of Route 7. Mary Coyle Schafer. General line.

Ascutney

The Château, Mrs. Mildred Nichols La Panne. General line, silver, painted tin. Open June 1 to October 15.

Bellows Falls

John J. Biernake, 26 Old Terrace, Route 121, one block off Route 5. Furniture in the rough, primitives, glass, china, unusual decorator items. Open daily 9 to 5, evening by appoinment. May to October 15.

Bennington

Matteson Antiques, 318 South Street, two blocks south of post office Route 7. Early furniture, accessories, glass, china, and cornices.

High Meadow Farm, West Road. Thelma S. Crosland. Pine, cherry, Pennsylvania cupboards, dry sinks, dough boxes, lamps, and accessories.

Echo Hill Antiques, two miles south of Bennington just off Route 7 behind Benn-View Motel. J. O. Linkletter. China, glass, and refinished furniture.

Bethel (East)

Florence Coutant, on Route 14. General line. Open all year.

Bradford

Brass Kettle Antiques, Route 5, twenty-four miles north of White River Junction. Paul Jenkins. Specializing in antique furniture and pine-framed mirrors. Open all year.

Brandon

Antique Art, 40 Park Street. S. S. and M. G. Lontos. China, glass, silver, pewter, bronzes, paintings, rare prints, and books.

Brattleboro

Mrs. S. V. Holden, Routes 5 and 9. Large general line.

Robert Kuhn, on U.S. 5, four miles south of Brattleboro. Almost anything, with emphasis on guns and coins.

Burlington

Ebenhart Antiques, 169 Cherry Street. Glass, china, brass, bottles, lamps, and some furniture.

The White House Antiques, Route 127, North Avenue. Marjorie M. Graves. General line.

Ethan Allen Antique Shop, South Burlington. General line.

Castleton

The Weathervane, just off Route 4. Natalie and Paul Sweitzer. General line.

J. W. McCullogh, on Route 4. Furniture and primitives.

1810 House, on Route 4. J. K. Ladd. Early American china, glass, and furniture.

Chester Depot

Dorothy E. McPeck, Route 103. Open daily. Antiques for the American home.

Clarendon

Red Shop Antiques, Route 7 opposite airport. Ada Herrick Stearns. Small antiques and small furniture.

Clarendon (East)

Airline Antique Shop, about five miles south of Rutland on Airport Road off Route 103. Madeline M. Squier. General line. Open all year.

Dorset

Colonial Antiques, Route 30. Gertrude Bickel. General line; Staffordshire boxes, colored glass, braided rugs.

Egidio's Shop, Dorset Hollow. Glass, china, Chinese export china, pewter, furniture, prints. Open daily 10 to 6.

Dorset (East)

Mary F. O'Neil, off Route 7, four miles from Manchester. Early glass, lamps, historical china, Meissen, onion pattern, primitives, and collectors' items.

Gaysville

Gay Hollow Farm Antiques, Route 107. Stanley E. Myers. General line, old tools, wrought iron.

Hartland

M. Hatch, in village on Route 5 near junction Route 12. Fine old furniture and early accessories.

Highgate Falls

Hurricane Hill Antiques, seven miles north of St. Albans on Highgate Road. Mrs. Eleanor Rice Smith. General line.

Ludlow

The Village Barn, 57 Depot Street. A. T. and M. S. Baker. General line.

Lyndonville

The Christmas Tree, East Burke Road at the foot of Burke Mountain, Route 114. William A. Avery and Samuel E. Kamens. Pewter, bottles, prints, maps, primitives, lighting items, general line of Americana. Open all year.

Manchester

Skyline Antiques, five miles south on Route 7. Kay and Bill Sweets. Glass, porcelains, silver jewelry, and small furniture.

Manchester Center

Brewsters' Antiques, Bonnet Street, Route 30. Robert and Cecile Brewster. Pattern glass, china, furniture.

The Old Tavern, Route 7. Walter Clemons. Furniture, glass, decorative items. Open all year.

Middlebury

Margaret Nichols, 5 College Street. Preferably by appointment. Eighteenth- and nineteenth-century items.

Newbury

The Oxbow Antiques, Elizabeth and Richard Darling. General line; rugs, and specializing in old lamps and shades.

Northfield

Carolyn Fernandez, 15 Union Street, Route 12. Furniture, copper, brass, bric-a-brac.

Orleans

The Craft Shop Antiques, Route 5, two miles north of Barton. Ray Lunge. Lamps, clocks, china, glass, furniture.

Orwell

Nellie B. Eddy Antiques, off Route 73. General line. Open May 1 to November.

Natalie Ramsey, decorative restoration of toleware and furniture. Antiques. Lamp accessories.

Pittsford

C. H. Kelley, Route 7. Guns and general line.

Academy House Antiques, Route 7. George H. Paul. Glass, china, English imports. Open May to November.

J. F. Hofmann Shop, Main Street. Old and rare books, coins, lamps, clocks.

Poultney

Andrew Vargish, off Route 22A halfway between Poultney and Fair Haven. Early American furniture, rough or finished.

Ripton

The Woodshed, one half mile off Route 125 near Bread Loaf. Mildred Inskip. Primitives, toys, glass, china. Open July through October 12.

Rochester

Vermont Antique Shop, Route 100. Clara Emily Cass. Specialty glass.

Rockingham

Robert Avery Smith, Route 103, between Bellows Falls and Chester. Early American antiques, primitives, rugs.

Rutland

Windy Ledge Antiques, 64 North Main Street, Route 7. Early Americana. Open from November to March. Appointment advised.

Hearthside Antiques, 78 South Main Street. Ruth and Ruby Lindholm. General line.

End of the Road Antiques, 1 Aiken Place off North Main Street. George and Clara Branchaud. General line.

Agnes Farrell, 3 Curtis Avenue, just off Route 7. China, glass.

Knapp Antiques, 407 West Street on Route 4, a half mile west of business section. General line of American antiques.

Charles F. Tuttle Co., 28-30 South Main Street. Old books, maps, prints, histories, genealogies, orientalia.

Hannibal Hodges, 79 Center Street. Specialty greeting cards. By appointment.

Spafford's Antiques, 30 Cottage Street. Marian and Jack Spafford. General line.

Shelburne

Gadhue's Antiques, in village on Route 7. Early items, including textiles and primitives.

Shoreham

Alice and Win Dibble, Route 74. Prints, paintings, painting restoration, custom frames. Open all year.

South Hero

Mrs. Florence Hall Schultz, three miles south of Four Corners in village. General line. Open May to September.

South Royalton

Slater's Antiques, Route 110. Irene Slater. Unusual antique items. Clock and mirror glasses authentically reproduced.

South Shaftsbury

The Copper Lamp Antiques, five miles north of Bennington on Route 7. Ethelyn Grassel. General line.

Springfield

Skitchewaug Antique Shop, on Route 10. Mildred and Maurice Crandall. General line including luster, Sandwich, dolls, primitives, Rockingham, and wrought iron.

St. Albans

The What Not Shop, 248 South Main Street. Mrs. Ward A. Post. Lamps, dolls, glass, and china.

St. Johnsbury

Stevens Antique Shop, 87 Eastern Avenue. General line.

Harold and Ione Penniman, 14 Saint John Street, just off Route 5. Early glass and china.

Starksboro
Old Mill Workshop, Mr. and Mrs. Robert Adsit. Large general line of early glass, china, and furniture.

Stowe
The Brick and Ell, Route 100. Madeline and Franklin Skinner. General line. Open all year.

Taftsville
Whitney's Antiques, three miles east of Woodstock on Route 4. General line. Open all year.

Morrill's Antiques, Route 4 east of Taftsville and junction of Routes 4 and 12. General line.

Underhill
The Valley Exchange Antiques, Wiley and Margaret Danforth. Fine general line of glass, china, primitives, and furniture.

Wallingford
The Paul Cary Fixer Shop, Route 7, a half mile north. Maud and Paul Cary. China, glass, furniture, general line. Open all year. Closed Wednesday and Sunday A.M.

Mary E. Taylor, 40 North Main Street, Route 7. General line. Also buttons.

The Dolphin, Route 7. Thomas Harris, Jr. General line.

Wallingford (South)
Golden Eagle, between Manchester and Rutland. Phyllis Frew. Furniture, rough and finished, china, glass, etc. Open all year.

Weathersford Bow
The Bow Antiques, Route 5. Helen and Bob Smurl. General line, with accent on primitives. Open April through November.

Westminster Station
Cram's Antique Shop, on Route 5. Don and Dot Cram. Specializing in dolls and dollhouses, coins, guns, as well as a general line of antiques.

Weston
The Browserie, opposite Farrar-Mansur House. Louise Mervin and Sarah Bailey. Diversified general line.

Gay Meadow Farm Antiques, Trout Club Road. General line. Closed Mondays. Open May 15 to October 15.

Williamsville
The Betty Lamp, eleven miles from Brattleboro. Betty Pancoast. Early country furniture and lighting devices. Open summers only.

Wilmington
Arthur Pospesil, junction Routes 8 and 118, twenty miles from Greenfield.

Woodstock

Winfred E. Harding, Route 12, two miles north of Woodstock, go right at cement garage for one mile. Large stock of early and fine pieces.

John H. Martin, 16 The Green, opposite Woodstock Inn. Historical Americana, prints, paintings, broadsides, furniture, etc.

Hillary Underwood, 21 Pleasant Street. American country furniture and accessories.

Marion Field, 37 Pleasant Street, Route 4. New England furniture and accessories, primitive paintings, garden furniture, etc.

Wigren and Barlow, 29 Pleasant Street, Route 4 in village. Jack Barlow and Charles A. Wigren. Country furniture, rough and refinished, general line, decorative items. Open May 1 to November 1.

Grace Lethbridge.

MASSACHUSETTS
CAPE COD

Barnstable

Mabel Whipple Bangs, Main Street.

Blue Blinds, Route 6A. Dorothy Colonna. General line.

Brewster

Walcliff Inc. General line distinctive antiques.

Corner Shop Antiques, Route 6A. General line. Open April to December.

The Packet Country Store, just off Route 6A after leaving E. Dennis. H. Bradford Clarke. General line, country-store items. Open April to January.

Buzzard's Bay

The Old House. General line, pattern glass.

Bennett's Twin Gateway, Routes 6 and 28, Cranberry Highway. W. W. Bennett and E. J. Thieren. General line and rare collectors' items. Open April to October. (November to March part time.)

Chatham

Olive Hannon Antiques, Route 28. Period furniture, china, glass. Open June 15 to October 15.

Dennis

The Goblet Shop, New Boston Road. Jane S. Chase. Specializing in goblets and Early American pressed glass. Open April to December.

Hope Lane Antiques, Ruth W. Potter and Ida C. Watson. General line; distinctive antiques, porcelains, glass. Open June to October.

Dennisport
  Glenn Haven Antiques, Route 28. Kathryn M. Lynch. General line; glass,
    china. Closed October to April.
  Good and Hutchinson. General line.
  Tryphosa Bassett House, Depot Street. General line; pattern and colored
    glass. Summers only.
East Brewster
  Flora McCready, Foster and Point of Rocks roads. Porcelains, glass,
    furniture, pewter. Open May 15 to October 15.
East Dennis
  Robert Eldred, Windswept.
  Ship's Wheel, Routes 6A and 134. Dora and Russ Sargent. General line
    and nautical items.
East Harwich
  Brown's Antiques, Pleasant Bay Road off Route 39 or 137. General line.
East Sandwich
  The Old Time Shop, Mrs. Walter Cullity. Primitives, clocks, Sandwich
    glass.
  William M. Janse. China, glass, small antiques.
Falmouth
  Coonamasset Inn Antique Shop, Helen S. Beaman and Allard W.
    Spencer. General line; lighting items. Open all year.
  The Antiquarium, 204 Palmer Avenue, Route 28. O. D. Garland.
    Eighteenth- and nineteenth-century items, European imports. Open
    May to January. Closed Sundays.
Harwich
  Harwich House, Main Street, Route 39. Mrs. Margaret G. Levins. Good
    general line.
Nantucket Island
  The Hen Coop, Madaket Road. C. L. Sibley. Seventeenth- and
    eighteenth-century furniture, glass, china, pewter, marine items,
    paintings, scrimshaw. Open May 30 to October 1. Closed Sundays.
  Four Winds, Straight Wharf. Whaling items, scrimshaw, books, prints.
    Open June 1 to September 15.
Orleans
  Wind Song Antiques, Rock Harbor Road. Early American glass, pine
    furniture, primitives, decorative items. Open all year.
Osterville
  The Old House. Antiques, imports, objets d'art, decorative items. Open
    all year.

The Good Luck Antiques Shop, Marie Birtwistle. Good general line; porcelains, glass. Closed November to May.

Sandwich

The Brown Jug, Main Street at Jarves. Dorothy May Haines. Glass. Closed winters.

Alice Hall, Main and Jarves Streets, opposite Sandwich Museum. Specializing in glass.

Santuit

The Lockes, Routes 28 and 130. Marion and Perry Locke. Interesting general line; Americana, primitives.

South Chatham

The Butlers, Forest Beach Extension, half a mile off Route 28. General line; early Americana, pine furniture, art glass, colored glass, china, lamps. Open daily, except Sundays, June 15 to September 15.

South Dennis

Robert Ellis. Authentic ship models.

Bass River Farm, Main Street. Ruth Gordon Ellis. Early Americana, primitive lighting, treen. Open all year.

South Harwich

The Althea House, Route 28. Perley D. Porter. Stamps, coins, buttons, cards, prints, primitives. Open all year.

South Orleans

Wallace H. Furman, Route 28. Porcelain, glass, prints, furniture. Open all year.

South Yarmouth

Louise Sawyer, Bridge Street and Route 28. General line; glass, furniture. Open all year.

West Barnstable

Richard Bourne, Route 6A. Auctioneer and retail dealer in general line. Open June 1 to September 1.

West Brewster

Hilary House, Route 6A. General line and decorative items.

West Dennis

Emily and Everett Durgin, Route 28. General line.

West Falmouth

The Red Barn Antiques, Mr. and Mrs. Carlton Bourne. General line. Open May to October. Closed Sundays.

Tic Tac Toe Shop, Route 28. Albert C. Libby and Don W. Edgerton. General line.

Yarmouth Port

The Gray Goose. Route 6A.

Leslie and Ruth Pfeiffer. Route 6A. Early American furniture, glass, rugs, primitives, mirrors, and fireplace items. Open May 15 to November 15. Closed Sundays.

O. L. Griswold, Main Street, Route 6A. Fine line porcelains, glass, furniture.

Salt Acre Antique Barn, Thacher Shore Road. Ruby Wallwork.

The Wayside Shop, 94 Main Street, Route 6A. Gertrude and William Covill. Pattern, art, and blown glass, china, bottles, furniture. Open daily all year.

Abington

Diane Springhette Antiques, 101 Clapp Street, Route 123. China, glass, Victorian lamps (banquet, piano, etc.). Open all year.

Amherst

Avery's Antique Clocks, 219 Lincoln Avenue. Clocks bought, sold, and restored.

R. and R. French, 657 South Pleasant Street, Route 116 across from old grist mill. Early items, primitives, pewter, textiles, wood, and metals. Open all year by appointment.

The Wood-Shed, 150-156 Montague Road, Route 63 off Routes 28 and 116. H. A. Wood, Sr. and Jr. General line; coins, books. Open daily.

Andover

The Amber Lantern, 10 Forbes Lane. General line.

Arlington

Margaret H. Johnston, 234 Pleasant Street. Small antiques, fabrics, fans, miniature items, soft paste and export porcelain. Open all year.

Ashby

Laurelwood Antiques, Route 31, four miles north of Fitchburg. Mr. and Mrs. L. I. Boudreau. General line. Open all year.

Ashley Falls

John Bihler and Henry Coger, Route 7. General line; unusual and collectors' items.

Athol

Mohawk Antique Shop, Dwight E. Parker. General line.

Attleboro Falls

Blue Spruce Antique Shop, 267 Commonwealth Avenue. General line; glass, china.

Auburn

Fairview Antiques, 38 Marshall Avenue. Glass, china.

Belchertown

Lift the Latch Antiques, Main Street. Katherine E. Bassett. Early blown and pressed glass, lacy, cup plates, china, etc.

The Loving Cup, Route 202 near Amherst. Eighteenth-century china, glass, dolls, furniture, paintings, fire items.

Belmont

The Brown Jug, 252 Trapelo Road. General line; pattern glass, Sandwich, amberina, Tiffany, tools, pewter, china, iron, musical instruments.

Bernardston

Four Columns Antiques, Route 5. General line; spills, spooners, unusual items.

Billerica

Rachel Farmer Rosatto, Farmer's Lane.

Boston

Otto Laxy and Kenneth Johnson, 179 Newbury Street.

The Boston Antique Shop, 63 A Charles Street. F. A. Stainforth. Pewter, copper, brass, rose medallion, and Canton china.

Joseph J. Carbone, 106 Charles Street.

D'Ehrmann's, 283 Dartmouth Street.

Gebelein Silversmiths, 79 Chestnut Street.

Marika's Antiques, 126 Charles Street.

Roach and Craven, 18 Arlington Street.

Shreve, Crump and Low Co., Boylston Street at Arlington Street.

Vose Galleries, 559 Boylston Street.

Weiner's Antique Shop, 11 Park Street.

The Howland Shop, 142 Townsend Street.

Faneuil Furniture Hardware, 64 Charles Street.

Pig and Saddle (also Kennebunkport)

Queen Ann Cottage, 3 River Street.

Old English Shop, 28 Church Street.

Firestone and Parson. The Ritz Carlton Hotel. Silver.

Brockton

The Tally-Ho Antique Shop, 1508 Main Street, Route 128 to Cape Cod. Virginia M. Sperco. Victorian furniture, Revolutionary and Civil War items, glass, china, pine. Open all year by appointment only.

Brookfield

John H. Powell, Rice Corner Road. General line.

Ruggles Farm Antiques, one mile west on Route 9. Large general line specializing in early furniture and art glass.

Cambridge

Treasures and Trifles Shop.

F. L. Ball, 984 Memorial Drive. Toys, banks.

Putnam's Antiques, 1134 Massachusetts Avenue. Choice furniture, glass, china, silver.

Hubley Galleries. General line.

Canton

Mrs. Herbert Landick. Nineteenth-century art glass.

Colrain

The Village Post, Griswaldville, Route 112, four miles north of Shelburne Falls. General line; dolls, jewelry. Open all year.

Conway

Sheila's Shop, Sheila M. Taber. Choice blown and pattern glass, china, furniture. Open daily except Tuesdays, April 15 to November 15.

Dedham

Dedham Antique Shop, 622 High Street.

Dracut

Country Store Antiques, Route 113, Lakeview Avenue. Beryl A. Gunther. General line; art glass, collectors' items. Open all year Monday through Friday. Holidays by appointment.

East Bridgewater

Edward N. Ellis, 37 North Bedford Street. Furniture, glass, china.

Easthampton

The Earl B. Osborns, Route 10. American antiques in the rough. Closed Mondays.

Nell Diamond, 21 Park Street. Glass, china, furniture. By appointment in January, February, and March.

The Old Time Shop, 46 Union Street. William Krais. General line; furniture, primitives.

Glaskowsky and Co., 180 Main Street, Route 10. General line; toys, primitives. Open all year.

East Haverhill

The 1670 Tavern, 22 Wharf Lane. General line; primitives, costumes, unusual items.

Fall River

The Red Velvet Shop, 187 Rock Street (rear). General line. Daily 1 to 5 P.M. or by appointment.

Florence

Bernard Plating Works, Riverside Drive. Old patterns in sterling, flat, and plated hollow ware.

Raymond F. Murphy, 12 Keyes Street, two and a half miles west of Northampton just off Route 9. General line; country furniture, decoys, primitives, paperweights, art glass, metals.

Foxboro

Kay Biehler, 129 Oak Street. Jewelry.

Gloucester

Gloucester Art Galleries. Distinctive pieces, objets d'art.

The Redcoat, 349 Western Avenue. Collectors' items, pewter, glass, furniture.

Granville

George Abraham and Gilbert May, Route 57, West Granville. Rare glass and china.

Great Barrington

Blue Hollow Antiques, North Plain Road, Route 41, toward Stockbridge. Florence Klemenger. General line; art glass, pattern glass, dolls, furniture, lamps, china, toys. Open daily. Closed December 25 to January 5.

Greenfield

Gray Cottage Antiques, 9 Homestead Avenue. The Borge Overgaards. General line; silhouettes, flint pattern, Sandwich, Victorian glass. Open evenings and weekends.

Groton

The Barretts, Farmers Row, Route 111.

Halifax

Poor Man's Shop, Route 106. General line; nautical, country-store items.

Hampden

Hilltop Antiques, Bennett Road, fifteen miles from Springfield on the Connecticut border. Mrs. Harold F. Helberg. China, glass, wood, iron, copper, brass, tin, silver, primitives. Pine furniture, restored plank-seat chairs. Open daily except Tuesdays and winter weekends from March to December.

Haverhill

Lynch and Graham, 426 Water Street. General line. Open 12 to 6 P.M.

Guerin's Antiques, 45-47 Haseltine Street, just off Route 125 in the Bradford district. Daniel L. Guerin. China, glass, bric-a-brac. Open daily all year.

E. B. Holt, 224 Groveland Street. General line.

Ann Clohisy's Antiques, 81 Water Street, Route 110. Ann Clohisy. Glass, china, guns. Open daily.

Holyoke

Richard's Art Shop, 2020 Northampton Street. General line.

River View Antique Shop, Route 5. I. Josephson and Son. Collectors' and decorators' items. Driftwood.

Pedlar Country Store. Routes 5 and 202. Pine, metals, and Early American inn items.

Pine Nook, 88 Cherry Street. General line; glass, china.

Housatonic

Helen M. White. Haviland, quilts, spreads.

Ipswich

Pevear House. Specializing in China trade items.

Clyde Nason, 75 High Street. Early Americana.

Kingston

Helen A. Ayer, 181 Main Street, Route 3A. Decorative items, early glass, pattern glass, china, oriental items, small furniture. Open summers only. By appointment.

Lawrence

Grace Hudson, 501 Lowell Street.

Leominster

The Hemenways, 59 Church Street, just off Merriam Avenue. Peggy and Dick Hemenway. China, glass, wood, jewelry, primitives. Open all year.

Littleton

Frances C. Upton, 275 King Street, Routes 2A and 110. Lamps, decorative items, reproductions, braided rugs, coin silver, documented wallpaper, and fabrics.

Longmeadow

Estey's Antiques, 663 Longmeadow Street. By appointment only.

Malden

Ruth L. Eaton, 117 Maple Street. General line.

Marblehead

Gold Eagle Antiques, 84 State Street, opposite police station. Mr. and Mrs. Howard J. Finerty. Pine and maple furniture, refinished or in the rough, small antiques, china, glass. Open daily April to November.

Marion

The Overflow, Point Road, Captain Hadley House, Routes 6 and 105. Jill M. Miller. General line. Open all year.

Marshfield
   The Lea-Rig, Route 3A next to country club. Mrs. Edith E. Melville.
      Pewter, brass, china, Staffordshire.
Marshfield Hills
   M. Beryl Rafuse Antique Shop, Route 3A. Cut glass, pattern glass, art
      glass, and bric-a-brac. Open daily May to December.
Medfield
   Amos Clark Kingsbury, Spring Street, Route 27 Medfield to Walpole.
      General line; primitives. Open all year Thursday through Sunday.
Middletown
   Max Webber Inc., East Street. Fine furniture, rugs.
Milford
   Francis J. Drugan, 78 Purchase Street.
Montague
   Mrs. Lee Smith, Orchard Farm (also Madison, Connecticut).
Montgomery
   Attic Treasures. General line. Open April to October.
Natick
   Harry Emmons and Richard Faber, 1 Sunnyside Road.
   The Lavender Window, 181 North Main Street. Betty Emmons.
   Phyllis E. Kaufman, 85 Park Avenue.
Needham
   The Stewarts of Needham, 190 Nehoiden Street. Items for advanced and
      beginning collectors.
New Bedford
   William Kranzler, Johnny Cake Hill opposite Whaling Museum. General
      line; whaling items.
Newton Center
   Rose Janse, 336 Dudley Road. Jewelry and collectors' items.
Newtonville
   Grace S. Sawyer, 403 Walnut Street.
Norfolk
   Elizabeth R. Cutler, Leland Road. General line; glass, china.
North Adams
   The Victorian Antique Shop, 104 East Main Street. Mrs. Mary L. Demp-
      sey. General line; books.
Northampton
   Wiggins Old Tavern, Route 10. Country-store pieces, primitives.
   Elko Shop, 21 Center Street. Constance Kocot. General line; china, glass,
      silver, jewelry. Open daily except Sundays and holidays.

Pines Inn Antique Shop, 82 Bridge Street. Mr. and Mrs. John Berestka. General line; dolls, jewelry.

North Andover

Roland B. Hammond, 169 Andover Street. Authentic Americana.

Northboro

G. L. Tilden. Sandwich, cup plates, salts, Staffordshire, cameo glass, paperweights.

North Dartmouth

George Considine, High Hill House, Faunce Corner Road off Route 6 Fall River—New Bedford Highway. Early American furniture, china, and decorative items.

Northfield

Wayside Antiques, Routes 10 and 63. Mr. and Mrs. L. J. Spaulding. General line; cut glass. Open daily March 1 to December 1.

North Hatfield

Mama's Antique Shop, Greenfield Road, Routes 5 and 10. China, glass, furniture. Open May 1 to December 10.

North Reading

Pauline Fraumeni, Sunset Arms. Jewelry, china.

Norton

Paul E. Bernheimer, 10 Library Street, Routes 123 and 140. Rare collectors' items. European and Asiatic pieces before 1830. Primitive art. Antiquities. By appointment only.

Orange

Kozy Korner Antique Shop. Glass, books, antique publications.

Petersham

1738 House Antiques, Routes 32 and 122. Arnold Johnson. Early furniture, china, glass, books. Closed Fridays.

Plymouth

Amanda's Antique Shop, 10 North Street. Glass, china, furniture.

Plympton

The Just-Right Farm, Antiques and Collectibles, Route 58 between Routes 44 and 106. General line. Open all year.

Rockport

The Dolphin, Pigeon Cove. Margaret M. Kuhn. American pieces. Open July 1 to September 6. By appointment September to July. Closed Sundays and Mondays.

The High Wheel, 4 South Street. Katherine A. Geddes. Early Americana. Open April to January 1.

The Salt Box, 6 South Street. Louis Polack. Early Americana.

Christian Hill Antique Shop, 97 Main Street. Marshall Griffith.

The Corner Cupboard, 83 Main Street, Route 128. Mary Sharp Fithian. General line. Open summers daily. Winter address 2413 West 12th Street, Wilmington, Delaware.

Royalston

Blue Horizon Antiques, just off Route 68, one quarter mile from post office. Mrs. Carlton K. Wilcox. Pattern glass. Open daily all year.

Salem

Rum Shop, 170 Derby Street. Edward B. Rushford. Early American pieces, primitives.

Scituate

Lois W. Spring, 277 Country Way.

Sharon

Marian M. Hitchins, 31 Norwood Street, Route 27 off Route 1. Art glass, china. Open all year.

Sheffield

Mr. and Mrs. Ralph G. Jones, Route 7. Country antiques, pewter, furniture.

South Hadley Falls

The Johnsons Antiques, 461 Granby Road, Route 202, three miles from Exit 5, Massachusetts Turnpike. Toys, dolls, early china, glass, metals, country and New England furniture. Open daily all year.

Southwick

Carl and Celia Jacobs, Route 202. General line; American and English pewter, early lighting.

Spencer

Bemis Antique Shop, 186 Main Street. Robert H. Bemis. General line; glass, furniture. Open all year.

Harry M. Grout, 39 Cherry Street. Blown and art glass, china.

Springfield

The China Closet, 38 Washington Road off Sumner Avenue. Hertha D. Lange. China, cut glass, art glass. By appointment only.

Irene M. Wing, 16 Northumberland Street, off Alden and Roosevelt avenues. China, glass, lamps, furniture.

Still River

Colonial Antiques, Depot Road. Marion C. Gray. Quality Early American furniture, primitives, glass, china. Open all year.

Stockbridge

Beatrice J. Lennon, Main and Elm streets. Fine line porcelains, mirrors, furniture, glass.

Evelyn Dietrich Oriental Antiques, West Main Street, Route 102. Oriental items, porcelains, figurines, lamps, scrolls, prints. Open all year. Appointment appreciated.

Red Lion Inn Gift Shop. Old pieces from the inn's attics.

Stoneham

Guy Cross, 31 High Street. General line.

Sturbridge

Lib and Lem's Antiques, Main Street near Route 30. J. Lorenzo and Elizabeth C. Lemmelin. General line. Open daily.

Sunderland

The William L. Hubbards, Main Street. Large general line.

Red Salt Box Antique Shop, Clifton and Olive C. Hubbard. General line; bric-a-brac, dolls, jewelry.

Swift River

Martin K. Howes, Route 9. Collectors' items in glass, china, wood, metal, textiles, and small primitives.

Tolland

Marie Whitney, Route 57. China, glass, metals. Open daily July to December. Florida winter shop.

Ware

Quabbin Antique and Book Shop, Routes 9 and 32. Don Howe. Early furniture, wood, iron, primitive paintings.

Parkview Antiques, 55 Church Street, Route 9. Martha F. Roberson. General line; unusual pieces.

Warwick

Gracemont Antiques, Northfield Road, Route 78, half mile west at general store. Dorothea and Vincent Gillmore. General line; country-store items, refinished furniture. Open all year.

Wellesley

The Den of Antiquity, 556 A Washington Street. Leslie David. General line of unusual pieces.

Antiques Gallery, 28 Grove Street, just off square at Routes 135 and 16. General finished antiques, specializing in Chinese porcelains and connoisseur pieces. Open weekdays.

Wellesley Antique Shop, 34 Church Street, one block off square. General line; large stock china, glass. Open Mondays through Saturdays, closed Saturdays in July and August.

Wellesley Hills

The Fifields. Pattern glass, early blown glass, Staffordshire, lusters, historical blue china. By appointment only.

Mrs. Ernest Weeks Roberts, 84 Abbott Road.

Westfield

Rooster Hill Antiques, 54 Loomis Street. Florence Guinasso. Brass, copper, iron, primitive lighting items.

The Little Red Hen, Old Feeding Hill Road, Route 187. General line; small antiques. Open April 1 to November 1.

Westford

The Country Craftsman, Carlisle Road, Route 25, twelve miles north of Route 128 from Exit 36 Massachusetts Turnpike. General line; specializing in country pine, maple and cherry furniture, hand-carved eagles, and cigar-store Indians.

West Medway

The Parson's Hobby Antiques, Main Street at Route 126. Tristan Paul Knight and Mildred Pysell Knight. Winter shop, St. Petersburg, Florida. Fine collections jewelry, paperweights, enamels, silver, pewter, Wedgwood, porcelains, early blown glass, historical china, clocks, seventeenth- and eighteenth-century furniture. Open daily except Mondays June 25 to September 10.

Westminster

Old Turnpike Antiques, 7 Nichols Street. General line; buttons, unusual items.

West Somerville

Mrs. Edson W. Sanborn, 66 Conwell Avenue, near Tufts College. Glass and china. Open Wednesdays or by appointment.

West Springfield

Antique Center, 988 Riverdale Road, Route 5. Mrs. Lloyd McDonald. General line; decorative items. Open daily, except Sundays, all year.

Sidney Richards, 26 Southworth Street. By appointment only.

Whately

The Red Brick Schoolhouse, Routes 5 and 10, seven miles north of Northampton. Fred A. Adams. General line of authentic pieces. Open daily. Holidays by appointment.

Whitman

Almira's Curiosities, 29 West Street. Small antiques, oddities, no imports. By appointment only.

Lois Spring and Charles F. Buchko, 351 Bedford Street, Routes 14 and 18 opposite Toll House Restaurant. Specializing in silver, obsolete patterns in sterling and flatware, estate silver, jewelry, glass, china, paintings. Open all year. Appointments advisable in summer months.

Worcester

Raymond S. Mentzer, 150 Lincoln Street. Summer address, 39 Rocky Neck Avenue, Gloucester. Continental and American pieces.

The Bird Cage, Bessie A. Harper, 18 High Ridge Road.

RHODE ISLAND

Ashaway

Bittersweet Farms Antiques, Chase Hill Road, off Route 3. Mrs. Katharine Fyfe. Glass, china, and pine furniture. Open 8 to 5:30 daily except Sundays, May to November.

Mary and Sarah Andrews, Main Street, Route 3. Early American pieces. Open June to October. By appointment October to June. Closed Sundays and Mondays.

Barrington

George Bidden. Music boxes.

Bradford

Mrs. Margaret Collings.

Carolina

Mr. James E. Scudder, Route 112, six miles from Kingston Interchange on Route 95. Furniture only, pine and maple. Open all year.

Charlestown

Salt Box Antiques, Post Road, Route 1. Charlotte and Chris Molloy. General line; pattern and art glass a specialty. Open daily, weekdays after 4 P.M.

Coventry

Louise's Country Antiques, Nooseneck, Route 3. Louise Handfield. General line; lamps. Open daily all year.

Salsbury Treasure Chest. General line.

East Greenwich

Shirley Frazier's Pine Primitives, 55 Atherton Road, east of Route 2. Wooden pieces rough and finished, small furniture, iron, flax wheels, no china. Open all year.

Mrs. Teresa M. Boesch, South Road, nine-tenths miles west of Route 2. Early American furniture, lamps, glass, china, copper, brass, and decorative items. Open daily all year. By appointment only.

Foster Center

Mr. Charles M. Borders, North Road. General line. Open daily all year.

Little Compton
  Mrs. Clark's Shop, Meeting House Lane. General line; prints, whaling items, unusual pieces.
Pawtucket
  Zalk's Antique Shop, 15 Patt Street. General line.
Providence
  Beccari Gallery, 263 Thayer Street. French furniture, objets d'art, connoisseur items.
  Millman Antiques, 265 Broad Street. General line; coins, jewelry.
  Mrs. Roselia Angelly, 173 Gallatin Street.
  Mrs. Majorie Hardy, 97 Williams Street.
Warwick
  Joseph Docekal Jr., 1734 Post Road. General line.
West Warwick
  Trader Bob Horn, 20 Center Street. General line.
Westerly
  Mrs. Philip Gingerella, 32 Linden Street.

CONNECTICUT

Ansonia
  George Arons and Bros., 234 Wakelee Avenue, Route 8, seven miles from Merritt Parkway. Very large general line.
Ashford
  The Grey House, Route 44. Eighteenth-century American furniture, rare porcelain and glass.
Berlin
  Horton Brasses. Good source for reproduction furniture hardware.
Bethel
  Helen Vaughn, Chestnut Ridge. Shaker and Continental furniture and accessories. Closed February and March.
Brookfield Center
  Margaret Whitton, Vale Road. Dolls.
Canaan
  Floyd Parmlee. Dolls.
Canton Center
  Sarah Hubbard Putnam. Victorian items, silver, and furniture.
Colchester
  Nathan Liverant and Son. General line; New England items.
  Scott's Barn, Lebanon Road. General line. Open daily and Sunday.

Cromwell

Dodges Antiques, 668 Main Street. General line.

Darien

East Lane Antique Shop, 336 Post Road.

Essex

Birchlands, 12 North Main Street. Ethel Hall Bjerkoe. General line.

Mrs. Walter Sands, Route 80, two and a half miles from Exit 67 Connecticut Turnpike. Eighteenth-century furniture and accessories. Appointment advisable.

Falls Village

Ferguson Schmidt, Main Street. Porcelains, decorative pieces.

Farmington

Hearts and Crowns, 22 High Street. Lillian Blankley Cogan. Early New England furniture, seventeenth- and eighteenth-century accessories. Open all year. Appointment advisable.

Franklin

Bramble Farm Shop. General line; dolls.

Georgetown

Bea's Antique Shop, Route 7. General line; coins.

Glastonbury

Madden and Austin, 1746 Main Street.

Glenbrook (Stamford)

Evelyn H. Bottome, 571 Glenbrook Road. Early glass, china, out-of-print books.

The Fieldstone Porch, 48 Oakdale Avenue. Cecily and Gerry Philpot. Art glass, lamps, furniture, and decorative items.

Granby

Ye Olde Furniture Shop, Routes 10 and 102 at Manitook Lake. Maude Wheeler Carroll. Early furniture. Open daily.

Greenwich

Norm Flayderman, 44 West Putnam Avenue. Guns. Civil War items.

Mrs. Virginia Lee Wood, Cornelia Drive, American eighteenth-century furniture and accessories. By appointment only.

Hamden (New Haven)

Joseph Pari, 3846 Whitney Avenue, Route 10, four miles off Merritt Parkway. General line. Auction every second Saturday.

Hartford

Grace Dyar, 20 Vernon Street. Dolls.

Mrs. Grace T. Spencer, West Hartford. Lamps, glass, Currier & Ives prints.

Eleanor T. St. John, 25 Atwood Street. Georgian and American silver, fine china. Open all year by appointment.

Lakeville

Questover Shop, Corell's, Middleton Road. General line.

Litchfield

F. W. and Jean C. Fuessenich, Route 25. By appointment only.

Thomas D. and Constance R. Williams, West Road. Pewter, homespuns, American fireplace items.

Madison

Mrs. Lee Smith (also Montague, Massachusetts)

Mansfield Depot

Knowlton Antiques, Route 44A. Unusual furniture, glass, early hardware.

Milford

Milford Antique Shop, 87 Forest Road. Doors, mantels, paneling, etc.

Morris (Litchfield)

Kenneth B. Way, Fairy lamps, pattern glass.

Mystic

The Lennox Shop, Seaport Store.

New Britain

John and Bill Antiques, 53 Ruth Road. Woodenware, iron, brass, copper, pottery, fabrics, primitives.

New Canaan

Conrad Stein Antiques, 121 Elm Street. American and English furniture, china, glass, etc.

Hilbert Brothers, 111 Main Street. General line.

Newtown

Lincoln B. Mitchell, Sandy Hook, Route 6A, Glen Road. General line of Americana.

Lilian Jones. By appointment only.

Tobin's Art Shop, 77 Nicoll Street. General line.

Noroton

Rose Ball, 1908 Post Road. Authentic general line, collectors' and decorative items. Closed Wednesdays and Sundays.

Norwalk

Gates More, River Road, Silvermine. Lighting reproductions. By appointment only.

Silvermine Tavern. New England and country furnishings.

Norwich

Antique Grandfather Clocks, 68 Broadway.

Norwichtown

Town Green Antique Shop, 16 Elm Avenue. Exit 82 Connecticut Turnpike. New England furniture and decorative items.

Old Greenwich

William's Antique Shop, Boston Post Road. William Richmond. American and English furniture, Eighteenth-century items. Open all year. Closed Sundays.

Old Lyme

Richard T. French, Exit 70 Connecticut Turnpike. By appointment only. David and Priscilla McCoy.

Old Saybrook

Jane Wilson, 1 Hammock Road.

Little House of Glass, Boston Post Road. Elsie B. Manning. Early American furniture and china. Open daily 3 to 5 P.M. All day Saturday and Sunday.

Plymouth

Plymouth Antique and Carriage House, Routes 6 and 202. The Cleavelands, H. Edson and Florence C. General line of Americana.

Putnam

Marjorie H. Nichols, 106 Grove Street, Connecticut Routes 44 and 12. Jewelry, unset stones, beads, charms, brooches. By appointment only.

Ridgefield

Florene Maine, Route 7. General line; period furniture, primitives, Americana, porcelains, etc.

B. H. Downing, Route 7. General line; rugs, beds.

Yellow Shutters Barn, Route 7, Danbury Road. Early American and English furniture and bric-a-brac.

The Rainsfords, 22 Silver Spring Road. Furniture and Gothic paintings of seventeenth century and French nineteenth century. Open March to December by appointment only.

Salisbury

Russell Carrell, Route 44 north of village. Americana and collectors' items. By appointment.

Sharon

Shrubbery Antiques, Route 41. Mrs. William Gavin. General line.

Simsbury

The Coat of Arms, College Highway, Routes 10 and 202. Furniture, glass, china, prints.

Paul W. Cooley (West Hartford), 982 B Farmington Avenue. Quality French furniture.

Southbury

I. M. Wiese, Route 3. Doors, mantels, paneling, etc.

Southington

Just Buttons Museum, Route 10. Open May to November. Sundays and Wednesdays.

Southport

Mary Allis, on harbor, one quarter mile off Exit 19 Connecticut Turnpike. American eighteenth-century furniture, primitives, paintings, sculpture.

Stamford

Avis and Rockwell Gardiner, 60 Mill Road, halfway between Merritt Parkway Exit 34 and Bedford Village, New York. Rare Americana, collectors' items, museum pieces, oil paintings, early craftsmen's tools. Open all year.

The Morris House, 1296 High Ridge Road. Joan Morris. American furniture and period accessories, seventeenth, eighteenth, and early nineteenth centuries, pewter, Delft, Whieldon, Wedgwood, etc.

Litchfield Fine Prints, 510 Glenbrook Road.

Stonington

Crossover Books. Miniature furniture, out-of-print juveniles.

Waterbury

Enie Antiques, 1800 Meriden Road. General line; dolls, toys, miniatures.

Watertown

Mary Atwood, 79 De Forest Street. Fine early furniture and accessories.

Westbrook

1799 House, Post Road. Mr. and Mrs. Rosenbloom. Silver, art glass, jewelry, bric-a-brac. Open June to September 15.

Weston

Church Street Galleries, English house represented by Margaret L. Marcott. Fine eighteenth-century furniture and paintings. By appointment only.

Westport

The Collector's Eye, Post Road. American and Continental collectors' items.

Dolle E. Gorin, 66 East State Street.

Marie Hakola, Sturges Highway, Easton Road. General line. By appointment only.

Wethersfield

Ida M. Thomson, 79 Southwell Road. Art glass, Danish Christmas plates. By appointment.

Wilton
　Deerfield House, Route 7. Decorative line of authentic antiques. By appointment only.
　Alice G. Fitzsimons, 379 Danbury Road.
Woodbury
　Kenneth Hammitt, Route 6. Early American furniture, accessories, folk art. Open Monday to Saturday.
　Moira Wallace, Route 6. American and English pieces, country furniture, lanterns.
　Isabel Mayer, Route 6. Oriental items, furniture, paintings, ceramics, and pewter.
　Henry D. Read, Route 47, one mile from Route 202. Early American furniture, Canton, china, prints. Open daily.
　S. N. Thompson, Route 6. American folk art, glass, pewter, copper, iron, and woodcarvings.

NEW YORK
LONG ISLAND

Bay Shore
　Copper Kettle Antiques, 228 East Union Street. Helen Bailey. General line, specializing in prints.
Belle Harbor
　Joseph Seabrook Tracey, 132–06 Rockaway Beach Boulevard. Period and country furniture, porcelains, chandeliers, quilts, glass, silver, and jewelry.
Bellerose
　Chris Winther, 250–72 Jericho Turnpike. Early American and English furniture and accessories.
Bellevue
　Rarity Shop, Mrs. Rathgeber.
Bellmore (North)
　Tillie Malkin, 900 Oakland Street. General line; specializing in jewelry, china, bric-a-brac.
Brooklyn
　Anna Olensky, 611 Lefferts Avenue. Bric-a-brac, china, lamps, cut glass, art glass, pattern glass, ironstone. Open all year.
　Tess Usatin, 95 Louisa Street. General line; decorative items, bric-a-brac.
　Bunny Winters, 568 Flatbush Avenue. Decorative pieces.
　Marion Auld, 2641 East Twenty-first Street.

Cambria Heights
Syd Sarisohn Antiques, 118–26 221st Street. General line; imports.

Cedarhurst
Ruth Lando, 669 Central Avenue.

Clayton
River Farm, Littlefield's Antiques, Route 12, two miles east of town. Glass, china, furniture, primitives. Open daily April through October.

Cold Spring Harbor
Patricia Priddy.

Far Rockaway
Irving Herman, 2011 Cornaga Avenue. Bronzes, wallpieces, oriental art, furniture, and decorative items.
Kitty Horlick, 1011 Neilson Street. Jewelry.

Floral Park
Ethel B. Bennett, 166 Cherry Street. Early American glass, furniture, art glass.

Flushing
Berenice Balaban, 69–50 198th Street. General line; decorative accessories.
Muriel Waldman, 168 Northern Boulevard. General line; specializing in cut glass.
The Laffans, 135 Roosevelt Avenue. Furniture, bric-a-brac.

Forest Hills
The Shack in the Back, Vera and Ed Wolfsohn. Continental antiques, lamps, chandeliers, wallpieces, paintings.
Bobbye Heckman, 110–23 65th Avenue. Decorative china, silver, bric-a-brac.

Freeport
Bertha Krudop, 43 Mill Road.

Glen Head
Bailiwick Antiques, Bailey Horse Farm.

Great Neck
Joan David, 83 Middle Neck Road. French and English porcelains, furniture.
The Showcase, 113 Middle Neck Road. Shirley Packales and Faye Schonbrunn. Decorative Continental furniture, accessories.
The Town Shop, 96 Middle Neck Road. Alex Spano and John Reid. English and French furniture, china, glass, and decorative items.
Beatrice Weinstock, 14 Brook Ridge Road.

Hempstead (West)
Betty L. Cohen, 103 Arden Boulevard. Jewelry.

Gertrude Rosenburg, 352 Laurel Road. General line; china, bric-a-brac; specializing in jewelry.

The Gift Horse, 715 Woodfield Road. Left from Exit 18 of Southern State Parkway. Early Americana, Victorian, Civil War items, and oddities.

Wisdom Acres, 23 Ingraham Street.

Hewlett

Florence Glassman, 1603 Hewlett Avenue. Brass and Early American chandeliers.

The Lennox Shop, 1127 Broadway.

Hicksville

Antiques Unlimited, 331 West John Street. Glass, china, bronzes.

Huntington

Valdemar F. Jacobsen, East Main Street, Route 25A, two miles east of village. Eighteenth-century American furniture, paintings, porcelains, collectors' items. Open weekdays and Sunday afternoons, all year.

Menninger's Antiques, 51 Oakland Street, off Route 110 (New York Avenue). Florence Menninger. Pine furniture cupboards to footstools, lamps, china, pattern glass, tin, wood. Open daily all year.

Little Candle Shop, 47 Wall Street.

Jamaica

Saljo Antiques, 79–22 164th Street. Selma Baungold. Jewelry, porcelains, oil paintings. Open Monday through Friday all year.

Minnie Beekman, 90 Sutphen Boulevard. Jewelry.

Strauss Antique Shop, 90 Parsons Boulevard.

Jericho

Lawrence Goldsmith, Jericho Turnpike, Route 7. Americana, country furniture rough and finished.

Little Neck

Edith Derman, 49–57 Annadale Lane. Porcelains, art glass, bric-a-brac, paintings, and unusual items. By appointment only.

Long Beach

David Leder, 24 East Park Avenue. Jewelry, table flatware, old patterns.

Long Valley

The Green Barn, Route 24. Ruth Marshall.

Manhasset

Helen Eisenberg, 13–72 Plandome Road. General line; specializing in glass.

Mrs. Margaret Zervas, 65 Plandome Road.

Gold Frame Studios, 103 Plandome Road.

Merrick

Molly V. Schwartz, 310 West Merrick Road. French and English furniture and accessories.

New Hyde Park

Mrs. Taylor, 411 Hillside Avenue.

Oceanside

Rockville Antique Shop, 57 Foxhurst Road, between Long Beach and Oceanside roads. General line. Open daily all year. Sundays 2 to 6.

Ozone Park

Joseph Walter Tuths, 101–21 93d Street. General line; signed glass, cut glass, Continental porcelains and curiosities. By appointment only.

Patchogue

Joseph Brode, 100 Cedar Avenue.

Port Washington

Boulevard Galleries, 1017 Port Washington Boulevard. Furniture, china, glass, decorative items. Open daily.

Barons Antiques, 639 Port Washington Boulevard. Furniture, lamps, decorative accessories.

Josephine Kugler, 7 Brookside Drive.

Queens Village

Dorothy M. Hamilton, 80–43 232d Street. Collectors' items, Victorian shoes, miniature lamps, souvenir spoons, art glass, porcelains, figurines, figural bottles. By appointment only.

Frances Tallman, 94–33 214th Place. General line; silver, books.

Rego Park

Amir and Co., 63–84 Saunders Street.

Cele Shapiro, 65–41 Saunders Street. Art glass, cut glass, jewelry, bric-a-brac.

Charlotte Stillman, 63 Booth Street.

Rockville Center

The Red Sleigh, 632 Sunrise Highway. P. Roberts Moore. Furniture, paintings, porcelains, glass, objets d'art.

St. James

Marjorie Ogden Budd, 53 Bayberry Avenue. Fans, fan cases, miniaturia.

Selden

The Attic Antiques, 505 Middle Country Road, Jericho Turnpike, Route 25. The Cadugans. General line; Americana. Open daily except Mondays.

Setauket

Haypath House, Phil Creelman. General line.

Southampton

Marie McLauchlen, Hill Street, Route 27. General line; specializing in Rogers groups. Open daily June through September.

Stony Brook

Island Trading Co., at Stony Brook Railroad station. Alexander Berenyi and Stephen Berenyi. General line. Open daily except Tuesdays.

Uniondale

Early American Antiques, 433 Uniondale Avenue, two miles east of Hempstead. Pine country furniture, primitives, copper, brass, wood, pewter, iron, bottles. Open daily 12 to 8 P.M. all year.

Valley Stream

Yellow Spinning Wheel, 21 East Valley Stream Boulevard. Unusual items. Open Tuesdays, Thursdays, Fridays, 1 to 10 P.M.

Wantagh

Cathryn Erath, 3445 Lufberry Avenue. Fine glass, china, luster.

Westbury

House of De Forest, 327 Winthrop Street, near Exit 32 Northern State Parkway. DeForest Cole. Eighteenth- and nineteenth-century American and English furniture, accessories. Gay Nineties country store, collectors' items, decorative accessories. Open 12 to 6 daily and by appointment.

Woodbury

Lawrence Goldsmith, Jericho Turnpike east of Woodbury Road. Eighteenth- and nineteenth-century American furniture and accessories. Open daily.

Woodside

Gertrude Kretz, 3230 Fifty-fifth Avenue.

NEW YORK STATE

Albany

Central Antique Exchange, 184 Washington Avenue. General line. Open daily all year or by appointment.

Ben Vener Antiques Importer, 126 Broadway (Rensselaer). American, French, and English furniture, china, metals.

Jean Fleisher, 351 Hackett Boulevard. Jewelry, silver.

Mollie Ruslander, 15 Hawthorne Avenue. Silver, jewelry, hand-painted items.

Schlesinger's Cottage Antiques, 632 Western Avenue, Route 30. Collectors' items, dolls, china, glass. Open daily all year.

Amsterdam

The Hobby Stall, Perth Road, Route 30. Hubert and Helen Harris. General line.

Serviss Homestead, 1740 Thruway Exit 27, Route 30 to Route 161.

Austerlitz

Robert Herron, Route 22, in post office. Fine early Americana.

Billings

Schuskill House, Route 55, two miles east of Taconic Parkway. Helene and Norris Schuskill. Hudson Valley Americana.

Bronxville

Americana, 47 Dellwood Road. By appointment only.

Burnt Hills

The Red Door Antiques, 184 Kingsley Road, eight miles north of Schenectady off Route 50. Concetta P. Humphrey. General line; furniture, country pine, cherry, china, pattern glass. Open daily all year.

Chappaqua

Joy Stanley Antiques, 11 Lero Road. Authentic eighteenth-century items.

Chatham

The Top Shelf, 21 Center Street (rear of McClellan Building). Furniture, glass, buttons, clocks, ironstone. Open Sundays and evenings all year.

Chelsea-on-Hudson

Robert Seymour. Primitives.

Circleville

Henderson's Barn. Mechanical Americana.

Cobleskill

Myra C. Tinklepaugh. Furniture and unusual items.

Cornwallville

Ethel M. Watson. Belleek, Tiffany, mocha, art glass. Open September and October by appointment.

Croton-on-Hudson

Verne House Antiques, Route 9. Select general line.

Ellenville

Mrs. Roy W. Ball, 7 Hermance Street. Specialty buttons.

Fultonville

Mildred Streeter Hinds, Riverside Drive, Thruway Exit 28. China, glass, lamps, and some furniture. Open daily.

Garrison-on-Hudson

East Point Antiques, Route 9 D. Allan Dewey. General line; decorative items. Open daily and Sunday all year.

Trifles and Treasures, Mrs. Belcher.

Germantown

Country Antiques, M. Berrick. Primitive Americana.

Gilboa

Florence Brandow. Fine china, glass.

Glens Falls

Shiffrin's Antiques, nine miles south on Route 9. Morris Shiffrin. General line; furniture, glass, china, paintings, guns, jewelry, silver. Open daily May through October.

Donald Stark, Ridge Road, Route 9L, seven miles north of town. General line; specialty clocks. Open all year.

William K. Storie's Antiques, 12 Keenan Street. Ken and Arlene Storie. Glass, china, collectibles. Open daily.

The Gold Eagle, Ridge Road. Americana.

Gloversville

Anna M. Fonda, 176 South Main Street. (No sign.) Choice items.

Goshen

Marion Lewis Cobb, Scotchtown Road. Early glass, china, furniture, small antiques. Open all year. Appointment advisable.

High Falls

Tow Path House, Elsy G. Stromp. China, glass.

Hoosick Falls

McKearin's, home of the late George McKearin, glass authority. Glass and other antiques.

Hudson

Anna Hendler. Victorian pieces and primitives.

E. P. Simonson, 316 Warren Street.

Hyde Park

Thurston Thatcher. Early paintings, Americana.

Johnstown

Shuler and Duross, 230 North Perry Street, Route 30 A. General line; glass, china, furniture rough and finished. Open daily all year. Sundays by appointment.

Kingston

Eugene Brossard, 39 Franklin Street. Americana, objets d'art.

Fred J. Johnston, 63 Main Street. Seventeenth- and eighteenth-century quality Americana.

Larchmont

Mrs. Elizabeth Bates, 1880 Palmer Avenue.

Frances H. Kraus, 67 Iselin Terrace. Unusual items for the connoisseur.

Latham

Wilber's Antiques, 820 New Louden Road, Route 9 north of Albany. General line. Open daily Monday through Saturday.

Middleburgh

Mrs. Harry Stevens. China, glass, furniture.

Middletown

Four Winds, Mrs. Helen Lippert, Route 17M. General line, paintings.

Denton Hill Antiques, Route 6 and 17M between Goshen and Middletown. Janis Tusten Horton. General line.

Marie W. Johnson, 38 Roosevelt Avenue. General line.

Seeley's Old Lamp Shop, 112 East Main Street.

A. B. Patterson, Route 211 at Howells. China, glass, objets d'art.

Millbrook

Mrs. Wentworth Bacon, Route 44 near Taconic Parkway. Fine early pieces, decorative items.

Charles Woolsey Lyon, Deep Hollow Road. Guaranteed American antiques. By appointment.

John C. R. Tompkins, from Taconic Parkway, Route 44 to 82 A and two miles on Shunpike. Eighteenth-century American and English furniture and accessories. Open all year.

Millerton

The Jack Johnstons, Route 22. General line; specializing in fine lamps.

Monsey

Jeanne Walker, Hillside Avenue. French and American pieces.

Montgomery

Locke's Stock and Barrel, 10 Bridge Street.

Mountainville

Ruth O. Kranz, Taylor Road, one mile west of Route 32. Quality furniture, porcelains, glass, bronzes, brasses, accessories. Open all year.

Mt. Vernon

Pauline Sobel, 211 Claremont Avenue.

Narrowsburg

Brick House Antiques, Route 97. David Barnes. China, glass, collectors' items. Open daily May through October.

Newburgh

Olde Stone House, Route 300. Early American homespuns, dolls, lighting items, furniture, decorative and unusual pieces.

John A. Wicks, 149 Grand Street. General line Americana. Appointment advisable.

Donald MacDonald, 208 Montgomery Street.

Balmville Antique Shop, Balmville Road. Connie Kahr.

New Scotland

Betty's Barn, Route 85. Betty M. Hotaling. General line; china, glass, furniture rough or finished, lamps, copper, brass, silver. Open daily 12.45 to 5 P.M. or by appointment April 15 to November 1.

Nyack

Hill House, 55–57 Burd Street.

Paul Gabel, 109 Sickles Avenue.

Old Chatham

Celeste and Edward Koster.

Palisades

Yonderhill Dwellers, Route 9W, old meetinghouse. William O'Neil. Eighteenth- and nineteenth-century Americana. Open daily all year except Mondays.

Peekskill

Timothy Trace, Red Mill Road. Old and rare books, especially on antique collecting. Antique scientific instruments. By appointment only.

Pelham

Bornand Music Box Company.

Pelham Manor

Doris Lurcott, 4784 Boston Post Road.

Louise Winkler-Prins, Bolton Priory Cottage.

Poughkeepsie

The Carriage House, North Road, Route 9. Opposite Hudson River State Hospital. Marjorie T. Plunkett. Full line American and Continental furniture, glass, china, bric-a-brac, paintings, silver. Open all year.

The Yellow House, 34 College Avenue near Vassar College. Marionne L. Boeckel. Fine glass, china. Open daily all hours.

Pound Ridge

Mildred and Herbert Kaufmann, Scotts Corners, Route 394. Country furniture and accessories. Open daily except Mondays.

Marjorie Shop, Scotts Corners.

Putnam Valley

Victor Young Antiques, Mill Street off Route 6 between Shrub Oak and Lake Mohegan. General line. Open daily year round except Thursdays.

August Antiques, Peekskill Hollow Road.

Red Hook

Irwin's Red Cottage Antiques, 84 South Broadway, Route 9. Country furniture, lamps, china, glass, collectors' items.

Rhinebeck

Minnie Mehlig Antiques, 38 Livingston Street, one and a half blocks off Route 9. General line; china, cut glass, pattern glass, silver. Open daily any time.

Kinner and Harrigan, Albany Post Road, one mile south of Beekman Arms. Early American furniture, china, glass, folk art, Hudson Valley items. Open daily except Tuesdays May 1 to November 10.

Riverdale

David Hollander, 5806 Mosholu Avenue. General line; collectors' items.

Roscoe

Cain's. General line.

Saratoga Springs

Mabel J. Cline, Lake Lonely. General line; pressed glass. Open all year.

Little Antique Shop, Gideon Putnam Hotel, Route 9 to Spa. Unusual china, mechanical banks, collectors' items. Open daily except Sunday. Other times by appointment March 1 through October 31.

Saugerties

Verna H. Elliott, Route 32, two miles from Thruway. Furniture, art glass, china, Victorian jewelry.

Scarsdale

Tyne Burne Shop, 10 Spencer Street. Lamps, shades, glass, china, Americana, French, English, Victorian furniture. Open daily except Wednesdays.

Mathilde K. Kuss, 1259 Post Road.

Schenectady

Betty Ball Spear, 1368 Keys Avenue. No sign. Silver, china, miniature furniture, Chinese items.

Betty Lee Ingraham, Route 5S. General line.

Beatrice Platt, 1027 Wendell Avenue.

Scotia

Palmer Welch, 213 Alexander Street. General line.

Idella Shaffer, 4 Washington Road.

Sidney

The Golden Yoke, E. E. Van Horne. Furniture.

Slate Hill

Mrs. Pearl Wickham, Routes 6 and 84. General line. Painted items.

Slingerlands

The Three Trivet Shop, 27 Bridge Street. Laura Jennings Garrison. Art glass, luster, Bristol, mocha.

South Salem

Antiques on Peaceable Street, near corner of Routes 123 and 125, Merritt Parkway to Route 123. Jack and Gretchen Sharp. Primitive or country furniture of eighteenth and early nineteenth century, pewter, wrought-iron fireplace equipment, gaudy china, pottery. Open daily all year.

Spencertown

Sallie Skyberg, Route 203. General line specializing in coronation items.

Staatsburg

Harry Sylvanie and Son, Pleasant Plains Road. Turn right from Route 9G. General line; guns, swords. Open all year.

Stone Ridge

Lillian Quick. Lamps.

Tarrytown

Alfred Arnold, Heritage House, Leroy Avenue. General line.

Elizabeth Edgette, 115 Grove Street.

Tivoli-on-Hudson

White Clay Kill Antiques, Route 9G. Americana, early glass, collectors' items, furniture. Open daily all year.

Troy

R. T. Westbrook, 161 Pinewoods Avenue. Early American furniture, Delft, glass.

Tuxedo

Helen McGehee, Route 17. By appointment.

Walden

The Stone House, Route 14. Eleanor Vanek. General line; china, glass, lamps, primitives, specialty furniture. Open daily all year.

Kidd's Antique Shop, 18 Ulster Avenue, Route 208, just north of traffic light. General line; Hudson Valley and local items, jewelry. Open all year. Appointment advised.

The Yankee Shop Antiques, North Montgomery Street, Route 52. Eleanor Phelps. General line. Open all year.

The Many's Antiques, Sycamore Place, Brown Road, between Route 17K and Route 52 west of Newburgh. General line; furniture refinished and in rough; windsor chairs. Open all year.

Walkill

The Windover Antique Shop, next to railroad. Mrs. E. Lester Mack.

Furniture, china, glass, bric-a-brac, primitives. Open all year. Appointment advised.

Washingtonville

Brewster Board, twelve miles from Thruway Exit 16 (Harriman). Eighteenth-century items.

White Plains

Pearl Miller, 102 West Chester Avenue, opposite Altman's. Authentic collectors' items in pewter, glass, china, lamps, pictures.

Joan Morris, 152 Davis Avenue.

Woodstock

Betty Collins Barnes.

Pauline Stone Summers. Toys.

Donald W. Johnson, Country Club Lane.

Red Barn Antiques.

NEW YORK CITY

Consult listing from *Antiques* magazine, also the New York Antique and Art Dealers' Association.

Add these names:

Leonard Rose, 3202 Kossuth Avenue, Brooklyn.

David Sid, 765 Third Avenue. Meissen.

Robert Abels. Armor and firearms.

David J. A. Raffe.

Harry Hirsch, 213 East 55th Street. Pewter.

Frank Lustig, 1122 Madison Avenue. Ivories and enamels.

Dorothy Rose, 49 East 12th Street. Bronzes, Wedgwood, stones.

Gerald Kornblau, 926 Second Avenue. Primitives.

Anton Hardt, 104 Christopher Street.

Churchill J. Brazelton, 924 Madison Avenue.

Hammer Galleries.

Rosella Baskind, 210 East 62nd Street.

Chimney Corners Antiques, 1057 Second Avenue. Americana.

duVerrier, 202 East 47th Street.

James A. Watson, 1039 Second Avenue.

Anne Benjamin, 1398 Third Avenue.

Dolphin Importers, 187 East 64th Street.

Hobby House, 103 West 44th Street.

Jarvis House, 172 East 75th Street.

The Opportunity Shop Inc., of C. S. S. 46 West 47th Street.

Bella Rosenblatt, 355 East 55th Street.

James Van Toor III, 419 East 54th Street.

Lee Wirth, 209 East 58th Street.

Timepieces Clock Shop, 1092 Third Avenue.

The Gilded Lily, 780 Madison Avenue.

Albert Hrdina, 1237 Park Avenue.

Martin's Antiques, 1085 Third Avenue.

Motamed and Frances Pratt Inc., 235 East 80th Street.

Alice Reiss, 233 West 77th Street.

Helen Schacter, Liberty Warehouse, 43 West 64th Street.

Rose Steinman, 114 Kensington Street, Brooklyn.

Louis A. Stuart.

Lord & Taylor, Now and Then Shop, Fifth Avenue at 38th Street.

Altman's, 34th Street and Fifth Avenue.

Plummer, Fifth Avenue at 57th Street.

W. and J. Sloane, Fifth Avenue at 47th Street.

B. Paleschuck, 37 Allen Street. Brass, metals.

Argosy Gallery, 119 East 59th Street. American primitive paintings.

Toby House, 955 Second Avenue. Wedgwood, bronzes, paperweights, nautical items.

The Old Print Shop, 150 Lexington Avenue. Harry Shaw Newman.

New York Women's Exchange, Collectors' Corner, 54th Street and Madison Avenue.

William H. Lautz, 206 East 61st Street. Eighteenth-century porcelains.

Ye Olde Mantel Shoppe, 327 East 48th Street. Fireplace items.

Ellsworth and Goldie Ltd., 210 East 58th Street. Eighteenth-century furniture, objets d'art.

Edwin Jackson, 159 East 54th Street. Fireplace equipment, mantels.

Ward and Rome, 63 East 57th Street. Tole lamps.

Authentic Designs, 139 East 61st Street.

The 5 Antique Shop, 347 Amsterdam Avenue.

M. Raphael of London, 832 A Lexington Avenue.

Garvin Mecking, 1123 Second Avenue.

Florence Goldman, 995 Second Avenue.

Don Brown Antiques, 202 East 61st Street.

Marie Hahn, 227 East 89th Street.

Four Seasons, 17 West 8th Street.

J. Miles, Gay Victorian, 249 East 78th Street.

Mary Jane Shoppe, 580 Third Avenue.

Al Lewis, 2 Horatio Street. Mochaware.

The Carousel, 343 Bleecker Street.

Webster Hill Antiques, 50 Greenwich Avenue.

Susan Reed and James Karen, 49 Greenwich Avenue.

Stuart Jensen Antiques, 325 Bleecker Street.

David Ordway, 389 Second Avenue. Country furniture.

Martin Task, 29 West 47th Street.

Soupcon, 203 East 61st Street. Faïence and porcelains.

Antonio Martin, 123 Allen Street.

Julia Kuttner, 228 East 51st Street.

Thedlow Inc., 146 East 55th Street.

Margaret M. Harper, 908 Madison Avenue.

18th Century Shop, 1024 Third Avenue.

Kay and Gross Antiques, 1333 Second Avenue.

AWVS Shop, American Women's Voluntary Services, 14 East 55th Street.

Rita Ford Inc., 907 Third Avenue.

Vieux Paris Ltd., 160 East 55th Street.

Amos W. Shepard, 22 East 60th Street.

Elinor Merrell, 18 East 69th Street. 823 Madison Avenue.

John L. McHugh, 26 East 56th Street.

Linlo House Inc., 11 East 55th Street.

Richard V. Hare, 927 Madison Avenue.

W. D. Gottlieb Inc., 1166 Second Avenue.

Philip Colleck of London, 122 East 57th Street.

Belgravia House.

Chrystian Aubusson Inc., 160A East 55th Street.

Charles Hall Inc., 1020 Madison Avenue.

Oliver Varner, Brooklyn.

Richard Camp, 306 East 53rd Street. Ironwork.

The Country Imports, 1143 First Avenue. Farm and country-house items.

Frederick-Thomas Associates, Inc., 210 East 60th Street. Signs and stoves.

Orchard House, 245 East 58th Street.

NEW JERSEY

Allaire State Park
Urban Lohnes, Deserted Village.

Allendale
Signet Antiques, 111 Allendale Avenue. Genuine oriental and European items, objets d'art. Open Tuesdays, Wednesdays, Fridays, and Saturdays.

Alpine
   Alpine Antiques, Closter Dock Road, off Route 9W. Mrs. E. B. Hille. General line. Closed Mondays.
Annandale
   Grandin Antique Shop, R. C. Apgar.
Atlantic City
   Ye Olde Trading Post Inc., Guarantee Trust Building, North Carolina and Atlantic avenues. Irene Ford. Rare and unusual jewelry. By appointment only.
Basking Ridge
   Ardis Leigh, Maple Avenue. American furniture and general distinctive line. Open weekends. Appointment suggested for weekdays.
   Mary Clarke Beattie, Lilac Hill. General line.
   Sutton's Antiques, 66 South Finley Avenue, across from post office. General line; country pine and cherry furniture. Open daily except Sundays and Mondays.
Bay Head
   The Bay Shop, Mount Street at Lake. Helen Tickner. Open all year. Winter weekday appointments advisable.
   Antiques Work Shop, 184 Bridge Avenue.
Bedminster
   Hanscom, Routes 202 and 206. Early china, prints, primitives.
   Claire O'Donnell, Lamington Road. China, glass, furniture.
Belvidere
   Homer Hicks, 427 Mansfield Street, just off Route 46, nine miles below Delaware Water Gap. General line. Open daily.
   Travelers' Rest, Mansfield Street at Second Street. Elizabeth G. Chamberlin. Americana.
Beverly
   Muriel de Fulio, Perkins Lane off Route 130. Country furniture, primitives, iron, tin. Open daily all year.
Blackwood
   Black Horse Antiques, 615 Black Horse Highway, Route 42 (Blenheim). General line; dolls, pistols, paintings.
Bloomfield
   Mabel Bielitz, 12 Barnet Street. China, glass, and decorative items.
Bogota
   Bergen County Art Galleries, 54 West Main Street. Gizella Siklost. China, objets d'art, cut glass, paintings, Chinese teak, bronzes. Open daily 11 to 7 P.M. Mondays and Thursdays 1 to 8 P.M.

Bordentown

Bordentown Antiques, Route 206.

Bridgeport

The Pedricks, 20 Main Street. General line. Open daily except Thursday 12:30 to 4:45 P.M. Tuesday, Wednesday, and Friday evenings.

Bridgeton

The Hitching Post, 81 North Pearl Street, Route 77. General line. Open daily 2 to 9 P.M. Other times by appointment.

The Camerons.

Brielle

Don Armstrong, 104 Union Avenue. Americana.

Caldwell

J. E. Currie, 417 Bloomfield Avenue. General line.

Califon

Louis and Martin, Anthony Road. Furniture, glass, china. Open weekends.

Cape May

Olivia Regar. Summers only. Winter shop, Collegeville, Pennsylvania.

Cape May Country Store, Jefferson and Columbia Avenues at end of Garden State Parkway. General line; country-store items. Open April 15 to December 31.

Washington Square Shop. J. D. Nelter. Furniture.

Cape May Courthouse

A. and A. Bezaar, two miles south on Route 9. S. G. Evan. Americana. Open daily all year.

Wilhelmina E. Powell, three miles north on Route 9. General line; furniture, glass, china, lamps, lampshades. Open all year, daily, evenings by appointment.

Sidney Ewan, Shore Road. General line.

Cape May Point

Mildred Steimle, Lake Drive. Americana, early glass a specialty. Open June 15 to October 1. Winter shop in New York City, 135 East 53rd Street.

Cedar Grove

Marion Korbelak, 479 Pompton Avenue.

Chatham

Quester Antiques, 6 Myrtle Avenue. Mrs. Bertha B. Anderson.

The Franklin House, John H. Keeley, 346 Main Street.

Karl and Doris Jacobi, 31 Ellers Drive. Early American furniture, glass.

Clifton

The Old China Shop, 1076 Main Avenue. Furniture, glass, china, prints. Open Tuesdays through Saturdays. Fridays to 9 P.M.

Clinton

Clinton Antique Shop, 46 Center Street. Mrs. Louise Mastrangel. General line; Early furniture, glass, china.

Closter

A. L. Curtis and Co., 110 Schraalenburgh Road, corner of Old Rock Road. Open weekdays 1 to 5.

Dover

Olive Rinehart Boyd, Millbrook Road, Route 10. Early American furniture, primitives, quilts. Open all year. Closed Sundays. Evenings by appointment.

James H. Stickles. General line.

Dunellen

Old Yankee Shop, Elmer C. Payne. Rare guns.

East Brunswick

Natalie and Ed Goodman, Marion Thomas, 155 Turnpike Road, Route 18.

East Orange

Stable Antique Shop, 343 Cleveland Street, Garden State Parkway to Park Avenue and to Cleveland. Primitives, esoterica, specializing in American Empire items.

Lillian Stewart, 17 Summit Street.

Englewood

William Barnett Antiques, 43½ North Dean Street. Americana, unusual items. Open 12 to 6.

The Old Stone House, 488 Grand Avenue, two miles west of George Washington Bridge, one block south of Route 4. Mrs. R. F. Viegener. Early American furniture and accessories.

Farmingdale

The 1807 House, on Route 527 four miles off Garden State Parkway via Exit 96 and Route 524. Betty and Ray Davies. Americana and interesting accessories. Open all year daily except Sundays and Mondays.

Flanders

Flanders Barn, Route 206 and Flanders Road.

Flemington

Straywinds Antiques, 3 Bridge Street, Reaville Road. Karl and Mai Engerud. General line; decorative items. Open daily.

Florham Park

Carriage House (1756), Columbia Turnpike and Crescent Road. Furniture, glass, china. Open daily 1 to 5.

Marion Stillwell's Old Country Store, Ridgevale Avenue. A. Bertelo. Lighting items, glass, prints, lamps.

Fords

Betty Papp, 665 Amboy Avenue. General line.

Freehold

The House with the Brick Wall, 57 South Street. E. H. Feltus 3rd. Seventeenth- and eighteenth-century American furniture and appointments.

Homestead Antiques, Ardena Road, Route 524. Mrs. William Fellenberg. Bric-a-brac, china, glass, flowing blue china, miniature oil lamps, Victorian furniture. Open all year, Mondays through Saturdays.

The Week End Shop, 59 South Street. Early American country furniture. Open weekends and holidays and after 4 P.M. on weekdays.

Glassboro

Little Eva's Antiques, 30 North Delsea Drive, Routes 47 and 322. Specializing in art glass, china, furniture.

Grandin

Grandin Antique Shop, Route 513. Robert C. and Kenneth Apgar. Pine furniture primitives. Open daily and Sundays.

Great Meadows

Mrs. Charles F. Edsall. General line; china, furniture.

Mary de Long, Shades of Death Road.

Hackensack

The Roadrunner, 837 Main Street, seven miles west of George Washington Bridge. Country furniture, early items.

Kay Zeilner, 51 Willow Avenue.

Hackettstown

Boxwood Antiques, Route 24, two miles south of town. Irene D. Ott. Pattern glass, primitives, art glass, metals, china, colored glass a specialty. Open daily.

Haddonfield

The Red Farm House, 500 King's Highway East, Route 41. Mrs. Eleanor W. Post. Primitives, furniture, glass, china, and decorative items. Open daily all year.

Sanski Galleries, 50 Tanner Village. Early American and European paintings.

Hanover

Marie B. Parker, 30 Preston Avenue.

Hopewell

At the Sign of the Black Kettle, 47 West Broad Street, Route 518. Eliza R. Moore. General line; early tools, metals, wood, lamps, accessories. Open all year, closed Sundays.

Virginia Holcombe.

Iona

Donald Streeter, wrought-iron hardware reproductions and lighting fixtures.

Irvington

Sophia C. Poppele, 45 Bruen Avenue.

Keyport

The Opportunity Shop, 115 Broadway.

La Fayette

Pumleye's Antique Shop, Route 15. Large general line. Open daily.

Lakewood

Florence B. Smith, 602 Seventh Street. China, cut glass, hand-painted china. Appointments advisable.

Fred B. Nadler, 2161 Highway 9 — Southard.

Pauline C. Ferber, 1225 Madison Avenue.

Lambertville

H and R Sandor Inc., 8 Bridge Street, Route 202. Superior stock of eighteenth-century American furniture. Open all year except Christmas Day.

High Button Shoes, 20 Bridge Street.

Laurel Springs

Country House Antiques, Chews Landing and Clementon Road, four miles from Exit 3 New Jersey Turnpike. William B. McCurdy. Furniture and decorative pieces. Open daily, all year. Appointment suggested.

Liberty Corner

Neher's Antiques, Mary Ann Neher. Furniture, clocks.

Long Valley

The Green Barn, Route 24. Ruth Marshall. Early items, specializing in lamps. Open afternoons all year except Sundays and Mondays.

Macopin

Macopin Homestead, Macopin Road. Fine furniture.

Madison

Rose W. Olstead, English and American porcelain, prints, quilts, fabrics, rugs, lamps, scrimshaw, period and country furniture.

Mamora

The Barn, Sarah R. Wood Antiques, Route 9, Shore Road just outside of Ocean City. General line; pattern glass. Open daily June 15 to September 15. In winters by appointment at home, 34 Finley Avenue, Trenton, New Jersey.

Manasquan

Town's End Shop, 100 Union Avenue, Route 71. Bernard Townsend. Americana, period furniture, glass, china, decorative items, French and Italian furniture, decoupage. Open all year.

Hilltop House, Route 35.

Maplewood

Ruth Harrison, 1876 Springfield Avenue. General line. Open Monday to Saturday all year.

Dilly Dally Antiques, 212 Laurel Avenue. Garry Johnson. China, glass, bric-a-brac, and decorative items.

Marie O'Neill.

Marlboro

Fred T. Schoch, Hudson Street and Vandenburg Road. Early Americana, primitives. Open daily except Sunday.

Matawan

Thru the Years Shop, 27 Main Street, Routes 34 and 79. The Welsteads. China, glass, art glass, furniture, specializing in cut glass.

Maywood

Stone House Antiques, 279 Maywood Avenue.

Mendham

Velma King, Hilltop Road.

Metuchen

Betty Gorham Kaye, 158 Maple Avenue. Glass. By appointment only.

Mickleton

Mrs. Mary B. Ward, Democrat Road.

Middletown

Apple Brook Shop, Sarah A. Moore. General line.

H. Gregory Gulick, Holland Road. Early Americana. By appointment only.

Millburn

Leda Gillette, 105 Main Street. Furniture, china, glass.

The Pewter Cupboard, 2 Taylor Street, off Main Street, one block south of Millburn Avenue. Alice R. Schmidt. Furniture, china, and specializing in pewter. Daily except Sundays. Evenings by appointment.

Pearl Phelps Brown, 83 Main Street. Collectors' items, glass, china, lead soldiers, Russian spoons, post cards, signs, miniatures on ivory. Open daily except Sundays.

Elderly Things, 87 Main Street. Ruth N. Durand. General line.

Millville

Marie R. Moore, Lairton Road.

Monmouth Junction

W. P. Reynolds, Ridge Road.

Montclair

Aladdin Antiques, 219 Glen Ridge Avenue. Mabel Bielitz. China, glass, decorative items.

The Axminster, Ltd., 8 South Fullerton Avenue. English, Irish, Scotch imports, Eighteenth-century china.

Sanford Smith.

Edith May Antiques Shop, 324 Orange Road. Edith May. General line; early American, French furniture, art glass. Open daily 10 to 5, except Wednesdays. Closed February.

Moorestown

Juliana Newman Antiques, 123 East Main Street. Furniture, glass, china, paintings, mirrors, decorative items, lamps and custom shades. Daily, Friday 9 P.M. Closed April 15 to September 15.

Alfred Firth, Bridgeboro Road. By appointment only.

Ray D. Cole, 325 South Church Street.

Morristown

Katherine Wiley, 17 Georgian Road, one block from Washington's Headquarters. Furniture, china, glass, primitives.

Turtle House Antiques, 5 Egbert Hill. Ruth Salny. Pottery, china, majolica, unusual collectors' items. By appointment only.

Mountainside

Dutch Oven Antiques, 1260 Route 22. American furniture. Closed Wednesdays.

Newark

The Manse, 55 Nairn Place. Mrs. Charles Frank Bazata. Prints, unusual items.

Mina Budish, 469 Elizabeth Avenue. Silver, brass, copper, china, jewelry.

Dorothea Rosenblatt, 72 Grummon Avenue.

Newfoundland
   Cobweb Corner Antiques, Harry and Betty Grosch. Primitives, lamps, decorative items. Open Friday to Monday.

North Branch
   Ken and Mary Lawrence. General line.

Nutley
   Hazel Giblin, 70 Newman Road.

Oakhurst
   Copper Kettle Antiques, 61 Monmouth Road, one mile east of Route 35. Americana, primitives, furniture, accessories. Open all year daily except Sundays.

Oakland
   Ahler's Corner Antique Shop, Route 202. General line; early American and Pennsylvania Dutch primitives.
   Penny Exchange, Route 202. Paul Penny. General line; early American, primitive, and Pennsylvania Dutch items.
   The Carriage House, Route 202. Ethel C. Proskey. Finished early furniture, pattern glass, silver, lamps, copper.
   Edward Proskey, East Oakland Avenue, one block from railroad station, Route 202. Primitives, rough and finished furniture.

Ocean View
   Elizabeth M. Lemont, Shore Road. General line; quilts, brass, copper, unusual items.

Old Bridge
   The Country Bazaar, Mae Eleanore Brown. Early American furniture, primitives, collectors' items.

Old Tappan
   Valerie Purgold's Antique Shop, Old Tappan Road, two miles out of Westwood. Pine furniture and primitives. Open Monday, Tuesday, Thursday, Friday, and Saturday; Wednesday 9 to 1 P.M.

Orange
   The Stable Antique Shop, 343 Cleveland Street. General line. Open evenings and weekends.

Palermo
   Fred Reech, Shore Road. General line; furniture.

Park Ridge
   Josephine Rossano Antiques, 131 Kinderkamack Road, twenty minutes from George Washington Bridge. China, glass, silver, fine furniture. Open daily. Fridays until 9 P.M. Closed Sundays.

Parsippany

Joan Madsen, 849 Lake Shore Drive.

Lorene Ruth Case, 360 Halsey Road. Furniture, glass, china. Closed Tuesdays.

Paterson

Skyland, 269 Faid Street. Glass, china, silver, jewelry.

Oscar Appel, 82 Preakness Avenue. Furniture, clocks, paintings, guns, and quilts.

Ann Aslan, 104 Lily Street. Art and pattern glass, steins, decorative pieces.

Margaret Mitchell, 642 Madison Avenue. Lamps, china, brass, marble-top furniture.

Phillipsburg

Zhender's Red Barn, 491–493 South Main Street. Country pine, primitives, Pennsylvania Dutch items.

Pittston

Fiddler's Forge, James R. Marsh. Lighting fixtures authentically reproduced.

Pompton Plains

Black Oak Antiques, Old Sheffield Farm Buildings, Route 202. Lou Kisch. General line; Pennsylvania and New England primitives.

Kay Schlichting, 543 Turnpike. China, glass, small antiques.

Princeton

Millstone Antique Shop, Harrison Street near Route 1. Country furniture. Open daily. Evenings by appointment.

Quakertown

Old Village Store, James F. Steenhill. Primitives, country-store items. Open daily except Monday and Wednesday.

Rahway

Jane Roosevelt, 717 West Milton Avenue.

John E. Herman, 806 Hamilton Street. General line; furniture.

Rancocas

Marie A. Richards.

Red Bank

Burson Wynkoop. Antique decorative items.

The Hudson Shop, 511 Broad Street. Americana, prints, maps, Jersey primitives. Open daily.

Marjorie West, 155 East Newman Springs Road.

Suburban House, 123 West Front Street.

Yankee Trader, 3 Clay Street. M. Morrill.

Ringoes
> Mrs. McKittrick-Wright, Route 69 between Flemington and Trenton. French and English antiques, also American pieces. Closed Tuesdays and Wednesdays. Appointment advisable.
>
> Les Deux Moulins, Pierre Dutel.

Riverdale
> Century House Antiques, Newark Turnpike. Dorothy Hildebrandt. General line.

River Edge
> Collectors' Finds, 648 Bogart Road, one mile north of Route 4. Lillian Hirschmann. Collectors' items of early dates, porcelains, brasses, prints, fabrics, needlework, treen, miniatures, Chinese export china. By appointment only.

Riverton
> Wm. and Helen Scholl, 1600 Riverton Road.

Roselle Park
> Mildred D. Clayton.

Rutherford
> John T. Staples Antiques, 12 West Park Place, just off Park Avenue. General line. Open daily.
>
> Myrtle Binns, 19 Raymond Avenue. General line.

Scotch Plains
> Browse Around Antiques. China, primitives, glass. Open daily.

Sicklerville
> Anne Russell, New Freedom Road, between Black Horse and White Horse pikes. Rare books, buttons, china, glass. Open daily, by chance or by appointment.

Somerville
> John Bouchard, Route 202 between Somerville and Flemington.

Southard
> Fred B. Nadler, Route 9.

South Orange
> Katherine Wells, 201 South Orange Avenue. Period furniture, early china, glass, prints, lamps, fabrics. By appointment only.
>
> Ray Burger, 303 Western Drive South.
>
> Sara Fiverson, 98 Rynda Road. Royal Worcester, ironstone, Staffordshire china.

Sparta
> Frances Mackie, 19 Main Street. China, glass, and unusual decorative items.

The Posts, Earl and Dora, 11 Main Street. Country furniture. Open daily Tuesday through Sunday.

Springfield

John A. Mendelson, 352 Morris Avenue. Collectors' items.

Squankum

The 1807 House, Garden State Parkway Exit 96, west on Route 524 past Allaire State Park, at blinker turn left on Route 547. Elizabeth L. Davies. Country furniture. Open daily except Sundays and Mondays by appointment.

Summit

M. S. Townley, 7 Linden Place. China, glass.

Tenafly

Alice R. MacKenzie, 35 Royden Street (side door). Imports from India.

Tom's River

Lillian M. Waters Antiques, 157 West Locust Street, one mile west of Exit 82, Garden State Parkway. Authentic glass, china, furniture. Open daily, Sundays and evenings.

Towaco

The Salt Box, Route 202. Florence and Ozzie Lower. Early Americana, primitives, Pennsylvania Dutch items.

Frank Weaver, furniture.

Trenton

L. L. Beans, 654 Stuyvesant Avenue. Paintings, folk art, tavern signs.

Bee S. Hoiles. By appointment.

Upper Montclair

Montclair Women's Exchange, 197 Bellevue Avenue. Verna Eichna. Orientals, porcelain, glass, paintings, furniture, objets d'art. Open Monday through Saturday.

Miss Osborne's Antique Shop, 581 Valley Road. General line; paintings, prints, silver, china, glass, fabrics, costumes.

Robert T. Berry, 590 Valley Road. Period furniture, glass, china. Open daily except Sunday. Evenings by appointment.

Dorothy Pontecorvo, 213 A Bellevue Avenue. Glass, china, furniture, lamps. Closed Wednesdays and Saturdays.

Cranetown Antiques, 104 Watchung Avenue. Isabelle Elvin. Pine furniture, marble-top coffee tables, art glass.

Kathryn Creighton Heyer, 606 Valley Road. Formal and pine furniture, china. Summer shop, Rio Grande and Swainton, New Jersey.

Verona
   Rose Rowe, 53 Pease Street. China, glass, collectors' items, prints.
   The Butlers, 23 Park Court.
Vineland
   Faber's Antiques, 742 South Delsea Drive. American art glass.
West Caldwell
   Anne R. Owen, 29 Clinton Road. Early china, glass, furniture, objets
      d'art. By appointment only.
West Englewood
   Evelyn Pfeiffer.
Westfield
   Herbert E. and Dorothy B. Stevenson, 189 Elm Street. Wallpaper print
      rollers for lamps.
   Marjorie C. Millen, 302 East Broad Street. Period furniture, lamps, early
      glass, accessories.
   Nelson Rapp, 741 Clark Street, one mile from town center. Pattern glass,
      small antiques. Open daily.
   Don Maxwel, 885 Mountain Avenue. Unusual items in furniture, glass,
      china.
West Orange
   Justin Gallander and Mel Siegel, 54 Main Street. General line.
Whippany
   Stanley R. Fort, Route 10.
   J. C. Seng and Son, Routes 37 and 10. Early American.
Whitehouse
   The Hulzigers, Route 22 at Oldwick Road. Early Americana and
      furniture.
Wildwood
   Avalon Antique Shop, Gertrude Avalon. Glass, china, furniture.
Williamstown
   Julia David, Lake Avenue.
   Aaron Frazier, Black Horse Pike. Victorian china, pattern glass, cut glass,
      silver, buttons, coins.
Woodstown
   Ye Olde Stage Coach, 68 North Main Street. Betty Hamilton Lippincott.
      General line; authentic pieces.
Wycoff
   Elizabeth B. Brickell, 440 West Main Street. Country items, early brass,
      primitives, country furniture. Appointment advisable.

PENNSYLVANIA

Abington

Abington Antique Shop, 1165 Old York Road. General line.

Ambler

Janet Harvan and Helen Nickel, Butler Pike and Susquehanna Road.

Ruth Roberts Dubbs, 404 Edgewood Drive. Glass, china, silver.

Dora Seeley, Broadaxe Antiques. General line.

Amityville

Merritt's Antiques. Very large general line. American and imported items.

Annville

Sam Yeagley, 44 East Main Street.

Aquetong

Maplecroft Farm Antiques, Route 202. George G. Dunn, Jr., and A. M. Lang.

Sheffield Shop, Route 202 near New Hope. Mrs. W. D. Barlow.

Audubon

The Wren's Nest, Pinetown Road (near Norristown). Mary Croll Moister. Glass, china, primitives, furniture.

Bainbridge

Helen S. Jourdet's Country Store, Route 441.

Bala-Cynwyd

John H. Dilks, Jr., 307 Tregaron Road.

Bareville

Mrs. Willis P. Bower, R. D. 1, five miles east of Lancaster, Route 222. General line; primitives. Open at all times.

Bethlehem

Rosemary Ryan Shop, 600 Forrest Street. Elizabeth D. De Angelis. Art glass.

Lamp Post Antiques, 620 North New Street (American Hotel Building). Joseph K. Peters. General line; primitives, Dutch country items, historical Staffordshire, soft paste china. Open evenings Monday through Friday, other times by appointment.

Birchrunville

James Boyd, three miles east of Route 100 (Pottstown–West Chester highway). Early Americana, primitives, iron, furniture.

Bristol

Sam Laidacker, 206 Otter Street. Early American china, glass, Staffordshire.

Helen S. Gould, Edgely Avenue.

Buckingham

Rowland's, Route 202. Mr. and Mrs. Bertram M. Rowland. Early American, English imports, unusual collectors' items.

Katy Houghton Antiques, Professional Building, Route 202. Mrs. Katy Houghton. Distinctive general line, American and English, pewter, furniture.

Edna's Antique Shop, Route 202. Mrs. Edna Wehmeyer. Glass.

Griffin's Antiques, Route 202. Mrs. Freda M. Griffin. General line. Open daily.

Stotz and Thiele, Route 202. Herman Stotz and Arch Thiele. Rough and refinished pine furniture. Open daily and Sunday all year.

Carlisle

Le Roy Comp, 164 East High Street. General line; furniture, glass, china.

Brown's Antiques, one and a half miles southeast on Route 74. General line; furniture, lamps, clocks, and small items.

Chadd's Ford

Brandywine House, three miles west on Route 1.

Charlestown Village

Barbara Corbett, south of Phoenixville. General line; distinctive china, glass, etc. By appointment only.

Chester

The Gordons, 10 Pennsylvania Avenue, Garden City.

Clark's Summit

Carol Connelly, Knapp Road off Route 611. Early furniture, china, glass, lamps, prints, collectors' items.

Coatesville

Edna Hoffman, 530 Elm Street, opposite railroad freight station. Painted pieces, tin.

Collegeville

Forge Antiques, Germantown Pike. Russell Jackson. Period pieces, silver, Sheffield plate.

Olivia Regar, The Hermitage, Pechin Mill Road. General line; glass, silver, and unusual items. Summer shop in Cape May, New Jersey.

Emma Nyce, Trappe–Collegeville, Routes 422 and 113. General line; buttons. Open daily and evenings except Thursday afternoon.

Cornwall Heights

A. L. Gessler, 1920 Virginia Avenue.

Whitehouse Antiques, 1962 Virginia Avenue.

Coventryville

The Corner Cupboard, Route 23. Mrs. Don Neilsen. General line; country furniture. Open daily and evenings.

Croydon

Kathryn C. Sutton, 3944 Bristol Pike. Clocks a specialty.

Cynwyd

Mrs. William Gundersheimer, 708 Fordham Road. Oriental pieces, china.

Dalton

The Little House, West Main Street, on old road between Dalton and Factoryville. General line; furniture, colored glass, china, prints, brass, copper, and decorative items. Open all year Monday through Saturday.

Delaware Water Gap

Ralph M. Meyer.

Delta

J. B. Stone Antiques, Route 74 near York. General line.

Dillsburg

Logan Stone House Antiques, Route 74, South Dillsburg by-pass to Dillsburg at junction of roads from Carlisle to York and Harrisburg to Gettysburg. Eastern Pennsylvania antiques. Open any time except Sundays.

Douglasville

Irene N. Fork, Gramarcy Gardens, Route 83. Decorative antiques. By appointment only.

Shadow Box Antiques, four miles west of Pottstown on Route 83. Betty and Joe Lenich. General line; primitives, china, glass, dolls and doll accessories, furniture, linens. Open all year daily.

Downingtown

Philip H. Bradley, East Lancaster Avenue, Route 30. Distinctive general line; period pieces.

Echo Glen Farm, Route 322, five miles west of Downingtown. Beatrice Leighton. China, glass, pine furniture, brass, copper, iron, old building materials. Open daily all year.

The Yesterday Shop, Route 30. Laura J. MacDonald. General line; early glass, china, furniture, brass, copper. Open daily except Sundays.

Howe's Antiques, 704 Lancaster Avenue, Route 30. W. W. Howe and M. L. Howe.

Doylestown

Heritage House, 167 South Main Street, Route 611. Elizabeth McCain. Refinished furniture, silver, china, glass, pewter, brass, copper. Open daily except Mondays; Sundays, 1 to 5.

Graham's Antiques, 363 North Main Street, Route 611. Lewis S. Graham. Furniture rough and finished. Open all year.

Sinexon Antiques, 46 West Court Street. Mildred Bolles Sinexon. Unusual pieces, metal items, specializing in pre-Columbian art and articles of primitive cultures. Open April through November.

The Rutherfords, 102 North Main Street. Mr. and Mrs. Russell G. Rutherford. Cherry and pine furniture, china. By appointment only.

Mrs. Albert A. Bliss, Jr., 485 North Main Street.

Drexel Hill

Pauline F. Williams, 532 Drexel Avenue. General line; glass, china, woodenware. Appointment advisable.

Gloria Greenberg, 4019 Sommers Avenue. China, glass, small antiques.

East Berlin

Myers Antiques, Route 234, one mile west of town. Nettie Myers. Firearms and general line. Closed Sundays.

East Stroudsburg

Bird in Hand, Audrey Vail, Franklin Hill.

Elizabethtown

Mrs. Daisy D. Crooks, 125 Washington Street, three-quarter block east of Route 230. General line.

Ephrata

Jake Borry, 222 Duke Street. General line.

Red Barn Antiques. Robert Lausch. General line; Pennsylvania Dutch items. Open weekends all year. Summer shop, Ocean View, New Jersey.

Erdenheim

Carolyn Lebrocq, 214 Heatherwood Road.

Exton

Myrtle B. Swannenburg, Ship Road north of Route 30. General line; items in good condition, no reproductions. Open daily all year except January and February.

Fleetwood

The Glockenspiel, Route 222 between Reading and Kutztown. General line.

Furlong

School House Antiques, Route 263. Mrs. Doris H. Yarborough. General line.

Gettysburg

The Hartlaubs, Route 30, three miles east of town. Furniture in the rough.

Hess Antiques, 233 Chambersburg Street. Glass, china, dolls, furniture, guns.

Mrs. George Miller, Red Pine Acres, Route 15, five miles south of town. General line.

Old Lamp Shop, Route 116, one mile from square.

N. L. Oyer, Route 30, two and a half miles east of town. Old coins and Civil War items.

Red Patch Antiques, West Confederate Avenue.

The Red Schoolhouse, Route 15, four miles south of town.

Weaver's White Barn, Route 30, three miles east of town. Furniture in the rough.

The Blackwells, twelve miles west of Gettysburg, Route 30. Glass and china.

Gladwyne

Margaret Swartz. General line; furniture, china, glass.

Glen Mills

Down East Antiques, Route 202, one-half mile south of Christy's Corner, Brandywine Summit. Furniture, brass, copper, china, glass. Open daily.

Green Lane

Colonial House Antiques, Routes 29 and 63. Stephen Szegda. General line. Open evenings, all day Saturday and Sunday.

Pennywell Farm Antiques, Route 29 just north of Eastern Bible Institute. Mrs. Mary E. Robinson. General line; rare china.

Gwynedd

Henry Clay, Route 202. General line; country furniture, decorative items.

Hanover

Joe Wisensale, 19 Pine Street. General line.

Gladys McCarney, 444 South Franklin Street. China, glass, bric-a-brac.

Bowman's Antiques, Route 116, China, glass, ironstone, furniture.

Markle's Antique Shop, Route 94, three miles south of town. General line.

Old Wagon Trail Antiques, Route 94, three miles south of town.

Harrisburg

Chestnut Tree Antique Shop, 3704 North Fourth Street (rear). Helen Fasolt. General line.

Dorothy K. Winemiller, 902 North Sixteenth Street. China, pattern glass, linens, silver, cut glass, collectors' items.

Hatboro

Harriet B. Off, Davisville Road. Early china, Staffordshire, spatter, gaudy, strawberry; unusual items.

Lillian C. Griffith, 332 North York Road. Brass, copper, lamps, country furniture.

Haverford

Hayestock House, 343 West Lancaster Avenue, Route 30. Eighteenth-century English furniture, Oriental export china, Worcester, Spode, Derby, lamps and accessories. Open daily except Sundays.

Neville Antiques, 369 Lancaster Avenue. C. Neville Lewis. American, English imports, Georgian silver, Sheffield, copper, brass, pewter, prints, frames, china, furniture.

Holicong

Hickory Bush Antiques, Holicong Road, Bucks County. Mr. A. M. Lang. Early Americana.

Holland

Heron Creek Antiques, 632 Buck Road, Route 532, between Newtown and Feasterville, Bucks County. Christine P. Horn. General line.

Horsham

John McGlinchey, Route 611. Restored furniture. Open daily all year.

Hummelstown

Olive R. Wagner, 507 West Main Street (near Harrisburg and Hershey). General line; primitives, furniture, glass, china, brass, copper. Open daily.

Huntingdon Valley

Hazel Schubert, 1023 Anna Road. By appointment only.

Jamison

Cello's Antiques, Almshouse Road, one-half mile west of York Road. General line; furniture, primitives. Open Saturdays and Sundays all year. Weekdays, knock on door.

Jenkintown

Lenne S. Feld and G. Hafter, 607 Balder Road.

Johnson's Corner

Valleyview Antiques, Route 202 near Delaware State line. William and Dorothy Kimmel. General line.

Jonestown

Freeman's Antique Shop. General line; early American, collectors' items.

King of Prussia

King of Prussia Antique Shop, Routes 202 and 23. Lucressa H. Morrison. General line; primitives, toys, furniture, glass, china, country-store items. Open daily all year except Sundays.

Kintnersville

Harriet Meginnes (near Route 611). Hooked rugs.

Kutztown

Robert Burkhardt, Route 222, at Monterey. Early Americana; period furniture, distinctive line.

Lamb's Mill Antiques, Krumsville Road between Route 22 and Route 222. Early Americana.

Edwin J. Bieber, one and a half miles west at Kutz's Mill. Pennsylvania Dutch furniture, primitives, early tools, guns, china.

Lafayette Hill

Mr. and Mrs. H. M. Lowry, 768 Germantown Pike. Early Americana furniture. Appointment advisable.

Terry Palma, 330 Ridge Pike.

Lahaska

Lippincott Antiques, at Route 263 and Street Road. Carroll E. Lippincott. Country furniture; unusual items rough or finished in pine, cherry; sinks, chests, tables, desks.

Crest Galleries, Inc., Route 202, three and a half miles west of New Hope. Early American paintings and antiques. Open daily.

The House of Tobys, Route 202. Morton B. Tobias. Fine eighteenth- and nineteenth-century furniture, china, glass, bibelots, jewelry, paintings, silver. Open daily and Sundays all year.

Mary Jennings Antiques, Route 202. Early local furniture with original paint and decoration; primitives, accessories; unusual items. Open daily except Monday after Christmas.

Mrs. Bruno Gonella, Route 202. General line; specialty pewter. Open daily all year.

Pearl Johnson, Route 202. Pine furniture, china, glass, fireplace equipment. Open daily all year.

Fryers' What Not Shop, Route 202. Mildred and Harold Fryers. French dolls, art glass, American, English, and French furniture; imported items. Open daily.

Yesterday's Treasures Shop, Route 202. Marguerite T. Bye. General line; china, glass, furniture; boxes a specialty. Open daily all year except Sundays.

Sterling's Antiques, Route 202. Paul Sterling. Furniture, glass, copper, brass, iron furniture and urns. Open daily all year.

Shelley's Antiques, Route 202. Shelley Bobinac. Americana. Open daily all year except Sundays.

Pilgrim's Progress, Route 202. Mrs. Stanley H. Rowe.

Lancaster Antique Shop, Route 202. Mr. Donald C. Moore.

French-American Antiques, Route 202. Mrs. W. H. Thayer.

Lancaster

Mabel S. Downing, 3021 Columbia Avenue. China, cut glass, dolls, prints, furniture.

Melvin Hubley, 534 North Duke Street. Colonial and federal period furniture and decorative items.

Dillinborger's, 2101 Columbia Avenue, Route 30, three miles west of square. Furniture, primitives, china, prints, cut and pattern glass.

Wolf's Antiques, 409 Atkins Avenue, one block west of Hamilton Watch Co. Mr. and Mrs. Clarence Wolf. Small antiques, glass, china, buttons, decorative items. By appointment only.

Clarence W. Hinden, six miles east of Lancaster on Route 30. China, glass, furniture rough and finished. Open all year.

Helen Warren Antique Shop, 725 North Duke Street, seven blocks north of monument. Mrs. Robert F. Warren. General line; small antiques, buttons, post cards, jewelry, china, glass, linens, primitives, books. Open daily all year.

Lansdale

Edna Victor, Sumneytown Pike. Dolls.

Mildred's Doll Hospital, 205 East Sixth Street.

Detweiler's Antiques, 341 Oak Park Road, Route 63. Glass, china, furniture.

The Rockers, 215 Susquehanna Avenue.

Gladys Dell, Hedrick Road.

Lansdowne

Mrs. Horace H. Mitchell, 5 Balfour Circle.

The Wagners, 59 Drexel Avenue.

Layfield

The Mill Antiques, Junction 663 and 73, north of Pottstown. J. and M. Miller. General line.

Lebanon

Nagle's White House Antiques, 701 South Lincoln Avenue, seven blocks south of Route 422. Elsa Nagle. China, cut glass, pressed glass, furniture rough and finished, Pennsylvania Dutch items. Open daily except Saturday P.M.

Lederach

The White House Antiques, Route 113. Eva K. Hess.

Lenape

Lenape Antiques, Creek Road. Mildred and Walter Shank. Glass, majolica, brass, furniture. Open daily from noon.

Laughing Waters on the Brandywine, Creek and Street roads, Route 100 south of West Chester. Harriette R. Glanding and Mildred E. M. Pike.

Lewiston

Theresa Redmond Antiques, 14 Sunset Road, Route 22 W. Glass and china. By appointment only.

Limerick

The Parsonage Shop, one mile west of Limerick on Route 422. Elaine and Nelson Weller. Early American furniture, china. Open daily all year.

Littlestown

The Little Antique Shop, 129 West King Street. General line. Cups and saucers.

Ludwig's Corners

Hobby House Antiques, Route 401 west of Route 100. Dorothy Dunstone (from Wellsville, New York). General line; primitives, frames, decorative items.

Lumberville

The Black Bass Antique Shop, River Road. Herbert Ward. Period pieces, imports, decorative items.

Larry Bates and H. B. Hartman (formerly the Spread Eagle at Montgomeryville), Fleecy Dale Road. Primitives, country furniture. By appointment only.

William Woolsey, 32 River Road.

Macungie

Country Cupboard at the Little Red Schoolhouse. Route 100 west of Allentown. M. Weidenfeld. General line.

Malvern

Mrs. Edna Phillips, 39 Conestoga Road, Route 401. General line; prints, guns.

Manheim

Hart's, 151 North Charlotte Street. Large authentic stock.

Maxatawny

Mrs. D. E. Frey, Route 222. Early American glass, china, furniture, jewelry, Pennsylvania Dutch pieces, linens, quilts.

Media

Morr Antiques, Bowling Green, two miles north of Route 1 at Media Inn. Mabelle Krain Orr. Small antiques, Staffordshire mugs and whistles, pattern, colored, and art glass, trivets, pewter. Open daily, no evenings.

Merion

Thelma E. Milde, 709 Montgomery Avenue. Glass, china, small antiques.

Middletown

Eisenhauer's Antiques, 649 Briarcliff Road, one and a half blocks north of Routes 2 and 30. Furniture, china, lamps, primitives, coins.

Mifflinburg

Seek and Find Shop, 253 Green Street. Glass, china, furniture, penny banks.

Milford

Elsie Atkins.

Montgomeryville

Fisher's, Cowpath Road, Route 463. General line.

Morrisville

William and Goldie H. Hickey, 330 East Birch Drive. Early glass, china, furniture, stamps, correspondence. By appointment only.

Narberth

Martin's Antiques, 913 Montgomery Avenue. Furniture, objets d'art, bric-a-brac.

New Britain

Bucks County Cabinet Shop, 134 Iron Hill Road, Route 202. Frank J. Udinski. General line. Open all year.

Wishing Well Antiques, Route 202.

New Hope

George S. Hobensack, Jr., Bridge Street, Route 202. Furniture, glass, china, silver, specializing in oriental rugs and garden appointments such as urns, fences, fountains. Open daily all year.

The Crawfords of Cintra, Route 202 opposite high school. Jean and Donald Crawford. Formal and informal antiques, no silver or jewelry. Open weekdays.

Washington Square Antiques, 44 West Mechanic Street. Lamps, custom shades, silver, china, period furniture. Open daily and Sundays all year.

Dorchester Antiques, 130 North Main Street. Furniture, Chinese export, and other fine porcelains, accessories. Open Tuesday through Saturday all year.

Grace D. Wilson-Lavery, Route 202. Carefully selected general line. Summer shop, Haverill, New Hampshire.

The Pink House, Route 202. Burwell and Louise Shepard. Fine early furniture, paintings, unusual decorative items.

House of Bargains, Main Street. Ruth Page.

Distelbird Antiques, Mechanic Street.

Colonial Arms Antiques, Route 202.

New Oxford

Antiques Folly, Routes 30 and 19 Lincoln Way East. Unusual items. Weekends and summer.

Antiques-on-the-Square, Route 30, a half block east of square. Collectors' items and Early American furniture.

Gleck's Antiques, Route 94, just south of Route 30. General line.

John C. Byers, 18 Lincoln Way East.

John Shultz, New Chester, four miles north of New Oxford. General line. Open daily every day; evenings Saturdays and Sundays.

New Providence

Baldwin Antiques, Route 222. Country antiques, glass, china, primitives, furniture. Open daily.

Newtown

The Hanging Lamp, 140 North State Street. Mr. and Mrs. Duane P. Stump. General line; imports.

Morrell's Antique Shop, 4 East Washington Avenue. R. Monroe Morrell. Furniture, brass, wood, copper, tin, iron, primitives. Country-store atmosphere. Open all year Monday through Saturday.

Newtown Square

The Little House Antiques, 3537 Rhoads Avenue. Rachel Mitchell. Specializing in small furniture and accessories for the small house.

Norristown

Jennie J. Schlumpf and Emma M. Kramer, 1009 West Airy Street. General line; glass, china.

Stephen Arena, 237 West Main Street next to New Shoppe. Pennsylvania pieces, antique firearms, clocks. Open all year Monday through Saturday.

Potshop Farm Antiques.

Evelyn S. Easton, 1637 Williams Way, off Route 422 at Jeffersonville. General line.

North Wales

Ray Leirer, 316 Upper Valley Road. General line; lamps, shades, Canton china.

Merrimac Shop, 112 South Main Street. Furniture, glass, china, silver, jewelry. Closed July and August.

Howard D. Finkle, North Wales Road.

Oley

Twin Birches, Pleasantville, Route 73. Kathryn N. Heist. General line; pattern glass, Dresden, lamps, primitives, buttons, post cards, furniture. The Oley Antique Shop, Daniel and Sadie Herzog. China, glass, Pennsylvania Dutch furniture, guns, dolls, coins.

Oreland

Margaret Bonz, 526 Papermill Road, Enfield.

Oxford

Parton Althouse, two miles south on Route 1. General line; glass, pottery, porcelain, barometers.

Paoli

Candle Shop Antiques, Route 30, four miles west of town. James and Kenneth Parrish. American, English, and French furniture; country pine; primitives, pewter, Canton, Wedgwood, paintings, rugs, garden pieces, and accessories.

Parkesburg

The Rocking Chair, Route 30 west of Sadburyville. Thomas U. Schock. Americana, coin glass, lithophanes, early china, unusual items.

Perkiomenville

Stanley C. Kircher, Kratz Road off Gravel Pike. General line; glass.

PHILADELPHIA

D. B. Neal, 1712 Rittenhouse Street. Early glass.

Alfred Bullard Inc., 1604 Pine Street. Period pieces.

J. E. Caldwell and Co., Chestnut and Juniper streets. Silver.

Charles B. Smith, 3818 Chestnut Street. Wedgwood.

Eugene Sussel, 1929 Chestnut Street. Distinctive general line.

Lily S. Ostroff, 1145 Pine Street. General line.

Reese's Antiques, The Horn of Plenty, 928–30 Pine Street. General line; popular pieces.

I. Taylor Associates Inc., 926 Pine Street.

M. Finkel Antiques, southeast corner 10th and Pine streets. Jewelry, guns, nautical items, oriental art, Americana, imports, and Civil War items.

Laura Witmer, 135 South 18th Street. Lamps, shades, china, furniture, early glass.

Helen D. Riggle, 1508 Roselyn Street.

Stella and Thomas von Trott, 101 West Rittenhouse Street, Germantown.

Taylor Gilbert, 6326 Germantown Avenue.

Ionic Antique Shop, 114 South 20th Street.

Robert Carlen, 323 South 16th Street.

Walter Eldridge, 2000 Clarkson Avenue.

Frieda and Harry Burke, 1726 Chestnut Street and 1628 Pine Street. Jewelry, silver, china, glass, objets d'art, collectors' items.

Sara Leff Karr, 1125 Lindley Avenue.

Oxford Antiques, 7826 Oxford Avenue. Choice American furniture, Pennsylvania Dutch primitives, china, lamps.

Three-Ways, 2020 North Broad Street. English imports, silver, porcelain, and pottery.

Terry Palmer, 45 East Chestnut Hill Avenue. Early American furniture, glass, china, silver, copper, brass, pewter, lamps.

Ruth M. Mandler, 4233 Devereaux Avenue. By appointment.

Schuylkill Book Service, 873 Belmont Avenue (44th Street and Lancaster Avenue). Books, prints, collectors' items.

Gladys Haftel, 1298 West Cheltenham Avenue. China, silver, jewelry.

Joseph Davidson, 1814 Chestnut Street. China, furniture, jewelry.

Avalon Antique Shoppe, 7108 Castor Avenue.

Edward G. Wilson, 1802 Chestnut Street. Jewelry, silver, pewter, objets d'art.

Benjamin Ginsberg, 1519 Roslyn Street.

Mrs. H. Carlton Antrim, 4721 Leiper Street.

Jane Kay MacAllister, 222 West Harvey Street, Germantown.

Freda Morris, 5310 Green Street, Germantown.

Miriam Rayvis, 425 West Upsal Street, Germantown.

Thurlow V. Staples, 118 West Rittenhouse Street, Germantown.

Lillian Weiner, 8252 Williams Avenue.

Emily and Earl Schommer, 6330 Ridge Avenue.

Helene Kelly, 6505 Germantown Avenue.

J. Donald VonNeida, 109 West Rittenhouse Street, Germantown.

Mrs. Lydia A. Worthington, 1234 Marlborough Street.

John and Edna Welthall, 5319 Green Street, Germantown.

Mrs. Beatrice E. Paine, 346 Berkley Street.

Mrs. Helen Zeitz, 2550 Ardsley Avenue, Ardsley.

The Candle Shop, 8523 Germantown Avenue.

Mary Elizabeth Keys, 7038 Cottage Street.

E. Emerson Bolton, 4701 Leiper Street.

Seal Simons, 473 West Ellet Street. Wedgwood.

Joan Saffiian.

Nettie Shyne, 1712 Pine Street.

Phoenixville

Lengle's, 113 South Main Street. Glass, china, majolica, lamps.

William S. Jones, Ellis Woods Road. Guns and accessories.

Schuylkill House, Black Rock Road. Eighteenth-century American furniture, silver, and accessories.

H. F. S. Clarke, White Horse Road. General line.

Franklin M. Roshon, 388 First Avenue. Locks, shackles, spurs, bronzes, books, prints.

Point Pleasant

Elizabeth R. Fay, River Road, eight miles north of New Hope. General line; decorative accessories. Open May to November. Winter shop in Riviera Beach, Florida.

Port Kennedy

Valley Forge Antiques, David Ellinger.

Portland

Elmer's Antiques.

Pottstown

Evelyn Trout Applegate, Harmonyville Road, three miles south off Route 100. Furniture, jewelry, decorative items.

Oliver Christman, High and Warren streets. Furniture, china, silver, Sheffield, glass, decorative items.

Paul Egolf, 351 Chestnut Street. General line; antiques and curios.

Green's Antique Shop, 866 High Street. General line; coins. Open daily 8 A.M. to 10 P.M.

Homespun Shop, Harmonyville Road, three miles south off Route 100. Jessie Boyer. Unusual items, primitives, country pieces, glass, collectors' pieces.

Merkel's Antiques, Route 663, two miles north. Early glass, china, art glass, guns, coins, lamps, furniture.

Louis Patrizi, 557 High Street. General line.

Mr. and Mrs. Richard A. Patrizi, 557 High Street. General line; painted pieces, decorative items.

Merle Wenrich, 1319 High Street. General line.

Stahl's Antiques, Route 422, three miles east, Saratoga. Large general line.

William Roup, 301 Grandview Road. Mechanical banks, iron toys.

Pughtown

The Seminary Shop, Mr. and Mrs. Raymond Tull. General line.

Quarryville

Sullivan's Antiques, 116 South Lime Street.

Rahn's

John Klein, Route 29 off Route 422. General line; primitives, early iron, lanterns, furniture.

Reading

Rhena L. Hinz, 613 Gordon Street. General line.

Bingaman's Antiques, 3602 Saint Lawrence Avenue, one mile east on Route 562. General line; Early American and Victorian furniture, Pennsylvania Dutch items, pattern, cut, art, and colored glass, early and decorative china.

Walter and Sarah Rothermel, Conestoga House, one mile north on Pricetown Road. Early American furniture, Pennsylvania Dutch primitives, mechanical banks, early china, clocks.

Sternbergh Antiques, Route 222, seven miles north. Pattern, cut, and colored glass, ironstone, decorative china, quilts, lamps, refinished furniture.

Helen Wenger, 128 South Ninth Street. Chandeliers, hanging lamps, decorative brass, china, Dutch, Empire, Victorian, and marble-top furniture, quilts, picture frames, primitives.

Emily Troutman, 325 North Sixth Street. Pattern glass, china.

Reinholds

Kattie K. Brunner, Route 897, three miles from Route 222 interchange.

Richlandtown

Gargoyle Antiques, Martha Hill Hommel. Rare books.

Roxborough

Schommer's Antiques, 6730 Ridge Avenue. Early American, Empire, and Victorian furniture.

Rydal

Mary Aloe, 1259 Cox Road. American furniture, English china, and accessories, eighteenth-century items. Open all year by appointment.

Sadsburyville

Randall's Old Barn, Route 30. Meda Randall. Early American china, glass. Open daily.

Schaefferstown

Clyde Youtz, one mile east of town, Route 897. Dry sinks, glass, china, coins. Open Wednesdays, Fridays, Sundays, all year.

Scranton

Fifty King Antiques, 332 Lackawanna Avenue. Early furniture, prints, rare books. Open daily except Sundays, evenings by appointment.

Shawnee-on-Delaware
  Charlotte and Edgar Sittig. Specializing in Americana and collectors' items.
Shillington
  L. W. Slaughter, 201 East Lancaster Avenue. Clocks. By appointment only.
Sinking Spring
  The Shipes, four blocks off Route 222, eight miles south of Reading. General line; Pennsylvania Dutch refinished furniture. Open Wednesdays, Saturdays, and Sundays. Other times by appointment.
  J. Russell Fegley, use Bern Road in Wyomissing to State Hill, three and a quarter miles. Specializing in cleaning old china.
Skippack
  The Skippack Pike Antique Shop, Mrs. Ambra Buck. Prints, maps, small antiques.
  Frances W. Hunt. General line.
  Charles Supplee, Route 73, Skippack Pike. General line.
  Towamencin Antiques, Hedrick Road. General line; glass, furniture in the rough. Open all year, by appointment only.
Slatington
  M. A. Behler, Route 29, off Route 22. General line; furniture finished and in the rough.
Spring City
  Mrs. Anna Cappalonga, Pikeland Avenue. China, glass, small antiques.
  The Reeds, 38 North Main Street. General line; small antiques.
Springfield
  Marple Store Antique Shop, 816 Springfield Road. Near by-pass Route 1. General line.
  Burman's Antique Mart, 237 Baltimore Pike, Route 1. Guns, jewelry, books, toys, clocks, collectors' items. Open daily; Sundays and evenings by appointment.
Spring Mill
  Spring Mill Antique Shop. Matthew and Elizabeth Sharpe. Early American china, glass, furniture. Chinese import china.
Spring Valley
  Charlotte N. Achey, Furlong Road, just off Route 202.
  Bob Selby Associates, Route 202. R. Selby, A. Frank, and T. Baldwin. Early Americana; period pieces.
  The Scofield Shop, Route 202. Mrs. Violetta S. Scofield.

Telford

A. J. Pennypacker, Route 309, Bethlehem Pike. Early American pieces, mostly Pennsylvania origin.

Trappe

Franklin House, 1639 Main Street. General line.

Upper Black Eddy

McCarty's Antiques, River Road, Route 32. Country antiques, pine and cherry pieces.

Upper Darby

Sallie Halpern, 115 North Fairview Avenue.

Valley Forge

R. E. Condon, Oakwood Lane. Hooked rugs.

Villa Nova

Gate House Antiques, 1502 Old Gulph Road. Mrs. J. M. Robinson. Early American, French, English furniture, accessories, lamps. Open all year.

Elinor Gordon, Lancaster Pike, Route 30. Chinese export china (oriental Lowestoft).

Wayne

Mary T. Connor, the Lady from Philadelphia, 667 Church Road. Summer shop, Assisi Bird Sanctuary, Route 90, Paradise Valley, Cresco, Pennsylvania. General line; small antiques.

West Chester

William J. Campbell Antiques, 1108 Pottstown Pike, Route 100, one mile north of town. Glass, china, refinished pine and cherry cottage furniture. Open daily except Sundays.

Charles P. Johns, Route 30 at Glen Loch, five miles west of Paoli, six miles north of West Chester. Eighteenth-century furniture.

George H. Bennett, Boot Road. Period furniture, china, luster, blown glass, wrought iron, locks, latches, hinges, quilts, homespun linen. Open daily except Sundays.

R. E. Swayne, Route 100, three miles north of town. Large general line; furniture, china, glass. Open daily all year.

Frank I. Getzman, 1101 Grove Street. General line; china, lamps. Summer shop, Warren, Maine.

Whitemarsh

Harry A. Prock, Hapwood. General line; objets d'art.

Whitford

Herbert Schiffer, Route 30, two miles east of Downingtown. Early American furniture, china, silver, Canton, period accessories.

Ball and Ball, Route 30. Authentic reproductions American hardware, original brasses.

Woodside

Edgewood Farms Antiques, John Exton and Milton Hatcher. Near Yardley on the Delaware River.

Worcester

The Granary Antique Shop, Route 73 between Routes 202 and 363. Irma A. Schultz. General line; early china, quilts.

Shiloh Antiques, Valley Forge Road. Clay and Irene Weiseenbach. Furniture.

Yardley

Hayes Lamp Shop, 69 South Main Street. Martin A. Hayes. Antique lamps. Open all year daily from 11 A.M.

York

Joe Kindig, Jr., 325 West Market Street. Large general line; guns.

The Long, Long Ago Shop, 347 East Market Street. Margaret J. Lichtenberger. Choice, authentic Americana.

Maravene's Antiques, Route 30, eight miles east of town. General line; glass, china, mechanical banks.

E. L. Ramsay, 882 East Market Street. General line; coins, imported items. Open daily all year.

The Priscilla Alden House, 720 Skyline Drive. Mrs. Frank L. Jarrell. Small antiques, collectors' items, political items, buttons, stereo views, deeds, toys, cards, hand-quilting service. Open daily all year. Advisable to call in advance.

Colonial Metal and Art Studio, 1821 West Market Street. C. C. Thomas. Early American furniture, primitives, Pennsylvania Dutch designing and refinishing. Open daily, Tuesday and Thursday evenings.

DELAWARE

Bear

Afton Antique Shop, Route 40.

Delaware City

Thomas J. Armstrong, Williams and Adams streets.

Dover

Mrs. James I. Flamm, Dupont Highway, three miles north of Dover. General line.

Frederica

Harry C. Hinkley, Market Street.

Houston
George W. Kirkley.

Lewes
Old Russell Farmhouse, 410 Pilot Town Road, seven miles along canal. Reba Russell Lynch. Period furniture, early glass, china. Open all year.

Middletown
Bay Head Antiques, near Bay View.

New Castle
Quality House, 124 Delaware Street. Vern Hagen and Lyall Bowers. Period furniture, unusual pieces, porcelains.
Mrs. Robert Crooks.

Newport
Wanda's Attic, 2202 Kirkwood Highway, Route 2 across from Veterans' Hospital. Wanda Gallo. China, cut glass, art glass. By appointment only.

Wilmington
David Stockwell, Inc., 3701 Kennett Pike. Period furniture, porcelains, unusual early pieces.
The Bells, 407 West Thirteenth Street, corner of Washington Street. Joseph Bell. Furniture, china, glass, bronzes, coins, jewelry. Open Monday through Saturday. Closed Saturdays in June, July, and August.
Books and Things, 103 West Twelfth Street. Books, paintings, bric-a-brac, oriental pieces.
Avenue Antiques, 601 South Maryland Avenue, Hayden Park. Margaret H. Doyle. General line; china, glass, brass, silver, linens, furniture. Open daily.
Hobby House, 4503 Weldin Road just off Route 202 at Blue Ball. Elbert and Florence Turner. Furniture rough or finished, china, early glass. Open daily, Sunday by appointment.
John Farrace, 815 West Seventh Street. Firearms, swords, documents, books, newspapers, locks and keys.
Antiques Studio, 244 Philadelphia Pike.
Corner Cupboard, 2413 West Seventeenth Street.
Lloyd-Walsh, 220 West Ninth Street.
Robert L. Quaintance, 16 North Broad Street.
Benjamin Sklut, 307 West Second Street. General line. Open daily.
Wilmington Art Shop, 513 Washington Street.

MARYLAND

Annapolis

Dorothy R. Luttrell, 39 Maryland Avenue. General line. Open Monday through Saturday.

Baltimore

(There are more than seventy-five dealers listed in the classified section of the Baltimore phone book. Here are a few of the better-known ones.)

Ray Rink, 2822 Maryland Avenue.

Berenice K. Goldsmith, 3505 Bancroft Road.

Ruth D. Harris, 229 West Read Street.

Thelma Judkins, 231 West Read Street.

Theresa Redmond, 4905 Liberty Heights Avenue.

Franklin Rappold, 8007 Liberty Road. Eighteenth-century American furniture. Open all year. Appointment preferred.

The Corner Cupboard, 5620 York Road, Route 111. Mrs. George Coleman. General line; pattern glass, furniture, china, primitives, collectors' items. Open Tuesday through Saturday. Evenings by appointment.

Richard and Virginia Wood, 4 Hillside Road. Distinctive collectors' items.

Read Antiques, 899 North Howard Street. Clocks, early furniture, porcelains, silver, glass.

Anne Walker, 408 West Cold Spring Lane. Eighteenth-century furniture, china, glass, Lowestoft, Worcester, Staffordshire, lamps.

Rote Betty Antiques, 919 Charles Street. General line; glass, china, furniture.

Null's Antique Shop, 1014 Hillen Street, east of 420 Fallsway. Cornelia E. Null. General line; furniture, china, glass. Open Monday through Saturday noon to 5 P.M.

Norton Asner, 891 North Howard Street. Early furniture, porcelains, glass, silver, guns, paintings, bronzes, collectors' items.

Edelson's Antique Shop, 4516 Reistertown Road. General line.

Cathedral Antiques, 1406 Park Avenue. Dolls.

Harris Galleries, 875 North Howard Street. Guns, swords, fireplace items, china, glass, bric-a-brac, toys.

Little Antique Shop, 1015 North Charles Street. Myrtle Seidel. Jewelry, silver, glass, furniture, early English china, snuffboxes, spoons.

Golden's Antique and Silver Shop, 863 North Howard Street. China, silver (to match old patterns), coins, jewelry.

Good Luck Antique Shop, 845 North Howard Street. General line; specializing in dolls and doll accessories.

Shirley Frieman, 867 North Howard Street. Rugs, paintings, silver, ivories, bronzes, jewelry, china, bric-a-brac, furniture.

Virginia E. Broome, 5862 Belair Road. Shades, lamp parts, glass, china. Open noon to 6 P.M. or by appointment.

Bethesda

Catherine Costella, 5911 Ryland Drive.

Mrs. Helen G. Teskey, 6509 River Road. General line.

Chevy Chase

Anna Lois Webber, 6024 Western Avenue. General line; china, glass.

Easton

Anna H. Buck, opposite Tidewater Inn. China, metals, furniture, lamps, shades, pewter. Open all year, Monday through Saturday.

Clara and Ben Stewart, 402 Goldsboro Street (rear).

Frederick

Harold B. Cahn, 108 West Third Street. Rare furniture, porcelains, silver, lamps, and decorative accessories.

Funkstown

Ruth's Antique Shop. English and Continental imports.

Glenelg

R. T. Matthews, Cloverfield. Early American lighting.

Hagerstown

Bee House Antiques, Route 40, two miles west of town. Beulah T. Myers. Furniture, collectors' items in china and glass.

Ruth's Antique Shop, Route 40, one mile east of town. Ruth and Roger Beckley.

Beckley Antique Shop, two and a half miles south on Route 11.

The Old Treasure Shop, four miles west of Route 40.

La Plata

Preference Antique Shop, three miles south of La Plata, Route 301.

Leonardtown

Vera C. Richardson. General line.

New Market

Ray and Mary Messanelle, Route 40. Fine oriental porcelain, glass, and American glass and pottery. Open all year.

Sullivans Antiques, Route 40. General line; furniture, china, glass, lamps, primitives. Open all year.

Frank Shaw, Old National Pike, one block north of Route 40.

Paul Staley, Old National Pike, one block north of Route 40.

Stoll Kemp, Old National Pike, one block north of Route 40.

Benjamin Palmer, Old National Pike, one block north of Route 40. Firearms and edged weapons.

Frank Perham, Old National Pike, one block north of Route 40. Furniture, silver.

Charles W. Wood, Old National Pike, one block north of Route 40. Antiques, books.

Camden Ramsburg, Old National Pike, one block north of Route 40. Civil War items.

William Moran, Old National Pike, one block north of Route 40. Edged weapons.

Raymond Smith, Jr., Old National Pike, one block north of Route 40. Gunsmith.

Eli Alper, Old National Pike.

Jean Zimmerman, Old National Pike.

B. E. Sullivan, Old National Pike.

Thrift shop, Old National Pike. Old china.

Surch House, Old National Pike.

Dorsey Griffith, Old National Pike.

Oxford

Candlelight Shop. General line; marine paintings.

Saddle Brook Shop. General line; linens.

Queen Anne

K. N. Grove. Early and unusual pieces of Americana.

Texas

Tollgate House, York Road. Furniture, primitives, lamps. Open 12 to 5, Tuesday, Thursday, Saturday, and Sunday.

Thurmont

Ruffles Antique Shop, 302 East Main Street, Route 77, two blocks east of square. Glass, china. Open daily.

Westminster

O'Farrell's Antique Shop, 43 Liberty Street.

Wheaton

Hermitage, 11419 Viers Mill Road. Early American pieces, Sandwich, pewter, glass, china, rare and unusual items.

WASHINGTON, D.C.

D. C. Penny's Treasure Chest.

Early American Shop, 1323 Wisconsin Avenue N.W.

Studio 33 Shop, 1626 Wisconsin Avenue N.W. Small antiques, art, and objets d'art. Open afternoons, closed Mondays.

Old Salzburg Music Boxes.

Mellina Studios, 1510 Wisconsin Avenue.

Dorothy Fitzer, 1310 Floral Street N.W.

Edna Crawford Johnson, 1247 20th Street. French and English eighteenth-century pieces.

Laura Reinhard, 3131 Military Road N.W.

The Old World Shop, R. J. Riddell.

Cranberry Shelf, Mrs. Wright.

Heritage House, Catharine L. Costello, 3207 O Street N.W.

VIRGINIA

Alexandria

Katharine Ryan Antiques, 910 Prince Street. Extensive collection of distinctive pieces.

Strawberry Hill Antiques, 3968 Duke Street.

Queen Elizabeth Antiques, 910 Prince Street.

The Apothecary Shop Antiques, 105 South Fairfax Street. Ceramics, brass, furniture. Open daily; Sundays by appointment.

The Distelbird Shop, David Sheedy.

Arlington

Thieves Market, 89 North Glebe Road. Henry Cohen. Extensive general line.

Bristol

Unique Art Shop, 1210 Massachusetts Avenue, Route 76.

Carrollton

The Steeple, Bailey's antique clocks and repairs. Routes 17 and 258.

Charlottesville

Doris Pugh, 610 Lyons Court.

Bernard Caperton, 2248 Ivy Road, Route 250. Early Americana, imports, unusual items.

Anne Woods, 1215 West Main Street. Period furniture, silver, Sheffield, glass, china, decorative items.

The Ivy Shop, 1111 West Main Street. Mrs. Donald S. Wallace. General line. Unusual items.

Piney Mountain Antique Shop, Route 29 North. Mrs. B. L. Jarman. General line of country furniture, glass, china.

Wilma DeMuth, 1113 West Main Street. Decorative antiques.

Culpeper

The Haphazard Cabin, 610 North Main Street. Mrs. Charles B. Payne. General line; furniture, glass, tin, prints, books, paintings.

Hudson's Shop, J. B. Hudson. General line including cut glass, brass, copper.

Mrs. Osborn Antiques, Route 3, near Zion Church.

Log Cabin, Route 3. Mr. and Mrs. Foster.

Fredericksburg

Ginnie's Shop, 107 William Street. Mrs. Kerah Proctor. General line; mostly glass and china.

Shirley's Antique Shop, Route 1 north of town.

Wayside Shop, four miles north on Route 1.

Front Royal

Virginia Grant Antiques, 403 East Main Street. General line.

Gloucester

Trophy Room Antiques, one mile south on Route 17. Rare eighteenth-century porcelains and pottery.

Hampton

Pembroke Antiques, 2538 West Pembroke Avenue. General line; early American and English furniture, lamps, primitives, accessories. Open daily.

Hanover Court House

The Pewter Mug, fourteen miles north of Richmond on Route 301. W. L. Tolerton and D. J. Bresline. Collectors' items, period pieces, decorative antiques.

Lynnhaven

Shomier's Antique Shop, Virginia Beach, Route 58, eleven miles east of Norfolk. John E. and Lela L. Shomier. General line featuring Early American pine.

McLean

Yankee Pedlar Antiques, 6710 Old Dominion Drive, three miles from Washington, D.C. China, glass, furniture, marble-top tables. Open daily except Sundays.

Virginia Co. Furniture Hardware. Authentic reproductions.

Middleburg

Mrs. Greer. Early American, English, and French pieces.

The Beaver Hat. Fine American glass, authentic general line.

Norfolk

Studios Incorporated, 807 Shirley Avenue. Silver, Sheffield plate.

Richmond

(More than thirty dealers are listed in the classified section of the Richmond phone book, of which these are some of the outstanding.)

Charles Navis, 19 East Main Street. Specializing in American pieces in the rough.

Reese's Antiques, 207 East Main Street. American, English, and French pieces, silver and Sheffield plate.

Sherwood Shoppe, 103 East Main Street. General line; fine furniture, unusual pieces.

The Millstone, Route 301, nine miles north of Richmond. Jean Javins and Lula Eubank. General line; lamps, shades.

Beck's Antique Shop, 218 West Broad Street. W. I. Beckum. Early American furniture, walnut, cherry, mahogany, early and late styles. Open Monday through Friday.

Cameo Antique Shop, 108 East Franklin Street. Wm. L. Pavon. Furniture, china, glass, prints, paintings. Open daily except Sundays.

The Home Wrecker, 1911 Porter Street, rear of Martin Chevrolet. Louis J. Caravati. Stained glass, leaded glass, bubbly and wavy windowpanes, shutters, old pine, ornamental iron, marble fireplaces, slate, lighting fixtures, general line of antiques.

Charles' Antiques, 504 West Broad Street, a half block east of Route 1. Charles R. Percivall. General line. Open all year.

Stone's Antique Shop, 5508 West Broad Street, west on Route 250. Glass, china. Open Monday through Saturday.

Tow-Path House, 3 East Main Street. American and English furniture. Open all year.

Zincone and Son, 3027 West Cary Street. Antiques and reproductions. Open daily.

Roanoke

Stage Coach Antiques, four miles north on Routes 11 and 220. Mrs. Chesley Dickinson. General line.

Shepherd's Antiques, 1216 Morningside Street N.E. Clelia P. Shepherd. General line; glass, china, brass, wood, furniture. Open all year.

Sabot

Antiques at Woodlawn, Route 250, seventeen miles west of Richmond. Janet B. Kennedy. Period furniture, mirrors, paintings, decorative items.

South Hill

Old Plank Road Antique Shop, Mrs. Sarah I. Cliborne. Glass, china, bisque, Staffordshire figures.

Staunton

Just Folks Doll House.

Suffolk

Wilson Picture Frame Shop, 1326 Holland Road. Fine frames, lamps, bric-a-brac. Closed Sundays.

Tazewell

The Treasure Chest, Routes 19, 46, and 16. Carefully selected authentic pieces.

Upperville

Golden Horse Shoe, Route 50, fifty miles from Washington, D.C. Furniture and accessories; collectors' items.

Warrenton

Clark Bros., Routes 15, 17, and 29, six miles south. General line; Civil War items.

Williamsburg

Cogar, Lewis, and Geiger Inc., 137 York Street. Eighteenth-century furniture and accessories.

Yorktown

The Swan Tavern Antique Shop, Main Street, across from court house. General line. Open daily all year.

NORTH CAROLINA

Albemarle

The McSwain Antique Shop, 813 Main Street, Routes 73 and 27 near Charlotte and Pinehurst. Mrs. C. H. McSwain. Early furniture, glass, decorative items. Open daily or by appointment.

Arden

Fort Shuford Antique Shop, Route 25 south of Asheville. Glass, china, bric-a-brac. Open daily April to November.

Asheville

J. K. Buckner's Antique and Reproduction Shop, 204 Tunnel Road, Routes 70 and 74. China, bric-a-brac, furniture, custom-built furniture. Open all year, daily, except Sundays.

Robert D. Bunn, Antiques and Interiors, 14 Biltmore Avenue. Eighteenth-century paintings, mirrors, frames, furniture, bronze. Open daily all year except Sundays.

Susquehanna Antique Co., 55 Biltmore Avenue. Furniture, silver, glass, china, stamps, coins. Open daily all year.

Mrs. Charles R. Hunter, 23 Buxton Road.

Bat Cave

The River Shed, Hickory Nut Gorge, Route 74, twenty-two miles east of Asheville. General line; pattern glass, china, furniture; unusual items. Open all year.

Boone

Burgess Antiques.

M and R Furniture Co., Route 421 at Vilas, four miles west of Boone. Ray A. Farthing. Furniture, china, glass, early Americana, cast iron, guns, coins. Open daily all year except Sundays.

Burlington

Louise Lorimer, 1704 Woodland Avenue. Glass, bric-a-brac, small antiques, unusual items. Open daily all year and by appointment.

Johnson's Furniture Shop, Route 70A, one mile west. W. A. Johnson. General line and reproductions. Open daily all year except Sundays.

Candler

Harrison Antiques, R. D. 2.

Chapel Hill

Whitehall Antique Shop, 1215 East Franklin Street, Routes 15 and 501. Mrs. George F. Bason. Eighteenth- and nineteenth-century furniture, china, silver, crystal, brass. Open daily all year except Sundays and holidays.

Blackberry Farm Antiques, Carrboro–Hillsboro Road, five miles out of town. H. W. Carroll. Authentic Americana, eighteenth-century furniture, collectors' porcelains, primitives, pewter, glass, Lowestoft, Chinese objets d'art. Open daily all year, evenings by appointment.

Charlotte

Mills Antique Shop, 1340 East Morehead Street. Period English, French, and American furniture, silver, crystal. Open daily, evenings by appointment.

The Lamplighter, 5703 North Tryon Street, Route 29 N. Betty and Bill Green. Prints, frames, lamps, furniture.

Lucy Moore Antiques, Crescent Extension.

Lawrence Antiques, South Mint Street.

Chimney Rock

Cox's Antiques, Route 74, twenty-five miles east of Asheville. Russell K. Cox. China, glass, clocks, early Americana, mountain items. Open daily all year.

China Grove

Earl Caton.

Edenton

Myrtle Davis Watson, 507 North Broad Street, Route 17. Dresden, Waterford, Meissen, gold leaf, decorators' items. Open daily all year.

Elizabeth City

Worth Britt's Antiques, 1506 North Toad Street. China, glass, furniture, reproductions. Summer shop, Nag's Head. Open April 15 to October 15.

Gastonia

Geneva's Antique Shop, 1400 Jackson Road. South of town off Route 321. China, furniture, specializing in lamps and custom-made shades. Open all year daily except Saturday afternoons in summer.

Gladys White Antiques, Charlotte R.D.

Greensboro

Otto Zenke, 215 South Eugene Street. Furniture, porcelains, lamps, no Victorian.

Jean Watson Antiques, 2605 West Market Street.

Mrs. Della W. Amos, 1101 Grayland Street. Hepplewhite, Victorian furniture, china, glass, bisque, silver. By appointment only.

Greenville

Kyzer Hearthside Antique Shop, 202 East Ninth Street. Early American pine, cherry, small furniture, pressed glass; frames, some Victorian furniture, collectors' items. Open daily all year.

Hendersonville

John Atha, Route 25, a half mile south. General line; Bassett pewter, primitives.

Hickory

Mrs. Kennedy's Antiques, Route 321 on way to Blowing Rock. Quality goods, small furniture, brass, pewter, gold-leaf and walnut frames. Open daily. Saturdays until noon.

High Point

Willis Stallings, Routes 29, 70, and 311. Eighteenth-century American, southern furniture and accessories.

Kannapolis

The Glass Shop, Main Street, Route 29 South. Mrs. Ruth Adams. China, gold-leaf frames, Victorian items. Open daily except Sundays and Tuesday afternoons.

The China Mart, 612 South 29. General line. Open daily. Sundays 2 to 7 P.M.

Lattimore

Bells Antiques.

Lenoir

Russell's Antiques, 100 Crestline Drive. Summer shop in Blowing Rock. The Clover Patch.

Lumberton

Frances Olsen's Antique and Gift Shop, Pine Street. General line. Open daily.

Monroe

Maud Funderburke.

Morganton

D. M. Munday.

New Bern

Bess Hyman Guion, 311 Johnson Street. General line; china, glass, period furniture.

Mrs. H. C. Waldrop, 701 Broad Street. Period furniture, silver, china, glass.

North Wilkesboro

Bare-Miller Antique Co., 307 Tenth Street, Route 421. Mr. and Mrs. Trent Crawford. French, Victorian, Chippendale, Empire furniture. Open daily.

Old Salem

Dan's Antique Shop, Salem Interiors, 527–529 South Main Street. In Old Salem Restoration. General line decorative antiques, lamps, shades, wallpaper, fabrics, paintings.

Salem Antique and Gift Shop, 531 South Main Street, near Wachovia Museum. General line. Open daily.

Pinehurst

Joseph Garnier Antiques. General line; books, objets d'art. Open daily October through May.

Raleigh

Lightfoot's Antiques, 2 Maiden Lane, opposite Memorial Tower just off Hillsboro Street. Furniture, china, bric-a-brac, frames, prints, mirrors. Open daily. Sundays by appointment.

Spinning Wheel Antique Shop, 3205 Hillsboro Street. Harrison Kauffman. China, glass, furniture. Open daily including Sundays.

Colonial Antique Shop, 504 East Jones Street. Two blocks east at Governor's Mansion, south at corner of East and Jones Streets. Mrs. Elizabeth B. Gatling. General line; furniture, glass, china. Open daily, except Sundays, all year.

Antique Corner, 549 North Person Street. Louise W. Solaneck. General line; glass, china, lamps, furniture. Open daily.

Smith's Antiques, Holly Springs Road, two miles south on Route 401.

Roxobel

Tyler's Antiques, five miles off Route 258 at Rich Square. John Edward Tyler. Furniture, prints, oil paintings, frames, lamps, oriental items, china, books, oddities. Open all year. Appointment advisable.

Salisbury

Mrs. T. Walter Grimes, 602 West Council Street. General line; glass, china, bric-a-brac, furniture.

Carter's Antiques, 530 West Council Street. Mrs. Stamey Carter. General line of authentic items. Open all year.

Mrs. William Stossel, Innes Street.

Mrs. C. I. Jones, Statesville Road.

Spencer

Lewis Antique Shop, 119 Fifth Street, one-fourth block off Route 29. General line; early American and period furniture. Open daily.

Sugar Grove

Mildred Farthing Antiques.

Tryon

Seven Hearths, Route 176. The Mills-Mossellers. Hooked rugs (antique and custom made). By appointment only.

John Adams.

Valdese

Powels Furniture and Antiques.

Wake Forest

Minta Holding Folk, 217 White Street. Period furniture, lamps, accessories. Appointment advised.

Warrenton

Scott's Antiques, Norlina Road, two miles north of town. Estelle and Robert Scott. General line; lamps, frames, mirrors. Open daily including Sundays, evenings by appointment.

Winston–Salem

Everett Parker Stutts, 1034 Burke Street. Authentic pieces and interiors.

SOUTH CAROLINA

Abbeville

Noah's Ark. Furniture in the rough, china, glass, bric-a-brac. Open Monday through Saturday.

Charleston

Porgy's Shop, 89 Church Street. Mrs. Wm. Sinkler. Fine china, glass, silver, and period furniture.

The Goat Cart, 94 Church Street. Outlet for good things sold on commission. Many antiques.

House and Garden Shop, 83 Church Street. Fine china, silver, glass, furniture, and decorative items.

The Century House, 77 Church Street. Good general line.

Schlinder's, 200 King Street. Extensive general line; collectors' items, Civil War items.

Colonial Antique Shop, 193 King Street. Mrs. Mary Schwerin. General line.

George C. Birlant and Co., 191 King Street. Silver, objets d'art.

Jack Patla Co., 181 King Street. Good general line, silver, garden pieces.

Clark's Hill

Partain's, Route 28, one mile south of town. Furniture, glass, china, brass, silver, Victorian chairs. Open daily and Sundays.

Columbia

Safran's Antique Galleries, 930 Gervais Street. English, American, and French furniture, silver. Open daily.

The Trading Post, 2340 Two Notch Road, Route 1, north of town, near Midland Shopping Center. Mr. and Mrs. R. E. Pannick. General line. Open weekdays except Thursday afternoon.

George's Antique Shop, 934 Gervais Street.

McDuffie's Antiques, 1811 Gervais Street.

Marion E. Green, 118 Taylor Street.

Sigg Conrad Antiques, 2228 Devine Street.

Darlington

The Plunder Shop, Route 401. General line; lamps, clocks, frames, Victorian furniture. Open daily.

Greenville

Cannon's Antique Shop, 552 West Washington Street, five blocks from Routes 25, 29, and 276. General line; furniture, frames, china, glass, bric-a-brac. Open daily except Sundays.

Boyd's Antique Shop, 313 Hamilton Street.

Piedmont Furniture Co., 115 North Brown Street.

Myrtle Beach

Treasure House Antiques, Route 17 N. Mrs. T. R. Cox and Mrs. W. C. Roberts. General line of distinctive pieces.

Rock Hill
Ferguson Antiques.
Taylor's
The Spinning Wheel Antiques, Route 29, four miles north of Greenville.
Mrs. Lois W. Garrison. General line; early furniture, glass, china. Open
daily except Sundays.

GEORGIA

Alpharetta
Sara Cherry Antiques.
Atlanta
Mary Akers, 1582 Piedmont Avenue N.E. Eighteenth- and nineteenth-
century pieces. Paintings.
Joe Barnes, 89 Ellis Street N.E. Traditional English and Continental
pieces. Decorators' items.
W. E. Browne Decorating Co., 443 Peachtree Street N.E. Fine furniture,
porcelains, and decorators' items.
Chenoweth Galleries, 1142 Peachtree Street N.W. Eighteenth- and
nineteenth-century pieces.
J. H. Elliot, 537 Peachtree Street N.E. Large general line.
Kenneth Garcia, 2297 Peachtree Street N.E. Fine English eighteenth-
century pieces, paintings.
Margaret Vickery, 1106 Crescent Avenue N.E. Traditional English and
French pieces.
Gordon Little, 2295 Peachtree Street N.E. Eighteenth- and nineteenth-
century pieces, decorators' items.
John Lachnitt, 1166 Peachtree Street N.W. Large general line, primitives.
Florence Routh, 1162 Peachtree Street N.W. General line.
Reese's Antiques, 507 Peachtree Street N.W. French and English imports,
china, crystal, silver, furniture.
Virginia Williams Antiques, 2291 Peachtree Street N.E. Fine old glass,
china, small antiques.
Strickland's, 47 West Pace's Ferry Road N.W. English, French, and Early
American.
Rudolph-Sparks Inc., 279 East Pace's Ferry Road, N.E. Decorators' items.
Specializing in fine English porcelains.
The Corner Shop, at Davison-Paxon Co., 180 Peachtree Street. Mrs.
Burns. Antiques and decorative items.
Henderson's Antique Shop, 1039 North Highland Avenue N.E.

Furniture-Antique Supply Co., 1243 Lee Street S.W. French and Victorian furniture, marble-top items, china cabinets, curio cabinets, lamps, tables, bric-a-brac. Open Monday through Friday, Saturdays until 2 P.M. Closed Sundays.

Mrs. Spencer Butler, 1385 Spring Street N.W.

Mrs. C. W. Hightower, 1824 Lenox Road N.E.

Barnesville

Mrs. John T. Middlebrooke, 852 Thomaston Street. American and English period furniture, decorative items. Also a shop in Columbus.

Columbus

Ellen Worrell Antiques, 1221 Third Avenue.

Decatur

Howard's Place.

Griffin

The Antique Shop, Route 41 North. Fred J. West. General line; furniture, china.

Newton Bell, 132 East College Avenue. General line; decorative items.

Macon

The Little Antique Shop, 350 Cotton Avenue. D. W. McIver. China, brass, glass, frames, furniture. Open all year.

McLean's Antiques, 2291 Ingleside Avenue, one block off Route 80. Mr. and Mrs. Norman P. McLean. China, glass, furniture, primitives, jewelry. Open daily, Sundays by appointment.

Beall Antiques, 2988 Houston Avenue. Mr. and Mrs. Dennis Beall. "Junk to jewels." Open daily, Sundays by appointment.

Mrs. Samuel Orr, 2263 Vineville Avenue.

Marietta

Rebel Ridge Ranch Antiques, Burnt Hickory Road. Mrs. Jennie Tate Anderson. General line; oriental rugs, oil paintings, silver, pewter. Open daily.

Savannah

Alida Harper Fowlkes, 326 Bull Street. Fine period furniture, imports, decorative items.

Rosemary Antique Shop, Inc., 29 West Liberty Street. Mrs. Miriam Pollard. Furniture, brass, china, glass, objets d'art. Continental imports.

Colonial Antiques, 23 Houston Street.

Schendel's.

FLORIDA

Altamonte Springs
   The Windsor Chair, Route 436. Earlah M. Smith. Pine and maple furniture, china, glass.

Belleview
   Golding's Antiques, Routes 441 and 27, eleven miles south of Ocala. Harry and Eleanor Golding. China, glass, copper, brass, guns.

Bradenton
   Marjorie B. Barney, 2309 Manatee Avenue. General line.

Clearwater
   Mrs. J. M. Brazington Antiques, 1222 Idlewild Drive. General line; lamp parts.

Clermont
   Jones Country Store, six miles north of Citrus Tower, Route 2. Ginny Lee Jones. Early American and country-store items.

Dade City
   Roberts Barn, Antiques and Stuff, four miles west on Lake Iola Road. Open weekends only, October through June. Other times by appointment. General line.
   Longfritz's Antique Shop, 1206 West Coleman Avenue, just off Route 52. Glass, china, silver.
   Maltby's Antiques, four miles south on Route 301. China, glass, furniture.

Dania
   Ely Antique Shop, 246 South Federal Highway, four miles south of Ft. Lauderdale. Bric-a-brac; lamps a specialty. Open all year.

Daytona Beach
   Winifred Harned Antiques, 648 South Ridgewood Street, Route 1. Furniture, glass, small antiques.
   Benson Antiques, 176 Broadway. General line.

Deerfield Beach
   Josephine R. Powis, 714 Southeast, Twentieth Avenue. China, glass.

De Land
   Miss Ann and Jack's Antiques, 115 East Euclid Avenue. Glass, china, Haviland.
   Breezy Hill Antiques, 1775 South Boulevard, one mile south. Jean W. Johnson. Clocks, lamps. Closed Wednesdays.
   Cornelia Moseley Antiques, 121 Rich Avenue. General line. Open all year.

Delray
Gwendolyn Maloney, Hibiscus Court Motel, Route 1. General line.
Ft. Lauderdale
Americana Gallery, 810 East Broward Street. Civil War items, maps, valentines.
Fruitland Park
The Briscoes Antiques, Routes 441 and 27 (next to Gulf station). China, glass, furniture.
Haines City
The Calico Cat, 106 First Street, just off Routes 17 and 92. Mrs. John E. Loucks. Bottles, glass, china, furniture, and "plunder." Closed Tuesdays and Fridays.
Hilliard
The River Shop, on Routes 101, 1, and 23, one and a half miles north. Furniture and bric-a-brac.
Indian River City
Red Shutters Antique Shop, 519 Washington Avenue, one block west of Route 1, nine blocks north of Route 50. L. McCarthy. China, glass, furniture.
Jacksonvillle
Hidden House Antiques, 1745 Girvin Road off Atlantic Boulevard. L. H. Engelhardt. Ironstone, brass, lamps, primitives, bric-a-brac, furniture. Open daily all year.
Helen P. Kennard, Antiques, 3575 St. John's Avenue (Avondale Shopping Center), two blocks from river. General line; cut glass, china, Dresden, Meissen, furniture.
Ann Nachman Galleries, Inc., 3106 Beach Boulevard, Route 90 east. Mrs. Frederick P. Nachman. Cut glass, art glass, porcelains, silver, oriental items, jewelry. Open daily. Sundays and evenings by appointment.
Colonial Shop, 2973 King's Avenue, Route 1 south. Mrs. William M. Arehart. General line. Open Monday through Friday.
Robert R. Story, 648 Cassat Avenue. General line. Open daily except Sundays. Auction every Saturday night.
Mrs. George H. Woods, 135 Third Avenue S.
The Amber Lantern, Ina Ward Antiques.
Mrs. Lake Randolph, 3572 Saint John's Avenue.
William McGinnis, 6349 Beach Boulevard.
Jacksonville Beach
Mr. and Mrs. George H. Wood, 135 Third Avenue S., one block east of Route AIA. Glass, china, furniture, and antique auto parts.

Key West

Old Island Trading Post, 301 Whitehead Street. Al and Ethel Brown. Imports, items from Old England and New England. Open all year.

Lakeland

Glass Shelf Anteekery, 124 South Ingraham Avenue, off Routes 92 and 98. Laura Chipman. China, glass, furniture, and primitives. Unusual collectors' items.

The Teagles Antique Shop, 1457 Gary Road, Route 92 east. Decorative, hand-painted, and Haviland china, cut glass. Open all year.

The Cheek House, 2307 Freemason Street in Lake Bonny Heights, east of town. Betty L. Cheek. Glass, china, bric-a-brac, and collectors' items. Open all year.

Largo

Howard Tanner, 2130 Ridge Road, southwest 24th Avenue, four blocks west of Alternate Route 19.

The Wagon Wheel, 1101 Ridge Road, one block east of Clearwater–Largo Road. Bert and Joline Leone Young. Open daily, 9 to 5. Large general line.

Leesburg

Curiosity Shop, Routes 27 and 441, next to Howard Johnson's. Dora Lee Grizzard. Lamps, furniture, brass.

Koss Manor Motel Antiques, Route 27, ten miles south of Leesburg. George J. Holzhauser. General line; lamps and vases.

Maitland

Dick Wood Antiques, Manor Road, Routes 17 and 92. China, glass, furniture, and primitives.

Sadler's Antiques, 201 West Horation Avenue. Glass, china, furniture.

Montgomery's Antiques, Routes 17 and 92 between Maitland and Fern Park. Early American and period furniture.

Miami

Gaslamp Antiques, The Ramers, Miami Avenue at 6 N.W. Sixty-second Street. Lamps, shades, china, and glass.

An Wise, 2298 Coral Way S.W. Twenty-second Street.

Miami Beach

Violet Davidson, 1426 Alton Road.

Mount Dora

Fletcher's Antiques, four miles northwest Route 441.

Margaret H. Knight, Antiques, Route 441, one and one tenth miles on Donnelly West, one and one tenth miles on Old Eustis–Mt. Dora Road. General line; pattern glass and lamps.

Ocala

Mrs. Eloise F. Griggs, Antiques, 2634 Silver Springs Boulevard Route 40 east. General line.

Juanita Akin, Antiques, three and a half miles west on Route 200. China, brass, bric-a-brac, and Victorian items.

Orlando

Marian Smith, Antiques, 804 Magnolia Avenue (turn north from Colonial Drive). Glass, china, furniture.

MacKoy's Authentic Antiques, 322 West Church Street. Charlotte Wesche. Colored glass, cut glass, jewelry, china, furniture, silver.

Alice Mundis, Antiques, 2501 Edgewater Drive (corner of Rugby and Edgewater). Art glass, cut glass, china, period furniture, Currier & Ives prints.

Hancock's Antiques, 715 Glendonjo Drive. Glass, dolls, lamps, period furniture.

Haviland Matching Service, 2340 Virginia Drive. Ethel A. Ranson. China, glass.

Grace Winter Jones, 130 North Rosalind Avenue. Colored glass, Haviland, furniture.

Darling's Antiques, seven miles west on Colonial Drive, Route 50. Russell Darling. American furniture, prints, oil paintings, primitives, china, glass.

Vonice Adams Taylor Antiques, 540 North Ferncreek Avenue. Colored glass, china, lamps, gold-leaf mirrors, bric-a-brac, and furniture. Closed Thursday mornings.

Palatka

Dancy's Antiques, 1225 Reid Street, north at intersection of Routes 17 and 100. Mr. and Mrs. D. F. Dancy. China, glass, furniture.

Riviera Beach

The Fays, 179 East Blue Heron Road, east of Route 1. General line and accessories. Open December 15 to April 15. Summer shop, Point Pleasant, Bucks County, Pennsylvania, eight miles north of New Hope.

Four Winds, 5000 Gulf of Mexico Drive, on Longboat Key. China, glass, silver, custard glass, checker books. By appointment only.

Sarasota

The English Shop, 75 South Palm Avenue. Silver, glass, china, maps, prints, music boxes.

St. Augustine

The Boxwood, at entrance to Lightner Museum. Mrs. Elizabeth T. Little. Fine general line, silver, oriental items, imports.

Pomar's Antiques, Route AIA, ten miles south. Specializing in art glass, furniture, cut glass, china dolls.

George Tedder's Studio, 64 Saint George Street. China, crystal, glass, marble-top furniture, decorative items. Fine reproductions.

Antiques Exchange, 65 Saint George Street. E. H. Smiley. General line; small antiques.

Pauline Graham Best, 12 Charlotte Street. General line; furniture. Open winter only, November to May.

Mrs. Lilian S. Smith, 38 Cordova Street. Dolls and miniatures.

Old Gold and Silver Shoppe, R. E. Jellison. Early silver and jewelry.

St. Petersburg

Jonathan's, 7283 Forty-sixth Avenue N. Irene and Martin J. Brice. Furniture and decorative items.

John and Edna Davis, 2012 Fourth Street N. (Fourth Street is main street to Gandy Bridge.) General line; Haviland, buttons.

Allicia Doll-O-Pedic Hospital, 448 Ninth Avenue. Museum. Unusual items for collectors. Open Tuesday through Friday, 11 to 6.

Sundial Antique Bazaar, 5900 Fifth Avenue N. at Alternate Route 19 and Tyronne Boulevard. John and Leila Bliss. General line.

Mardelena Antiques, 2930 Tangerine Avenue. American, European, and oriental furniture and decorative items.

Thomas Antiques, 2903 Tangerine Avenue S. Small antiques, brass, copper, iron, china, glass, silver, books, prints. Open daily 11 to 5.

The Parson's Hobby Antiques, 2900 Tangerine Avenue S. Early Americana. Collectors' items in Audubon and Gould prints, Wedgwood, glass, china, silver, jewelry, furniture. Winter only. (Summer shop June to September in West Medway, Massachusetts.)

St. Petersburg Beach

Marie Whitney Antiques. 3112 Gulf Boulevard. (Summer shop Tolland, Massachusetts.) Open January 15 to April 15. China, glass, decorative items.

Tampa

Katherine Nunez, 5409 Seminole Avenue, one block north of Route 92. Furniture, bric-a-brac, and art glass.

Venice

The Lazy Susan Shop, 106 Nokomis Avenue, two blocks west of traffic light on Route 41. China, glass, lamps, furniture.

Winter Park

Cobweb Antiques, 348 Park Avenue N. Hidden Garden. R. T. Rademacher. Porcelains, fine metals, colored glass, furniture.

Ferris Galleries, 334 Park Avenue and Hidden Garden. European imports.

The Jewel Box, 654 Orange Avenue. Mrs. Doherty. Jewelry, china, and glass. Closed Wednesdays.

Zephyrhills

Anderson's Antiques. Early American and Victorian furniture, glass, china.

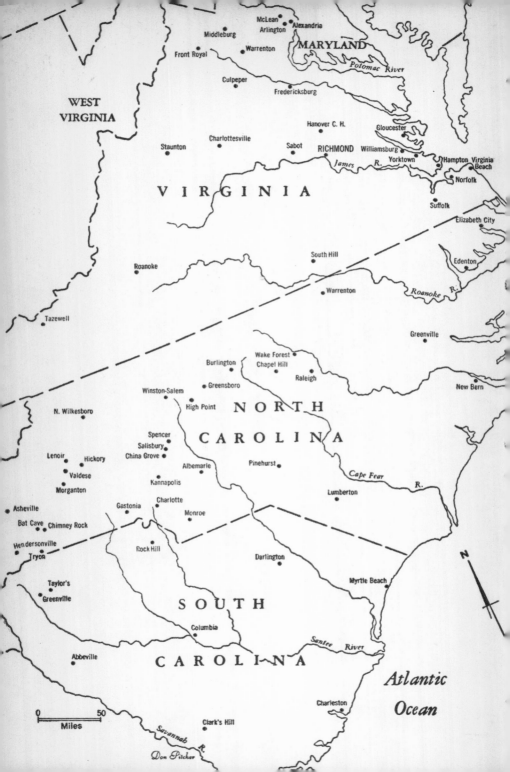